Complex Fuzzy Rough Sets and Their Applications

RIVER PUBLISHERS SERIES IN MATHEMATICAL, STATISTICAL AND COMPUTATIONAL MODELLING FOR ENGINEERING

Series Editors:

MANGEY RAM
Graphic Era University
India

Applied mathematical techniques along with statistical and computational data analysis has become vital skills across the physical sciences. The purpose of this book series is to present novel applications of numerical and computational modelling and data analysis across the applied sciences. We encourage applied mathematicians, statisticians, data scientists and computing engineers working in a comprehensive range of research fields to showcase different techniques and skills, such as differential equations, finite element method, algorithms, discrete mathematics, numerical simulation, machine learning, probability and statistics, fuzzy theory, etc.

Books published in the series include professional research monographs, edited volumes, conference proceedings, handbooks and textbooks, which provide new insights for researchers, specialists in industry, and graduate students.

Topics included in this series are as follows:-

- Discrete mathematics and computation
- Fault diagnosis and fault tolerance
- Finite element method (FEM) modeling/simulation
- Fuzzy and possibility theory
- Fuzzy logic and neuro-fuzzy systems for relevant engineering applications
- Game Theory
- Mathematical concepts and applications
- Modelling in engineering applications
- Numerical simulations
- Optimization and algorithms
- Queueing systems
- Resilience
- Stochastic modelling and statistical inference
- Stochastic Processes
- Structural Mechanics
- Theoretical and applied mechanics

For a list of other books in this series, visit www.riverpublishers.com

Complex Fuzzy Rough Sets and Their Applications

Tahir Mahmood
International Islamic University Islamabad, Pakistan

Jabbar Ahmmad
National University of Modern Languages (NUML), Islamabad, Pakistan

Ubaid Ur Rehman
University of Management and Technology, Lahore, Punjab, Pakistan

Harish Garg
Thapar Institute of Engineering & Technology, Patiala, Punjab, India

River Publishers

Routledge
Taylor & Francis Group
NEW YORK AND LONDON

Published 2026 by River Publishers
River Publishers
Broagervej 10, 9260 Gistrup, Denmark
www.riverpublishers.com

Distributed exclusively by Routledge
605 Third Avenue, New York, NY 10017, USA
4 Park Square, Milton Park, Abingdon, Oxon OX14 4RN

Complex Fuzzy Rough Sets and Their Applications / by Tahir Mahmood, Jabbar Ahmmad, Ubaid Ur Rehman, Harish Garg.

Routledge is an imprint of the Taylor & Francis Group, an informa business

ISBN 978-87-4380-781-0 (hardback)
ISBN 978-87-4380-786-5 (paperback)
ISBN 978-87-4380-783-4 (online)
ISBN 978-87-4380-782-7 (master ebook)

DOI 10.1201/9788743807827

Dedicated to Our Families and Teachers

Contents

Preface xi

Acknowledgement xv

List of Figures xvii

List of Tables xix

List of Abbreviations xxi

1 Fundamental Concepts of Fuzzy Sets and Rough Sets 1
1.1 Characteristic Function 1
1.2 Fuzzy Set 2
1.3 Rough Set 2
1.4 Fuzzy Rough Set 4
1.5 Complex Fuzzy Set 5
1.6 Complex Fuzzy Rough Set 5
1.7 Some Basic T-norms and T-conorms 6
1.8 Scope and Organization of the Book 8

2 WASPAS Approach Based on Complex Fuzzy Rough Aggregation Operators and their Application to Cybersecurity 11
2.1 Hamacher Operational Rules Based on CFRNs 11
2.2 Complex Fuzzy Rough Hamacher Arithmetic and Geometric Aggregation 12
2.3 Application of Developed Approach 23
2.3.1 WASPAS approach 23
2.3.2 Numerical example 25
2.4 Comparative Analysis 29
2.5 Conclusion 32

3 Integrating Complex Fuzzy Rough Yager Aggregation Operators with Neural Networks for Improved AI Predictive Models **33**
3.1 Complex Fuzzy Rough Yager Power AOs 34
3.1.1 Properties of CFRYPA operator 37
3.1.2 Properties of CRFYPWA operator 39
3.1.3 Properties of CRFYPG operator 43
3.2 MCDM Approach Within the Framework of CFRS 44
3.2.1 Case study (selection of neural network framework for AI predictive models) 46
3.3 Comparison 51
3.4 Conclusion 54

4 Innovative Approaches to Prioritizing Financial Tools for Business Growth and Sustainability through Complex Fuzzy Rough Structure **55**
4.1 Sine Trigonometric Operational Laws for CFRNs 55
4.2 Sine Trigonometric AOs for CFR Sets 57
4.3 Sine Trigonometric Complex Fuzzy Rough Weighted Geometric AOs 60
4.4 Application of the Proposed Theory 62
4.4.1 Decision-making algorithm 63
4.4.2 Numerical example 63
4.5 Comparative Analysis of the Proposed Study 68
4.6 Conclusion 71

5 A Framework for Prioritizing Tools and Techniques in Electrical Engineering Design and Analysis: An Application of Complex Fuzzy Rough Sets **73**
5.1 Aczel-Alsina Operations of CFRNs 73
5.2 Aczel-Alsina Aggregation Operators using CFR Information 79
5.3 Application of the Proposed Theory in Multiattribute Decision-making (MADM) 82
5.3.1 Decision-making procedure 83
5.3.2 Illustrated example 83
5.4 Comparative Analysis 87
5.5 Conclusion 90

6 Innovative AI Solutions through the Utilization of Complex Fuzzy Rough Set Theory 91
6.1 Power AOs for CFRNs 92
6.1.1 Properties of CFRPA operator 94
6.1.2 Properties of CFRPWA operator 95
6.1.3 Properties of CRFPG operator 97
6.1.4 Properties of CRFPWG operator 99
6.2 MCDM Approach based on Power Operators within CFRS . 99
6.2.1 Case study (selection of AI solution) 101
6.3 Comparative Analysis 105
6.4 Conclusion 107

7 Advanced Data Science Techniques with Complex Fuzzy Rough Sets: Applications and Insights 109
7.1 Einstein Operators for CFRS 109
7.2 CFR Einstein Weighted Average and Geometric Aggregation Operators 110
7.2.1 Properties of CFREWA AOs 113
7.2.2 CFREWG AOs 116
7.3 The WASPAS Technique based on CFRE AOs 118
7.3.1 Algorithm of the proposed study 119
7.3.2 Numerical example 120
7.4 Comparative Analysis 125
7.5 Conclusion 127

8 Tackling the Challenges of Environmental Complexity: A Complex Fuzzy Rough Set Approach to Ecosystem Management 129
8.1 Dombi AOs within the Framework of CFRS 130
8.1.1 Properties of CFRDPA operator 134
8.1.2 Properties of CRFDPG operator 137
8.2 MCDM Approach based on Dombi Power Operators within CFRS 139
8.2.1 Case study (selection of protected forest management strategy in national reserve) 140
8.3 Comparative Study 145
8.4 Conclusion 147

9 Empowering Robotic Decision-making with Complex Fuzzy Rough Sets: Toward Autonomous Industrial Applications 149
9.1 Frank AOs within the Framework of CFRSs 150
9.1.1 Properties of CFRFPA operator 155
9.1.2 Properties of CFRFPWA operator 157
9.1.3 MADM Approach for the Developed Notions 159
9.1.4 Case study (selection of robotic automation solution) 160
9.2 Comparative Study 166
9.3 Conclusion 169

References 171

Index 175

About the Authors 177

Preface

In real life, there are many situations where it is not possible to make some decision by following the binary logic that is "No" or "Yes." For example, consider the statements "Rahul is tall," "Sara is intelligent," and "Thomas is healthy." Now these statements cannot be answered by just "No" or "Yes," because the terms "tall," "intelligent," and "healthy" are not the well-defined terms, as these terms have variable meanings by person to person. To handle such type of uncertain and vague information in 1965, Zadeh initiated the notion of fuzzy sets. Fuzzy sets model imprecision by assigning a membership degree between 0 and 1 to each element. One can then represent very complex, vague concepts like "tall," "intelligent," and "healthy." The flexibility makes fuzzy sets useful for applications in decision-making, control systems, image processing, and artificial intelligence. This helps in places where human reasoning along with linguistic terms have to be mathematically modeled. They bridge the gap between binary logic and the vagueness of the real world, making fuzzy sets a highly powerful tool in solving problems of many domains.

The motivation for using rough sets results from the need to deal with uncertainty, imprecision, and incomplete information arising during data analysis whenever classical mathematical models fail to account for reality. Rough set theory, advanced by Pawlak in the early 1980s, constitutes a system for reasoning based on vague or indeterminate information and focuses essentially on the process of approximating sets. Unlike fuzzy sets, which deal with gradual membership, rough sets are based on the indiscernibility relation and are especially well suited to analyzing data without requiring additional subjective or external information like membership degrees or probability distributions. Rough set theory classifies an object into two approximations: a lower approximation that contains objects that certainly belong to the target set and an upper approximation that includes objects that possibly belong to it. The difference between such approximations acts as a notation for capturing the uncertainty in the classification process. This framework is very effective for feature selection, attribute reduction, and decision-making in systems where relationships between variables are not explicitly known. It has found applications in machine learning, pattern recognition, data mining, and knowledge discovery. For example, rough sets can identify the important attributes in a large dataset while improving computational efficiency and interpretability without losing much information. The most important characteristic of rough sets is that they are free from any a priori assumptions regarding data, thus being able to operate directly with raw information. This is helpful in application areas like medical diagnosis, fault detection, and market analysis, where data commonly contain or are associated with inconsistencies or ambiguities. Rough sets supply a mathematical basis for approximating uncertain concepts and make it easier for us to model, analyze, and decide within complex environments.

Fuzzy rough sets are an emergent tool to deal with uncertainty and imprecision that fills the gap between rough set theory and fuzzy set theory. Motivation: They address some limitations of classical rough sets in handling vague or imprecise boundaries, as well as the limitations of traditional fuzzy sets in handling granularity in data without strong mechanisms. Fuzzy rough sets offer a more profound analysis of complex systems with ambiguity and overlapping features by incorporating the strengths of both frameworks. This hybrid approach helps most in decision-making, pattern recognition, and data classification where vagueness and boundary uncertainty can be appropriately incorporated. Fuzzy sets of excellence perform better in applications relying on multicriteria evaluation as trade-offs have to be solved under uncertainty among conflicting objectives. They can easily handle real-world datasets, with inherent imprecision, making them a cornerstone for advancements in artificial intelligence, machine learning, and optimization. This paradigm becomes attractive to most researchers because it captures complex relationships of variables and induces meaningful insights that may be hiding in ambiguous data. Fuzzy rough sets are applied in many sectors such as medical diagnosis and image processing, as well as managing cybersecurity and supply chains where the significance of decision under uncertainty is critical in most of its applications. Further advances continue to enrich both the conceptual and practical worth of fuzzy sets, making their contribution to building intelligent systems into a cornerstone area.

Motivation: the idea behind developing Ramot complex fuzzy set, as classical fuzzy sets have inadequacies for dealing with uncertainties and ambiguities present in many problems related to decision-making processes. The motivation is to eradicate shortcomings of the classical fuzzy set regarding the issues related to the uncertainties and ambiguity that accompany decision-making processes when the problem complexity rises. Ramot introduced complex-valued membership functions, which in contrast to the traditional fuzzy sets that use real-valued membership functions, add further dimensions of information, including amplitude and phase. This improvement makes it possible to represent uncertainty more subtly, especially in dynamic systems with oscillatory or periodic behavior. It ends up being most applied in signal processing, control systems, and quantum computing, where the magnitudes and phases play a very important role. It extends the expressiveness of fuzzy sets, which makes it possible to model imprecise and complex phenomena more fittingly. CFS ends up facilitating advanced aggregation and reasoning techniques, hence becoming a powerful tool for doing multidisciplinary research. The CFS presents more fertile grounds for handling real-world vagueness by using geometric intuition in the world of complex numbers. This somehow brings innovation into the breakthrough that extends new grounds toward not only further abstract developments but applications practically in lots of fields of specialization. Another perspective about the notion of CFS was Tamir's CFS notion in which the range of membership grades belongs to unit square rather than unit circle. The idea behind this notion was to cover more information as compared to Ramot's CFS notions. In the case of Tamir's CFS if we take the value of membership grade as $0.9{+}\iota 0.7$ then we can see that the amplitude term in Ramot's CFS does not belong to [0, 1]. We can observe that $r{=}\sqrt{0.9^2{+}0.7^2}{=}\ 1.3{\notin}\ [0,\ 1]$. Hence Tamir's CFS provides more space to decision-makers to cover more advanced information.

The idea of the complex fuzzy rough set (CFRS) has been developed based on the idea of Tamir's CFS that can cover the upper and lower approximation making the structure more advanced than both Ramot's CFS and Tamir's CFS ideas. CFRS is based on complex fuzzy relations and Tamir's CFS. This idea reduces the chance of data loss in the sense of providing the upper and lower approximation of the data. As decision making is very important to every field of life and making an accurate decision in recent days is very important. The decision-makers are relying on an advanced structure that can provide them more space to handle vague and imprecise information. In this case, the notion of CFRS does not only discuss the two-dimensional information but also covers the lower and upper information effectively making this idea more reliable and valuable in different domains.

Motivated by the idea of CFRS, and to provide more aggregation theories for CFRSs, the authors of this book have analyzed and delivered the different aggregation theories based on different t-norms and t-conforms. We have provided the basic operational laws for complex fuzzy rough numbers (CFRNs) and then developed the aggregation theory based on these introduced operational operations.

Acknowledgement

We would like to express our appreciation to all my family members for their love and blessings to see me scaling greater heights of my life.

Above all, we would thank Almighty for blessing such affectionate and efficient people who have been playing a great role in accomplishing our dreams.

Tahir Mahmood, Jabbar Ahmmad, Ubaid Ur Rehman, and Harish Garg

List of Figures

Figure 2.1	Graphical representation of ranking results.	29
Figure 2.2	A graphical representation of data given in Table 2.3.	31
Figure 3.1	Graphical interpretation of operator.	51
Figure 3.2	The comparison among existing and proposed theories.	53
Figure 4.1	Graphical representation of data given in Table 4.3.	68
Figure 4.2	Graphical representation of results given in Table 4.5.	70
Figure 5.1	Graphical representation of data given in Table 5.4.	87
Figure 5.2	Graphical representation of data given in Table 5.6.	89
Figure 6.1	The graphical interpretation of the score values and ranking of the AI solutions through different proposed operators.	105
Figure 6.2	The comparison of the score values of AI solutions obtained by existing and proposed work.	106
Figure 7.1	Graphical representation of results.	124
Figure 7.2	Graphical representation of results given in Table 7.3.	126
Figure 8.1	The graphical interpretation of score values of forest management strategies.	145
Figure 8.2	The graphical interpretation of score values obtained by proposed and existing methods.	147
Figure 9.1	The graphical representation of score values of robotic systems.	165
Figure 9.2	The graphical interpretation of comparison.	167

List of Tables

Table 2.1	Attributes and their description.	27
Table 2.2	CFR data.	28
Table 2.3	Score values and ranking results of interpreted and existing work.	30
Table 3.1	The neural network frameworks along with explanation.	47
Table 3.2	The criteria of neural network frameworks.	48
Table 3.3	The assessment values of neural network frameworks, interpreted by experts.	49
Table 3.4	The aggregated outcomes of neural network frameworks.	50
Table 3.5	The score values of neural network frameworks.	50
Table 3.6	The ranking of neural network frameworks.	51
Table 3.7	The score values of existing and proposed theory.	52
Table 3.8	The ranking of proposed theories and existing ones.	52
Table 4.1	CFR data.	67
Table 4.2	Aggregated outcomes.	67
Table 4.3	Score values.	67
Table 4.4	Ranking result.	68
Table 4.5	Comparative analysis results.	69
Table 5.1	Attributes and their explanations.	86
Table 5.2	CFR data.	86
Table 5.3	Aggregated results by using CFRAAWA or CFRAAOWA AOs.	87
Table 5.4	Shown the SVs of the aggregated values.	87
Table 5.5	Ranking results.	87
Table 5.6	Mentioned the comparison between proposed and existing work.	88
Table 6.1	The AI solutions along with an explanation.	101
Table 6.2	The criteria of the AI solutions.	102

Table 6.3 The assessment values of AI solutions are interpreted by experts. 102
Table 6.4 The aggregated outcomes of AI solutions. 104
Table 6.5 The score values of AI solutions. 104
Table 6.6 The ranking of AI solutions. 104
Table 6.7 The score values of existing and proposed theory. . . 106
Table 6.8 The ranking of proposed theories and existing ones. . 106
Table 7.1 Description of attributes. 123
Table 7.2 Data proposed by experts in the form of CFRNs. . . . 123
Table 7.3 Overall results. 125
Table 8.1 The forest management strategies with explanation. . 141
Table 8.2 The criteria of forest management strategies. 142
Table 8.3 The assessment values of forest management strategies are interpreted by the experts of the committee. 143
Table 8.4 The aggregated outcomes of management strategy. . 144
Table 8.5 The score values of forest management strategies. . . 144
Table 8.6 The ranking of management strategies. 145
Table 8.7 The score values of existing and proposed theory. . . 146
Table 8.8 The ranking of proposed theories and existing ones. . 146
Table 9.1 The robotic solutions along with an explanation. . . . 161
Table 9.2 The criteria of robotic solutions. 162
Table 9.3 The assessment values of robotic solutions are interpreted by experts. 163
Table 9.4 The aggregated outcomes of robotic solutions. 164
Table 9.5 The score values of neural network frameworks. . . . 165
Table 9.6 The ranking of robotic solutions. 165
Table 9.7 The score values of existing and proposed theories. . . 167
Table 9.8 The ranking of proposed theories and existing ones. . 167

List of Abbreviations

AAO	Arithmetic aggregation operator
ACL	Access control list
AI	Artificial intelligence
AO	Aggregation operator
CFRDPA	Complex fuzzy rough dombi power averaging
CFRDPG	Complex fuzzy rough dombi power geometric
CFRDPWA	Complex fuzzy rough dombi power weighted averaging
CFRDPWG	Complex fuzzy rough dombi power weighted geometric
CFREWA	Complex fuzzy rough einstein weighted average
CFRFPA	Complex fuzzy rough frank power averaging
CFRFPG	Complex fuzzy rough frank power geometric
CFRFPWA	Complex fuzzy rough frank power weighted averaging
CFRFPWG	Complex fuzzy rough frank power weighted geometric
CFRHWA	Complex fuzzy rough hamacher weighted average
CFRHWG	Complex fuzzy rough hamacher weighted geometric
CFRN	Complex fuzzy rough number
CFRPA	Complex fuzzy rough power averaging
CFRPG	Complex fuzzy rough power geometric
CFRPWA	Complex fuzzy rough power weighted averaging
CFRPWG	Complex fuzzy rough power weighted geometric
CFRS	Complex fuzzy rough set
CFRWA	Complex fuzzy rough weighted average
CFRYPA	Complex fuzzy rough yager power averaging
CFRYPG	Complex fuzzy rough yager power geometric

CFRYPWA	Complex fuzzy rough yager power weighted averaging
CFRYPWG	Complex fuzzy rough yager power weighted geometric
CFS	Complex fuzzy set
DFMC	Department of forest management and conservation
FEWA	Fuzzy einstein weighted average
FEWG	Fuzzy einstein weighted geometric
FN	Fuzzy number
FREWA	Fuzzy rough einstein weighted average
FREWG	Fuzzy rough einstein weighted geometric
FRN	Fuzzy rough number
FRS	Fuzzy rough set
FS	Fuzzy set
GDPR	General data protection regulation
GTS	Global tech services
HIPAA	Health insurance portability and accountability act
IC	Integrated circuit
IoT	Internet of things
MADM	Multiattribute decision-making
MCDM	Multi-criteria decision-making
NEPA	National environmental protection agency
NIES	National institute of environmental studies
NLP	Neural language process
NPV	Net present value
PLC	Programmable logic controller
RS	Rough set
SDN	Software-defined networking
STCFRHA	Sine trigonometric complex fuzzy rough hybrid averaging
STCFRHG	Sine trigonometric complex fuzzy rough hybrid geometric
STCFROWA	Sine trigonometric complex fuzzy rough hybrid averaging
STCFROWG	Sine trigonometric complex fuzzy rough ordered weighted geometric

STCFRWA	Sine trigonometric complex fuzzy rough weighted averaging
STCFRWG	Sine trigonometric complex fuzzy rough weighted geometric
TRS	Techno-robotics solutions
UAV	Unmanned aerial vehicle
WASPAS	Weighted aggregated sum product assessment
WV	Weight vector
ZTA	Zero trust architecture

1

Fundamental Concepts of Fuzzy Sets and Rough Sets

This chapter consists of fundamental notions that will help in the subsequent chapters and will make the book self-contained. Here we have discussed the fundamental notion of the characteristic function, FS, RS, CFS, FRS, and CFRS. Moreover, the fundamental operational laws based on these theories have been used to provide the foundation of aggregation theory.

1.1 Characteristic Function

Definition 1.1: For a universal set $\mathcal{U}$ the mapping f: $\mathcal{U} \to \{0, 1\}$ is called a characteristic function. For any characteristic function, we can define the unique subset of $\mathcal{U}$ as

$$A_{\mathrm{f}} = \{v \in \mathcal{U} : \mathrm{f}(v) = 1\}.$$

Similarly for any A $\subset \mathcal{U}$, we can define a unique characteristic function on $\mathcal{U}$ defined as

$$f_{\mathrm{A}} = \begin{cases} 1 & \text{if } v \in \mathcal{U} \\ 0 & \text{if } v \notin \mathcal{U} \end{cases}.$$

Remark 1.1: If f and g are two characteristic functions on $\mathcal{U}$, then

- $f \bigvee g$ is a characteristic function defined by $(f \bigvee g)(v) = f(v) \bigvee g(v)$
- $f \bigwedge g$ is a characteristic function defined by $(f \bigwedge g)(v) = f(v) \bigwedge g(v)$
- f' is the characteristic function given by $f'(v) = 1 - f(v)$

DOI: 10.1201/9788743807827-1

1.2 Fuzzy Set

In crisp set theory, if an element belongs to any set, then we propose its membership value equal to 1 and if an element does not belong to any set, then its membership value is equal to 0. It means that there is no chance of in between 0 and 1. But in many decision-making situations where the data is ambiguous, for example, Akram is healthy or Ali is rich. In these examples, the terms healthy and rich are imprecise or fuzzy in the sense that they can never be sharply defined. However, we do make sense of this information and use it in decision-making. The mathematical modeling of FS was first delivered by Zadeh [1] in 1965. The ideas of FS not only led to a revolution in other areas of science and technology but also in mathematics and logic. FS deals with imprecise information more efficiently since the MG falls in the unit interval [0, 1].

Definition 1.2: [1] For a universal set $\mathcal{U}$, FS is of the form $\mathcal{A} = \{(a(v)) : v \in \mathcal{U}\}$, where $a(v)$ is called MG and $a : \mathcal{U} \rightarrow [0, 1]$. For simplicity, the notion $\mathcal{A} = \{(a(v))\} = \{(a)\}$ is called a fuzzy number (FN).

Definition 1.3: [1] Assume that $\mathcal{A}_1 = \{a_1(v)\}$ and $\mathcal{A}_2 = \{a_2(v)\}$ are two FNs. The basic operational laws like sum, product, union, intersection, inclusion operation, and complement of the FS is given by:

(1) $\mathcal{A}_1 \subseteq \mathcal{A}_2$ iff $a_1(v) \leq a_2(v)$ for all $v \in \mathcal{U}$
(2) $\mathcal{A}_1 \cup \mathcal{A}_2 = \{\max(a_1(v), a_2(v))\}$
(3) $\mathcal{A}_1 \cap \mathcal{A}_2 = \{\min(a_1(v), a_2(v))\}$
(4) $\mathcal{A}_1^c = \{1 - a_1(v)\}$ where $\mathcal{A}_1^c$ denote the complement of $\mathcal{A}_1$.
(5) $\mathcal{A}_1 \oplus \mathcal{A}_2 = \{a_1(v) + a_2(v) - a_1(v)\, a_2(v)\}$
(6) $\mathcal{A}_1 \bigotimes \mathcal{A}_2 = \{a_1(v)\ a_2(v)\}$

1.3 Rough Set

The rough set theory, which was first introduced by Pawlak [2] in 1982, is a powerful mathematical framework for dealing with uncertainty and imprecision in data analysis. It is motivated especially by the need to handle incomplete, inconsistent, or vague information without requiring any prior assumptions, such as probability distributions or membership grades. Unlike classical set theory, concepts in rough sets are approximated by lower and upper bounds. This enables proper categorization of objects into very accurate and vague categories; the approach is very practically applicable in real-world issues like machine learning, decision-making, and data mining. The motivation behind such discoveries lies in the fact that the method can discover hidden patterns in the data, reduce dimensional spaces, and extract new knowledge. They complement other uncertainty-based models, such as fuzzy sets and probabilistic approaches, by offering a noninvasive, data-driven methodology. Their simplicity, reliance on discrete data, and interpretability make rough sets preferred solutions for solving classification and reasoning problems. This explains why the theory of rough sets still has relevance in modern applications related to artificial intelligence, big data analysis, and information systems.

The formal definition is given by:

Definition 1.4: [2] Assume that $\mathcal{U}_1$ and $\mathcal{U}_2$ are two nonempty subsets and $\mathcal{U}_1 \times \mathcal{U}_2$ is the Cartesian product given by $\{(v_1,\ v_2) : v_1 \in \mathcal{U}_1 \text{ and } v_2 \in \mathcal{U}_2\}$. A subset of a Cartesian product is referred to as a binary relation $\mathcal{R}_e$. If $(v_1,\ v_2) \in \mathcal{R}_e$ then we write $v_1 \mathcal{R}_e v_2$.

A relation $\mathcal{R}_e$ on $\mathcal{U}$ is called an equivalence relation if it satisfies the following conditions:

(1) Reflexive if $(v,\ v) \in \mathcal{R}_e$ for all $v \in \mathcal{R}_e$
(2) Symmetric if $(v_1,\ v_2) \in \mathcal{R}_e$ then $(v_2,\ v_1) \in \mathcal{R}_e$ for any $v_1,\ v_2 \in \mathcal{U}$
(3) Transitive if $(v_1,\ v_2) \in \mathcal{R}_e$ and $(v_2,\ v_3) \in \mathcal{R}_e$ then $(v_1,\ v_3) \in \mathcal{R}_e$ for any $v_1,\ v_2,\ v_3 \in \mathcal{U}$

The equivalence class of $v \in \mathcal{U}$, denoted by $[v]_{\mathcal{R}_e}$ is given by

$$[v]_{\mathcal{R}_e} = \{v \in \mathcal{U} \text{ such that } v\mathcal{R}_e v\}.$$

Definition 1.5: [2] Let $\mathcal{U}$ and $\mathcal{R}_e$ represent the universal set and an equivalence relation respectively, then a pair $(\mathcal{U},\ \mathcal{R}_e)$ is referred to as approximation space. For $\mathbb{A} \subset \mathcal{U}$, the set $\mathbb{A}$ is called definable if $\mathbb{A}$ can be written as a union of some equivalence classes of $\mathcal{U}$. Otherwise, $\mathbb{A}$ is not definable. If $\mathbb{A}$ is not definable $\mathbb{A}$ can be approximated into definable subsets known as lower and upper approximations as

$$\underline{\mathcal{R}_e}(\mathbb{A}) = \left\{\left(v \in \mathcal{U} : [v]_{\mathcal{R}_e} \subseteq \mathbb{A}\right)\right\},$$

$$\overline{\mathcal{R}_e}(\mathbb{A}) = \left\{\left(v \in \mathcal{U} :\ [v]_{\mathcal{R}_e} \cap \mathbb{A} \neq \emptyset\right)\right\}.$$

The set $\mathcal{R}_e(\mathbb{A}) = \left(\underline{\mathcal{R}_e}(\mathbb{A}),\ \overline{\mathcal{R}_e}(\mathbb{A})\right)$ is called RS, where $\underline{\mathcal{R}_e}(\mathbb{A}) \neq \overline{\mathcal{R}_e}(\mathbb{A})$.

Example 1.1: Let $\mathcal{U} = \{v_1, v_2, v_3\}$ is the universal set. Let $\mathcal{R}_e = \{(v_1, v_1), (v_1, v_3), (v_3, v_1), (v_2, v_2), (v_3, v_3)\}$ is the equivalence relation. Now equivalence classes are as follows:

$$[v_1]_{\mathcal{R}_e} = \{v_1, v_3\}, [v_2]_{\mathcal{R}_e} = \{v_2\}, [v_3]_{\mathcal{R}_e} = \{v_1, v_3\}.$$

Let $\mathbb{A} = \{v_1, v_2\} \subset \mathcal{U}$.

Therefore, we get $\underline{\mathcal{R}_e}(\mathbb{A}) = \{v_2\}$ and $\overline{\mathcal{R}_e}(\mathbb{A}) = \{v_1, v_2, v_3\}$. As we can see that $\underline{\mathcal{R}_e}(\mathbb{A}) \neq \overline{\mathcal{R}_e}(\mathbb{A})$. Hence the set $\mathcal{R}_e(\mathbb{A}) = \left(\underline{\mathcal{R}_e}(\mathbb{A}), \overline{\mathcal{R}_e}(\mathbb{A})\right)$ is called RS.

Theorem 1.1: [2] For any two equivalence relations $\mathcal{R}_{e_1}$ and $\mathcal{R}_{e_2}$ on a nonempty set $\mathcal{U}$ and $\mathbb{A}_1, \mathbb{A}_2 \subseteq \mathcal{U}$. The underneath statements hold:

(1) $\underline{\mathcal{R}_e}(\mathbb{A}_1) \subseteq \mathbb{A}_1 \subseteq \overline{\mathcal{R}_e}(\mathbb{A}_1)$
(2) $\overline{\mathcal{R}_e}(\mathbb{A}_1 \cup \mathbb{A}_2) = \overline{\mathcal{R}_e}(\mathbb{A}_1) \cup \overline{\mathcal{R}_e}(\mathbb{A}_2)$
(3) $\underline{\mathcal{R}_e}(\mathbb{A}_1 \cap \mathbb{A}_2) = \underline{\mathcal{R}_e}(\mathbb{A}_1) \cap \underline{\mathcal{R}_e}(\mathbb{A}_2)$
(4) If $\mathbb{A}_1 \subseteq \mathbb{A}_2$ then $\overline{\mathcal{R}_e}(\mathbb{A}_1) \subseteq \overline{\mathcal{R}_e}(\mathbb{A}_2)$
(5) $\underline{\mathcal{R}_e}(\mathbb{A}_1 \cup \mathbb{A}_2) \supseteq \underline{\mathcal{R}_e}(\mathbb{A}_1) \cup \underline{\mathcal{R}_e}(\mathbb{A}_2)$
(6) $\overline{\mathcal{R}_e}(\mathbb{A}_1 \cap \mathbb{A}_2) \subseteq \overline{\mathcal{R}_e}(\mathbb{A}_1) \cap \overline{\mathcal{R}_e}(\mathbb{A}_2)$

1.4 Fuzzy Rough Set

In this section, we have discussed the definition of FRS and its fundamental laws. Here we have discussed the notion of fuzzy relation on a universal set and based on this relation we have discussed the idea of a fuzzy rough set. The overall theory is given by

Definition 1.6: [3] A fuzzy set subset $a_{\mathcal{R}_e}$ of $\mathcal{U}^2$ defined by a mapping $a_{\mathcal{R}_e} : \mathcal{U} \times \mathcal{U} \to [0, 1]$ is called fuzzy relation and it is called

(1) Reflexive if and only if $a_{\mathcal{R}_e}(v, v) = 1$
(2) Symmetric if and only if $a_{\mathcal{R}_e}(u, v) = a_{\mathcal{R}_e}(v, u)$
(3) Transitive if $a_{\mathcal{R}_e}(u, w) \geq a_{\mathcal{R}_e}(u, v) \bigwedge a_{\mathcal{R}_e}(v, w)$

Here, $a_{\mathcal{R}_e}$ is membership function and $a_{\mathcal{R}_e}(v, v)$ is called membership value for any $v \in \mathcal{U}$. A fuzzy relation is said to be an equivalence relation if it is reflexive, symmetric, and transitive.

Definition 1.7: [3] Assume that $\mathcal{R}_e$ is a fuzzy relation and $\mathcal{U}$ is a universal set. Then $(\mathcal{U}, \mathcal{R}_e)$ is called fuzzy approximation space. Now for any FS

$\mathcal{A} = \{(a(v)) : v \in \mathcal{U}\}$, the upper and lower approximation of $\mathcal{A}$ concerning approximation space $(\mathcal{U}, \mathcal{R}_e)$ is given by

$$\overline{\mathcal{R}_e}(v) = \bigvee_{v \in \mathcal{U}} \left\{a_{\mathcal{R}_e}(u, v) \bigwedge a(v)\right\},$$
$$\underline{\mathcal{R}_e}(v) = \bigwedge_{v \in \mathcal{U}} \left\{1 - a_{\mathcal{R}_e}(u, v) \bigvee a(v)\right\}.$$

Then the pair $\left(\overline{\mathcal{R}_e}(v), \underline{\mathcal{R}_e}(v)\right)$ is called fuzzy rough set (FRS). For the sake of simplicity, fuzzy rough number (FRN) is denoted by $\mathcal{A} = \{(\overline{a}, \underline{a})\}$.

1.5 Complex Fuzzy Set

In this section, we have discussed the notion of CFS that was based on Ramot et al.'s [4] approach and Tamir et al.'s [5] approach. Both ideas are given by

Definition 1.8: [4] Let $\mathcal{U}$ be a universal set. Then the notion of CFS is given by

$$\mathcal{A} = \left\{a(v) = r(v)\, e^{2\pi\theta(v)} : v \in \mathcal{U}\right\},$$

where $a(v)$ is an MG and it is defined in the sense that $a(v) = r(v)\, e^{2\pi\theta(v)}$ such that $r(v)$ and $\theta(v)$ are called amplitude terms and phase terms respectively with the condition that $r(v), \theta(v) \in [0, 1]$.

Definition 1.9: [5] For a universal set $\mathcal{U}$, the notion of CFS delivered by Tamir et al. [5] is of the form:

$$\mathcal{A} = \{(v, a(v) + \iota b(v)) \mid 0 \leq a(v) \leq 1 \text{ and } 0 \leq b(v) \leq 1\},$$

where $a(v)$ denotes the real part of the MG and $a : U \to [0, 1]$ and $b(v)$ denote imaginary part of the MG with $b : U \to [0, 1]$.

1.6 Complex Fuzzy Rough Set

In this section, we have discussed two different forms of CFRS. Moreover, we have discussed the basic operational laws of these developed ideas. Here we have discussed the notion of complex fuzzy relation. Then based on this relation we have discussed the notion of CFRSs in two different forms.

Definition 1.10: [6] Let $\mathcal{U}$ be the universal set, then any complex fuzzy subset $\mathcal{R}_e$ of $U \times U$ referred to as $\mathcal{R}_e = \{(u, v), \beta(u, v) \mid \beta(u, v) = \alpha(u, v) + \iota b(u, v)\}$, where $\alpha(u, v) > 0$, $b(u, v) > 0$ and $\beta(u, v) : \mathcal{U} \times \mathcal{U} \to [0, 1] + \iota [0, 1]$ is called complex fuzzy relation (CFR) on $\mathcal{U}$.

Definition 1.11: [6] For universal set $\mathcal{U}$ and CFR "$\mathcal{R}_e$" the pair $(\mathcal{U}, \mathcal{R}_e)$ is called complex fuzzy approximation space. Then for any CFS $\mathcal{A} = \{(v, a_{\mathcal{A}}(v) + \iota b_{\mathcal{A}}(v)) \mid 0 \leq a_{\mathcal{A}}(v) \leq 1 \text{ and } 0 \leq b_{\mathcal{A}}(v) \leq 1\}$, the upper and lower approximation of v for $(\mathcal{U}, \mathcal{R}_e)$ are defined by

$$\overline{\mathcal{R}_e}(\mathcal{A}) = \left\{ \left(v, \mathrm{M}_{\overline{\mathcal{R}_e}}(v)\right) \middle| v \in \mathcal{U} \right\},$$

$$\underline{\mathcal{R}_e}(\mathcal{A}) = \left\{ \left(v, \mathrm{M}_{\underline{\mathcal{R}_e}}(v)\right) \middle| v \in \mathcal{U} \right\},$$

where

$$\mathrm{M}_{\overline{\mathcal{R}_e}}(v) = \bigvee_{v \in \mathcal{U}} \left[\alpha(u, v) \bigwedge a_{\mathcal{A}}(v)\right] + \iota \bigvee_{v \in \mathcal{U}} \left[b(u, v) \bigwedge b_{\mathcal{A}}(v)\right],$$

$$\mathrm{M}_{\underline{\mathcal{R}_e}}(v) = \bigwedge\nolimits_{v \in \mathcal{U}} [1 - \alpha(u, v) \bigvee a_{\mathcal{A}}(v)] + \iota \bigwedge\nolimits_{v \in \mathcal{U}} [1 - b(u, v) \bigvee b_{\mathcal{A}}(v)].$$

The pair $\left(\overline{\mathcal{R}_e}(\mathcal{A}), \underline{\mathcal{R}_e}(\mathcal{A})\right)$ is CFRS if $\overline{\mathcal{R}_e}(\mathcal{A}) \neq \underline{\mathcal{R}_e}(\mathcal{A})$. For the sake of simplicity, complex fuzzy rough number (CFRN) is denoted by $\mathcal{A} = \left\{\left(\overline{a} + \iota\overline{b}, \underline{a} + \iota\underline{b}\right)\right\}$.

Definition 1.12: [6] For a CFRN $\mathcal{A} = \left\{\left(\overline{a} + \iota\overline{b}, \underline{a} + \iota\underline{b}\right)\right\}$, the idea of score function and accuracy function is defined by

$$\text{Scor.}(\mathcal{A}_1) = \frac{1}{4}\left(\overline{a} + \underline{a} + \overline{b} + \underline{b}\right) \in [0, 1],$$

and

$$Accr.(\mathcal{A}_1) = \frac{1}{4}\left(\overline{a} + \underline{a} - \overline{b} - \underline{b}\right) \in [-1, 1].$$

1.7 Some Basic T-norms and T-conorms

In this section of the chapter, we will discuss the basic definitions of t-norm and t-conorm. Moreover, some fundamental t-norms and t-conorms like Hamacher t-norm and t-conorm, Aczel-Alsina t-norm and t-norm, and Einstein t-norm and t-conorm.

Definition 1.13: [7] A function $\mathfrak{T} : [0, 1] \times [0, 1] \to [0, 1]$ is called t-norm if the following conditions hold:

(1) $\mathfrak{T}(s, t) = \mathfrak{T}(t, s)$ for all $s, t \in [0, 1]$

(2) $\mathfrak{T}(\mathfrak{T}(s, t), \mathrm{t}) = \mathfrak{T}(s, \mathfrak{T}(t, \mathrm{t}))$ for all $s, t, \mathrm{t} \in [0, 1]$

(3) For all $s, t, s^*, t^* \in [0, 1]$, If $s \leq t$ and $s^* \leq t^*$, then $\mathfrak{T}(s, s^*) \leq \mathfrak{T}(t, t^*)$

(4) $\mathfrak{T}(s,\ 1) = s$ for all $s \in [0,\ 1]$.

Definition 1.14: [8] A function $\mathfrak{T}^* : [0,\ 1] \times [0,\ 1] \to [0,\ 1]$ is called t-conorm if the following conditions hold:

(1) $\mathfrak{T}^*(s,t) = \mathfrak{T}^*(t,s)$ for all $s,\ t \in [0,\ 1]$

(2) $\mathfrak{T}^*(\mathfrak{T}^*(s,t), \mathrm{t}) = \mathfrak{T}^*(s, \mathfrak{T}^*(t, \mathrm{t}))$ for all $s,\ t, \mathrm{t} \in [0,\ 1]$

(3) For all $s, t,\ s^*,\ t^* \in [0,\ 1]$, If $s \leq t$ and $s^* \leq t^*$, then $\mathfrak{T}^*(s,\ s^*) \leq \mathfrak{T}^*(t,\ t^*)$

(4) $\mathfrak{T}^*(s,\ 0) = s$ for all $s \in [0,\ 1]$.

Definition 1.15: [9] Hamacher t-norm and t-conorm are defined respectively by

$$\mathfrak{T}(s_1,\ s_2) = s_1 \oplus s_2 = \frac{(s_1 + s_2 - s_1 s_2) - (1-\rho)\, s_1 s_2}{1 - (1-\rho)\, s_1 s_2}.\ \rho > 0.$$

$$\mathfrak{T}^*(s_1,\ s_2) = s_1 \otimes s_2 = \frac{s_1 s_2}{\rho + (1-\rho)(s_1 + s_2 - s_1 s_2)},\ \rho > 0.$$

Definition 1.16: [8, 10] Average and geometric t-norm and t-conorm are defined respectively by

$$\mathfrak{T}(s_1,\ s_1) = s_1 \oplus s_2 = (s_1 + s_2 - s_1 s_2).$$

$$\mathfrak{T}^*(s_1,\ s_2) = s_1 \otimes s_2 = s_1 s_2.$$

Definition 1.17: [11] Aczel-Alsina discussed the notions of t-norm and t-conorm based on functional equations given by

$$\mathfrak{T}(s_1,\ s_2) = \begin{cases} \mathfrak{T}(s_1,\ s_2) & \text{if } \rho = 0 \\ \min(s_1,\ s_2) & \text{if } \rho = \infty \\ e^{-((-\log\, s_1\,)^\rho + (-\log\, s_2\,)^\rho)^{\frac{1}{\rho}}}, & \text{otherwise} \end{cases}$$

$$\mathfrak{T}^*(s_1,\ s_2) = \begin{cases} \mathfrak{T}^*(s_1,\ s_2) & \text{if } \rho = 0 \\ \max(s_1,\ s_2) & \text{if } \rho = \infty \\ 1 - e^{-((-\log(1-\varepsilon_1)\,)^\rho + (-\log(1-\varepsilon_2)\,)^\rho)^{\frac{1}{\rho}}}, & \text{otherwise} \end{cases}$$

where $\rho \in [0,\ \infty]$.

Definition 1.18: [12] Einstein t-norm and t-conorm are defined respectively by

$$\mathfrak{T}(s_1,\ s_2) = s_1 \oplus s_2 = \frac{(s_1 + s_2)}{1 + s_1 s_2},$$
$$\mathfrak{T}^*(s_1,\ s_2) = s_1 \otimes s_2 = \frac{s_1 s_2}{1 + (1 - s_1)(1 - s_2)},$$

where $s_1,\ s_2 \in [0,\ 1]$.

1.8 Scope and Organization of the Book

This book, titled "*Complex Fuzzy Rough Sets and its Applications*" aims to provide a comprehensive understanding of dealing with the uncertainties using the pairs of fuzzy rough sets. It will cover the theoretical foundation, practical implementation, and real-world applications of these techniques. This book is intended for researchers, engineers, and practitioners working in the fields of decision-making, computational intelligence, fuzzy set theory, and soft computing. It assumes a basic understanding of fuzzy set concepts and decision-making approaches. The book is organized into nine chapters:

Chapter 1 consists of fundamental notions that can help us to define the aggregation theory. Here we have discussed the fundamental notion of the characteristic function, fuzzy set (FS) by Zadeh, rough set (RS), fuzzy rough set (FRS), complex fuzzy set (CFS), and complex fuzzy rough set (CFRS). Moreover, the fundamental operational laws based on these theories have been used to provide the foundation of aggregation theory.

In Chapter 2, the WASPAS approach with complex fuzzy rough aggregation operators is proposed and we have provided its applications in the government and defense sectors to provide a more robust decision-making framework regarding cybersecurity issues. By using CFRS, this technique models multifaceted parameters like threat severity, vulnerability exploitation likelihood, and resource criticality. In government and defense, it ensures the proper evaluation and prioritization of cybersecurity risks and, therefore, proactive mitigation of threats. This model has been applied to classify and assess cyber-resilient network architectures where data is imprecise and decisions are time-critical.

In Chapter 3, a new MCDM framework has been proposed for the selection of the neural network framework. Additionally, we have proposed four innovative aggregation operators, for example, complex fuzzy rough Yager power averaging (CFRYPA), complex fuzzy rough Yager power weighted averaging (CFRYPWA), complex fuzzy rough Yager power geometric (CFRYPG), and complex fuzzy rough Yager power weighted geometric (CFRYPWG). We have provided a detailed case study of the selection of the neural network frameworks for AI predictive models. The case study demonstrates how our MCDM technique can process fuzzy rough information to assess and rank the best neural network frameworks according to the criteria.

In Chapter 4, we have defined the notion of sine trigonometric complex fuzzy rough weighted averaging (STCFRWA), sine trigonometric complex fuzzy rough ordered weighted averaging (STCFROWA), sine trigonometric complex fuzzy rough hybrid averaging (STCFRHA), sine trigonometric complex fuzzy rough weighted geometric (STCFRWG), sine trigonometric complex fuzzy rough ordered weighted geometric (STCFROWG), sine trigonometric complex fuzzy rough hybrid geometric (STCFRHG) operators. To discuss the application perspective of the developed theory, we have initiated an algorithm for the developed approach.

In Chapter 5, we have delivered the basic operational laws for CFRNs based on Aczel-Alsina t-norm and t-conorm. We have delivered the notion of complex fuzzy rough Aczel-Alsina weighted, ordered weighted, and hybrid aggregation operators. We have proposed the application of the delivered approaches by defining an algorithm. We have provided an illustrative example through which we can classify the different technologies and tools in electrical engineering design and analysis.

In Chapter 6, we have developed several sophisticated operators: These aggregation operators are complex fuzzy rough power averaging (CFRPA), complex fuzzy rough power weighted averaging (CFRPWA), complex fuzzy rough power geometric (CFRPG), and complex fuzzy rough power weighted geometric (CFRPWG). In addition, we have presented a detailed MCDM approach that can efficiently handle problems with complex fuzzy rough data, especially concerning AI solution selection. This integrated framework not only improves the decision-making process for selecting AI solutions but also defines a new paradigm for AI solution evaluation and implementation in different domains.

Data science advancements have changed aerospace engineering. It now helps in accurate decision-making and optimization of complex systems. Chapter 7, introduces advanced data science techniques integrated with the complex fuzzy rough WASPAS approach for solving MCDM problems in aerospace applications. We have developed the Einstein aggregation theory based on CFRNs and then used these aggregation operators to develop the WASPAS approach. The outcomes show that this hybrid method provides more accuracy along with adaptability, giving opportunities for intelligent and resilient solutions in aerospace.

Chapter 8 offers a new strategy to address the environmental challenges by proposing the CFRS theory to design new sophisticated aggregation operators. We have proposed complex fuzzy rough Dombi power averaging (CFRDPA), complex fuzzy rough Dombi power weighted averaging (CFRDPWA), complex fuzzy rough Dombi power geometric (CFRDPG), and complex fuzzy rough Dombi power weighted geometric (CFRDPWG) aggregation operators. Based on these operators, we have constructed an integrated MCDM method for environmental decision-making situations involving fuzzy rough data.

In Chapter 9, we have proposed a novel theoretical framework for enhancing robotic decision-making using CFRS, especially in the context of autonomous industrial environments where uncertainty, roughness, and complexity of information are inevitable. We have introduced the notions of complex fuzzy rough Frank power averaging (CFRFPA), complex fuzzy rough Frank power weighted averaging (CFRFPWA), complex fuzzy rough Frank power geometric (CFRFPG), and complex fuzzy rough Frank power weighted geometric (CFRFPWG) operators. This chapter demonstrates how the proposed approach can be applied to solve practical problems in industrial automation decision-making where uncertainty and imprecision are inevitable.

Overall, this book aims to provide a comprehensive and in-depth understanding of complex fuzzy rough sets for decision-making approaches.

2

WASPAS Approach Based on Complex Fuzzy Rough Aggregation Operators and their Application to Cybersecurity

In this chapter, the use and effectiveness of the WASPAS approach in different decision-making problems will be discussed and especially the WASPAS technique with complex fuzzy rough aggregation operators will be used in the government and defense sectors to provide a more robust decision-making framework regarding cybersecurity issues. This method combines in itself the strengths of fuzzy logic, rough sets, and multicriteria decision-making to address issues of uncertainty and vagueness in cyber security issues. By using complex fuzzy rough sets, it models multifaceted parameters like threat severity, vulnerability exploitation likelihood, and resource criticality. It is the methodology of WASPAS that combines both weighted sum and weighted product strategies for evaluating and ranking potential countermeasures or system configurations under uncertain conditions. In government and defense, it ensures the proper evaluation and prioritization of cybersecurity risks and, therefore, proactive mitigation of threats. The model has been applied to classify and assess cyber-resilient network architectures where data is imprecise and decisions are time-critical.

2.1 Hamacher Operational Rules Based on CFRNs

This section of the chapter is devoted to defining the basic operational rules based on the Hamacher t-norm and t-conorm. The defined operational rules are given by

Definition 2.1: Let $\mathcal{A}_1 = \left\{\left(\overline{a_1} + \iota\overline{b_1},\ \underline{a_1} + \iota\underline{b_1}\right)\right\}$ and $\mathcal{A}_2 = \left\{\left(\overline{a_2} + \iota\overline{b_2},\ \underline{a_2} + \iota\underline{b_2}\right)\right\}$ be two CFRNs with $s > 0$ and $t > 0$, then

DOI: 10.1201/9788743807827-2

$$\text{a) } \mathcal{A}_1 \oplus \mathcal{A}_2 = \left(\begin{array}{c} \frac{\overline{a_1}+\overline{a_2}-\overline{a_1}\ \overline{a_2}-(1-t)\overline{a_1}\ \overline{a_2}}{1-(1-t)\overline{a_1}\ \overline{a_2}} + \iota \frac{\overline{b_1}+\overline{b_2}-\overline{b_1}\ \overline{b_2}-(1-t)\overline{b_1}\ \overline{b_2}}{1-(1-t)\overline{b_1}\ \overline{b_2}}, \\ \frac{\underline{a_1}+\underline{a_2}-\underline{a_1}\ \underline{a_2}-(1-t)\underline{a_1}\ \underline{a_2}}{1-(1-t)\underline{a_1}\ \underline{a_2}} + \iota \frac{\underline{b_1}+\underline{b_2}-\underline{b_1}\ \underline{b_2}-(1-t)\underline{b_1}\ \underline{b_2}}{1-(1-t)\underline{b_1}\ \underline{b_2}} \end{array} \right),$$

$$\text{b) } \mathcal{A}_1 \otimes \mathcal{A}_2 = \left(\begin{array}{c} \frac{\overline{a_1}\ \overline{a_2}}{t+(1-t)(\overline{a_1}+\overline{a_2}-\overline{a_1}\ \overline{a_2})} + \iota \frac{\overline{b_1}\ \overline{b_2}}{t+(1-t)\left(\overline{b_1}+\overline{b_2}-\overline{b_1}\ \overline{b_2}\right)}, \\ \frac{\underline{a_1}\ \underline{a_2}}{t+(1-t)\left(\underline{a_1}+\underline{a_2}-\underline{a_1}\ \underline{a_2}\right)} + \iota \frac{\underline{b_1}\ \underline{b_2}}{t+(1-t)\left(\underline{b_1}+\underline{b_2}-\underline{b_1}\ \underline{b_2}\right)} \end{array} \right),$$

c) $s\mathcal{A}_1$

$$= \left(\begin{array}{c} \frac{(1+(t-1)\overline{a_1})^s-(1-\overline{a_1})^s}{(1+(t-1)\overline{a_1})^s+(t-1)(1-\overline{a_1})^s} + \iota \frac{\left(1+(t-1)\overline{b_1}\right)^s-\left(1-\overline{b_1}\right)^s}{\left(1+(t-1)\overline{b_1}\right)^s+(t-1)\left(1-\overline{b_1}\right)^s}, \\ \frac{\left(1+(t-1)\underline{a_1}\right)^s-\left(1-\underline{a_1}\right)^s}{\left(1+(t-1)\underline{a_1}\right)^s+(t-1)\left(1-\underline{a_1}\right)^s} + \iota \frac{\left(1+(t-1)\underline{b_1}\right)^s-\left(1-\underline{b_1}\right)^s}{\left(1+(t-1)\underline{b_1}\right)^s+(t-1)\left(1-\underline{b_1}\right)^s} \end{array} \right),$$

d) $(\mathcal{A}_1)^s$

$$= \left(\begin{array}{c} \frac{t(\overline{a_1})^s}{(1+(t-1)(1-\overline{a_1}))^s+(t-1)(\overline{a_1})^s} + \iota \frac{t\left(\overline{b_1}\right)^s}{\left(1+(t-1)\left(1-\overline{b_1}\right)\right)^s+(t-1)\left(\overline{b_1}\right)^s}, \\ \frac{t\left(\underline{a_1}\right)^s}{\left(1+(t-1)\left(1-\underline{a_1}\right)\right)^s+(t-1)\left(\underline{a_1}\right)^s} + \iota \frac{t\left(\underline{b_1}\right)^s}{\left(1+(t-1)\left(1-\underline{b_1}\right)\right)^s+(t-1)\left(\underline{b_1}\right)^s} \end{array} \right).$$

2.2 Complex Fuzzy Rough Hamacher Arithmetic and Geometric Aggregation Operators

This section of the chapter is devoted to defining the notion of complex fuzzy rough Hamacher weighted average (CFRHWA) and complex fuzzy rough Hamacher weighted geometric (CFRHWG) aggregation operators. This section of the chapter is about the aggregation theory of CFRNs based on the developed operational laws for CFRNs. Throughout in our next study, $\mathcal{A}_j = \left\{\left(\overline{a_j} + \iota\overline{b_j},\ \underline{a_j} + \iota\underline{b_j}\right)\right\}$ $(j = 1,\ 2, \ldots,\ n)$ be a family of CFRNs and $\omega = (\omega_1,\ \omega_2, \ldots,\ \omega_n)$ be a weight vector of $\mathcal{A}_j$ $(j = 1,\ 2, ..,\ n)$ with $\omega_j \in [0,\ 1]$ and $\sum_{j=1}^{n} \omega_j = 1$.

The defined theory is given by

Definition 2.2: The CFRHWA operator is defined by

$$\text{CFRHWA}_\omega\left(\mathcal{A}_1,\ \mathcal{A}_2,\ \mathcal{A}_3,\ \ldots,\ \mathcal{A}_n\right) = \bigoplus_{j=1}^{n}\left(\omega_j \mathcal{A}_j\right). \tag{2.1}$$

Theorem 2.1: The aggregated result obtained by using eqn (2.1) is again CFRN and it is given by

$$\mathrm{CFRHWA}_{\omega}\left(\mathcal{A}_1,\ \mathcal{A}_2,\ \mathcal{A}_3,\ \ldots,\ \mathcal{A}_n\right)=\bigoplus_{j=1}^{n}\left(\omega_j\mathcal{A}_j\right),$$

$$=\left(\begin{array}{c}\dfrac{\left(\begin{array}{c}\prod_{j=1}^{n}\left(1+(t-1)\overline{a_j}\right)^{\omega_j}\\-\prod_{j=1}^{n}\left(1-\overline{a_j}\right)^{\omega_j}\end{array}\right)}{\left(\begin{array}{c}\prod_{j=1}^{n}\left(1+(t-1)\overline{a_j}\right)^{\omega_j}+\\(t-1)\prod_{j=1}^{n}\left(1-\overline{a_j}\right)^{\omega_j}\end{array}\right)}+\iota\dfrac{\left(\begin{array}{c}\prod_{j=1}^{n}\left(1+(t-1)\overline{b_j}\right)^{\omega_j}\\-\prod_{j=1}^{n}\left(1-\overline{b_j}\right)^{\omega_j}\end{array}\right)}{\left(\begin{array}{c}\prod_{j=1}^{n}\left(1+(t-1)\overline{b_j}\right)^{\omega_j}+\\(t-1)\prod_{j=1}^{n}\left(1-\overline{b_j}\right)^{\omega_j}\end{array}\right)},\\\dfrac{\left(\begin{array}{c}\prod_{j=1}^{n}\left(1+(t-1)\underline{a_j}\right)^{\omega_j}\\-\prod_{j=1}^{n}\left(1-\underline{a_j}\right)^{\omega_j}\end{array}\right)}{\left(\begin{array}{c}\prod_{j=1}^{n}\left(1+(t-1)\underline{a_j}\right)^{\omega_j}+\\(t-1)\prod_{j=1}^{n}\left(1-\underline{a_j}\right)^{\omega_j}\end{array}\right)}+\iota\dfrac{\left(\begin{array}{c}\prod_{j=1}^{n}\left(1+(t-1)\underline{b_j}\right)^{\omega_j}\\-\prod_{j=1}^{n}\left(1-\underline{b_j}\right)^{\omega_j}\end{array}\right)}{\left(\begin{array}{c}\prod_{j=1}^{n}\left(1+(t-1)\underline{b_j}\right)^{\omega_j}+\\(t-1)\prod_{j=1}^{n}\left(1-\underline{b_j}\right)^{\omega_j}\end{array}\right)}\end{array}\right). \tag{2.2}$$

Proof: We will prove it through mathematical induction.

Let $n=1$, so we get that $\omega_1=1$ and eqn (2.2) becomes:

$$\mathrm{CFRHWA}_{\omega}\left(\mathcal{A}_1,\ \mathcal{A}_2,\ \mathcal{A}_3,\ \ldots,\ \mathcal{A}_n\right)=\mathcal{A}_1$$

$$=\left(\begin{array}{c}\dfrac{\left(\begin{array}{c}\left(1+(t-1)\overline{a_j}\right)\\-\left(1-\overline{a_j}\right)\end{array}\right)}{\left(\begin{array}{c}\left(1+(t-1)\overline{a_j}\right)+\\(t-1)\left(1-\overline{a_j}\right)\end{array}\right)}+\mathrm{i}\dfrac{\left(\begin{array}{c}\left(1+(t-1)\overline{b_j}\right)\\-\left(1-\overline{b_j}\right)\end{array}\right)}{\left(\begin{array}{c}\left(1+(t-1)\overline{b_j}\right)+\\(t-1)\left(1-\overline{b_j}\right)\end{array}\right)},\\\dfrac{\left(\begin{array}{c}\left(1+(t-1)\underline{a_j}\right)\\-\left(1-\underline{a_j}\right)\end{array}\right)}{\left(\begin{array}{c}\left(1+(t-1)\underline{a_j}\right)+\\(t-1)\left(1-\underline{a_j}\right)\end{array}\right)}+\mathrm{i}\dfrac{\left(\begin{array}{c}\left(1+(t-1)\underline{b_j}\right)\\-\left(1-\underline{b_j}\right)\end{array}\right)}{\left(\begin{array}{c}\left(1+(t-1)\underline{b_j}\right)+\\(t-1)\left(1-\underline{b_j}\right)\end{array}\right)}\end{array}\right).$$

Thus, for $n=1$ (2.2) holds.

Next, suppose that eqn (2.2) holds for $n=m$:

$$\mathrm{CFRHWA}_{\omega}\left(\mathcal{A}_1,\ \mathcal{A}_2,\ \mathcal{A}_3,\ \ldots,\ \mathcal{A}_m\right)=\bigoplus_{j=1}^{m}\left(\omega_j\mathcal{A}_j\right)$$

$$= \left(\frac{\frac{\left(\prod_{j=1}^{m}(1+(t-1)\overline{a_j})^{\omega_j} - \prod_{j=1}^{m}(1-\overline{a_j})^{\omega_j}\right)}{\left(\prod_{j=1}^{m}(1+(t-1)\overline{a_j})^{\omega_j} + (t-1)\prod_{j=1}^{m}(1-\overline{a_j})^{\omega_j}\right)} + \mathrm{i}\frac{\left(\prod_{j=1}^{m}(1+(t-1)\overline{b_j})^{\omega_j} - \prod_{j=1}^{m}(1-\overline{b_j})^{\omega_j}\right)}{\left(\prod_{j=1}^{m}(1+(t-1)\overline{b_j})^{\omega_j} + (t-1)\prod_{j=1}^{m}(1-\overline{b_j})^{\omega_j}\right)},}{\frac{\left(\prod_{j=1}^{m}\left(1+(t-1)\underline{a_j}\right)^{\omega_j} - \prod_{j=1}^{m}\left(1-\underline{a_j}\right)^{\omega_j}\right)}{\left(\prod_{j=1}^{m}\left(1+(t-1)\underline{a_j}\right)^{\omega_j} + (t-1)\prod_{j=1}^{m}\left(1-\underline{a_j}\right)^{\omega_j}\right)} + \mathrm{i}\frac{\left(\prod_{j=1}^{m}\left(1+(t-1)\underline{b_j}\right)^{\omega_j} - \prod_{j=1}^{m}\left(1-\underline{b_j}\right)^{\omega_j}\right)}{\left(\prod_{j=1}^{m}\left(1+(t-1)\underline{b_j}\right)^{\omega_j} + (t-1)\prod_{j=1}^{m}\left(1-\underline{b_j}\right)^{\omega_j}\right)}} \right).$$

Now let $n = m + 1$. Then we have:

$$\begin{aligned} &\mathrm{CFRHWA}_{\omega}\left(\mathcal{A}_1, \mathcal{A}_2, \mathcal{A}_3, \ldots, \mathcal{A}_m, \mathcal{A}_{m+1}\right) \\ &= \bigoplus_{j=1}^{m}\left(\omega_j \mathcal{A}_j\right) \oplus \left(\omega_{m+1}\, \mathcal{A}_{m+1}\right) \end{aligned}$$

$$= \left(\frac{\frac{\left(\prod_{j=1}^{m}(1+(t-1)\overline{a_j})^{\omega_j} - \prod_{j=1}^{m}(1-\overline{a_j})^{\omega_j}\right)}{\left(\prod_{j=1}^{m}(1+(t-1)\overline{a_j})^{\omega_j} + (t-1)\prod_{j=1}^{m}(1-\overline{a_j})^{\omega_j}\right)} + \mathrm{i}\frac{\left(\prod_{j=1}^{m}(1+(t-1)\overline{b_j})^{\omega_j} - \prod_{j=1}^{m}(1-\overline{b_j})^{\omega_j}\right)}{\left(\prod_{j=1}^{m}(1+(t-1)\overline{b_j})^{\omega_j} + (t-1)\prod_{j=1}^{m}(1-\overline{b_j})^{\omega_j}\right)},}{\frac{\left(\prod_{j=1}^{m}\left(1+(t-1)\underline{a_j}\right)^{\omega_j} - \prod_{j=1}^{m}\left(1-\underline{a_j}\right)^{\omega_j}\right)}{\left(\prod_{j=1}^{m}\left(1+(t-1)\underline{a_j}\right)^{\omega_j} + (t-1)\prod_{j=1}^{m}\left(1-\underline{a_j}\right)^{\omega_j}\right)} + \mathrm{i}\frac{\left(\prod_{j=1}^{m}\left(1+(t-1)\underline{b_j}\right)^{\omega_j} - \prod_{j=1}^{m}\left(1-\underline{b_j}\right)^{\omega_j}\right)}{\left(\prod_{j=1}^{m}\left(1+(t-1)\underline{b_j}\right)^{\omega_j} + (t-1)\prod_{j=1}^{m}\left(1-\underline{b_j}\right)^{\omega_j}\right)}} \right)$$

$$\oplus\left(\begin{array}{c}\dfrac{\left(\begin{array}{c}(1+(t-1)\,\overline{a_j})^{\omega_{m+1}}\\ -(1-\overline{a_j})^{\omega_{m+1}}\end{array}\right)}{\left(\begin{array}{c}(1+(t-1)\,\overline{a_j})^{\omega_{m+1}}\\ +(t-1)\,(1-\overline{a_j})^{\omega_{m+1}}\end{array}\right)}+\mathrm{i}\dfrac{\left(\begin{array}{c}(1+(t-1)\,\overline{b_j})^{\omega_{m+1}}\\ -(1-\overline{b_j})^{\omega_{m+1}}\end{array}\right)}{\left(\begin{array}{c}(1+(t-1)\,\overline{b_j})^{\lambda}\\ +(t-1)\,(1-\overline{b_j})^{\lambda}\end{array}\right)},\\ \dfrac{\left(\begin{array}{c}\left(1+(t-1)\,\underline{a_j}\right)^{\omega_{m+1}}\\ -\left(1-\underline{a_j}\right)^{\omega_{m+1}}\end{array}\right)}{\left(\begin{array}{c}\left(1+(t-1)\,\underline{a_j}\right)^{\omega_{m+1}}\\ +(t-1)\left(1-\underline{a_j}\right)^{\omega_{m+1}}\end{array}\right)}+\mathrm{i}\dfrac{\left(\begin{array}{c}\left(1+(t-1)\,\underline{b_j}\right)^{\omega_{m+1}}\\ -\left(1-\underline{b_j}\right)^{\omega_{m+1}}\end{array}\right)}{\left(\begin{array}{c}\left(1+(t-1)\,\underline{b_j}\right)^{\lambda}\\ +(t-1)\left(1-\underline{b_j}\right)^{\lambda}\end{array}\right)}\end{array}\right)$$

$$=\left(\begin{array}{c}\dfrac{\left(\begin{array}{c}\prod_{j=1}^{m+1}(1+(t-1)\,\overline{a_j})^{\omega_j}\\ -\prod_{j}^{m+1}(1-\overline{a_j})^{\omega_j}\end{array}\right)}{\left(\begin{array}{c}\prod_{j=1}^{m+1}(1+(t-1)\,\overline{a_j})^{\omega_j}+\\ (t-1)\prod_{j=1}^{m+1}(1-\overline{a_j})^{\omega_j}\end{array}\right)}+\mathrm{i}\dfrac{\left(\begin{array}{c}\prod_{j=1}^{m+1}(1+(t-1)\,\overline{b_j})^{\omega_j}\\ -\prod_{j}^{m+1}(1-\overline{b_j})^{\omega_j}\end{array}\right)}{\left(\begin{array}{c}\prod_{j=1}^{m+1}(1+(t-1)\,\overline{b_j})^{\omega_j}+\\ (t-1)\prod_{j=1}^{m+1}(1-\overline{b_j})^{\omega_j}\end{array}\right)},\\ \dfrac{\left(\begin{array}{c}\prod_{j=1}^{m+1}\left(1+(t-1)\,\underline{a_j}\right)^{\omega_j}\\ -\prod_{j}^{m+1}\left(1-\underline{a_j}\right)^{\omega_j}\end{array}\right)}{\left(\begin{array}{c}\prod_{j=1}^{m+1}\left(1+(t-1)\,\underline{a_j}\right)^{\omega_j}+\\ (t-1)\prod_{j=1}^{m+1}\left(1-\underline{a_j}\right)^{\omega_j}\end{array}\right)}+\mathrm{i}\dfrac{\left(\begin{array}{c}\prod_{j=1}^{m+1}\left(1+(t-1)\,\underline{b_j}\right)^{\omega_j}\\ -\prod_{j}^{m+1}\left(1-\underline{b_j}\right)^{\omega_j}\end{array}\right)}{\left(\begin{array}{c}\prod_{j=1}^{m+1}\left(1+(t-1)\,\underline{b_j}\right)^{\omega_j}+\\ (t-1)\prod_{j=1}^{m+1}\left(1-\underline{b_j}\right)^{\omega_j}\end{array}\right)}\end{array}\right).$$

Thus, for $n = m + 1$, (2.2) holds. $\Rightarrow$ (2.2) holds, for all n.

The notion of CFRHWA operator satisfies the following three properties.

Theorem 2.2: (Idempotency) If all $\mathcal{A}_j$ $(j = 1,\ 2,\ 3,\ \ldots,\ n)$ are identical, that is $\mathcal{A}_j = \mathcal{A}\ \forall\ j$, then:

$$\mathrm{CFRHWA}_\omega\left(\mathcal{A}_1,\ \mathcal{A}_2,\ \mathcal{A}_3,\ \ldots,\ \mathcal{A}_m\right) = \mathcal{A}.$$

Proof: As $\mathcal{A}_j = \mathcal{A}\ \forall\ j$, then we get: $\overline{a_j} = \overline{a}, \overline{b_j} = \overline{b},\ \underline{a_j} = \underline{a}$ and $\underline{b_j} = \underline{b}$ and

$$\mathrm{CFRHWA}_\omega\left(\mathcal{A}_1,\ \mathcal{A}_2,\ \mathcal{A}_3,\ \ldots,\ \mathcal{A}_m\right) =$$

$$\left(\begin{array}{c} \dfrac{\left(\begin{array}{c}\prod_{j=1}^{m+1}(1+(t-1)\overline{a_j})^{\omega_j}\\ -\prod_{j}^{m+1}(1-\overline{a_j})^{\omega_j}\end{array}\right)}{\left(\begin{array}{c}\prod_{j=1}^{m+1}(1+(t-1)\overline{a_j})^{\omega_j}+\\ (t-1)\prod_{j=1}^{m+1}(1-\overline{a_j})^{\omega_j}\end{array}\right)}+\mathrm{i}\dfrac{\left(\begin{array}{c}\prod_{j=1}^{m+1}(1+(t-1)\overline{b_j})^{\omega_j}\\ -\prod_{j}^{m+1}(1-\overline{b_j})^{\omega_j}\end{array}\right)}{\left(\begin{array}{c}\prod_{j=1}^{m+1}(1+(t-1)\overline{b_j})^{\omega_j}+\\ (t-1)\prod_{j=1}^{m+1}(1-\overline{b_j})^{\omega_j}\end{array}\right)},\\ \dfrac{\left(\begin{array}{c}\prod_{j=1}^{m+1}\left(1+(t-1)\underline{a_j}\right)^{\omega_j}\\ -\prod_{j}^{m+1}\left(1-\underline{a_j}\right)^{\omega_j}\end{array}\right)}{\left(\begin{array}{c}\prod_{j=1}^{m+1}\left(1+(t-1)\underline{a_j}\right)^{\omega_j}+\\ (t-1)\prod_{j=1}^{m+1}\left(1-\underline{a_j}\right)^{\omega_j}\end{array}\right)}+\mathrm{i}\dfrac{\left(\begin{array}{c}\prod_{j=1}^{m+1}\left(1+(t-1)\underline{b_j}\right)^{\omega_j}\\ -\prod_{j}^{m+1}\left(1-\underline{b_j}\right)^{\omega_j}\end{array}\right)}{\left(\begin{array}{c}\prod_{j=1}^{m+1}\left(1+(t-1)\underline{b_j}\right)^{\omega_j}+\\ (t-1)\prod_{j=1}^{m+1}\left(1-\underline{b_j}\right)^{\omega_j}\end{array}\right)}\end{array}\right)$$

$$=\left(\begin{array}{c}\frac{(1+(t-1)\overline{a}-(1-\overline{a}))}{((1+(t-1)\overline{a})+(t-1)(1-\overline{a}))}+\mathrm{i}\frac{\left(1+(t-1)\overline{b}-\left(1-\overline{b}\right)\right)}{\left((1+(t-1)\overline{b})+(t-1)\left(1-\overline{b}\right)\right)},\\ \frac{(1+(t-1)\underline{a}-(1-\underline{a}))}{((1+(t-1)\underline{a})+(t-1)(1-\underline{a}))}+\mathrm{i}\frac{(1+(t-1)\underline{b}-(1-\underline{b}))}{((1+(t-1)\underline{b})+(t-1)(1-\underline{b}))}\end{array}\right)$$

$$=\left(\begin{array}{c}\frac{((t)\overline{a})}{t}+\mathrm{i}\frac{((t)\overline{b})}{t},\\ \frac{(t\underline{a})}{t}+\mathrm{i}\frac{(t\underline{b})}{t}\end{array}\right)=\left\{\left(\overline{a}+\iota\overline{b},\ \underline{a}+\iota\underline{b}\right)\right\}=\mathcal{A}.$$

Hence:

$$\mathrm{CFRHWA}_{\omega}\left(\mathcal{A}_1,\ \mathcal{A}_2,\ \mathcal{A}_3,\ \ldots,\ \mathcal{A}_m\right)=\mathcal{A}.$$

Theorem 2.3: (Monotonicity) Let $\mathcal{A}_j = \left\{\left(\overline{a_j}+\iota\overline{b_j},\ \underline{a_j}+\iota\underline{b_j}\right)\right\}$ and $\mathcal{A}_j^* = \left\{\left(\overline{a_j^*}+\iota\overline{b_j^*},\ \underline{a_j^*}+\iota\underline{b_j^*}\right)\right\}$ $(j = 1,\ 2,\ 3,\ \ldots,\ n)$ be two collections of CFRNs. If $\overline{a_j} \leq \overline{a_j^*}$, $\overline{b_j} \leq \overline{b_j^*}$, $\underline{a_j} \leq \underline{a_j^*}$, and $\underline{b_j} \leq \underline{b_j^*}$ for all j. Then:

$$\mathrm{CFRHWA}_{\omega}\left(\mathcal{A}_1,\ \mathcal{A}_2,\ \ldots,\ \mathcal{A}_n\right) \leq \mathrm{CFRHWA}_{\omega}\left(\mathcal{A}_1^*,\ \mathcal{A}_2^*,\ldots,\ \mathcal{A}_n^*\right).$$

Proof: As $\overline{a_j} \leq \overline{a_j^*}$, $\overline{b_j} \leq \overline{b_j^*}$, $\underline{a_j} \leq \underline{a_j^*}$, and $\underline{b_j} \leq \underline{b_j^*}$ for all j then:

$$
\begin{aligned}
&\mathrm{CFRHWA}_{\omega}\left(\mathcal{A}_1,\ \mathcal{A}_2,\ \mathcal{A}_3,\ \ldots,\ \mathcal{A}_n\right)\\
&=\begin{pmatrix}
\dfrac{\begin{pmatrix}\prod_{j=1}^{m+1}\left(1+(t-1)\,\overline{a_j}\right)^{\omega_j}\\ -\prod_{j}^{m+1}\left(1-\overline{a_j}\right)^{\omega_j}\end{pmatrix}}{\begin{pmatrix}\prod_{j=1}^{m+1}\left(1+(t-1)\,\overline{a_j}\right)^{\omega_j}+\\ (t-1)\prod_{j=1}^{m+1}\left(1-\overline{a_j}\right)^{\omega_j}\end{pmatrix}}+\mathrm{i}\dfrac{\begin{pmatrix}\prod_{j=1}^{m+1}\left(1+(t-1)\,\overline{b_j}\right)^{\omega_j}\\ -\prod_{j}^{m+1}\left(1-\overline{b_j}\right)^{\omega_j}\end{pmatrix}}{\begin{pmatrix}\prod_{j=1}^{m+1}\left(1+(t-1)\,\overline{b_j}\right)^{\omega_j}+\\ (t-1)\prod_{j=1}^{m+1}\left(1-\overline{b_j}\right)^{\omega_j}\end{pmatrix}},\\
\dfrac{\begin{pmatrix}\prod_{j=1}^{m+1}\left(1+(t-1)\,\underline{a_j}\right)^{\omega_j}\\ -\prod_{j}^{m+1}\left(1-\underline{a_j}\right)^{\omega_j}\end{pmatrix}}{\begin{pmatrix}\prod_{j=1}^{m+1}\left(1+(t-1)\,\underline{a_j}\right)^{\omega_j}+\\ (t-1)\prod_{j=1}^{m+1}\left(1-\underline{a_j}\right)^{\omega_j}\end{pmatrix}}+\mathrm{i}\dfrac{\begin{pmatrix}\prod_{j=1}^{m+1}\left(1+(t-1)\,\underline{b_j}\right)^{\omega_j}\\ -\prod_{j}^{m+1}\left(1-\underline{b_j}\right)^{\omega_j}\end{pmatrix}}{\begin{pmatrix}\prod_{j=1}^{m+1}\left(1+(t-1)\,\underline{b_j}\right)^{\omega_j}+\\ (t-1)\prod_{j=1}^{m+1}\left(1-\underline{b_j}\right)^{\omega_j}\end{pmatrix}}
\end{pmatrix}.
\end{aligned}
$$

Now

$$
\frac{\begin{pmatrix}\prod_{j=1}^{m+1}\left(1+(t-1)\,\overline{a_j}\right)^{\omega_j}\\ -\prod_{j}^{m+1}\left(1-\overline{a_j}\right)^{\omega_j}\end{pmatrix}}{\begin{pmatrix}\prod_{j=1}^{m+1}\left(1+(t-1)\,\overline{a_j}\right)^{\omega_j}+\\ (t-1)\prod_{j=1}^{m+1}\left(1-\overline{a_j}\right)^{\omega_j}\end{pmatrix}}\leq\frac{\begin{pmatrix}\prod_{j=1}^{m+1}\left(1+(t-1)\,\overline{a_j^*}\right)^{\omega_j}\\ -\prod_{j}^{m+1}\left(1-\overline{a_j^*}\right)^{\omega_j}\end{pmatrix}}{\begin{pmatrix}\prod_{j=1}^{m+1}\left(1+(t-1)\,\overline{a_j^*}\right)^{\omega_j}+\\ (t-1)\prod_{j=1}^{m+1}\left(1-\overline{a_j^*}\right)^{\omega_j}\end{pmatrix}},
$$

and

$$
\frac{\begin{pmatrix}\prod_{j=1}^{m+1}\left(1+(t-1)\,\overline{b_j}\right)^{\omega_j}\\ -\prod_{j}^{m+1}\left(1-\overline{b_j}\right)^{\omega_j}\end{pmatrix}}{\begin{pmatrix}\prod_{j=1}^{m+1}\left(1+(t-1)\,\overline{b_j}\right)^{\omega_j}+\\ (t-1)\prod_{j=1}^{m+1}\left(1-\overline{b_j}\right)^{\omega_j}\end{pmatrix}}\leq\frac{\begin{pmatrix}\prod_{j=1}^{m+1}\left(1+(t-1)\,\overline{b_j^*}\right)^{\omega_j}\\ -\prod_{j}^{m+1}\left(1-\overline{b_j^*}\right)^{\omega_j}\end{pmatrix}}{\begin{pmatrix}\prod_{j=1}^{m+1}\left(1+(t-1)\,\overline{b_j^*}\right)^{\omega_j}+\\ (t-1)\prod_{j=1}^{m+1}\left(1-\overline{b_j^*}\right)^{\omega_j}\end{pmatrix}}.
$$

Also:

$$\frac{\left(\prod_{j=1}^{m+1}\left(1+(t-1)\underline{a_j}\right)^{\omega_j} - \prod_{j}^{m+1}\left(1-\underline{a_j}\right)^{\omega_j}\right)}{\left(\prod_{j=1}^{m+1}\left(1+(t-1)\underline{a_j}\right)^{\omega_j} + (t-1)\prod_{j=1}^{m+1}\left(1-\underline{a_j}\right)^{\omega_j}\right)} \leq \frac{\left(\prod_{j=1}^{m+1}\left(1+(t-1)\underline{a_j^*}\right)^{\omega_j} - \prod_{j}^{m+1}\left(1-\underline{a_j^*}\right)^{\omega_j}\right)}{\left(\prod_{j=1}^{m+1}\left(1+(t-1)\underline{a_j^*}\right)^{\omega_j} + (t-1)\prod_{j=1}^{m+1}\left(1-\underline{a_j^*}\right)^{\omega_j}\right)},$$

and

$$\frac{\left(\prod_{j=1}^{m+1}\left(1+(t-1)\underline{b_j}\right)^{\omega_j} - \prod_{j}^{m+1}\left(1-\underline{b_j}\right)^{\omega_j}\right)}{\left(\prod_{j=1}^{m+1}\left(1+(t-1)\underline{b_j}\right)^{\omega_j} + (t-1)\prod_{j=1}^{m+1}\left(1-\underline{b_j}\right)^{\omega_j}\right)} \leq \frac{\left(\prod_{j=1}^{m+1}\left(1+(t-1)\underline{b_j^*}\right)^{\omega_j} - \prod_{j}^{m+1}\left(1-\underline{b_j^*}\right)^{\omega_j}\right)}{\left(\prod_{j=1}^{m+1}\left(1+(t-1)\underline{b_j^*}\right)^{\omega_j} + (t-1)\prod_{j=1}^{m+1}\left(1-\underline{b_j^*}\right)^{\omega_j}\right)}$$

$$\Rightarrow \left(\begin{array}{c} \dfrac{\left(\prod_{j=1}^{m+1}\left(1+(t-1)\overline{a_j}\right)^{\omega_j} - \prod_{j}^{m+1}\left(1-\overline{a_j}\right)^{\omega_j}\right)}{\left(\prod_{j=1}^{m+1}\left(1+(t-1)\overline{a_j}\right)^{\omega_j} + (t-1)\prod_{j=1}^{m+1}\left(1-\overline{a_j}\right)^{\omega_j}\right)} + \mathrm{i}\dfrac{\left(\prod_{j=1}^{m+1}\left(1+(t-1)\overline{b_j}\right)^{\omega_j} - \prod_{j}^{m+1}\left(1-\overline{b_j}\right)^{\omega_j}\right)}{\left(\prod_{j=1}^{m+1}\left(1+(t-1)\overline{b_j}\right)^{\omega_j} + (t-1)\prod_{j=1}^{m+1}\left(1-\overline{b_j}\right)^{\omega_j}\right)}, \\ \dfrac{\left(\prod_{j=1}^{m+1}\left(1+(t-1)\underline{a_j}\right)^{\omega_j} - \prod_{j}^{m+1}\left(1-\underline{a_j}\right)^{\omega_j}\right)}{\left(\prod_{j=1}^{m+1}\left(1+(t-1)\underline{a_j}\right)^{\omega_j} + (t-1)\prod_{j=1}^{m+1}\left(1-\underline{a_j}\right)^{\omega_j}\right)} + \mathrm{i}\dfrac{\left(\prod_{j=1}^{m+1}\left(1+(t-1)\underline{b_j}\right)^{\omega_j} - \prod_{j}^{m+1}\left(1-\underline{b_j}\right)^{\omega_j}\right)}{\left(\prod_{j=1}^{m+1}\left(1+(t-1)\underline{b_j}\right)^{\omega_j} + (t-1)\prod_{j=1}^{m+1}\left(1-\underline{b_j}\right)^{\omega_j}\right)} \end{array}\right)$$

$$\leq \left(\begin{array}{c} \frac{\left(\prod_{j=1}^{m+1}\left(1+(t-1)\overline{a_j^*}\right)^{\omega_j} - \prod_{j}^{m+1}\left(1-\overline{a_j^*}\right)^{\omega_j}\right)}{\left(\prod_{j=1}^{m+1}\left(1+(t-1)\overline{a_j^*}\right)^{\omega_j} + (t-1)\prod_{j=1}^{m+1}\left(1-\overline{a_j^*}\right)^{\omega_j}\right)} + \mathrm{i}\frac{\left(\prod_{j=1}^{m+1}\left(1+(t-1)\overline{b_j^*}\right)^{\omega_j} - \prod_{j}^{m+1}\left(1-\overline{b_j^*}\right)^{\omega_j}\right)}{\left(\prod_{j=1}^{m+1}\left(1+(t-1)\overline{b_j^*}\right)^{\omega_j} + (t-1)\prod_{j=1}^{m+1}\left(1-\overline{b_j^*}\right)^{\omega_j}\right)}, \\ \frac{\left(\prod_{j=1}^{m+1}\left(1+(t-1)\underline{a_j^*}\right)^{\omega_j} - \prod_{j}^{m+1}\left(1-\underline{a_j^*}\right)^{\omega_j}\right)}{\left(\prod_{j=1}^{m+1}\left(1+(t-1)\underline{a_j^*}\right)^{\omega_j} + (t-1)\prod_{j=1}^{m+1}\left(1-\underline{a_j^*}\right)^{\omega_j}\right)} + \mathrm{i}\frac{\left(\prod_{j=1}^{m+1}\left(1+(t-1)\underline{b_j^*}\right)^{\omega_j} - \prod_{j}^{m+1}\left(1-\underline{b_j^*}\right)^{\omega_j}\right)}{\left(\prod_{j=1}^{m+1}\left(1+(t-1)\underline{b_j^*}\right)^{\omega_j} + (t-1)\prod_{j=1}^{m+1}\left(1-\underline{b_j^*}\right)^{\omega_j}\right)} \end{array} \right).$$

Hence:

$$\mathrm{CFRHWA}_{\omega}\left(\mathcal{A}_1, \mathcal{A}_2, \mathcal{A}_3, \ldots, \mathcal{A}_n\right) \leq \mathrm{CFRHWA}_{\omega}\left(\mathcal{A}_1^*,\ \mathcal{A}_2^*, \mathcal{A}_3^*, \ldots, \mathcal{A}_n^*\right).$$

Theorem 2.4: (Boundedness) Let $\mathcal{A}^- = \mathrm{min_j}\mathcal{A}_j$, $\mathcal{A}^+ = \mathrm{max_j}\mathcal{A}_j$. Then:

$$\mathcal{A}^- \leq \mathrm{CFRHWA}_{\omega}\left(\mathcal{A}_1,\ \mathcal{A}_2,\ \mathcal{A}_3,\ \ldots,\ \mathcal{A}_m\right) \leq \mathcal{A}^+.$$

Proof: Using Theorems 2.3 and 2.4, we get:

$$\mathrm{CFRHWA}_{\omega}\left(\mathcal{A}_1,\ \mathcal{A}_2,\ \mathcal{A}_3,\ \ldots,\ \mathcal{A}_m\right) \leq \mathcal{A}^+,$$

and

$$\mathcal{A}^- \leq \mathrm{CFRHWA}_{\omega}\left(\mathcal{A}_1,\ \mathcal{A}_2,\ \mathcal{A}_3,\ \ldots,\ \mathcal{A}_m\right).$$

Hence

$$\mathcal{A}^- \leq \mathrm{CFRHWA}_{\omega}\left(\mathcal{A}_1,\ \mathcal{A}_2,\ \mathcal{A}_3,\ \ldots,\ \mathcal{A}_m\right) \leq \mathcal{A}^+.$$

Particular cases: Here, we have discussed some particular cases for CFRHWA operators given by

1. For $t = 1$, the CFRHWA operator transforms into the complex fuzzy rough weighted average (CFRWA) operator given by

$$\mathrm{CFRWA}_{\omega}\left(\mathcal{A}_1,\ \mathcal{A}_2,\ \mathcal{A}_3,\ \ldots,\ \mathcal{A}_n\right) = \bigoplus_{j=1}^{n}\left(\omega_j \mathcal{A}_j\right)$$

$$= \begin{pmatrix} 1-\prod_{j=1}^{n}\left(1-\overline{a_j}\right)^{\omega_j} + \mathrm{i}\, 1-\prod_{j=1}^{n}\left(1-\overline{b_j}\right)^{\omega_j}, \\ 1-\prod_{j=1}^{n}\left(1-\underline{a_j}\right)^{\omega_j} + \mathrm{i}\, 1-\prod_{j=1}^{n}\left(1-\underline{b_j}\right)^{\omega_j} \end{pmatrix}.$$

2. For $t = 2$, the CFRHWA operator transforms into a complex fuzzy rough Einstein weighted average (CFREWA) operator:

$$\mathrm{CFREWA}_{\omega}\left(\mathcal{A}_1, \mathcal{A}_2, \mathcal{A}_3, \ldots, \mathcal{A}_n\right) = \bigoplus_{j=1}^{n}\left(\omega_j \mathcal{A}_j\right)$$

$$= \begin{pmatrix} \dfrac{\left(\prod_{j=1}^{n}\left(1+\overline{a_j}\right)^{\omega_j} - \prod_{j=1}^{n}\left(1-\overline{a_j}\right)^{\omega_j}\right)}{\left(\prod_{j=1}^{n}\left(1+\overline{a_j}\right)^{\omega_j} + \prod_{j=1}^{n}\left(1-\overline{a_j}\right)^{\omega_j}\right)} + \mathrm{i}\dfrac{\left(\prod_{j=1}^{n}\left(1+\overline{b_j}\right)^{\omega_j} - \prod_{j=1}^{n}\left(1-\overline{b_j}\right)^{\omega_j}\right)}{\left(\prod_{j=1}^{n}\left(1+\overline{b_j}\right)^{\omega_j} + \prod_{j=1}^{n}\left(1-\overline{b_j}\right)^{\omega_j}\right)}, \\ \dfrac{\left(\prod_{j=1}^{n}\left(1+\underline{a_j}\right)^{\omega_j} - \prod_{j=1}^{n}\left(1-\underline{a_j}\right)^{\omega_j}\right)}{\left(\prod_{j=1}^{n}\left(1+\underline{a_j}\right)^{\omega_j} + \prod_{j=1}^{n}\left(1-\underline{a_j}\right)^{\omega_j}\right)} + \mathrm{i}\dfrac{\left(\prod_{j=1}^{n}\left(1+\underline{b_j}\right)^{\omega_j} - \prod_{j=1}^{n}\left(1-\underline{b_j}\right)^{\omega_j}\right)}{\left(\prod_{j=1}^{n}\left(1+\underline{b_j}\right)^{\omega_j} + \prod_{j=1}^{n}\left(1-\underline{b_j}\right)^{\omega_j}\right)} \end{pmatrix}.$$

Definition 2.3: The CFRHWG aggregation operator is defined by

$$\mathrm{CFRHWG}_{\omega}\left(\mathcal{A}_1, \mathcal{A}_2, \mathcal{A}_3, \ldots, \mathcal{A}_n\right) = \bigotimes_{j=1}^{n}\left(\mathcal{A}_j\right)^{\omega_j}. \tag{2.3}$$

Theorem 2.5: The aggregated result obtained by using eqn (2.3) is again CFRN and it is given by

$$\mathrm{CFRHWG}_{\omega}\left(\mathcal{A}_1, \mathcal{A}_2, \mathcal{A}_3, \ldots, \mathcal{A}_n\right) = \bigotimes_{j=1}^{n}\left(\mathcal{A}_j\right)^{\omega_j}$$

$$= \left(\begin{array}{c} \dfrac{t \prod_{j=1}^{n} (\overline{a_j})^{\omega_j}}{\left(\begin{array}{c} \prod_{j=1}^{n} (1 + (t-1)(1-\overline{a_j}))^{\omega_j} \\ + (t-1) \prod_{j=1}^{n} (\overline{a_j})^{\omega_j} \end{array} \right)} + \iota \dfrac{t \prod_{j=1}^{n} (\overline{b_j})^{\omega_j}}{\left(\begin{array}{c} \prod_{j=1}^{n} (1 + (t-1)(1-\overline{b_j}))^{\omega_j} \\ + (t-1) \prod_{j=1}^{n} (\overline{b_j})^{\omega_j} \end{array} \right)}, \\ \dfrac{t \prod_{j=1}^{n} (\underline{a_j})^{\omega_j}}{\left(\begin{array}{c} \prod_{j=1}^{n} (1 + (t-1)(1-\underline{a_j}))^{\omega_j} \\ + (t-1) \prod_{j=1}^{n} (\underline{a_j})^{\omega_j} \end{array} \right)} + \iota \dfrac{t \prod_{j=1}^{n} (\underline{b_j})^{\omega_j}}{\left(\begin{array}{c} \prod_{j=1}^{n} (1 + (t-1)(1-\underline{b_j}))^{\omega_j} \\ + (t-1) \prod_{j=1}^{n} (\underline{b_j})^{\omega_j} \end{array} \right)} \end{array} \right). \quad (2.4)$$

Proof: We will prove it through mathematical induction.

Let $n = 1$, so we get that $\omega_1 = 1$ and eqn (2.4) becomes:

$$\text{CFRHWG}_\omega (\mathcal{A}_1, \mathcal{A}_2, \mathcal{A}_3, \ldots, \mathcal{A}_n) = \mathcal{A}_1$$

$$= \left(\begin{array}{c} \dfrac{t(\overline{a_j})}{\begin{array}{c}(1 + (t-1)(1-\overline{a_j})) \\ + (t-1)\overline{a_j}\end{array}} + \mathrm{i} \dfrac{t(\overline{b_j})}{\begin{array}{c}(1 + (t-1)(1-\overline{b_j})) \\ + (t-1)\overline{b_j}\end{array}}, \\ \dfrac{t(\underline{a_j})}{\begin{array}{c}(1 + (t-1)(1-\underline{a_j})) \\ + (t-1)\underline{a_j}\end{array}} + \mathrm{i} \dfrac{t(\underline{b_j})}{\begin{array}{c}(1 + (t-1)(1-\underline{b_j})) \\ + (t-1)\underline{b_j}\end{array}} \end{array} \right).$$

Thus, for $n = 1$ (2.4) holds.

Assume that eqn (2.4) holds for $n = m$:

$$\text{CFRHW}G_\omega (\mathcal{A}_1, \mathcal{A}_2, \mathcal{A}_3, \ldots, \mathcal{A}_m) = \bigotimes_{j=1}^{n} (\mathcal{A}_j)^{\omega_j}$$

$$= \left(\begin{array}{c} \dfrac{t \prod_{j=1}^{m} (\overline{a_j})^{\omega_j}}{\left(\begin{array}{c} \prod_{j=1}^{m} (1 + (t-1)(1-\overline{a_j}))^{\omega_j} \\ + (t-1) \prod_{j=1}^{m} (\overline{a_j})^{\omega_j} \end{array} \right)} + \mathrm{i} \dfrac{t \prod_{j=1}^{m} (\overline{b_j})^{\omega_j}}{\left(\begin{array}{c} \prod_{j=1}^{m} (1 + (t-1)(1-\overline{b_j}))^{\omega_j} \\ + (t-1) \prod_{j=1}^{m} (\overline{b_j})^{\omega_j} \end{array} \right)}, \\ \dfrac{t \prod_{j=1}^{m} (\underline{a_j})^{\omega_j}}{\left(\begin{array}{c} \prod_{j=1}^{m} (1 + (t-1)(1-\underline{a_j}))^{\omega_j} \\ + (t-1) \prod_{j=1}^{m} (\underline{a_j})^{\omega_j} \end{array} \right)} + \mathrm{i} \dfrac{t \prod_{j=1}^{m} (\underline{b_j})^{\omega_j}}{\left(\begin{array}{c} \prod_{j=1}^{m} (1 + (t-1)(1-\underline{b_j}))^{\omega_j} \\ + (t-1) \prod_{j=1}^{m} (\underline{b_j})^{\omega_j} \end{array} \right)} \end{array} \right).$$

Now for $n = m + 1$, we get:

$$\text{CFRHWA}_\omega (\mathcal{A}_1, \mathcal{A}_2, \ldots, \mathcal{A}_m, \mathcal{A}_{m+1}) = \bigotimes_{j=1}^{n} (\mathcal{A}_j)^{\omega_j} \otimes (\mathcal{A}_{m+1})^{\omega_{m+1}}$$

$$= \left(\begin{array}{c} \dfrac{t\prod_{j=1}^{m}(\overline{a_j})^{\omega_j}}{\left(\begin{array}{c}\prod_{j=1}^{m}(1+(t-1)(1-\overline{a_j}))^{\omega_j} \\ +(t-1)\prod_{j=1}^{m}(\overline{a_j})^{\omega_j}\end{array}\right)} + i\dfrac{t\prod_{j=1}^{m}(\overline{b_j})^{\omega_j}}{\left(\begin{array}{c}\prod_{j=1}^{m}\left(1+(t-1)\left(1-\overline{b_j}\right)\right)^{\omega_j} \\ +(t-1)\prod_{j=1}^{m}\left(\overline{b_j}\right)^{\omega_j}\end{array}\right)}, \\ \dfrac{t\prod_{j=1}^{m}\left(\underline{a_j}\right)^{\omega_j}}{\left(\begin{array}{c}\prod_{j=1}^{m}\left(1+(t-1)\left(1-\underline{a_j}\right)\right)^{\omega_j} \\ +(t-1)\prod_{j=1}^{m}\left(\underline{a_j}\right)^{\omega_j}\end{array}\right)} + i\dfrac{t\prod_{j=1}^{m}\left(\underline{b_j}\right)^{\omega_j}}{\left(\begin{array}{c}\prod_{j=1}^{m}\left(1+(t-1)\left(1-\underline{b_j}\right)\right)^{\omega_j} \\ +(t-1)\prod_{j=1}^{m}\left(\underline{b_j}\right)^{\omega_j}\end{array}\right)} \end{array} \right)$$

$$\otimes \left(\begin{array}{c} \dfrac{t(\overline{a_j})^{\omega_{m+1}}}{\left(\begin{array}{c}(1+(t-1)(1-\overline{a_j}))^{\omega_{m+1}} \\ +(t-1)(\overline{a_j})^{\omega_{m+1}}\end{array}\right)} + i\dfrac{t(\overline{b_j})^{\omega_{m+1}}}{\left(\begin{array}{c}\left(1+(t-1)\left(1-\overline{b_j}\right)\right)^{\omega_{m+1}} \\ +(t-1)\left(\overline{b_j}\right)^{\omega_{m+1}}\end{array}\right)}, \\ \dfrac{t\left(\underline{a_j}\right)^{\omega_{m+1}}}{\left(\begin{array}{c}\left(1+(t-1)\left(1-\underline{a_j}\right)\right)^{\omega_{m+1}} \\ +(t-1)\left(\underline{a_j}\right)^{\omega_{m+1}}\end{array}\right)} + i\dfrac{t\left(\underline{b_j}\right)^{\omega_{m+1}}}{\left(\begin{array}{c}\left(1+(t-1)\left(1-\underline{b_j}\right)\right)^{\omega_{m+1}} \\ +(t-1)\left(\underline{b_j}\right)^{\omega_{m+1}}\end{array}\right)} \end{array} \right)$$

$$= \left(\begin{array}{c} \dfrac{t\prod_{j=1}^{m+1}(\overline{a_j})^{\omega_j}}{\left(\begin{array}{c}\prod_{j=1}^{m+1}(1+(t-1)(1-\overline{a_j}))^{\omega_j} \\ +(t-1)\prod_{j=1}^{m+1}(\overline{a_j})^{\omega_j}\end{array}\right)} + i\dfrac{t\prod_{j=1}^{m+1}(\overline{b_j})^{\omega_j}}{\left(\begin{array}{c}\prod_{j=1}^{m+1}\left(1+(t-1)\left(1-\overline{b_j}\right)\right)^{\omega_j} \\ +(t-1)\prod_{j=1}^{m+1}\left(\overline{b_j}\right)^{\omega_j}\end{array}\right)}, \\ \dfrac{t\prod_{j=1}^{m+1}\left(\underline{a_j}\right)^{\omega_j}}{\left(\begin{array}{c}\prod_{j=1}^{m+1}\left(1+(t-1)\left(1-\underline{a_j}\right)\right)^{\omega_j} \\ +(t-1)\prod_{j=1}^{m+1}\left(\underline{a_j}\right)^{\omega_j}\end{array}\right)} + i\dfrac{t\prod_{j=1}^{m+1}\left(\underline{b_j}\right)^{\omega_j}}{\left(\begin{array}{c}\prod_{j=1}^{m+1}\left(1+(t-1)\left(1-\underline{b_j}\right)\right)^{\omega_j} \\ +(t-1)\prod_{j=1}^{m+1}\left(\underline{b_j}\right)^{\omega_j}\end{array}\right)} \end{array} \right).$$

Thus, for $n = m + 1$, (2.4) holds. $\Rightarrow$ (2.4) holds, for all n.

The notion of CFRHWG operator satisfies the following three properties.

Remark 2.1. The notion of CFRHWG AOs satisfies the properties of idempotency, monotonicity, and boundedness.

Particular cases: The idea of CFRHWG operator transforms into the following cases

(1) For $t = 1$, the CFRHWG operator transforms into the complex fuzzy rough weighted geometric (CFRWG) operator:

$$\text{CFRWG}_{\omega}(\mathcal{A}_1, \mathcal{A}_2, \mathcal{A}_3, \ldots, \mathcal{A}_n) = \bigotimes_{j=1}^{n} (\mathcal{A}_j)^{\omega_j}$$

$$= \begin{pmatrix} \prod_{j=1}^{n} \left(\overline{a_j}\right)^{\omega_j} + \mathrm{i} \prod_{j=1}^{n} \left(\overline{b_j}\right)^{\omega_j}, \\ \prod_{j=1}^{n} \left(\underline{a_j}\right)^{\omega_j} + \mathrm{i} \prod_{j=1}^{n} \left(\underline{b_j}\right)^{\omega_j} \end{pmatrix}.$$

(2) For $t = 2$, the notion of CFRHWG operator transforms into the complex fuzzy rough Einstein weighted geometric CFREWG) operator:

$$\mathrm{CFREWG}_{\omega}\left(\mathcal{A}_1, \mathcal{A}_2, \mathcal{A}_3, \ldots, \mathcal{A}_n\right) = \bigotimes_{j=1}^{n} \left(\mathcal{A}_j\right)^{\omega_j}$$

$$= \begin{pmatrix} \dfrac{2\prod_{j=1}^{n}\left(\overline{a_j}\right)^{\omega_j}}{\left(\prod_{j=1}^{n}\left(2-\overline{a_j}\right)^{\omega_j} + \prod_{j=1}^{n}\left(\overline{a_j}\right)^{\omega_j}\right)} + \mathrm{i}\, \dfrac{2\prod_{j=1}^{n}\left(\overline{b_j}\right)^{\omega_j}}{\left(\prod_{j=1}^{n}\left(2-\overline{b_j}\right)^{\omega_j} + \prod_{j=1}^{n}\left(\overline{b_j}\right)^{\omega_j}\right)}, \\ \dfrac{2\prod_{j=1}^{n}\left(\underline{a_j}\right)^{\omega_j}}{\left(\prod_{j=1}^{n}\left(2-\underline{a_j}\right)^{\omega_j} + \prod_{j=1}^{n}\left(\underline{a_j}\right)^{\omega_j}\right)} + \mathrm{i}\, \dfrac{2\prod_{j=1}^{n}\left(\underline{b_j}\right)^{\omega_j}}{\left(\prod_{j=1}^{n}\left(2-\underline{b_j}\right)^{\omega_j} + \prod_{j=1}^{n}\left(\underline{b_j}\right)^{\omega_j}\right)} \end{pmatrix}.$$

2.3 Application of Developed Approach

In this section, we will discuss the application of the defined approach and we will discuss an algorithm for the WASPAS approach to discuss the utilization of defined aggregation theory. We have discussed the numerical example in this regard to validate the defined approach.

2.3.1 WASPAS approach

Assume that there are m alternatives and a set of alternatives is given by $\mathfrak{L} = \{\mathfrak{L}_1, \mathfrak{L}_2, \ldots, \mathfrak{L}_m\}$. The n attributes of these alternatives are denoted by $\mathbb{T} = \{\mathbb{T}_1, \mathbb{T}_2, \ldots, \mathbb{T}_n\}$. The weights of these attributes $\omega_j = (\omega_1, \omega_2, \ldots, \omega_n)^T$ such that $\sum_{j=1}^{n} \omega_j = 1$ and $\omega_j \in [0, 1]\ \forall\ j$. Assume that the decision analyst provides theory assessment in the form of CFRNs given by $\mathcal{A}_{ij} = \left\{\left(\overline{a_{ij}} + \iota\overline{b_{ij}},\ \underline{a_{ij}} + \iota\underline{b_{ij}}\right)\right\}$ for $i = 1, 2, .., m$ and $j = 1, 2, 3, \ldots, n$. Now step-wise algorithm is given by

Step 1: Collect the information in the form of CFRNs proposed by decision makers and arrange it in the form of matric given by

$$\mathcal{M} = \begin{bmatrix} \mathcal{A}_{11} & \mathcal{A}_{12} & \dots & \mathcal{A}_{1n} \\ \mathcal{A}_{21} & \mathcal{A}_{22} & \dots & \mathcal{A}_{2n} \\ \vdots & \ddots & \dots & \vdots \\ \mathcal{A}_{m1} & \mathcal{A}_{m2} & & \mathcal{A}_{mn} \end{bmatrix}.$$

Step 2: Utilize the following formula, if there is a need to normalize the information based on the information of cost type or benefit type attributes. The formulas are given by

$$\mathcal{N} = \begin{cases} \mathcal{A}_{ij} & \text{for benefit type attributes} \\ (\mathcal{A}_{ij})^c & \text{for cost type attributes} \end{cases},$$

where $(\mathcal{A}_{ij})^c = \left\{\left(\left(1 - \underline{a_{ij}}\right) + \iota\left(1 - \underline{b_{ij}}\right), (1 - \overline{a_{ij}}) + \iota\left(1 - \overline{b_{ij}}\right)\right)\right\}$ represent the complement of $\mathcal{A}_{ij}$.

Step 3: Find out the relative importance of the alternatives relying on the WSM by the formula given by

$$(\mathcal{A}_j)^{\mathrm{WS}} = \mathrm{CFRHWA}_\omega(\mathcal{A}_1, \mathcal{A}_2, \mathcal{A}_3, \dots, \mathcal{A}_n) = \bigoplus_{j=1}^{n} (\omega_j \mathcal{A}_j)$$

$$= \left(\begin{array}{c} \dfrac{\left(\begin{array}{c}\prod_{j=1}^{n}(1+(t-1)\overline{a_j})^{\omega_j} \\ -\prod_{j=1}^{n}(1-\overline{a_j})^{\omega_j}\end{array}\right)}{\left(\begin{array}{c}\prod_{j=1}^{n}(1+(t-1)\overline{a_j})^{\omega_j}+ \\ (t-1)\prod_{j=1}^{n}(1-\overline{a_j})^{\omega_j}\end{array}\right)} + \iota \dfrac{\left(\begin{array}{c}\prod_{j=1}^{n}(1+(t-1)\overline{b_j})^{\omega_j} \\ -\prod_{j=1}^{n}(1-\overline{b_j})^{\omega_j}\end{array}\right)}{\left(\begin{array}{c}\prod_{j=1}^{n}(1+(t-1)\overline{b_j})^{\omega_j}+ \\ (t-1)\prod_{j=1}^{n}(1-\overline{b_j})^{\omega_j}\end{array}\right)}, \\ \dfrac{\left(\begin{array}{c}\prod_{j=1}^{n}\left(1+(t-1)\underline{a_j}\right)^{\omega_j} \\ -\prod_{j=1}^{n}\left(1-\underline{a_j}\right)^{\omega_j}\end{array}\right)}{\left(\begin{array}{c}\prod_{j=1}^{n}\left(1+(t-1)\underline{a_j}\right)^{\omega_j}+ \\ (t-1)\prod_{j=1}^{n}\left(1-\underline{a_j}\right)^{\omega_j}\end{array}\right)} + \iota \dfrac{\left(\begin{array}{c}\prod_{j=1}^{n}\left(1+(t-1)\underline{b_j}\right)^{\omega_j} \\ -\prod_{j=1}^{n}\left(1-\underline{b_j}\right)^{\omega_j}\end{array}\right)}{\left(\begin{array}{c}\prod_{j=1}^{n}\left(1+(t-1)\underline{b_j}\right)^{\omega_j}+ \\ (t-1)\prod_{j=1}^{n}\left(1-\underline{b_j}\right)^{\omega_j}\end{array}\right)} \end{array} \right).$$

Step 4: Find out the relative importance of the alternatives relying on the WSP by the formula given by

$$(\mathcal{A}_j)^{\mathrm{WP}} = \mathrm{CFRHWG}_{\omega}(\mathcal{A}_1, \mathcal{A}_2, \mathcal{A}_3, \ldots, \mathcal{A}_n) = \bigotimes_{j=1}^{n} (\mathcal{A}_j)^{\omega_j}$$

$$= \left(\begin{array}{c} \dfrac{t \prod_{j=1}^{n} (\overline{a_j})^{\omega_j}}{\left(\begin{array}{c} \prod_{j=1}^{n} (1 + (t-1)(1-\overline{a_j}))^{\omega_j} \\ + (t-1) \prod_{j=1}^{n} (\overline{a_j})^{\omega_j} \end{array} \right)} + \iota \dfrac{t \prod_{j=1}^{n} (\overline{b_j})^{\omega_j}}{\left(\begin{array}{c} \prod_{j=1}^{n} \left(1 + (t-1)\left(1-\overline{b_j}\right)\right)^{\omega_j} \\ + (t-1) \prod_{j=1}^{n} \left(\overline{b_j}\right)^{\omega_j} \end{array} \right)}, \\ \dfrac{t \prod_{j=1}^{n} \left(\underline{a_j}\right)^{\omega_j}}{\left(\begin{array}{c} \prod_{j=1}^{n} \left(1 + (t-1)\left(1-\underline{a_j}\right)\right)^{\omega_j} \\ + (t-1) \prod_{j=1}^{n} \left(\underline{a_j}\right)^{\omega_j} \end{array} \right)} + \iota \dfrac{t \prod_{j=1}^{n} \left(\underline{b_j}\right)^{\omega_j}}{\left(\begin{array}{c} \prod_{j=1}^{n} \left(1 + (t-1)\left(1-\underline{b_j}\right)\right)^{\omega_j} \\ + (t-1) \prod_{j=1}^{n} \left(\underline{b_j}\right)^{\omega_j} \end{array} \right)} \end{array} \right).$$

Step 5: The importance of each alternative is evaluated by using the WASPAS technique using the following formula:

$$\mathcal{A}_j = \frac{(\mathcal{A}_j)^{\mathrm{WS}} + (\mathcal{A}_j)^{\mathrm{WP}}}{2}.$$

Step 6: Find out the score values by using the formula given in definition 1.12.

Step 7: Rank the alternatives according to the result obtained through step 6 and obtain the best alternative according to ranking order.

2.3.2 Numerical example

Cyber-resilient network architectures are planned to withstand, adapt, and recover from cyber threats and disruptions while maintaining essential operations. These architectures integrate state-of-the-art technologies including artificial intelligence, blockchain, and complex fuzzy logic into identifying vulnerabilities, predicting potential attacks, and strong defense mechanisms. Adaptive frameworks and redundancy measures enable these networks to function seamlessly in stressful conditions, thereby reducing risk and minimizing downtime. In addition, they also focus on proactive threat management, which involves continuous monitoring and real-time responses to changing cyber challenges. Such resilience is very important in safeguarding critical infrastructures in the finance, health care, and national security sectors. The bottom line is that cyber-resilient networks will ensure operational continuity and maintain data integrity in an ever-changing. The most famous cyber-resilient network architectures as an alternative are given by

- *Zero trust architecture (ZTA)*:

In summary, with Zero Trust as the philosophy, "Never trust, always verify," access must be granted once users, devices, and applications successfully authenticate. Continuously, MFA is used within ZTA together with continuous monitoring and micro-segmentation. Separating the network zones limits lateral movement. It assumes breaches are imminent, and therefore, operates under the assumption of least privilege. Its security policies are regularly updated to ensure continued adaptability to threats. Its robust defense mechanisms make it a favorite for critical infrastructure. By centralizing access control, ZTA eliminates reliance on perimeter-only defenses. ZTA also enhances data visibility and reduces insider threat risks. Its scalability makes it suitable for both small and large organizations.

- *Software-defined networking (SDN)*:

Software-defined networking breaks the control and data planes into networks, which provide centralized control to dynamically configure and manage them. It enhances resiliency through real-time reconfigurations of the network due to threats. A central controller can automatically enforce policies to block suspicious traffic. Due to programmability, SDN supports the instant deployment of security patches and updates. The fine-grained traffic management that SDN provides assures network segmentation, which eventually blocks the attack spread. The compromised components are isolated through virtualization in SDN. Further dynamic rerouting of traffic is accomplished in the case of cyberattacks for fault tolerance. It supports proactive security by incorporating IDS. Its adaptability also suits the changing cyber-resilient needs. SDN further supports cloud-native security architectures.

- *Segmented network architecture*:

This methodology segments the network into small isolated parts or zones to hold threats. Segmentation prevents one breach in a segment from affecting the whole network. Firewalls and access control lists (ACLs) are often used to control communications between the segments. The sensitive data, such as the information of the customers, is kept in high-security zones. Network segmentation also simplifies the monitoring as anomalies become easy to identify. It also supports the regulation of laws such as GDPR and

HIPAA, protecting certain sets of data. This architecture is cost-effective in securing legacy systems. Coupling it with IPS will improve its resilience. It is extensively used in the health care and financial sectors due to the robust data protection it provides. It reduces attack surfaces, making overall cybersecurity better.

- *Cloud-native network architecture*:

This design uses cloud infrastructure and its native security tools to enhance cyber resilience. Built-in redundancy, automated threat detection, and elastic scaling all work together to counter attacks. Decentralization of resources reduces the occurrence of single points of failure in cloud-native architectures. Features such as containerization isolate workloads, which prevent compromise spillovers. Security automation, like patch management and vulnerability scanning, strengthens defenses. AI-powered analytics continuously monitor and predict threats. Data is mostly encrypted in both transit and at rest, providing high confidentiality. This architecture makes it easier to integrate into DevSecOps pipelines for secure application development. Cloud-native approaches suit modern businesses relying on distributed systems. Its resilience is further enhanced by disaster recovery and backup solutions in multicloud environments.

The attributes of these alternatives are given in Table 2.1.

Table 2.1 Attributes and their description.

Attributes	Description	Relevance to cybersecurity
Fault tolerance	The ability to function even when cyberattacks or hardware and software failures take place.	Reduces downtime and avoids the disruptions of the whole system.
Proactive defence	Instead of reacting, focus on preventing and controlling the attacks before they have the chance to occur.	Improves response times and reduces attack surface.
Adaptability	The ability to keep adapting to changes in network environments and the threat landscapes	Reduces changing risks and ensures the system is secure at all times
Zero trust enforcement	Installation of data and backup systems that ensure availability in the case of a failure	Eliminates single points of failure that improve system reliability.

Based on this information, assume that the WVs for these attributes are $(0.24, 0.22, 0.31, 0.23)$. Now we apply the step-wise WASPAS algorithm for the execution of the developed approach.

Step 1: The information provided by the decision analyst in the form of CFRNs is described in Table 2.2.

Table 2.2 CFR data.

	$\mathbb{T}_1$	$\mathbb{T}_2$	$\mathbb{T}_3$	$\mathbb{T}_4$
$\mathfrak{L}_1$	$\begin{pmatrix} 0.17+\iota\,0.12, \\ 0.19+\iota 0.16 \end{pmatrix}$	$\begin{pmatrix} 0.21+\iota\,0.37, \\ 0.22+\iota 0.35 \end{pmatrix}$	$\begin{pmatrix} 0.38+\iota\,0.53, \\ 0.39+\iota 0.52 \end{pmatrix}$	$\begin{pmatrix} 0.54+\iota\,0.69, \\ 0.55+\iota 0.68 \end{pmatrix}$
$\mathfrak{L}_2$	$\begin{pmatrix} 0.2+\iota\,0.12, \\ 0.3+\iota 0.16 \end{pmatrix}$	$\begin{pmatrix} 0.23+\iota\,0.34, \\ 0.24+\iota 0.33 \end{pmatrix}$	$\begin{pmatrix} 0.40+\iota\,0.51, \\ 0.41+\iota 0.50 \end{pmatrix}$	$\begin{pmatrix} 0.56+\iota\,0.67, \\ 0.57+\iota 0.66 \end{pmatrix}$
$\mathfrak{L}_3$	$\begin{pmatrix} 0.1+\iota\,0.52, \\ 0.2+\iota 0.46 \end{pmatrix}$	$\begin{pmatrix} 0.26+\iota\,0.32, \\ 0.27+\iota 0.36 \end{pmatrix}$	$\begin{pmatrix} 0.42+\iota\,0.49, \\ 0.43+\iota 0.48 \end{pmatrix}$	$\begin{pmatrix} 0.58+\iota\,0.65, \\ 0.59+\iota 0.64 \end{pmatrix}$
$\mathfrak{L}_4$	$\begin{pmatrix} 0.23+\iota\,0.42, \\ 0.31+\iota 0.32 \end{pmatrix}$	$\begin{pmatrix} 0.28+\iota\,0.31, \\ 0.29+\iota 0.30 \end{pmatrix}$	$\begin{pmatrix} 0.44+\iota\,0.47, \\ 0.45+\iota 0.46 \end{pmatrix}$	$\begin{pmatrix} 0.60+\iota\,0.63, \\ 0.61+\iota 0.62 \end{pmatrix}$

Step 2: Since all attributes are benefit type so no need to normalize the information and we get the same data as given in Table 2.2.

Step 3: Find out the relative importance of the alternatives by using the formula given in eqn (2.2):

$$(\mathcal{A}_1)^{\text{WS}} = \begin{pmatrix} 0.\ 3326+\iota\,0.4475\ , \\ 0.3454+\iota\,0.4459 \end{pmatrix}, (\mathcal{A}_2)^{\text{WS}} = \begin{pmatrix} 0.\ 3558+\iota\,0.\ 4281, \\ 0.3872+\iota\,0.4288 \end{pmatrix},$$

$$(\mathcal{A}_3)^{\text{WS}} = \begin{pmatrix} 0.3501\ +\iota\,0.5027, \\ 0.3822+\iota\,0.4904 \end{pmatrix}, (\mathcal{A}_4)^{\text{WS}} = \begin{pmatrix} 0.\ 3973+\iota\,0.4651, \\ 0.4237+\iota\,0.4341 \end{pmatrix}.$$

Step 4: Find out the relative importance of the alternatives by using the formula given in eqn (2.4):

$$(\mathcal{A}_1)^{\text{WP}} = \begin{pmatrix} 0.\ 3078+\iota\,0.\ 3891, \\ 0.\ 3210+\iota\,0.4000 \end{pmatrix}, (\mathcal{A}_2)^{\text{WP}} = \begin{pmatrix} 0.\ 3370+\iota\,0.\ 3735, \\ 0.\ 3710+\iota\,0.3860 \end{pmatrix},$$

$$(\mathcal{A}_3)^{\text{WP}} = \begin{pmatrix} 0.\ 3068+\iota\,0.4847\ , \\ 0.3570+\iota\,0.4810 \end{pmatrix}, (\mathcal{A}_4)^{\text{WP}} = \begin{pmatrix} 0.\ 3791+\iota\,0.\ 4456, \\ 0.\ 4070+\iota\,0.4180 \end{pmatrix}.$$

Step 5: The evaluated overall significance of every alternative is:

$$\mathcal{A}_1 = \begin{pmatrix} 0.\ 3152+\iota\,0.4185, \\ 0.3332+\iota\,0.4231 \end{pmatrix}, \mathcal{A}_2 = \begin{pmatrix} 0.\ 3664+\iota\,0.4010, \\ 0.\ 3791+\iota\,0.4075 \end{pmatrix},$$

$$\mathcal{A}_3 = \begin{pmatrix} 0.\ 3285+\iota\,0.\ 4937, \\ 0.3696+\iota\,0.4857 \end{pmatrix}, \mathcal{A}_4 = \begin{pmatrix} 0.\ 3882+\iota\,0.\ 4553, \\ 0.4153+\iota\,0.4260 \end{pmatrix}.$$

Step 6: Find out the score values by using the formula given in definition (1.12). Hence score value for each alternative $\mathcal{A}_j,\ j = 1,\ 2,\ 3,\ 4$ are given by

$$\text{Scor.}\,(\mathcal{A}_1) = 0.3725,\ \text{Scor.}\,(\mathcal{A}_2) = 0.3835,$$
$$\text{Scor.}\,(\mathcal{A}_3) = 0.4194,\ \text{Scor.}\,(\mathcal{A}_4) = 0.4212.$$

Step 7: Rank the alternatives according to the result obtained through step 6 and obtain the best alternative according to ranking order. Based on the results we can conclude that the ranking results are $\mathcal{A}_4 > \mathcal{A}_3 > \mathcal{A}_2 > \mathcal{A}_1$. Thus, $\mathcal{A}_4$ is the best alternative.

The graphical representation of the results is presented in Figure 2.1.

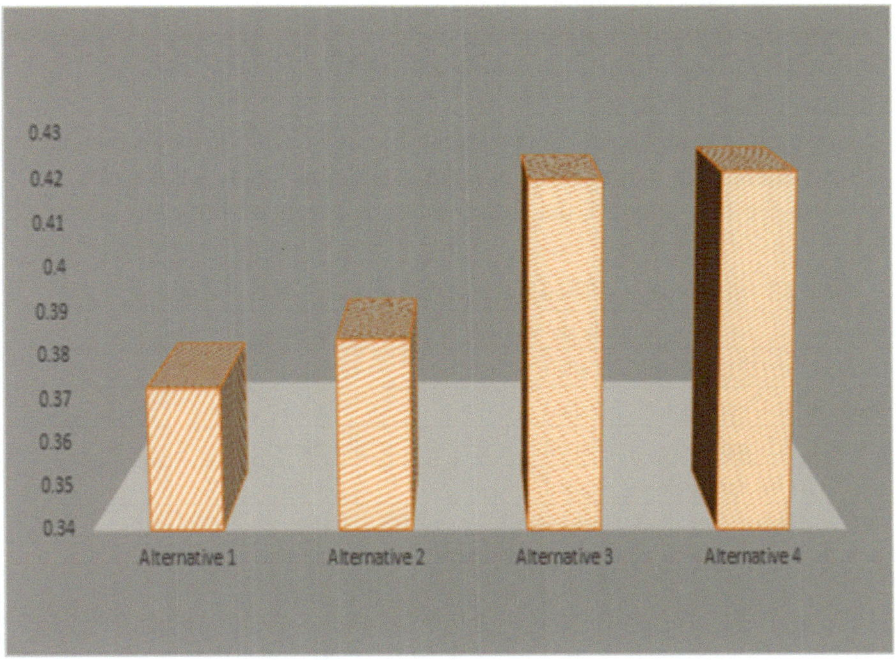

Figure 2.1 Graphical representation of ranking results.

2.4 Comparative Analysis

In this section of the chapter, we will discuss the comparative analysis of the proposed study and discuss the importance and need of the introduced work.

Here, we will compare our work with Mardani et al. [13] approach, Khan et al. [14] approach, Hadi et al. [15] approach, and Zhou et al. [16] approach.

(1) In the case of Mardani et al. [13] approach, we can see that this approach relies on fuzzy aggregation theory, but these notions are less applicable as compared to the defined approach. The defined approaches can handle more advanced data and this approach can discuss the two-dimensional information as well while the existing approach is free from this characteristic. Hence the existing approach has some drawbacks.

(2) In the case of the Khan et al. [14] approach we can observe that this approach is based on the complex idea of Ramot et al. [4] and Ramot et al. [4] approach has the condition that amplitude term $r \in [0,\ 1]$. In the case of the developed approach, we can observe that the defined approach is based on Tamir's complex fuzzy idea, and in the case of the information $0.7 + \iota 0.8$ the amplitude term $r \notin [0,\ 1]$. Hence, the existing approach can never cover these problems and the initiated approach can discover these problems.

(3) In the case of Hadi et al. [15] approach, this study is based on Fermatean fuzzy Hamacher aggregation operators and this approach is free to discuss the two-dimensional information as given in Table 2.2. Also,

Table 2.3 Score values and ranking results of interpreted and existing work.

Methods	**Score values**	**Ranking**
Mardani et al. [13] approach	Failed	Failed
Khan et al. [14] approach	Failed	Failed
Hadi et al. [15] approach	Failed	Failed
Zhou et al. [16] approach	Failed	Failed
CFRHWA AOs (proposed approach)	$\text{Scor.}(\mathcal{A}_1) = 0.3930$, $\text{Scor.}(\mathcal{A}_2) = 0.4000$, $\text{Scor.}(\mathcal{A}_3) = 0.4310$ $\text{Scor.}(\mathcal{A}_4) = 0.4300$	$\mathcal{A}_3 > \mathcal{A}_4 > \mathcal{A}_2 > \mathcal{A}_1$
CFRHWG AOs (proposed approach)	$\text{Scor.}(\mathcal{A}_1) = 0.3540$, $\text{Scor.}(\mathcal{A}_2) = 0.3670$, $\text{Scor.}(\mathcal{A}_3) = 0.4070$ $\text{Scor.}(\mathcal{A}_4) = 0.4120$	$\mathcal{A}_4 > \mathcal{A}_3 > \mathcal{A}_2 > \mathcal{A}_1$
The WASPAS approach (proposed)	$\text{Scor.}(\mathcal{A}_1) = 0.3725$, $\text{Scor.}(\mathcal{A}_2) = 0.3835$, $\text{Scor.}(\mathcal{A}_3) = 0.4194$ $\text{Scor.}(\mathcal{A}_4) = 0.4212$	$\mathcal{A}_4 > \mathcal{A}_3 > \mathcal{A}_2 > \mathcal{A}_1$

this approach can never discuss the upper and lower approximation of data. Hence we can see that the chance of data loss increases in the case of Hadi et al. [15] approach. On the other hand, the delivered work can cover both possibilities and provide the opportunity for decision-makers to take more advance in their decision-making problems that rely on two-dimensional information.

(4) Zhou et al. [16] approach is based on hesitant fuzzy Hamacher aggregation operators. Although this approach is more advanced than fuzzy information. But we can observe that this approach can never discuss the two-dimensional scenario-based problems that make this approach limited and it is the drawback of these defined notions. The defined work is superior to these existing notions because these notions can cover all such difficulties. Hence the advantages of the initiated work are obvious in any case.

The results of the study are given in Table 2.3

Moreover, the graphical representation of the information in Table 2.3 is given in Figure 2.2.

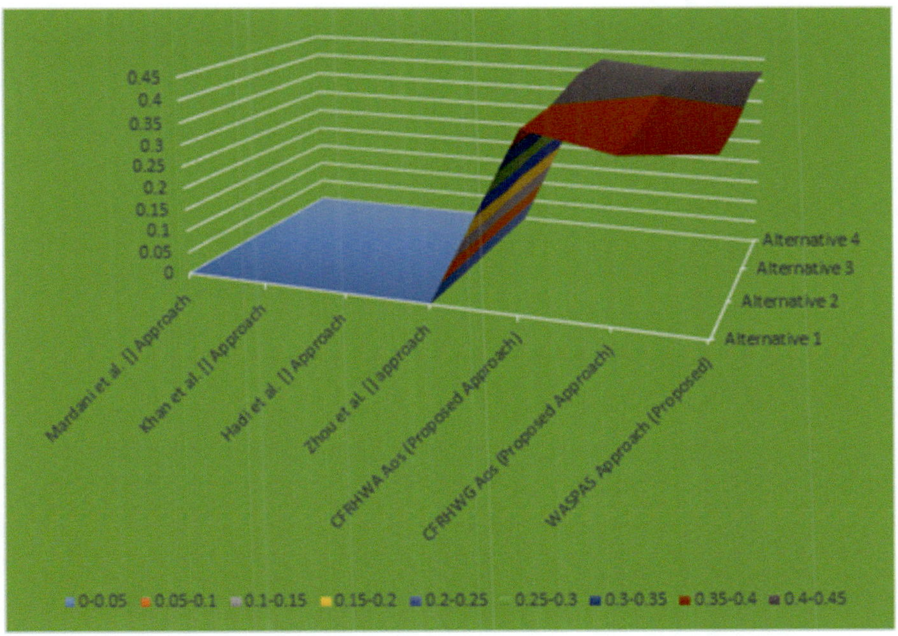

Figure 2.2 A graphical representation of data given in Table 2.3.

2.5 Conclusion

This new study on combining complex fuzzy rough Hamacher aggregation operators with the WASPAS approach introduces a novel framework in the area of cyber-resilient network architecture prioritization. This method integrates the strengths of complex fuzzy rough set theory in handling nuanced issues of uncertainty and imprecision in evaluating cybersecurity. The model ensures a balanced and adaptive decision by utilizing the Hamacher aggregation operators, especially in situations where criteria conflict. Further improving the computational efficiency and accuracy of the framework that robustly prioritizes the architectures against cyber threats is achieved with the WASPAS approach. This work serves to close the gap between the theory of advancements and their application in real life, hence the provision of a systematic way by which network designers identify their optimum solutions. Its relevance spreads as it covers critical infrastructure sectors for which cyber-resilience matters. Overall, the research provides a great step toward incorporating AI-driven methodologies into planning and the decision-making process in cybersecurity.

3

Integrating Complex Fuzzy Rough Yager Aggregation Operators with Neural Networks for Improved AI Predictive Models

When it comes to predictive modeling, choosing the most suitable neural network models is even more important in the age of expanded artificial intelligence. Neural networks as basic components of the modern AI systems themselves presuppose the proper selection of the framework regarding multiple criteria starting from the scalability and ending with computational performance and integration possibilities. This chapter meets this crucial challenge in two ways: first, by proposing a new MCDM framework for the selection of the neural network framework; and second, by developing the theoretical underpinnings of the complex fuzzy rough set theory. We propose four innovative aggregation operators: The proposed novel operators are complex fuzzy rough Yager power averaging (CFRYPA), complex fuzzy rough Yager power weighted averaging (CFRYPWA), complex fuzzy rough Yager power geometric (CFRYPG), and complex fuzzy rough Yager power weighted geometric (CFRYPWG). These operators expand conventional methodologies by including advanced fuzzy rough information processing functions which are useful in making enhanced decisions during situations involving uncertain and imprecise data. This is supported by the theoretical analysis of the properties of these operators and their mathematical proofs that describe their performance. As a proof of concept of the proposed framework, we provide a detailed case study of the selection of neural network frameworks for AI predictive models. The case study demonstrates how our MCDM technique can process fuzzy rough information to assess and rank the best neural network frameworks according to the criteria. In addition, we also perform a detailed comparison with the other methods to show the effectiveness and improvement of the proposed method. The combination of complex fuzzy rough Yager power operators with the selection of the

DOI: 10.1201/9788743807827-3

neural network framework is a major improvement in theoretical and practical aspects of AI system development. This chapter narrows the gap between theoretical mathematical models and practical AI applications, offering practitioners effective and reliable instruments to make proper decisions in the NN framework choice and, at the same time, developing the field of fuzzy mathematics and decision-making theory.

3.1 Complex Fuzzy Rough Yager Power AOs

In this section, we interpret the Yager power AOs within the framework of CFRS. These operations are CFRYPA, CFRYPWA, CFRYPG, and CFRYPWG operators.

Definition 3.1: For two CFRNs $\mathcal{A}_1 = \left\{\left(\overline{a_1} + \iota\overline{b_1},\ \underline{a_1} + \iota\underline{b_1}\right)\right\}$ and $\mathcal{A}_2 = \left\{\left(\overline{a_2} + \iota\overline{b_2},\ \underline{a_2} + \iota\underline{b_2}\right)\right\}$, the algebraic operations by employing Yager t-norm and co-norm are inferred as

(1) $\mathcal{A}_1 \oplus \mathcal{A}_2 =$

$$\begin{pmatrix} \min\left(1,\ \left(\left(\overline{a_1}\right)^{\partial} + \left(\overline{a_2}\right)^{\partial}\right)^{\frac{1}{\partial}}\right) + \iota \min\left(1,\ \left(\left(\overline{b_1}\right)^{\partial} + \left(\overline{b_2}\right)^{\partial}\right)^{\frac{1}{\partial}}\right), \\ \min\left(1,\ \left(\left(\underline{a_1}\right)^{\partial} + \left(\underline{a_2}\right)^{\partial}\right)^{\frac{1}{\partial}}\right) + \iota \min\left(1,\ \left(\left(\underline{b_1}\right)^{\partial} + \left(\underline{b_2}\right)^{\partial}\right)^{\frac{1}{\partial}}\right) \end{pmatrix}.$$

(2)

$$\mathcal{A}_1 \otimes \mathcal{A}_2 = \begin{pmatrix} 1 - \min\left(1,\ \left((1 - \overline{a_1})^{\partial} + (1 - \overline{a_2})^{\partial}\right)^{\frac{1}{\partial}}\right) \\ +\iota\left(1 - \min\left(1,\ \left((1 - \overline{b_1})^{\partial} + (1 - \overline{b_2})^{\partial}\right)^{\frac{1}{\partial}}\right)\right), \\ 1 - \min\left(1,\ \left((1 - \underline{a_1})^{\partial} + (1 - \underline{a_2})^{\partial}\right)^{\frac{1}{\partial}}\right) \\ +\iota\left(1 - \min\left(1,\ \left((1 - \underline{b_1})^{\partial} + (1 - \underline{b_2})^{\partial}\right)^{\frac{1}{\partial}}\right)\right) \end{pmatrix}.$$

$$\text{(3) } k\mathcal{A}_1 = \begin{pmatrix} \min\left(1,\ \left(k(\overline{a_1})^{\partial}\right)^{\frac{1}{\partial}}\right) + \iota\left(\min\left(1,\ \left(k(\overline{b_1})^{\partial}\right)^{\frac{1}{\partial}}\right)\right), \\ \min\left(1,\ \left(k(\underline{a_1})^{\partial}\right)^{\frac{1}{\partial}}\right) + \iota\left(\min\left(1,\ \left(k(\underline{b_1})^{\partial}\right)^{\frac{1}{\partial}}\right)\right) \end{pmatrix}.$$

(4) ${\mathcal{A}_1}^k$

$$= \begin{pmatrix} 1-\min\left(1,\ \left(k(1-\overline{a_1})^{\partial}\right)^{\frac{1}{\partial}}\right)+\iota\left(1-\min\left(1,\ \left(k(1-\overline{b_1})^{\partial}\right)^{\frac{1}{\partial}}\right)\right), \\ 1-\min\left(1,\ \left(k(1-\underline{a_1})^{\partial}\right)^{\frac{1}{\partial}}\right)+\iota\left(1-\min\left(1,\ \left(k(1-\underline{b_1})^{\partial}\right)^{\frac{1}{\partial}}\right)\right) \end{pmatrix}.$$

Employing these operations, we initiate CFRYPA, CFRYPWA, CFRYPG, and CFRYPWG operators.

Definition 3.2: Let an assembly $\mathcal{A}_j = \left\{\left(\overline{a_j}+\iota\overline{b_j},\ \underline{a_j}+\iota\underline{b_j}\right)\right\}$, $(j = 1,\ 2,\ \ldots,\ n)$ of CFRNs. Then the CFRYPA operator is scrutinized as

$$\text{CFRYPA}\left(\mathcal{A}_1,\ \mathcal{A}_2,\ \mathcal{A}_3,\ \ldots,\ \mathcal{A}_n\right) = \bigoplus_{j=1}^{n} \frac{1+T\left(\mathcal{A}_j\right)}{\sum_{j=1}^{n}\left(1+T\left(\mathcal{A}_j\right)\right)}\mathcal{A}_j.$$

Observe that $\mathrm{T}\left(\mathcal{A}_j\right) = \sum_{\substack{j=1 \\ j\neq r}}^{n} \mathrm{Sup}\left(\mathcal{A}_j, \mathcal{A}_r\right)$ and $\mathrm{Sup}\left(\mathcal{A}_j,\ \mathcal{A}_r\right)$infers the support for $\mathcal{A}_j$ from $\mathcal{A}_r$ with the axioms given below:

- $\mathrm{Sup}\left(\mathcal{A}_j,\ \mathcal{A}_r\right) \in [0,\ 1]$;
- $\mathrm{Sup}\left(\mathcal{A}_j,\ \mathcal{A}_r\right) = \mathrm{Sup}\left(\mathcal{A}_r,\ \mathcal{A}_j\right)$;
- $\mathrm{Sup}\left(\mathcal{A}_j,\ \mathcal{A}_r\right) \geq \mathrm{Sup}\left(\mathcal{A}_{j'},\ \mathcal{A}_{r'}\right)$ if $\text{đ}\left(\mathcal{A}_j,\ \mathcal{A}_r\right) < \text{đ}\left(\mathcal{A}_{j'},\ \mathcal{A}_{r'}\right)$, đ can be a distance measure among CFRSs that is:

$$\text{đ}\left(\mathcal{A}_1,\ \mathcal{A}_2\right) = \frac{1}{4}\left(\left|\overline{a_1}-\overline{a_2}\right| + \left|\overline{b_1}-\overline{b_2}\right| + \left|\underline{a_1}-\underline{a_2}\right| + \left|\underline{b_1}-\underline{b_2}\right|\right),$$

where $\mathcal{A}_j = \left\{\left(\overline{a_j}+\iota\overline{b_j},\ \underline{a_j}+\iota\underline{b_j}\right)\right\}$, $(j = 1,\ 2)$.

In this book, to make things easy, we will use:

$$\chi_{\mathbb{J}} = \frac{1+T\left(\mathcal{A}_j\right)}{\sum_{j=1}^{n}\left(1+T\left(\mathcal{A}_j\right)\right)}.$$

Theorem 3.1: Let an assembly $\mathcal{A}_j = \left\{\left(\overline{a_j}+\iota\overline{b_j},\ \underline{a_j}+\iota\underline{b_j}\right)\right\}$, $(j = 1,\ 2,\ \ldots,\ n)$ of CFRNs. Then the usage of the CFRYPA operator over $\mathcal{A}_j$ will give a CFRN that is:

$\text{CFRYPA}\left(\mathcal{A}_1,\ \mathcal{A}_2,\ \mathcal{A}_3,\ \ldots,\ \mathcal{A}_n\right)$

$$= \begin{pmatrix} \min\left(1, \left(\sum_{j=1}^{n}\left(\chi_j(\overline{a_j})^{\partial}\right)\right)^{\frac{1}{\partial}}\right) + \iota \min\left(1, \left(\sum_{j=1}^{n}\left(\chi_j\left(\overline{b_j}\right)^{\partial}\right)\right)^{\frac{1}{\partial}}\right), \\ \min\left(1, \left(\sum_{j=1}^{n}\left(\chi_j\left(\underline{a_j}\right)^{\partial}\right)\right)^{\frac{1}{\partial}}\right) + \min\left(1, \left(\sum_{j=1}^{n}\left(\chi_j\left(\underline{b_j}\right)^{\partial}\right)\right)^{\frac{1}{\partial}}\right), \end{pmatrix}. \tag{3.1}$$

Proof: Let $n = 2$. Then, we have:

$$\text{CFRYPA}\,(\mathcal{A}_1,\ \mathcal{A}_2) = \chi_1\mathcal{A}_1 \oplus \chi_2\mathcal{A}_2,$$

and as

$$\chi_1\mathcal{A}_1 = \begin{pmatrix} \min\left(1, \left(\chi_1(\overline{a_1})^{\partial}\right)^{\frac{1}{\partial}}\right) + \iota\left(\min\left(1, \left(\chi_1\left(\overline{b_1}\right)^{\partial}\right)^{\frac{1}{\partial}}\right)\right), \\ \min\left(1, \left(\chi_1\left(\underline{a_1}\right)^{\partial}\right)^{\frac{1}{\partial}}\right) + \iota\left(\min\left(1, \left(\chi_1\left(\underline{b_1}\right)^{\partial}\right)^{\frac{1}{\partial}}\right)\right) \end{pmatrix}.$$

$$\chi_2\mathcal{A}_2 = \begin{pmatrix} \min\left(1, \left(\chi_2(\overline{a_2})^{\partial}\right)^{\frac{1}{\partial}}\right) + \iota\left(\min\left(1, \left(\chi_2\left(\overline{b_2}\right)^{\partial}\right)^{\frac{1}{\partial}}\right)\right), \\ \min\left(1, \left(\chi_2\left(\underline{a_2}\right)^{\partial}\right)^{\frac{1}{\partial}}\right) + \iota\left(\min\left(1, \left(\chi_2\left(\underline{b_2}\right)^{\partial}\right)^{\frac{1}{\partial}}\right)\right) \end{pmatrix}.$$

This implies that,

$$\chi_1\mathcal{A}_1 \oplus \chi_2\mathcal{A}_2 = \begin{pmatrix} \min\left(1, \left(\chi_1(\overline{a_1})^{\partial}\right)^{\frac{1}{\partial}}\right) + \iota\left(\min\left(1, \left(\chi_1\left(\overline{b_1}\right)^{\partial}\right)^{\frac{1}{\partial}}\right)\right), \\ \min\left(1, \left(\chi_1\left(\underline{a_1}\right)^{\partial}\right)^{\frac{1}{\partial}}\right) + \iota\left(\min\left(1, \left(\chi_1\left(\underline{b_1}\right)^{\partial}\right)^{\frac{1}{\partial}}\right)\right) \end{pmatrix}$$

$$\oplus \begin{pmatrix} \min\left(1, \left(\chi_2(\overline{a_2})^{\partial}\right)^{\frac{1}{\partial}}\right) + \iota\left(\min\left(1, \left(\chi_2\left(\overline{b_2}\right)^{\partial}\right)^{\frac{1}{\partial}}\right)\right), \\ \min\left(1, \left(\chi_2\left(\underline{a_2}\right)^{\partial}\right)^{\frac{1}{\partial}}\right) + \iota\left(\min\left(1, \left(\chi_2\left(\underline{b_2}\right)^{\partial}\right)^{\frac{1}{\partial}}\right)\right) \end{pmatrix}$$

$$= \begin{pmatrix} \min\left(1, \left(\chi_1\,(\overline{a_1})^{\partial} + \chi_2(\overline{a_2})^{\partial}\right)^{\frac{1}{\partial}}\right) + \iota \min\left(1, \left(\chi_1\left(\overline{b_1}\right)^{\partial} + \chi_2\left(\overline{b_2}\right)^{\partial}\right)^{\frac{1}{\partial}}\right), \\ \min\left(1, \left(\chi_1\left(\underline{a_1}\right)^{\partial} + \chi_2\left(\underline{a_2}\right)^{\partial}\right)^{\frac{1}{\partial}}\right) + \iota \min\left(1, \left(\chi_1\left(\underline{b_1}\right)^{\partial} + \chi_2\left(\underline{b_2}\right)^{\partial}\right)^{\frac{1}{\partial}}\right) \end{pmatrix}$$

$$= \begin{pmatrix} \min\left(1, \left(\sum_{j=1}^{2}\left(\chi_j(\overline{a_j})^{\partial}\right)\right)^{\frac{1}{\partial}}\right) + \iota \min\left(1, \left(\sum_{j=1}^{2}\left(\chi_j\left(\overline{b_j}\right)^{\partial}\right)\right)^{\frac{1}{\partial}}\right), \\ \min\left(1, \left(\sum_{j=1}^{2}\left(\chi_j\left(\underline{a_j}\right)^{\partial}\right)\right)^{\frac{1}{\partial}}\right) + \iota \min\left(1, \left(\sum_{j=1}^{2}\left(\chi_j\left(\underline{b_j}\right)^{\partial}\right)\right)^{\frac{1}{\partial}}\right) \end{pmatrix}.$$

Thus, eqn (3.1) holds for $n = 2$. Next let for $n = r$, eqn (3.1) holds. Then:

$$\text{CFRYPA}(\mathcal{A}_1, \mathcal{A}_2, \mathcal{A}_3, \ldots, \mathcal{A}_r)$$

$$= \begin{pmatrix} \min\left(1, \left(\sum_{j=1}^{r}\left(\chi_j(\overline{a_j})^{\partial}\right)\right)^{\frac{1}{\partial}}\right) + \iota \min\left(1, \left(\sum_{j=1}^{r}\left(\chi_j(\overline{b_j})^{\partial}\right)\right)^{\frac{1}{\partial}}\right), \\ \min\left(1, \left(\sum_{j=1}^{r}\left(\chi_j\left(\underline{a_j}\right)^{\partial}\right)\right)^{\frac{1}{\partial}}\right) + \iota \min\left(1, \left(\sum_{j=1}^{r}\left(\chi_j\left(\underline{b_j}\right)^{\partial}\right)\right)^{\frac{1}{\partial}}\right) \end{pmatrix}.$$

Finally, let $n = r + 1$. Then:

$$\text{CFRYPA}(\mathcal{A}_1, \mathcal{A}_2, \mathcal{A}_3, \ldots, \mathcal{A}_r, \mathcal{A}_{r+1})$$

$$= \begin{pmatrix} \min\left(1, \left(\sum_{j=1}^{r}\left(\chi_j(\overline{a_j})^{\partial}\right)\right)^{\frac{1}{\partial}}\right) + \iota \min\left(1, \left(\sum_{j=1}^{r}\left(\chi_j(\overline{b_j})^{\partial}\right)\right)^{\frac{1}{\partial}}\right), \\ \min\left(1, \left(\sum_{j=1}^{r}\left(\chi_j\left(\underline{a_j}\right)^{\partial}\right)\right)^{\frac{1}{\partial}}\right) + \iota \min\left(1, \left(\sum_{j=1}^{r}\left(\chi_j\left(\underline{b_j}\right)^{\partial}\right)\right)^{\frac{1}{\partial}}\right) \end{pmatrix}$$

$$\oplus \begin{pmatrix} \min\left(1, \left(\chi_{r+1}(\overline{a_{r+1}})^{\partial}\right)^{\frac{1}{\partial}}\right) + \iota \left(\min\left(1, \left(\chi_{r+1}(\overline{b_{r+1}})^{\partial}\right)^{\frac{1}{\partial}}\right)\right), \\ \min\left(1, \left(\chi_{r+1}\left(\underline{a_{r+1}}\right)^{\partial}\right)^{\frac{1}{\partial}}\right) + \iota \left(\min\left(1, \left(\chi_{r+1}\left(\underline{b_{r+1}}\right)^{\partial}\right)^{\frac{1}{\partial}}\right)\right) \end{pmatrix}$$

$$= \begin{pmatrix} \min\left(1, \left(\sum_{j=1}^{r+1}\left(\chi_j(\overline{a_j})^{\partial}\right)\right)^{\frac{1}{\partial}}\right) + \iota \min\left(1, \left(\sum_{j=1}^{r+1}\left(\chi_j(\overline{b_j})^{\partial}\right)\right)^{\frac{1}{\partial}}\right), \\ \min\left(1, \left(\sum_{j=1}^{r+1}\left(\chi_j\left(\underline{a_j}\right)^{\partial}\right)\right)^{\frac{1}{\partial}}\right) + \iota \min\left(1, \left(\sum_{j=1}^{r+1}\left(\chi_j\left(\underline{b_j}\right)^{\partial}\right)\right)^{\frac{1}{\partial}}\right) \end{pmatrix}.$$

$\Longrightarrow$ Eqn (3.1) is true for n.

3.1.1 Properties of CFRYPA operator

The notion of CFRYPA satisfies the following properties.

Idempotency: Let an assembly $\mathcal{A}_j = \left\{\left(\overline{a_j} + \iota\overline{b_j},\, \underline{a_j} + \iota\underline{b_j}\right)\right\}$, $(j = 1, 2, \ldots, n)$ of CFRNs. If $\mathcal{A}_j = \mathcal{A}$, $\forall\, j$ then:

$$\text{CFRYPA}(\mathcal{A}_1, \mathcal{A}_2, .., \mathcal{A}_n) = \mathcal{A}.$$

Boundedness: Let an assembly $\mathcal{A}_j = \left(\overline{a_j} + \iota\overline{b_j}, \underline{a_j} + \iota\underline{b_j}\right), (j = 1, 2, \ldots, n)$, of CFRNs and $\mathcal{A}^- = \left(\min_j \{\overline{a_j}\} + \iota \min_j \{\overline{b_j}\}, \min_j \left\{\underline{a_j}\right\} + \iota \min_j \left\{\underline{b_j}\right\}\right)$, and $\mathcal{A}^+ = \left(\max_j \{\overline{a_j}\} + \iota \max_j \{\overline{b_j}\}, \max_j \left\{\underline{a_j}\right\} + \iota \max_j \left\{\underline{b_j}\right\}\right)$.

Then:

$$\mathcal{A}^- \leq \text{CFRYPA}\left(\mathcal{A}_1,\ \mathcal{A}_2, \ldots, \mathcal{A}_n\right) \leq \mathcal{A}^+.$$

Monotonicity: Let two assemblies $\mathcal{A}_j = \left(\overline{a_j} + \iota\,\overline{b_j}, \underline{a_j} + \iota\underline{b_j}\right)$ and $\mathcal{A}_j^{'} = \left(\overline{a_j^{'}} + \iota\,\overline{b_j^{'}}, \underline{a_j^{'}} + \iota\underline{b_j^{'}}\right),\ (j = 1,\ 2,\ \ldots,\ n)$, of CFRNs. If $\underline{a_j} \leq \underline{a_j^{'}}, \underline{b_j} \leq \underline{b_j^{'}}$, $\overline{a_j} \leq \overline{a_j^{'}}, \overline{b_j} \leq \overline{b_j^{'}}\ \forall\ j$ then:

$$\text{CFRYPA}\left(\mathcal{A}_1,\ \mathcal{A}_2,\ ..,\ \mathcal{A}_n\right) \leq \text{CFRYPA}\left(\mathcal{A}_1^{'},\ \mathcal{A}_2^{'},\ ..,\ \mathcal{A}_n^{'}\right).$$

Definition 3.3: Let an assembly $\mathcal{A}_j = \left\{\left(\overline{a_j} + \iota\overline{b_j},\ \underline{a_j} + \iota\underline{b_j}\right)\right\},\ (j = 1,\ 2,\ \ldots, n)$ of CFRNs. Then the CFRYPWA operator is scrutinized as

$$\text{CFRYPWA}\left(\mathcal{A}_1,\ \mathcal{A}_2,\ \mathcal{A}_3,\ \ldots,\ \mathcal{A}_n\right) = \bigoplus_{j=1}^{n} \frac{\omega_j\left(1 + T\left(\mathcal{A}_j\right)\right)}{\sum_{j=1}^{n} \omega_j\left(1 + T\left(\mathcal{A}_j\right)\right)} \mathcal{A}_j.$$

Notice that $\omega = \left(\omega_1,\ \omega_2,\ \ldots,\ \omega_n\right)^T$ is a weight vector such that $\sum_{j=1}^{n} \omega_j = 1$ and $0 \leq \omega_j \leq 1$.

Theorem 3.2: Let an assembly $\mathcal{A}_j = \left\{\left(\overline{a_j} + \iota\overline{b_j},\ \underline{a_j} + \iota\underline{b_j}\right)\right\},\ (j = 1,\ 2,\ \ldots,\ n)$ of CFRNs. Then the usage of the CFRYPWA operator over $\mathcal{A}_j$ will give a CFRN that is:

$$\text{CFRYPWA}\left(\mathcal{A}_1,\ \mathcal{A}_2,\ \mathcal{A}_3,\ \ldots,\ \mathcal{A}_n\right) =$$

$$\begin{pmatrix} \min\left(1, \left(\sum_{j=1}^{n}\left(\frac{\omega_j(1+T(\mathcal{A}_j))}{\sum_{j=1}^{n}\omega_j(1+T(\mathcal{A}_j))}(\overline{a_j})^{\partial}\right)\right)^{\frac{1}{\partial}}\right) \\ +\iota\min\left(1, \left(\sum_{j=1}^{n}\left(\frac{\omega_j(1+T(\mathcal{A}_j))}{\sum_{j=1}^{n}\omega_j(1+T(\mathcal{A}_j))}(\overline{b_j})^{\partial}\right)\right)^{\frac{1}{\partial}}\right), \\ \min\left(1, \left(\sum_{j=1}^{n}\left(\frac{\omega_j(1+T(\mathcal{A}_j))}{\sum_{j=1}^{n}\omega_j(1+T(\mathcal{A}_j))}(\underline{a_j})^{\partial}\right)\right)^{\frac{1}{\partial}}\right) \\ +\iota\min\left(1, \left(\sum_{j=1}^{n}\left(\frac{\omega_j(1+T(\mathcal{A}_j))}{\sum_{j=1}^{n}\omega_j(1+T(\mathcal{A}_j))}(\underline{b_j})^{\partial}\right)\right)^{\frac{1}{\partial}}\right) \end{pmatrix}.$$

3.1.2 Properties of CRFYPWA operator

The notion of CFRYPWA satisfies the following properties.

Idempotency: Let an assembly $\mathcal{A}_j = \left\{\left(\overline{a_j} + \iota\overline{b_j},\ \underline{a_j} + \iota\underline{b_j}\right)\right\}$, $(j = 1,\ 2,\ \ldots,\ n)$ of CFRNs. If $\mathcal{A}_j = \mathcal{A}, \forall\ j$ then:

$$\text{CFRYPWA}\left(\mathcal{A}_1,\ \mathcal{A}_2,\ ..,\ \mathcal{A}_n\right) = \mathcal{A}.$$

Boundedness: Let an assembly $\mathcal{A}_j = \left(\overline{a_j} + \iota\,\overline{b_j}, \underline{a_j} + \iota\underline{b_j}\right)$, $(j = 1,\ 2,\ \ldots,\ n)$, of CFRNs and $\mathcal{A}^- = \left(\min_j\{\overline{a_j}\} + \iota\min_j\{\overline{b_j}\}, \min_j\left\{\underline{a_j}\right\} + \iota\min_j\left\{\underline{b_j}\right\}\right)$, and $\mathcal{A}^+ = \left(\max_j\{\overline{a_j}\} + \iota\max_j\{\overline{b_j}\}, \max_j\left\{\underline{a_j}\right\} + \iota\ \max_j\left\{\underline{b_j}\right\}\right)$. Then:

$$\mathcal{A}^- \leq \text{CFRYPWA}\left(\mathcal{A}_1,\ \mathcal{A}_2,\ ..,\ \mathcal{A}_n\right) \leq \mathcal{A}^+.$$

Monotonicity: Let two assemblies $\mathcal{A}_j = \left(\overline{a_j} + \iota\,\overline{b_j}, \underline{a_j} + \iota\underline{b_j}\right)$ and $\mathcal{A}_j^{'} = \left(\overline{a_j^{'}} + \iota\,\overline{b_j^{'}}, \underline{a_j^{'}} + \iota\underline{b_j^{'}}\right)$, $(j = 1,\ 2,\ \ldots,\ n)$, of CFRNs. If $\underline{a_j} \leq \underline{a_j^{'}}$, $\underline{b_j} \leq \underline{b_j^{'}}$, $\overline{a_j} \leq \overline{a_j^{'}}$, $\overline{b_j} \leq \overline{b_j^{'}}\ \forall\ j$ then:

$$\text{CFRYPWA}\left(\mathcal{A}_1,\ \mathcal{A}_2,\ ..,\ \mathcal{A}_n\right) \leq \text{CFRYPWA}\left(\mathcal{A}_1^{'},\ \mathcal{A}_2^{'},\ ..,\ \mathcal{A}_n^{'}\right).$$

Definition 3.4: Let an assembly $\mathcal{A}_j = \left\{\left(\overline{a_j} + \iota \overline{b_j},\ \underline{a_j} + \iota \underline{b_j}\right)\right\}$, $(j = 1,\ 2,\ \ldots,\ n)$ of CFRNs. Then the CFRYPG operator is scrutinized as

$$\text{CFRYPG}\left(\mathcal{A}_1,\ \mathcal{A}_2,\ \mathcal{A}_3,\ \ldots,\ \mathcal{A}_n\right) = \bigotimes_{j=1}^{n} (\mathcal{A}_j)^{\chi_j}.$$

Theorem 3.3: Let an assembly $\mathcal{A}_j = \left\{\left(\overline{a_j} + \iota \overline{b_j},\ \underline{a_j} + \iota \underline{b_j}\right)\right\}$, $(j = 1,\ 2,\ \ldots,\ n)$ of CFRNs. Then the usage of the CFRYPG operator over $\mathcal{A}_j$ will give a CFRN that is:

$$\begin{aligned}
&\text{CFRYPG}\left(\mathcal{A}_1,\ \mathcal{A}_2,\ \mathcal{A}_3,\ \ldots,\ \mathcal{A}_n\right) \\
&= \begin{pmatrix}
1 - \min\left(1,\ \left(\sum_{j=1}^{n} \chi_j (1 - \overline{a_j})^{\partial}\right)^{\frac{1}{\partial}}\right) \\
\quad + \iota \left(1 - \min\left(1,\ \left(\sum_{j=1}^{n} \chi_j (1 - \overline{b_j})^{\partial}\right)^{\frac{1}{\partial}}\right)\right), \\
1 - \min\left(1,\ \left(\sum_{j=1}^{n} \chi_j \left(1 - \underline{a_j}\right)^{\partial}\right)^{\frac{1}{\partial}}\right) \\
\quad + \iota \left(1 - \min\left(1,\ \left(\sum_{j=1}^{n} \chi_j \left(1 - \underline{b_j}\right)^{\partial}\right)^{\frac{1}{\partial}}\right)\right)
\end{pmatrix}.
\end{aligned} \tag{3.2}$$

Proof: Let $n = 2$. Then we have

$$\text{CFRYPG}\left(\mathcal{A}_1,\ \mathcal{A}_2\right) = \chi_1 \mathcal{A}_1 \otimes \chi_2 \mathcal{A}_2,$$

and as

$$\begin{aligned}
&{\mathcal{A}_1}^{\chi_1} = \\
&\begin{pmatrix}
1 - \min\left(1, \left(\chi_1 (1 - \overline{a_1})^{\partial}\right)^{\frac{1}{\partial}}\right) + \iota \left(1 - \min\left(1, \left(\chi_1 (1 - \overline{b_1})^{\partial}\right)^{\frac{1}{\partial}}\right)\right), \\
1 - \min\left(1,\ \left(\chi_1 (1 - \underline{a_1})^{\partial}\right)^{\frac{1}{\partial}}\right) + \iota \left(1 - \min\left(1, \left(\chi_1 (1 - \underline{b_1})^{\partial}\right)^{\frac{1}{\partial}}\right)\right)
\end{pmatrix} \\
&{\mathcal{A}_2}^{\chi_2} =
\end{aligned}$$

$$\begin{pmatrix} 1-\min\left(1,\left(\chi_2(1-\overline{a_2})^{\partial}\right)^{\frac{1}{\partial}}\right)+\iota\left(1-\min\left(1,\left(\chi_2(1-\overline{b_2})^{\partial}\right)^{\frac{1}{\partial}}\right)\right), \\ 1-\min\left(1,\left(\chi_2(1-\underline{a_2})^{\partial}\right)^{\frac{1}{\partial}}\right)+\iota\left(1-\min\left(1,\left(\chi_2(1-\underline{b_2})^{\partial}\right)^{\frac{1}{\partial}}\right)\right) \end{pmatrix}.$$

This implies that

$\mathcal{A}_1{}^{\chi_1}\otimes\mathcal{A}_2{}^{\chi_2}=$

$$\begin{pmatrix} 1-\min\left(1,\left(\chi_1(1-\overline{a_1})^{\partial}\right)^{\frac{1}{\partial}}\right)+\iota\left(1-\min\left(1,\left(\chi_1(1-\overline{b_1})^{\partial}\right)^{\frac{1}{\partial}}\right)\right), \\ 1-\min\left(1,\left(\chi_1(1-\underline{a_1})^{\partial}\right)^{\frac{1}{\partial}}\right)+\iota\left(1-\min\left(1,\left(\chi_1(1-\underline{b_1})^{\partial}\right)^{\frac{1}{\partial}}\right)\right) \end{pmatrix}$$

$$\otimes\begin{pmatrix} 1-\min\left(1,\left(\chi_2(1-\overline{a_2})^{\partial}\right)^{\frac{1}{\partial}}\right)+\iota\left(1-\min\left(1,\left(\chi_2(1-\overline{b_2})^{\partial}\right)^{\frac{1}{\partial}}\right)\right), \\ 1-\min\left(1,\left(\chi_2(1-\underline{a_2})^{\partial}\right)^{\frac{1}{\partial}}\right)+\iota\left(1-\min\left(1,\left(\chi_2(1-\underline{b_2})^{\partial}\right)^{\frac{1}{\partial}}\right)\right) \end{pmatrix}$$

$$=\begin{pmatrix} 1-\min\left(1,\left(\chi_1(1-\overline{a_1})^{\partial}+\chi_2(1-\overline{a_2})^{\partial}\right)^{\frac{1}{\partial}}\right) \\ +\iota\left(1-\min\left(1,\left(\chi_1(1-\overline{b_1})^{\partial}+\chi_2(1-\overline{b_2})^{\partial}\right)^{\frac{1}{\partial}}\right)\right), \\ 1-\min\left(1,\left(\chi_1(1-\underline{a_1})^{\partial}+\chi_2(1-\underline{a_2})^{\partial}\right)^{\frac{1}{\partial}}\right) \\ +\iota\left(1-\min\left(1,\left(\chi_1(1-\underline{b_1})^{\partial}+\chi_2(1-\underline{b_2})^{\partial}\right)^{\frac{1}{\partial}}\right)\right), \end{pmatrix}$$

$$=\begin{pmatrix} 1-\min\left(1,\left(\sum_{j=1}^{2}\chi_j(1-\overline{a_j})^{\partial}\right)^{\frac{1}{\partial}}\right) \\ +\iota\left(1-\min\left(1,\left(\sum_{j=1}^{2}\chi_j(1-\overline{b_j})^{\partial}\right)^{\frac{1}{\partial}}\right)\right), \\ 1-\min\left(1,\left(\sum_{j=1}^{2}\chi_j\left(1-\underline{a_j}\right)^{\partial}\right)^{\frac{1}{\partial}}\right) \\ +\iota\left(1-\min\left(1,\left(\sum_{j=1}^{2}\chi_j\left(1-\underline{b_j}\right)^{\partial}\right)^{\frac{1}{\partial}}\right)\right) \end{pmatrix}.$$

Thus, (3.2) holds for $n=2$. Next, let for $n=r$, eqn (3.2) holds:

$\text{CFRYPG}\,(\mathcal{A}_1,\ \mathcal{A}_2,\ \mathcal{A}_3,\ \ldots,\ \mathcal{A}_r)=$

$$\left(\begin{array}{l} 1-\min\left(1,\ \left(\sum_{j=1}^{r}\chi_j(1-\overline{a_j})\right)^{\frac{1}{\partial}}\right) \\ \qquad +\iota\left(1-\min\left(1,\ \left(\sum_{j=1}^{r}\chi_j(1-\overline{b_j})^{\partial}\right)^{\frac{1}{\partial}}\right)\right), \\ 1-\min\left(1,\ \left(\sum_{j=1}^{r}\chi_j\left(1-\underline{a_j}\right)^{\partial}\right)^{\frac{1}{\partial}}\right) \\ \qquad +\iota\left(1-\min\left(1,\ \left(\sum_{j=1}^{r}\chi_j\left(1-\underline{b_j}\right)^{\partial}\right)^{\frac{1}{\partial}}\right)\right) \end{array}\right).$$

Then finally, let $n = r + 1$. Then:

$$\text{CFRYPG}\left(\mathcal{A}_1,\ \mathcal{A}_2,\ \mathcal{A}_3,\ \ldots,\ \mathcal{A}_r,\ \mathcal{A}_{r+1}\right) =$$

$$\left(\begin{array}{l} 1-\min\left(1,\ \left(\sum_{j=1}^{r}\chi_j(1-\overline{a_j})^{\partial}\right)^{\frac{1}{\partial}}\right) \\ \qquad +\ \iota\left(1-\min\left(1,\ \left(\sum_{j=1}^{r}\chi_j(1-\overline{b_j})^{\partial}\right)^{\frac{1}{\partial}}\right)\right), \\ 1-\min\left(1,\ \left(\sum_{j=1}^{r}\chi_j\left(1-\underline{a_j}\right)^{\partial}\right)^{\frac{1}{\partial}}\right) \\ \qquad +\ \iota\left(1-\min\left(1,\ \left(\sum_{j=1}^{r}\chi_j\left(1-\underline{b_j}\right)^{\partial}\right)^{\frac{1}{\partial}}\right)\right) \end{array}\right)$$

$$\otimes\left(\begin{array}{l} 1-\min\left(1,\ \left(\chi_{z+1}(1-\overline{a_{z+1}})^{\partial}\right)^{\frac{1}{\partial}}\right) \\ \qquad +\iota\left(1-\min\left(1,\ \left(\chi_{z+1}(1-\overline{b_{z+1}})^{\partial}\right)^{\frac{1}{\partial}}\right)\right), \\ 1-\min\left(1,\ \left(\chi_{z+1}\left(1-\underline{a_{z+1}}\right)^{\partial}\right)^{\frac{1}{\partial}}\right) \\ \qquad +\iota\left(1-\min\left(1,\ \left(\chi_{z+1}\left(1-\underline{b_{z+1}}\right)^{\partial}\right)^{\frac{1}{\partial}}\right)\right) \end{array}\right)$$

$$= \begin{pmatrix} 1-\min\left(1, \left(\sum_{j=1}^{r+1} \chi_j (1-\overline{a_j})^{\partial}\right)^{\frac{1}{\partial}}\right) \\ +\iota \left(1-\min\left(1, \left(\sum_{j=1}^{r+1} \chi_j (1-\overline{b_j})^{\partial}\right)^{\frac{1}{\partial}}\right)\right), \\ 1-\min\left(1, \left(\sum_{j=1}^{r+1} \chi_j \left(1-\underline{a_j}\right)^{\partial}\right)^{\frac{1}{\partial}}\right) \\ +\iota \left(1-\min\left(1, \left(\sum_{j=1}^{r+1} \chi_j \left(1-\underline{b_j}\right)^{\partial}\right)^{\frac{1}{\partial}}\right)\right) \end{pmatrix}.$$

$\Longrightarrow$ (3.2) is true for n.

3.1.3 Properties of CRFYPG operator

The notion of CFRYPG satisfies the following properties.

Idempotency: Let an assembly $\mathcal{A}_j = \left\{\left(\overline{a_j} + \iota\overline{b_j},\ \underline{a_j} + \iota\underline{b_j}\right)\right\}$, $(j = 1,\ 2,\ \ldots,\ n)$ of CFRNs. If $\mathcal{A}_j = \mathcal{A}$, $\forall\ j$ then:

$$\text{CFRYPG}\left(\mathcal{A}_1,\ \mathcal{A}_2,\ ..,\ \mathcal{A}_n\right) = \mathcal{A}.$$

Boundedness: Let an assembly $\mathcal{A}_j = \left(\overline{a_j} + \iota\overline{b_j}, \underline{a_j} + \iota\underline{b_j}\right)$, $(j = 1, 2, \ldots, n)$, of CFRNs and $\mathcal{A}^- = \left(\min_j \{\overline{a_j}\} + \iota\ \min_j \{\overline{b_j}\}, \min_j \left\{\underline{a_j}\right\} + \iota\ \min_j \left\{\underline{b_j}\right\}\right)$, and $\mathcal{A}^+ = \left(\max_j \{\overline{a_j}\} + \iota\ \max_j \{\overline{b_j}\}, \max_j \left\{\underline{a_j}\right\} + \iota\ \max_j \left\{\underline{b_j}\right\}\right)$. Then:

$$\mathcal{A}^- \leq \text{CFRYPG}\left(\mathcal{A}_1,\ \mathcal{A}_2,\ ..,\ \mathcal{A}_n\right) \leq \mathcal{A}^+.$$

Monotonicity: Let two assemblies $\mathcal{A}_j = \left(\overline{a_j} + \iota\,\overline{b_j}, \underline{a_j} + \iota\underline{b_j}\right)$ and $\mathcal{A}_j^{'} = \left(\overline{a_j^{'}} + \iota\,\overline{b_j^{'}}, \underline{a_j^{'}} + \iota\underline{b_j^{'}}\right)$, $(j = 1,\ 2,\ \ldots,\ n)$, of CFRNs. If $\underline{a_j} \leq \underline{a_j^{'}}$, $\underline{b_j} \leq \underline{b_j^{'}}$, $\overline{a_j} \leq \overline{a_j^{'}}$, $\overline{b_j} \leq \overline{b_j^{'}}$ $\forall\ j$ then:

$$\text{CFRYPG}\left(\mathcal{A}_1,\ \mathcal{A}_2,\ ..,\ \mathcal{A}_n\right) \leq \text{CFRYPG}\left(\mathcal{A}_1^{'},\ \mathcal{A}_2^{'},\ ..,\ \mathcal{A}_n^{'}\right).$$

Definition 3.5: Let an assembly $\mathcal{A}_j = \left\{\left(\overline{a_j} + \iota\overline{b_j},\ \underline{a_j} + \iota\underline{b_j}\right)\right\}$, $(j = 1, 2, \ldots, n)$ of CFRNs. Then the CFRYPWG operator is scrutinized as

$$\text{CFRYPWG}\left(\mathcal{A}_1, \mathcal{A}_2, \mathcal{A}_3, \ldots, \mathcal{A}_n\right) = \bigotimes_{j=1}^{n} \left(\mathcal{A}_j\right)^{\frac{\omega_j\left(1+T\left(\mathcal{A}_j\right)\right)}{\sum_{j=1}^{n}\omega_j\left(1+T\left(\mathcal{A}_j\right)\right)}}.$$

Theorem 3.4: Let an assembly $\mathcal{A}_j = \left\{\left(\overline{a_j} + \iota\overline{b_j},\ \underline{a_j} + \iota\underline{b_j}\right)\right\}$, $(j = 1, 2, \ldots, n)$ of CFRNs. Then the usage of the CFRYPWG operator over $\mathcal{A}_j$ will give a CFRN that is:

$$\text{CFRYPWG}\left(\mathcal{A}, \mathcal{A}_2, \mathcal{A}_3, \ldots, \mathcal{A}_n\right) =$$

$$\left(\begin{array}{c} 1-\min\left(1, \left(\sum_{j=1}^{n}\frac{\omega_j(1+T(\mathcal{A}_j))}{\sum_{j=1}^{n}\omega_j(1+T(\mathcal{A}_j))}\left(1-\overline{a_j}\right)^{\partial}\right)^{\frac{1}{\partial}}\right) \\ +\iota\left(1-\min\left(1, \left(\sum_{j=1}^{n}\frac{\omega_j(1+T(\mathcal{A}_j))}{\sum_{j=1}^{n}\omega_j(1+T(\mathcal{A}_j))}\left(1-\overline{b_j}\right)^{\partial}\right)^{\frac{1}{\partial}}\right)\right), \\ 1-\min\left(1, \left(\sum_{j=1}^{n}\frac{\omega_j(1+T(\mathcal{A}_j))}{\sum_{j=1}^{n}\omega_j(1+T(\mathcal{A}_j))}\left(1-\underline{a_j}\right)^{\partial}\right)^{\frac{1}{\partial}}\right) \\ +\iota\left(1-\min\left(1, \left(\sum_{j=1}^{n}\frac{\omega_j(1+T(\mathcal{A}_j))}{\sum_{j=1}^{n}\omega_j(1+T(\mathcal{A}_j))}\left(1-\underline{b_j}\right)^{\partial}\right)^{\frac{1}{\partial}}\right)\right) \end{array}\right).$$

The CFRYPWG operator also holds the idempotency, boundedness, and monotonicity.

3.2 MCDM Approach Within the Framework of CFRS

Let $\mathfrak{L} = \{\mathfrak{L}_1, \mathfrak{L}_2, \ldots, \mathfrak{L}_m\}$ be an assembly of alternatives and for these alternatives, let $\mathbb{T} = \{\mathbb{T}_1, \mathbb{T}_2, \ldots, \mathbb{T}_n\}$ be an assembly of criteria that will be utilized for the assessment of the considered alternatives. In these alternatives, the decision analyst has to get the finest and best alternative. For that, the decision analyst will assess these alternatives based on their criteria and interpret their values in the framework of CFRNs that is $\mathcal{A} = \left(\overline{a} + \iota\overline{b}, \underline{a} + \iota\underline{b}\right)$, where $\overline{a}, \overline{b}, \underline{a}, \underline{b} \in [0,\ 1]$. As each criterion has its weight the decision expert will provide the weight to each of the criteria which is $\omega_j = (\omega_1, \omega_2, \ldots, \omega_n)^T$ such that $\sum_{j=1}^{n} \omega_j = 1$ and $\omega_j \in [0,\ 1]\ \forall\ j$. Now to solve this, this MCDM approach has the underneath steps.

Step 1: As the assessment values are in the form of CFRNs, so develop a complex fuzzy rough decision matrix (CFRDM) $\mathfrak{D}$ by employing these assessment values. In this CFRDM, the first entry will represent the assessment value of the first alternative against the first criteria.

Step 2: Standardization of the CFRDM will be performed in this step by employing the given underneath formula. Standardization is needed because the data can be benefit and cost types.

$$D^{\mathcal{N}} = \begin{cases} \left(\overline{a} + \iota\overline{b}, \underline{a} + \iota\underline{b}\right) & \text{for benefit kind} \\ \left(\overline{a} + \iota\overline{b}, \underline{a} + \iota\underline{b}\right)^c & \text{for cost kind} \end{cases}.$$

Step 3: Here, the support of each $\mathcal{A}_j$ would be interpreted as

$$\text{Sup}\left(\mathcal{A}_{jr},\ \mathcal{A}_{jl}\right) = 1 - \text{đ}\left(\mathcal{A}_{jr},\ \mathcal{A}_{jl}\right),\ r,\ l = 1,\ 2,\ \ldots, n,\ r \neq l,$$

where $\text{đ}\left(\mathcal{A}_{jr}, \mathcal{A}_{jl}\right) = \frac{1}{4}\left(\left|\overline{a_{jr}} - \overline{a_{jl}}\right| + \left|\overline{b_{jr}} - \overline{b_{jl}}\right| + \left|\underline{a_{jr}} - \underline{a_{jl}}\right| + \left|\underline{b_{jr}} - \underline{b_{jl}}\right|\right)$.

Step 4: Interpret

$$\text{T}\left(\mathcal{A}_{jr}\right) = \sum_{\substack{l=1 \\ l \neq r}}^{n} \text{Sup}\left(\mathcal{A}_{jr},\ \mathcal{A}_{jl}\right).$$

Noticed that $j = 1,\ 2,\ \ldots, m\ ; r,\ l = 1,\ 2,\ \ldots,\ n$ and $r \neq l$.

Step 5: Achieve the associated weight as follows:

$$\chi_{jr} = \frac{\left(1 + T\left(\mathcal{A}_{jr}\right)\right)}{\sum_{l=1}^{n}\left(1 + T\left(\mathcal{A}_{jl}\right)\right)},$$

or

$$\chi'_{jr} = \frac{\hat{\text{W}}_{\omega-jr}\left(1 + T\left(\mathcal{A}_{jr}\right)\right)}{\sum_{l=1}^{n} \hat{\text{W}}_{\omega-jl}\left(1 + T\left(\mathcal{A}_{jl}\right)\right)}.$$

Step 6: Aggregate the CFRDM with the assistance of any of the devised operators that is CFRYPA, CFRYPWA, CFRYPG, and CFRYPWG operators.

Step 7: Employing score function to achieve the score values of aggregated outcomes of each alternative. In case of the same score values, achieve the accuracy values by employing the accuracy function.

Step 8: Rank all alternatives by considering their score or accuracy values and select the finest and best alternative.

3.2.1 Case study (selection of neural network framework for AI predictive models)

In the dynamic area of AI, organizations are presented with crucial choices when it comes to choosing the right neural network frameworks to use in creating prediction models. A mid-size financial technology firm plans to use artificial intelligence in predictive analytical tools for fraud and customer profiling. The choice of a proper framework is critical because the optimization of development processes and the model's performance can be significantly influenced by the framework, along with the future costs of maintaining the latter. For this, the company hired a decision analyst, who shortlisted the 4 neural network frameworks, which are displayed in Table 3.1.

To assess these frameworks, the decision analyst considered 4 criteria, which are displayed in Table 3.2.

The decision expert will assess these neural network frameworks and provide their values in the form of CFRNs. Also, the expert provides the weight to the criteria based on their preference that weight is $(0.18,\ 0.25,\ 0.34,\ 0.23)$. To solve this, we have the underneath steps.

Step 1: The decision analyst assessed the neural network frameworks and provided their values in the structure of CFRNs which form CFRDM as shown in Table 3.3.

Step 2: As the data is benefit-kind, so after the standardization, the CFRDM will remain the same.

Step 3: The support of each $\mathcal{Z}_j$ for $j = 1$

$$\text{Sup}\,(\mathcal{Z}_{11},\ \mathcal{Z}_{12}) = 0.698, \text{Sup}\,(\mathcal{Z}_{11},\ \mathcal{Z}_{13}) = 0.795, \text{Sup}\,(\mathcal{Z}_{11},\ \mathcal{Z}_{14}) = 0.82,$$

$$\text{Sup}\,(\mathcal{Z}_{12},\ \mathcal{Z}_{11}) = 0.698, \text{Sup}\,(\mathcal{Z}_{12},\ \mathcal{Z}_{13}) = 0.548, \text{Sup}\,(\mathcal{Z}_{12},\ \mathcal{Z}_{14}) = 0.798,$$
$$\text{Sup}\,(\mathcal{Z}_{13},\ \mathcal{Z}_{11}) = 0.795, \text{Sup}\,(\mathcal{Z}_{13},\ \mathcal{Z}_{12}) = 0.548, \text{Sup}\,(\mathcal{Z}_{13},\ \mathcal{Z}_{14}) = 0.62,$$

Table 3.1 The neural network frameworks along with explanation.

Notations	Neural network frameworks	Explanation
$\mathcal{Z}_1$	Tensor Flow	The Tensor Flow of Google is an open-source framework that provides all the necessary tools an engineer may need to build and release neural networks. This promotes the support of distributing computing and production deployment through Tensor Flow Serving. Various facilities such as the Tensor Board used for visualization and debugging are also covered as a part of the proposed framework that can be extremely useful for large-scale enterprise applications. It has excellent compatibility with cloud platforms and can be deployed on mobile through Tensor Flow Lite.
$\mathcal{Z}_2$	PyTorch	Created by the Facebook AI Research department, PyTorch focuses on dynamic computation graphs and ease of use. It has a simple approach to debugging and is backed by a great community. It shines in research settings and when prototyping and it supports the most-used Python libraries without any issues. Unlike Tensor-flow, PyTroch supports an eager execution mode this is important in the development phase to inspect model variables without having to run a session.
$\mathcal{Z}_3$	Keras	Being a high-level API able to work with different backends Keras has a great focus on convenience and consistency. It greatly minimizes the time taken in developing through its user-friendly, unchanging interface and comprehensive documentation. While it might compromise on fine-grained control, what it gains is the ability to implement changes quickly and on Bowman's gentle learning slope for new developers.
$\mathcal{Z}_4$	JAX	A somewhat newer framework that is based on the integration of Autograd and XLA for applied machine learning research. JAX has strong AD and fast linear algebra capabilities by default. This Operating System supports modern hardware acceleration and also parallel processing most probably more suitable for mathematical computations and research exercises.

$$\text{Sup}\left(\mathcal{Z}_{14},\ \mathcal{Z}_{11}\right) = 0.82, \text{Sup}\left(\mathcal{Z}_{14},\ \mathcal{Z}_{12}\right) = 0.798, \text{Sup}\left(\mathcal{Z}_{14},\ \mathcal{Z}_{13}\right) = 0.62,$$

for $j = 2$

Table 3.2 The criteria of neural network frameworks.

Notations	Criteria	Explanation
$\mathbb{T}_1$	Learning curve and documentation	This criterion assesses the simplicity of integrating the framework of the development team; good documentation, available tutorials, community resources, and the amount of time needed to familiarize the developers with the framework. It also examines the accessibility of learning resources and the framework's ability to keep records up to date.
$\mathbb{T}_2$	Performance and scalability	Here, this aspect focuses on how well the framework performs more so in terms of the scalability of the current and future large-scale solutions. Some of them are training speed, inference time, the capability of handling distributed computing, and its optimization with available hardware. The optimization criterion also takes into account the scalability characteristic of the chosen framework as the amount of data and complexity of models increases.
$\mathbb{T}_3$	Support and ecosystem in the community	This measure quantifies the size of the established community and the activity level, as well as the support of ready models and third-party libraries. This looks at the compatibility of the update frequency, the bug frequencies, and the quick rates of the community in attending to issues. A crucial component is downloadable plugins, tools, and extensions which defines or measures how productive the development environment is.
$\mathbb{T}_4$	Production deployment capabilities	Based on this criterion, it is determined how the framework's functionalities for deploying, supervising, and updating models in the live environment are implemented. It includes things like model serialization, and versioning, support for the deployment platforms, and optimization tools. It also takes into account the stability of the framework in production environments and the extent to which they are supported by various deployment modes.

$$\mathrm{Sup}(\mathcal{Z}_{21}, \mathcal{Z}_{22}) = 0.635, \mathrm{Sup}(\mathcal{Z}_{21}, \mathcal{Z}_{23}) = 0.795, \mathrm{Sup}(\mathcal{Z}_{21}, \mathcal{Z}_{24}) = 0.76,$$

$$\mathrm{Sup}(\mathcal{Z}_{22}, \mathcal{Z}_{21}) = 0.635, \mathrm{Sup}(\mathcal{Z}_{22}, \mathcal{Z}_{23}) = 0.7, \mathrm{Sup}(\mathcal{Z}_{22}, \mathcal{Z}_{24}) = 0.71,$$

$$\mathrm{Sup}(\mathcal{Z}_{23}, \mathcal{Z}_{21}) = 0.795, \mathrm{Sup}(\mathcal{Z}_{23}, \mathcal{Z}_{22}) = 0.7, \mathrm{Sup}(\mathcal{Z}_{23}, \mathcal{Z}_{24}) = 0.915,$$

$$\mathrm{Sup}(\mathcal{Z}_{24}, \mathcal{Z}_{21}) = 0.755, \mathrm{Sup}(\mathcal{Z}_{24}, \mathcal{Z}_{22}) = 0.71, \mathrm{Sup}(\mathcal{Z}_{24}, \mathcal{Z}_{23}) = 0.915,$$

for $j = 3$

Table 3.3 The assessment values of neural network frameworks, interpreted by experts.

	$\mathbb{T}_1$	$\mathbb{T}_2$	$\mathbb{T}_3$	$\mathbb{T}_4$
$\mathcal{Z}_1$	$\begin{pmatrix} 0.78 + \iota\, 0.38, \\ 0.74 + \iota\, 0.26 \end{pmatrix}$	$\begin{pmatrix} 0.35 + \iota\, 0.72, \\ 0.38 + \iota\, 0.17 \end{pmatrix}$	$\begin{pmatrix} 0.92 + \iota\, 0.27, \\ 0.62 + \iota\, 0.72 \end{pmatrix}$	$\begin{pmatrix} 0.56 + \iota\, 0.77, \\ 0.83 + \iota\, 0.27 \end{pmatrix}$
$\mathcal{Z}_2$	$\begin{pmatrix} 0.28 + \iota\, 0.62, \\ 0.29 + \iota\, 0.17 \end{pmatrix}$	$\begin{pmatrix} 0.86 + \iota\, 0.72, \\ 0.72 + \iota\, 0.52 \end{pmatrix}$	$\begin{pmatrix} 0.72 + \iota\, 0.37, \\ 0.26 + \iota\, 0.27 \end{pmatrix}$	$\begin{pmatrix} 0.63 + \iota\, 0.32, \\ 0.26 + \iota\, 0.46, \end{pmatrix}$
$\mathcal{Z}_3$	$\begin{pmatrix} 0.48 + \iota\, 0.37, \\ 0.82 + \iota\, 0.84, \end{pmatrix}$	$\begin{pmatrix} 0.47 + \iota\, 0.28, \\ 0.74 + \iota\, 0.63, \end{pmatrix}$	$\begin{pmatrix} 0.17 + \iota\, 0.73, \\ 0.74 + \iota\, 0.16, \end{pmatrix}$	$\begin{pmatrix} 0.91 + \iota\, 0.62, \\ 0.15 + \iota\, 0.66, \end{pmatrix}$
$\mathcal{Z}_4$	$\begin{pmatrix} 0.48 + \iota\, 0.69, \\ 0.27 + \iota\, 0.93, \end{pmatrix}$	$\begin{pmatrix} 0.82 + \iota\, 0.84, \\ 0.27 + \iota\, 0.26, \end{pmatrix}$	$\begin{pmatrix} 0.55 + \iota\, 0.32, \\ 0.62 + \iota\, 0.53, \end{pmatrix}$	$\begin{pmatrix} 0.96 + \iota\, 0.17, \\ 0.52 + \iota\, 0.59, \end{pmatrix}$

$$\mathrm{Sup}\,(\mathcal{Z}_{31},\ \mathcal{Z}_{32}) = 0.903, \mathrm{Sup}\,(\mathcal{Z}_{31},\ \mathcal{Z}_{33}) = 0.643, \mathrm{Sup}\,(\mathcal{Z}_{31},\ \mathcal{Z}_{34}) = 0.618,$$

$$\mathrm{Sup}\,(\mathcal{Z}_{32},\ \mathcal{Z}_{31}) = 0.903, \mathrm{Sup}\,(\mathcal{Z}_{32},\ \mathcal{Z}_{33}) = 0.695, \mathrm{Sup}\,(\mathcal{Z}_{32},\ \mathcal{Z}_{34}) = 0.65,$$
$$\mathrm{Sup}\,(\mathcal{Z}_{33},\ \mathcal{Z}_{31}) = 0.643, \mathrm{Sup}\,(\mathcal{Z}_{33},\ \mathcal{Z}_{32}) = 0.695, \mathrm{Sup}\,(\mathcal{Z}_{33},\ \mathcal{Z}_{34}) = 0.515,$$
$$\mathrm{Sup}\,(\mathcal{Z}_{34},\ \mathcal{Z}_{31}) = 0.778, \mathrm{Sup}\,(\mathcal{Z}_{34},\ \mathcal{Z}_{32}) = 0.65, \mathrm{Sup}\,(\mathcal{Z}_{34},\ \mathcal{Z}_{33}) = 0.515,$$

for $j = 4$

$$\mathrm{Sup}\,(\mathcal{Z}_{41},\ \mathcal{Z}_{42}) = 0.71, \mathrm{Sup}\,(\mathcal{Z}_{41},\ \mathcal{Z}_{43}) = 0.703, \mathrm{Sup}\,(\mathcal{Z}_{41},\ \mathcal{Z}_{44}) = 0.603,$$
$$\mathrm{Sup}\,(\mathcal{Z}_{42},\ \mathcal{Z}_{41}) = 0.71, \mathrm{Sup}\,(\mathcal{Z}_{42},\ \mathcal{Z}_{43}) = 0.648, \mathrm{Sup}\,(\mathcal{Z}_{42},\ \mathcal{Z}_{44}) = 0.653,$$
$$\mathrm{Sup}\,(\mathcal{Z}_{43},\ \mathcal{Z}_{41}) = 0.703, \mathrm{Sup}\,(\mathcal{Z}_{43},\ \mathcal{Z}_{42}) = 0.648, \mathrm{Sup}\,(\mathcal{Z}_{43},\ \mathcal{Z}_{44}) = 0.82,$$
$$\mathrm{Sup}\,(\mathcal{Z}_{44},\ \mathcal{Z}_{41}) = 0.65, \mathrm{Sup}\,(\mathcal{Z}_{44},\ \mathcal{Z}_{42}) = 0.653, \mathrm{Sup}\,(\mathcal{Z}_{44},\ \mathcal{Z}_{43}) = 0.82,$$

Step 4: Interpreted $T\,(\mathcal{Z}_{jr})$

$$T\,(\mathcal{Z}_{11}) = 2.313, \mathrm{T}\,(\mathcal{Z}_{12}) = 2.043, \mathrm{T}\,(\mathcal{Z}_{13}) = 1.963, \mathrm{T}\,(\mathcal{Z}_{14}) = 2.238,$$
$$\mathrm{T}\,(\mathcal{Z}_{21}) = 2.19, \mathrm{T}\,(\mathcal{Z}_{22}) = 2.045, \mathrm{T}\,(\mathcal{Z}_{23}) = 2.41, \mathrm{T}\,(\mathcal{Z}_{24}) = 2.38,$$
$$\mathrm{T}\,(\mathcal{Z}_{31}) = 2.163, \mathrm{T}\,(\mathcal{Z}_{32}) = 2.248, \mathrm{T}\,(\mathcal{Z}_{33}) = 1.853, \mathrm{T}\,(\mathcal{Z}_{34}) = 1.943,$$
$$\mathrm{T}\,(\mathcal{Z}_{41}) = 2.015, \mathrm{T}\,(\mathcal{Z}_{42}) = 2.01, \mathrm{T}\,(\mathcal{Z}_{43}) = 2.17, \mathrm{T}\,(\mathcal{Z}_{44}) = 2.123,$$

Step 5: The associated weights are:

$$\chi_{11} = 0.264, \chi_{12} = 0.242, \chi_{13} = 0.236, \chi_{14} = 0.258,$$
$$\chi_{21} = 0.245, \chi_{22} = 0.234, \chi_{23} = 0.261, \chi_{24} = 0.26,$$

$$\chi_{31} = 0.259, \chi_{32} = 0.266, \chi_{33} = 0.234, \chi_{34} = 0.241,$$
$$\chi_{41} = 0.245, \chi_{42} = 0.244, \chi_{43} = 0.257, \chi_{44} = 0.254.$$

After that analyst weight of each criterion is $(0.18,\ 0.25,\ 0.34,\ 0.23)$, the associated weights are:

$$\chi'_{11} = 0.192, \chi'_{12} = 0.245, \chi'_{13} = 0.323, \chi'_{14} = 0.24,$$
$$\chi'_{21} = 0.175, \chi'_{22} = 0.233, \chi'_{23} = 0.354, \chi'_{24} = 0.238,$$
$$\chi'_{31} = 0.188, \chi'_{32} = 0.268, \chi'_{33} = 0.32, \chi'_{34} = 0.224,$$
$$\chi'_{41} = 0.176, \chi'_{42} = 0.243, \chi'_{43} = 0.349, \chi'_{44} = 0.232.$$

Step 6: The aggregated outcome of each neural network framework after employing CFRYPA, CFRYPWA, CFRYPG, and CFRYPWG operators is displayed in Table 3.4.

Table 3.4 The aggregated outcomes of neural network frameworks.

Operators	Scor. (Z_1)	Scor. (Z_2)	Scor. (z_3)	Scor. (Z_4)
CFRYPA	0.618	0.525	0.634	0.627
CFRYPWA	0.628	0.525	0.626	0.618
CFRYPG	0.648	0.405	0.438	0.464
CFRYPWG	0.468	0.412	0.424	0.465

Step 7: The score values of neural network frameworks are interpreted in Table 3.5.

Table 3.5 The score values of neural network frameworks.

Operators	Scor. (Z_1)	Scor. (Z_2)	Scor. (Z_3)	Scor. (Z_4)
CFRYPA	0.618	0.525	0.634	0.627
CFRYPWA	0.628	0.525	0.626	0.618
CFRYPG	0.648	0.405	0.438	0.464
CFRYPWG	0.468	0.412	0.424	0.465

Step 8: The ranking of neural network frameworks is devised in Table 3.6.

From the ranking of neural network frameworks, the analyst decided that $\mathcal{Z}_1$ is the finest and best framework. The graphical interpretation is given in Figure 3.1.

Table 3.6 The ranking of neural network frameworks.

Operators	**Ranking**
CFRYPA	$Z_3 > Z_4 > Z_1 > Z_2$
CFRYPWA	$Z_1 > Z_3 > Z_4 > Z_2$
CFRYPG	$Z_1 > Z_4 > Z_3 > Z_2$
CFRYPWG	$Z_1 > Z_4 > Z_3 > Z_2$

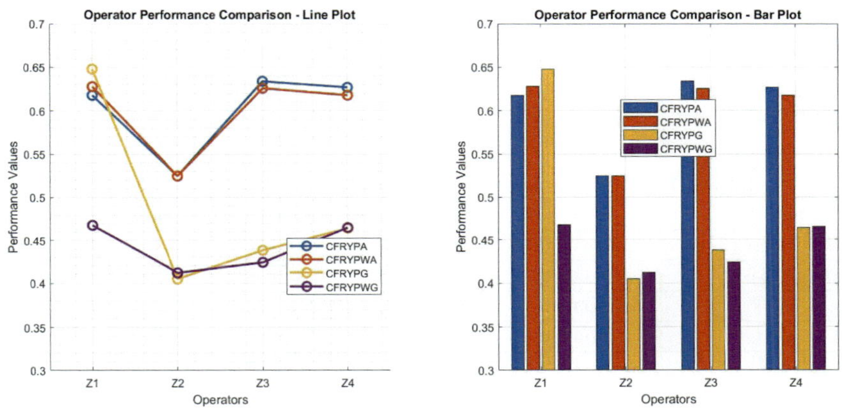

Figure 3.1 Graphical interpretation of operator.

3.3 Comparison

To indicate that the proposed theory is not only needed but also better than other techniques in the field, the following sections are dedicated to comparing our method with the existing ones. The following prominent approaches are considered for comparison:

(1) Power geometric operators

- Created by Xu and Yager [22].
- Whilst it is primarily a system that is designed for "crisp" information processing

(2) Probability complex fuzzy AOs

- Introduced by Rehman [23]
- With a feature that can aggregate Tamir's complex fuzzy information.

(3) Complex fuzzy geometric and arithmetic AOs

- Developed by Bi et al. [17, 18] in two distinct research works.
- To aggregate complex fuzzy information in polar form.

(4) These operators are analyzed and called complex fuzzy power AOs

- Devised by Hu et al. [24]
- They mainly handle polar form information and can find weight through proper formulas.

* *Experimental validation*

These existing operators are applied to the dataset in Table 3.3. Our results indicate that no proposed operator can adequately process the given information and on the other hand, the method proposed in this chapter was able to aggregate the data. The results can be seen in Tables 3.7 and 3.8 and Figure 3.2.

Table 3.7 The score values of existing and proposed theory.

Operators	Scor. (Z_1)	Scor. (Z_2)	Scor. (Z_3)	Scor. (Z_4)
Xu and Yager [22]	No result	No result	No result	No result
Rehman [23]	No result	No result	No result	No result
Bi et al. [17]	No result	No result	No result	No result
Bi et al. [18]	No result	No result	No result	No result
Hu et al. [24]	No result	No result	No result	No result
CFRYPA	0.618	0.525	0.634	0.627
CFRYPWA	0.628	0.525	0.626	0.618
CFRYPG	0.648	0.405	0.438	0.464
CFRYPWG	0.468	0.412	0.424	0.465

Table 3.8 The ranking of proposed theories and existing ones.

Operators	**Ranking result**
Xu and Yager [22]	No result
Rehman [23]	No result
Bi et al. [17]	No result
Bi et al. [18]	No result
Hu et al. [24]	No result
CFRYPA	$\mathcal{Z}_3 > \mathcal{Z}_4 > \mathcal{Z}_1 > \mathcal{Z}_2$
CFRYPWA	$\mathcal{Z}_1 > \mathcal{Z}_3 > \mathcal{Z}_4 > \mathcal{Z}_2$
CFRYPG	$\mathcal{Z}_1 > \mathcal{Z}_4 > \mathcal{Z}_3 > \mathcal{Z}_2$
CFRYPWG	$\mathcal{Z}_1 > \mathcal{Z}_4 > \mathcal{Z}_3 > \mathcal{Z}_2$

This comes as a result of limitations of the existing approaches which will be discussed in detail below.

(1) Power geometric operators

- Primary limitation: Lack of learning on how to comprehend CFR information

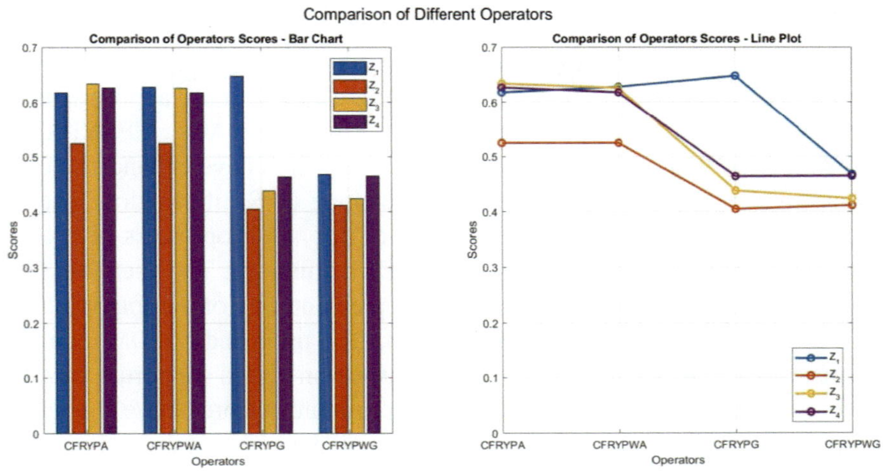

Figure 3.2 The comparison among existing and proposed theories.

- Limited to aggregate just crisp information

(2) Probability complex fuzzy operators

- Can work with complex information but does not take into account roughness
- Have a weak framework for the process of weighing them
- Incapable to decode integrated CFR information.

(3) Complex fuzzy geometric and arithmetic operators

- Cannot aggregate roughness of complex fuzzy information
- There is no systematic prevention or pardoning mechanism for failure to determine weight

(4) Complex fuzzy power operators

- This manages well when it comes to power components
- Restricted by the roughness which the apparatus could not process
- Cannot handle Tamir's complex numbers
- Thematic for processing of complete information about CFR

This comparison reveals the shortcomings of the current approaches and justifies the need for the method we describe for multifaceted CFR information processing.

3.4 Conclusion

This chapter has provided a major contribution to the theory and application of CFRS theory and its application in the selection of an appropriate AI framework. In this chapter, we have proposed new AOs, CFRYPA, CFRYPWA, CFRYPG, and CFRYPWG operators, which have enhanced the functionality of Yager power operators for managing CFR information. The mathematical characteristics and proofs derived for these operators give a theoretical background for their usage in MCDM situations. The usefulness of our work is shown through its successful implementation of the important task of choosing the neural network framework. The proposed MCDM technique encapsulates all the aspects of CFR information and is supported by a detailed case study on the selection of an appropriate AI predictive model framework. This practical implementation closes the gap between theory development and application and offers insights for practitioners. Comparing our work with other approaches outlined above clearly shows the effectiveness of the proposed operators in managing CFR information. The proposed operators can handle the complexity of CFR information processing which existing methods were unable to do. This enhancement in the management of intricate data is a major advancement in the area of fuzzy mathematics and decision-making. The combination of CFR Yager power operators with the selection of the neural network framework is a major development in decision-making methodological frameworks for AI systems. As offering both the theoretical analysis and the application, this work is beneficial to researchers and practitioners in the fields of fuzzy mathematics, decision theory, and artificial intelligence. The successful integration of theory with practice in this research makes this work especially timely in the current high-tech environment where decision-making tools for AI system development are becoming more critical. This comprehensive approach to handling CFR information in MCDM problems, especially in AI system development not only answers the current practical questions but also provides the base for future investigations in this field. The application of the methodology to neural network framework selection is a clear indication of its applicability in future advancements in AI and machine learning, which is a major advancement in the development of decision-making tools for complex technological systems.

4

Innovative Approaches to Prioritizing Financial Tools for Business Growth and Sustainability through Complex Fuzzy Rough Structure

The notion of the complex fuzzy rough set is a valuable and significant tool for discussing more advanced information. Aggregation theory plays a vital role in decision-making. In many decision-making situations, we have to deliver such kind of idea or structure that can handle more advanced data and, in this case, the chance of data loss is reduced and more accurate results can be obtained. The fundamental laws for sine trigonometric aggregation operators based on CFRS have been delivered. Moreover based on these operational laws we have defined the notion of sine trigonometric complex fuzzy rough weighted averaging (STCFRWA), sine trigonometric complex fuzzy rough ordered weighted averaging (STCFROWA), sine trigonometric complex fuzzy rough hybrid averaging (STCFRHA), sine trigonometric complex fuzzy rough weighted geometric (STCFRWG), sine trigonometric complex fuzzy rough ordered weighted geometric (STCFROWG), sine trigonometric complex fuzzy rough hybrid geometric (STCFRHG) operators. To discuss the application perspective of the developed theory, we have initiated an algorithm for the developed. Moreover, we have elaborated on the case study of prioritization of financial tools for business growth to strengthen the application of the developed theory. To discuss the results, we have established the comparative analysis section to deliver the validity and advancement of the initiated work.

4.1 Sine Trigonometric Operational Laws for CFRNs

In this section, we have to deliver the notion of operational laws that can help to discuss the aggregation theory.

DOI: 10.1201/9788743807827-4

Definition 4.1: Let $\mathcal{A} = \{(\overline{a} + \iota\overline{b},\ \underline{a} + \iota\underline{b})\}$ be a complex fuzzy rough number. Then the developed notion:

$$\sin(\mathcal{A}) = \left\{ \begin{pmatrix} \sin\left(\frac{\pi}{2}\overline{a}\right) + \iota \sin\left(\frac{\pi}{2}\overline{b}\right), \\ \sin\left(\frac{\pi}{2}\underline{a}\right) + \iota \sin\left(\frac{\pi}{2}\underline{b}\right) \end{pmatrix} \right\}. \tag{4.1}$$

The eqn (4.1) is called sine trigonometric operational law, where: $\overline{a} : \mathcal{U} \rightarrow [0,1]$, $\overline{b} : \mathcal{U} \rightarrow [0,1]$, $\underline{a} : \mathcal{U} \rightarrow [0,1]$, $\underline{b} : \mathcal{U} \rightarrow [0,1]$ and the trigonometric functions are: $\sin\left(\frac{\pi}{2}\overline{a}\right) : \mathcal{U} \rightarrow [0,1]$, $\sin\left(\frac{\pi}{2}\overline{b}\right) : \mathcal{U} \rightarrow [0,1]$, $\sin\left(\frac{\pi}{2}\underline{a}\right) : \mathcal{U} \rightarrow [0,1]$, $\sin\left(\frac{\pi}{2}\underline{b}\right) : \mathcal{U} \rightarrow [0,1]$ while:

$$\sin(\mathcal{A}) = \left\{ \begin{pmatrix} \sin\left(\frac{\pi}{2}\overline{a}\right) + \iota \sin\left(\frac{\pi}{2}\overline{b}\right), \\ \sin\left(\frac{\pi}{2}\underline{a}\right) + \iota \sin\left(\frac{\pi}{2}\underline{b}\right) \end{pmatrix} \right\}. \tag{4.2}$$

represents the CFRS.

Definition 4.2: Let $\mathcal{A} = \{(\overline{a} + \iota\overline{b},\ \underline{a} + \iota\underline{b})\}$ be a complex fuzzy rough number, then we call the function $\sin\mathcal{A}$ a sine trigonometric operator if:

$$\sin\mathcal{A} = \left\{ \begin{pmatrix} \sin\left(\frac{\pi}{2}\overline{a}\right) + \iota \sin\left(\frac{\pi}{2}\overline{b}\right), \\ \sin\left(\frac{\pi}{2}\underline{a}\right) + \iota \sin\left(\frac{\pi}{2}\underline{b}\right) \end{pmatrix} \right\}. \tag{4.3}$$

Definition 4.3: Assume that $\sin(\mathcal{A}_1) = \left\{ \begin{pmatrix} \sin\left(\frac{\pi}{2}\overline{a}_1\right) + \iota \sin\left(\frac{\pi}{2}\overline{b}_1\right), \\ \sin\left(\frac{\pi}{2}\underline{a}_1\right) + \iota \sin\left(\frac{\pi}{2}\underline{b}_1\right) \end{pmatrix} \right\}$ and $\sin(\mathcal{A}_2) = \left\{ \begin{pmatrix} \sin\left(\frac{\pi}{2}\overline{a}_2\right) + \iota \sin\left(\frac{\pi}{2}\overline{b}_2\right), \\ \sin\left(\frac{\pi}{2}\underline{a}_2\right) + \iota \sin\left(\frac{\pi}{2}\underline{b}_2\right) \end{pmatrix} \right\}$ be two STCFRNs, then the operational laws are given by

1. $\sin(\mathcal{A}_1) \oplus \sin(\mathcal{A}_2)$
$$= \begin{pmatrix} 1 - \left(1 - \sin\left(\frac{\pi}{2}\overline{a}_1\right)\right)\left(1 - \sin\left(\frac{\pi}{2}\overline{a}_2\right)\right) \\ +\iota\left(1 - \left(1 - \sin\left(\frac{\pi}{2}\overline{b}_1\right)\right)\left(1 - \sin\left(\frac{\pi}{2}\overline{b}_2\right)\right)\right), \\ 1 - \left(1 - \sin\left(\frac{\pi}{2}\underline{a}_1\right)\right)\left(1 - \sin\left(\frac{\pi}{2}\underline{a}_2\right)\right) \\ +\iota\left(1 - \left(1 - \sin\left(\frac{\pi}{2}\underline{b}_1\right)\right)\left(1 - \sin\left(\frac{\pi}{2}\underline{b}_2\right)\right)\right) \end{pmatrix}.$$
2. $\sin\ (\mathcal{A}_1) \otimes \sin(\mathcal{A}_2)$
$$= \begin{pmatrix} \sin\left(\frac{\pi}{2}\overline{a}_1\right)\sin\left(\frac{\pi}{2}\overline{a}_2\right) + \iota \sin\left(\frac{\pi}{2}\overline{b}_1\right)\sin\left(\frac{\pi}{2}\overline{b}_2\right), \\ \sin\left(\frac{\pi}{2}\underline{a}_1\right)\sin\left(\frac{\pi}{2}\underline{a}_2\right) + \iota \sin\left(\frac{\pi}{2}\underline{b}_1\right)\sin\left(\frac{\pi}{2}\underline{b}_2\right) \end{pmatrix}.$$
3. $s\sin(\mathcal{A}_1)^T$
$$= \begin{pmatrix} 1 - \left(1 - \sin\left(\frac{\pi}{2}\overline{a}_1\right)\right)^s + \iota\left(1 - \left(1 - \sin\left(\frac{\pi}{2}\overline{b}_1\right)\right)^s\right), \\ 1 - \left(1 - \sin\left(\frac{\pi}{2}\underline{a}_1\right)\right)^s + \iota\left(1 - \left(1 - \sin\left(\frac{\pi}{2}\underline{b}_1\right)\right)^s\right) \end{pmatrix}.$$
4. $(\sin(\mathcal{A}_1))^s = \begin{pmatrix} \left(\sin\left(\frac{\pi}{2}\overline{a}_1\right)\right)^s + \iota\left(\sin\left(\frac{\pi}{2}\overline{b}_1\right)\right)^s, \\ \left(\sin\left(\frac{\pi}{2}\underline{a}_1\right)\right)^s + \iota\left(\sin\left(\frac{\pi}{2}\underline{a}_1\right)\right)^s \end{pmatrix}.$

Now based on these operations, we can define the aggregation theory.

4.2 Sine Trigonometric AOs for CFR Sets

This section of the chapter is devoted to defining the notion of average and geometric aggregation operators based on the operational laws defined in definition (4.3). The proposed aggregation theory is named sine trigonometric complex fuzzy rough weighted average, sine trigonometric complex fuzzy rough ordered weighted average, sine trigonometric complex fuzzy rough weighted geometric, and sine trigonometric complex fuzzy rough ordered weighted geometric AOs. Here for simplicity, we will denote the weight vector by $\omega = (\omega_1, \omega_2, \ldots, \omega_n)^T$ such that $\sum_{j=1}^{n} \omega_j = 1$.

Definition 4.4: Let $\mathcal{A}_j = \left\{ \left(\overline{a_j} + \iota \overline{b}_j,\ \underline{a_j} + \iota \underline{b_j} \right) \right\}$ be the collection of complex fuzzy rough numbers $(j = 1, 2, 3, \ldots, n)$. The STCFRWA aggregation operator is defined by

$$\begin{aligned} &\text{STCFRWA}\,(\mathcal{A}_1, \mathcal{A}_2, \mathcal{A}_3, \ldots, \mathcal{A}_n) \\ &= \omega_1 \cdot \sin(\mathcal{A}_1) \oplus \omega_2 \cdot \sin(\mathcal{A}_2) \oplus \cdots \oplus \omega_n \cdot \sin(\mathcal{A}_n). \end{aligned} \tag{4.4}$$

Theorem 4.1: Let $\mathcal{A}_j = \left\{ \left(\overline{a_j} + \iota \overline{b}_j,\ \underline{a_j} + \iota \underline{b_j} \right) \right\}$ be the collection of complex fuzzy rough numbers $(j = 1, 2, 3, \ldots, n)$. The outcome using Equation (4.4) is again a CFRN given by

$$\begin{aligned} &\text{STCFRWA}\,(\mathcal{A}_1, \mathcal{A}_2, \mathcal{A}_3, \ldots, \mathcal{A}_n) \\ &= \begin{pmatrix} 1 - \prod_{j=1}^{n} \left(1 - \sin\left(\frac{\pi}{2}\overline{a_j}\right)\right)^{\omega_j} + \iota \left(1 - \prod_{j=1}^{n} \left(1 - \sin\left(\frac{\pi}{2}\overline{b}_j\right)\right)^{\omega_j}\right), \\ 1 - \prod_{j=1}^{n} \left(1 - \sin\left(\frac{\pi}{2}\underline{a_j}\right)\right)^{\omega_j} + \iota \left(1 - \prod_{j=1}^{n} \left(1 - \sin\left(\frac{\pi}{2}\underline{b}_j\right)\right)^{\omega_j}\right) \end{pmatrix}. \end{aligned} \tag{4.5}$$

Proof: The result of eqn (4.5) is proved by using the notion of mathematical induction.

Step 1: For $n = 2$, we get:

$$\begin{aligned} &\omega_1 \sin \mathcal{A}_1 \\ &= \begin{pmatrix} 1 - \left(1 - \sin\left(\frac{\pi}{2}\overline{a_1}\right)\right)^{\omega_1} + \iota \left(1 - \left(1 - \sin\left(\frac{\pi}{2}\overline{b_1}\right)\right)^{\omega_1}\right), \\ 1 - \left(1 - \sin\left(\frac{\pi}{2}\underline{a_1}\right)\right)^{\omega_1} + \iota \left(1 - \left(1 - \sin\left(\frac{\pi}{2}\underline{b_1}\right)\right)^{\omega_1}\right) \end{pmatrix}, \end{aligned}$$

$$\omega_2 \sin \mathcal{A}_2 = \left(\begin{array}{c} 1-\left(1-\sin\left(\frac{\pi}{2}\overline{a_2}\right)\right)^{\omega_2} + \iota\left(1-\left(1-\sin\left(\frac{\pi}{2}\overline{b_2}\right)\right)^{\omega_2}\right) \\ 1-\left(1-\sin\left(\frac{\pi}{2}\underline{a_2}\right)\right)^{\omega_1} + \iota\left(1-\left(1-\sin\left(\frac{\pi}{2}\underline{b_2}\right)\right)^{\omega_1}\right) \end{array} \right).$$

$$\omega_1 \sin \mathcal{A}_1 \oplus \omega_2 \sin \mathcal{A}_2 = \left(\begin{array}{c} 1-\left(1-\sin\left(\frac{\pi}{2}\overline{a_1}\right)\right)^{\omega_1}\left(1-\sin\left(\frac{\pi}{2}\overline{a_2}\right)\right)^{\omega_2} \\ +\iota\left(1-\left(1-\sin\left(\frac{\pi}{2}\overline{b_1}\right)\right)^{\omega_1}\left(1-\sin\left(\frac{\pi}{2}\overline{b_2}\right)\right)^{\omega_2}\right), \\ 1-\left(1-\sin\left(\frac{\pi}{2}\underline{a_1}\right)\right)^{\omega_1}\left(1-\sin\left(\frac{\pi}{2}\underline{a_2}\right)\right)^{\omega_2} \\ +\iota\left(1-\left(1-\sin\left(\frac{\pi}{2}\underline{b_1}\right)\right)^{\omega_1}\left(1-\sin\left(\frac{\pi}{2}\underline{b_2}\right)\right)^{\omega_2}\right) \end{array} \right)$$

$$= \left(\begin{array}{c} 1-\prod_{j=1}^{2}\left(1-\sin\left(\frac{\pi}{2}\overline{a_j}\right)\right)^{\omega_j} + \iota\left(1-\prod_{j=1}^{2}\left(1-\sin\left(\frac{\pi}{2}\overline{b_j}\right)\right)^{\omega_j}\right), \\ 1-\prod_{j=1}^{2}\left(1-\sin\left(\frac{\pi}{2}\underline{a_j}\right)\right)^{\omega_j} + \iota\left(1-\prod_{j=1}^{2}\left(1-\sin\left(\frac{\pi}{2}\underline{b_j}\right)\right)^{\omega_j}\right) \end{array} \right).$$

Step 2: Suppose eqn (4.5) is true for $n = r$ that is:

$$\text{STCFRWA}\left(\mathcal{A}_1, \mathcal{A}_2, \mathcal{A}_3, \ldots, \mathcal{A}_r\right) = \left(\begin{array}{c} 1-\prod_{j=1}^{r}\left(1-\sin\left(\frac{\pi}{2}\overline{a_j}\right)\right)^{\omega_j} + \iota\left(1-\prod_{j=1}^{r}\left(1-\sin\left(\frac{\pi}{2}\overline{b_j}\right)\right)^{\omega_j}\right), \\ 1-\prod_{j=1}^{r}\left(1-\sin\left(\frac{\pi}{2}\underline{a_j}\right)\right)^{\omega_j} + \iota\left(1-\prod_{j=1}^{r}\left(1-\sin\left(\frac{\pi}{2}\underline{b_j}\right)\right)^{\omega_j}\right) \end{array} \right).$$

Step 3: Now we prove that eqn (4.5) is true for $n = r + 1$:

$$\text{STCFRWA}\left(\mathcal{A}_1, \mathcal{A}_2, \mathcal{A}_3, \ldots, \mathcal{A}_r, \mathcal{A}_{r+1}\right) = \left(\begin{array}{c} 1-\prod_{j=1}^{r}\left(1-\sin\left(\frac{\pi}{2}\overline{a_j}\right)\right)^{\omega_j} + \iota\left(1-\prod_{j=1}^{r}\left(1-\sin\left(\frac{\pi}{2}\overline{b_j}\right)\right)^{\omega_j}\right), \\ 1-\prod_{j=1}^{r}\left(1-\sin\left(\frac{\pi}{2}\underline{a_j}\right)\right)^{\omega_j} + \iota\left(1-\prod_{j=1}^{r}\left(1-\sin\left(\frac{\pi}{2}\underline{b_j}\right)\right)^{\omega_j}\right) \end{array} \right)$$
$$\oplus \left(\begin{array}{c} 1-\left(1-\sin\left(\frac{\pi}{2}\overline{a_{r+1}}\right)\right)^{\omega_{r+1}} + \iota 1-\left(1-\sin\left(\frac{\pi}{2}\overline{b_{r+1}}\right)\right)^{\omega_{r+1}}, \\ 1-\left(1-\sin\left(\frac{\pi}{2}\underline{a_{r+1}}\right)\right)^{\omega_{r+1}} + \iota 1-\left(1-\sin\left(\frac{\pi}{2}\underline{b_{r+1}}\right)\right)^{\omega_{r+1}} \end{array} \right)$$

$$= \begin{pmatrix} 1 - \prod_{j=1}^{r+1} \left(1 - \sin\left(\frac{\pi}{2}\overline{a_j}\right)\right)^{\omega_j} + \iota \left(1 - \prod_{j=1}^{r+1} \left(1 - \sin\left(\frac{\pi}{2}\overline{b_j}\right)\right)^{\omega_j}\right), \\ 1 - \prod_{j=1}^{r+1} \left(1 - \sin\left(\frac{\pi}{2}\underline{a_j}\right)\right)^{\omega_j} + \iota \left(1 - \prod_{j=1}^{r+1} \left(1 - \sin\left(\frac{\pi}{2}\underline{b_j}\right)\right)^{\omega_j}\right) \end{pmatrix}.$$

Hence the statement is true $n = r + 1$. So eqn (4.5) is valid for all n.

Remark 4.1. The notion of STCFRWA AOs can satisfy the following properties of idempotency, monotonicity, and boundedness.

Definition 4.5: Let $\mathcal{A}_j = \left\{\left(\overline{a_j} + \iota\,\overline{b}_j,\ \underline{a_j} + \iota\,\underline{b_j}\right)\right\}$ be the collection of complex fuzzy rough numbers $(j = 1, 2, 3, \ldots, n)$. The sine trigonometric complex fuzzy rough ordered weighted averaging AO for the group of CFRNs is given by

$$\text{STCFROWA}(\mathcal{A}_1, \mathcal{A}_2, \ldots, \mathcal{A}_n)$$
$$= \omega_1 \sin\left(\mathcal{A}_{\mathbb{O}(1)}\right) \oplus \omega_2 \sin\left(\mathcal{A}_{\mathbb{O}(2)}\right) \oplus \cdots \oplus \omega_n \sin\left(\mathcal{A}_{\mathbb{O}(n)}\right)$$
$$= \begin{pmatrix} 1 - \prod_{j=1}^{n} \left(1 - \sin\left(\frac{\pi}{2}\overline{a_{\mathbb{O}(j)}}\right)\right)^{\omega_j} + \iota \left(1 - \prod_{j=1}^{n} \left(1 - \sin\left(\frac{\pi}{2}\overline{b}_{\mathbb{O}(j)}\right)\right)^{\omega_j}\right), \\ 1 - \prod_{j=1}^{n} \left(1 - \sin\left(\frac{\pi}{2}\underline{a_{\mathbb{O}(j)}}\right)\right)^{\omega_j} + \iota \left(1 - \prod_{j=1}^{n} \left(1 - \sin\left(\frac{\pi}{2}\underline{b}_{\mathbb{O}(j)}\right)\right)^{\omega_j}\right) \end{pmatrix}.$$

Here, $(\mathbb{O}(1), \mathbb{O}(2), \mathbb{O}(3), \ldots, \mathbb{O}(n))$ is a permutation of $(1, 2, \ldots, n)$ such that $\mathcal{A}_{\mathbb{O}(j-1)} \geq \mathcal{A}_{\mathbb{O}(j)}$ for all j.

Remark 4.2. The notion of STCFROWA AOs satisfies the properties of idempotency, monotonicity, and boundedness.

Definition 4.6: For the family of CFRNs $\mathcal{A}_j = \left\{\left(\overline{a_j} + \iota\,\overline{b}_j,\ \underline{a_j} + \iota\,\underline{b_j}\right)\right\}$, $(j = 1, 2, 3, \ldots, n)$, the sine trigonometric complex fuzzy rough hybrid averaging AO for the collection of CFRNs is given by

$$\text{STCFRHA}(\mathcal{A}_1, \mathcal{A}_2, \mathcal{A}_3, \ldots, \mathcal{A}_n) = \omega_1 \sin \mathcal{A}^*_{\mathbb{O}(1)} \oplus \omega_2 \sin \mathcal{A}^*_{\mathbb{O}(2)} \oplus \cdots \oplus \omega_n \sin \mathcal{A}^*_{\mathbb{O}(n)}$$
$$= \begin{pmatrix} 1 - \prod_{j=1}^{n} \left(1 - \sin\left(\frac{\pi}{2}\,\overline{a_{\mathbb{O}(j)}}^*\right)\right)^{\omega_j} + \iota \left(1 - \prod_{j=1}^{n} \left(1 - \sin\left(\frac{\pi}{2}\,\overline{b}^*_{\mathbb{O}(j)}\right)\right)^{\omega_j}\right), \\ 1 - \prod_{j=1}^{n} \left(1 - \sin\left(\frac{\pi}{2}\,\underline{a_{\mathbb{O}(j)}}^*\right)\right)^{\omega_j} + \iota \left(1 - \prod_{j=1}^{n} \left(1 - \sin\left(\frac{\pi}{2}\,\underline{b}^*_{\mathbb{O}(j)}\right)\right)^{\omega_j}\right) \end{pmatrix}.$$

Here, $\mathcal{A}^*_j = n\,\omega_j\,\mathcal{A}_j$. The sequence $(\mathbb{O}(1), \mathbb{O}(2), \mathbb{O}(3), \ldots, \mathbb{O}(n))$ is a permutation of $(1, 2, \ldots, n)$ such that $\mathcal{A}_{\mathbb{O}(j-1)} \geq \mathcal{A}_{\mathbb{O}(j)}$ for all j.

4.3 Sine Trigonometric Complex Fuzzy Rough Weighted Geometric AOs

The motive of this section is to deliver the idea of sine trigonometric complex fuzzy rough weighted geometric aggregation operators. Here in this section, we have proposed the notion of STCFRWG, STCFROWG, and STCFRHWG AOs.

Definition 4.7: For the family of CFRNs $\mathcal{A}_j = \left\{\left(\overline{a_j} + \iota\bar{b}_j,\ \underline{a_j} + \iota\underline{b}_j\right)\right\}$, $(j = 1,\ 2,\ 3, \ldots,\ n)$, the sine trigonometric complex fuzzy rough weighted geometric AO is defined as

$$\begin{aligned}&\text{STCFRWG}\left(\mathcal{A}_1,\ \mathcal{A}_2,\ \mathcal{A}_3,\ \ldots,\ \mathcal{A}_n\right)\\&= \left(\sin \mathcal{A}_1\right)^{\omega_1} \bigotimes \left(\sin \mathcal{A}_2\right)^{\omega_2} \bigotimes \cdots \bigotimes \left(\sin \mathcal{A}_n\right)^{\omega_n}.\end{aligned} \tag{4.6}$$

Theorem 4.2: For the family of CFRNs $\mathcal{A}_j = \left\{\left(\overline{a_j} + \iota\bar{b}_j,\ \underline{a_j} + \iota\underline{b}_j\right)\right\}$, $(j = 1,\ 2,\ 3, \ldots,\ n)$, the result obtained by using the notion of eqn (4.6) is again a CFRN, given by

$$\begin{aligned}&\text{STCFRWG}\left(\mathcal{A}_1,\ \mathcal{A}_2,\ \mathcal{A}_3,\ \ldots,\ \mathcal{A}_n\right)\\&= \left(\begin{array}{c}\prod_{j=1}^{n}\left(\sin\left(\frac{\pi}{2}\overline{a_j}\right)\right)^{\omega_j} + \iota\prod_{j=1}^{n}\left(\sin\left(\frac{\pi}{2}\bar{b}_j\right)\right)^{\omega_j},\\ \prod_{j=1}^{n}\left(\sin\left(\frac{\pi}{2}\underline{a_j}\right)\right)^{\omega_j} + \iota\prod_{j=1}^{n}\left(\sin\left(\frac{\pi}{2}\underline{b}_j\right)\right)^{\omega_j}\end{array}\right).\end{aligned} \tag{4.7}$$

Proof: We have proved this result using the mathematical induction technique.

Step 1: For $n = 2$, we get:

$$\left(\sin \mathcal{A}_1\right)^{\omega_1} = \left(\begin{array}{c}\left(\sin\left(\frac{\pi}{2}\overline{a_1}\right)\right)^{\omega_1} + \iota\left(\sin\left(\frac{\pi}{2}\bar{b}_1\right)\right)^{\omega_1},\\ \left(\sin\left(\frac{\pi}{2}\underline{a_1}\right)\right)^{\omega_1} + \iota\left(\sin\left(\frac{\pi}{2}\underline{b}_1\right)\right)^{\omega_1}\end{array}\right),$$

$$\left(\sin \mathcal{A}_2\right)^{\omega_2} = \left(\begin{array}{c}\left(\sin\left(\frac{\pi}{2}\overline{a_2}\right)\right)^{\omega_2} + \iota\left(\sin\left(\frac{\pi}{2}\bar{b}_2\right)\right)^{\omega_2},\\ \left(\sin\left(\frac{\pi}{2}\underline{a_2}\right)\right)^{\omega_2} + \iota\left(\sin\left(\frac{\pi}{2}\underline{b}_2\right)\right)^{\omega_2}\end{array}\right).$$

$$\begin{aligned}&\left(\sin \mathcal{A}_1\right)^{\omega_1} \otimes \left(\sin \mathcal{A}_2\right)^{\omega_2}\\&= \left(\begin{array}{c}\left(\sin\left(\frac{\pi}{2}\overline{a_1}\right)\right)^{\omega_1} + \iota\left(\sin\left(\frac{\pi}{2}\bar{b}_1\right)\right)^{\omega_1},\\ \left(\sin\left(\frac{\pi}{2}\underline{a_1}\right)\right)^{\omega_1} + \iota\left(\sin\left(\frac{\pi}{2}\underline{b}_1\right)\right)^{\omega_1}\end{array}\right)\end{aligned}$$

$$\otimes\begin{pmatrix} \left(\sin\left(\frac{\pi}{2}\overline{a_2}\right)\right)^{\omega_2}+\iota\left(\sin\left(\frac{\pi}{2}\overline{b}_2\right)\right)^{\omega_2}, \\ \left(\sin\left(\frac{\pi}{2}\underline{a_2}\right)\right)^{\omega_2}+\iota\left(\sin\left(\frac{\pi}{2}\underline{b}_2\right)\right)^{\omega_2} \end{pmatrix}$$

$$\begin{pmatrix} \left(\sin\left(\frac{\pi}{2}\overline{a_1}\right)\right)^{\omega_1}\left(\sin\left(\frac{\pi}{2}\overline{a_2}\right)\right)^{\omega_2}, +\iota\left(\left(\sin\left(\frac{\pi}{2}\overline{b_1}\right)\right)^{\omega_1}, \left(\sin\left(\frac{\pi}{2}\overline{b_2}\right)\right)^{\omega_2}\right) \\ \left(\sin\left(\frac{\pi}{2}\underline{a_1}\right)\right)^{\omega_1}\left(\sin\left(\frac{\pi}{2}\underline{a_2}\right)\right)^{\omega_2}+\iota\left(\left(\sin\left(\frac{\pi}{2}\underline{b_1}\right)\right)^{\omega_1}, \left(\sin\left(\frac{\pi}{2}\underline{b_2}\right)\right)^{\omega_2}\right) \end{pmatrix}$$

$$=\begin{pmatrix} \prod_{j=1}^{2}\left(\sin\left(\frac{\pi}{2}\overline{a_j}\right)\right)^{\omega_j}+\iota\prod_{j=1}^{2}\left(\sin\left(\frac{\pi}{2}\overline{b}_j\right)\right)^{\omega_j}, \\ \prod_{j=1}^{2}\left(\sin\left(\frac{\pi}{2}\underline{a_j}\right)\right)^{\omega_j}+\iota\prod_{j=1}^{2}\left(\sin\left(\frac{\pi}{2}\underline{b}_j\right)\right)^{\omega_j} \end{pmatrix}.$$

Step 2: Assume that eqn (4.7) is true for $n = r$, that is:

$$\text{STCFRWG}(\mathcal{A}_1, \ldots, \mathcal{A}_r) = \begin{pmatrix} \prod_{j=1}^{r}\left(\sin\left(\frac{\pi}{2}\overline{a_j}\right)\right)^{\omega_j}+\iota\prod_{j=1}^{r}\left(\sin\left(\frac{\pi}{2}\overline{b}_j\right)\right)^{\omega_j}, \\ \prod_{j=1}^{r}\left(\sin\left(\frac{\pi}{2}\underline{a_j}\right)\right)^{\omega_j}+\iota\prod_{j=1}^{r}\left(\sin\left(\frac{\pi}{2}\underline{b}_j\right)\right)^{\omega_j} \end{pmatrix}.$$

Step 3: Now for $n = r + 1$, we get:

$$\text{STCFRWG}(\mathcal{A}_1, \ldots, \mathcal{A}_r, \mathcal{A}_{r+1}) =$$

$$=\begin{pmatrix} \prod_{j=1}^{r}\left(\sin\left(\frac{\pi}{2}\overline{a_j}\right)\right)^{\omega_j}+\iota\prod_{j=1}^{r}\left(\sin\left(\frac{\pi}{2}\overline{b}_j\right)\right)^{\omega_j}, \\ \prod_{j=1}^{r}\left(\sin\left(\frac{\pi}{2}\underline{a_j}\right)\right)^{\omega_j}+\iota\prod_{j=1}^{r}\left(\sin\left(\frac{\pi}{2}\underline{b}_j\right)\right)^{\omega_j} \end{pmatrix}$$

$$\otimes\begin{pmatrix} \left(\sin\left(\frac{\pi}{2}\overline{a_{r+1}}\right)\right)^{\omega_{r+1}}+\iota\left(\sin\left(\frac{\pi}{2}\overline{b_{r+1}}\right)\right)^{\omega_{r+1}}, \\ \left(\sin\left(\frac{\pi}{2}\underline{a_{r+1}}\right)\right)^{\omega_{r+1}}+\iota\left(\sin\left(\frac{\pi}{2}\underline{b_{r+1}}\right)\right)^{\omega_{r+1}} \end{pmatrix}$$

$$=\begin{pmatrix} \prod_{j=1}^{r+1}\left(\sin\left(\frac{\pi}{2}\overline{a_j}\right)\right)^{\omega_j}+\iota\prod_{j=1}^{r+1}\left(\sin\left(\frac{\pi}{2}\overline{a}_j\right)\right)^{\omega_j}, \\ \prod_{j=1}^{r+1}\left(\sin\left(\frac{\pi}{2}\underline{a_j}\right)\right)^{\omega_j}+\iota\prod_{j=1}^{r+1}\left(\sin\left(\frac{\pi}{2}\underline{b}_j\right)\right)^{\omega_j} \end{pmatrix}.$$

Hence the statement is true for $n = r + 1$. So eqn (4.7) is true for all n.

Remark 4.3. The notion of STCFRWG AOs satisfies the properties of idempotency, monotonicity, and boundedness.

Definition 4.8: For the family of CFRNs $\mathcal{A}_j = \left(\overline{a_j} + \iota\overline{b_j},\ \underline{a_j} + \iota\underline{b_j}\right)$ where $j = 1, 2, 3, \ldots, n$, the sine trigonometric complex fuzzy rough ordered weighted geometric AO is defined as:

$$\begin{aligned} &\text{SCFROWG}\left(\mathcal{A}_1,\ \mathcal{A}_2,\ \ldots,\ \mathcal{A}_n\right) \\ &= \left(\sin \mathcal{A}_{\mathbb{O}(1)}\right)^{\omega_1} \otimes \left(\sin \mathcal{A}_{\mathbb{O}(2)}\right)^{\omega_2} \otimes \cdots \otimes \left(\sin \mathcal{A}_{\mathbb{O}(n)}\right)^{\omega_n} \\ &= \left(\begin{array}{c} \prod_{j=1}^{n} \left(\sin\left(\frac{\pi}{2}\overline{a_{\mathbb{O}(j)}}\right)\right)^{\omega_j} + \iota \prod_{j=1}^{n} \left(\sin\left(\frac{\pi}{2}\overline{b_{\mathbb{O}(j)}}\right)\right)^{\omega_j}, \\ \prod_{j=1}^{n} \left(\sin\left(\frac{\pi}{2}\underline{a_{\mathbb{O}(j)}}\right)\right)^{\omega_j} + \iota \prod_{j=1}^{n} \left(\sin\left(\frac{\pi}{2}\underline{b_{\mathbb{O}(j)}}\right)\right)^{\omega_j} \end{array} \right). \end{aligned}$$

Here, $(\mathbb{O}(1),\ \mathbb{O}(2),\ \ldots,\ \mathbb{O}(n))$ is a permutation of $(1,\ 2,\ \ldots,\ n)$ such that $\mathcal{A}_{\mathbb{O}(j-1)} \geq \mathcal{A}_{\mathbb{O}(j)}$ for all j.

Remark 4.4. The notion of STCFROWG AOs satisfies the properties of idempotency, monotonicity, and boundedness.

Definition 4.9: For the family of CFRNs $\mathcal{A}_j = \left(\overline{a_j} + \iota\overline{b_j},\ \underline{a_j} + \iota\underline{b_j}\right)$ where $j = 1, 2, 3, \ldots, n$, the sine trigonometric complex fuzzy rough hybrid geometric AO is defined as:

$$\begin{aligned} &\text{STCFRHG}\left(\mathcal{A}_1,\ \mathcal{A}_2,\ \ldots,\ \mathcal{A}_n\right) \\ &= \left(\sin \mathcal{A}^*_{\mathbb{O}(1)}\right)^{\omega_1} \otimes \left(\sin \mathcal{A}^*_{\mathbb{O}(2)}\right)^{\omega_2} \otimes \cdots \otimes \left(\sin \mathcal{A}^*_{\mathbb{O}(n)}\right)^{\omega_n} \\ &= \left(\begin{array}{c} \prod_{j=1}^{n} \left(\sin\left(\frac{\pi}{2}\overline{a^*_{\mathbb{O}(j)}}\right)\right)^{\omega_j} + \iota \prod_{j=1}^{n} \left(\sin\left(\frac{\pi}{2}\overline{b^*_{\mathbb{O}(j)}}\right)\right)^{\omega_j}, \\ \prod_{j=1}^{n} \left(\sin\left(\frac{\pi}{2}\underline{a^*_{\mathbb{O}(j)}}\right)\right)^{\omega_j} + \iota \prod_{j=1}^{n} \left(\sin\left(\frac{\pi}{2}\underline{b^*_{\mathbb{O}(j)}}\right)\right)^{\omega_j} \end{array} \right). \end{aligned}$$

Here, $\mathcal{A}^*_j = n \cdot \omega_j \cdot \mathcal{A}_j$, and $(\mathbb{O}(1),\ \mathbb{O}(2),\ \ldots,\ \mathbb{O}(n))$ is a permutation of $(1,\ 2,\ \ldots,\ n)$ such that $\mathcal{A}_{\mathbb{O}(j-1)} \geq \mathcal{A}_{\mathbb{O}(j)}$ for all j.

4.4 Application of the Proposed Theory

Our main goal in this study innovative approaches to prioritizing financial tools for business growth and sustainability. To achieve the desired goal, we have proposed an algorithm that can help us to prioritize the financial tools for business and suitability and show the importance and usability of the imitated work. The overall discussion is given below.

4.4.1 Decision-making algorithm

Assume that there are m alternatives and a set of alternatives is given by $\mathfrak{L} = \{\mathfrak{L}_1, \mathfrak{L}_2, \ldots, \mathfrak{L}_m\}$. The "$n$" attributes of these alternatives are denoted by $\mathbb{T} = \{\mathbb{T}_1, \mathbb{T}_2, \ldots, \mathbb{T}_n\}$. The weights of these attributes are $\omega_j = (\omega_1, \omega_2, \ldots, \omega_n)^T$ such that $\sum_{j=1}^{n} \omega_j = 1$, and $\omega_j \in [0, 1]\ \forall j$. Assume that the decision analyst provides theory assessment in the form of CFRNs given by $\mathcal{A}_{ij} = \left\{\left(\overline{a_{ij}} + \iota\, \overline{b}_{ij}, \underline{a_{ij}} + \iota\, \underline{b}_{ij}\right)\right\}$ for $i = 1, 2, 3, \ldots, m$ and $j = 1, 2, 3, \ldots, n$. Now, the step-wise algorithm is given by:

Step 1: Collect the information in the form of CFRNs proposed by decision makers and arrange it in the form of matric given by

$$\mathcal{M} = \begin{bmatrix} \mathcal{A}_{11} & \mathcal{A}_{12} & \cdots & \mathcal{A}_{1n} \\ \mathcal{A}_{21} & \mathcal{A}_{22} & \cdots & \mathcal{A}_{2n} \\ \vdots & \ddots & \cdots & \vdots \\ \mathcal{A}_{m1} & \mathcal{A}_{m2} & & \mathcal{A}_{mn} \end{bmatrix}.$$

Step 2: Utilize the following formula, if there is a need to normalize the information based on the information of cost type or benefit type attributes. The formulas are given by

$$\mathcal{N} = \begin{cases} \mathcal{A}_{rj} & \text{for benefit type attributes} \\ (\mathcal{A}_{rj})^c & \text{for cost type attributes} \end{cases},$$

where $(\mathcal{A}_{rj})^c = \left\{\left(\left(1 - \underline{a_{rj}}\right) + \iota\left(1 - \underline{b_{rj}}\right), (1 - \overline{a_{rj}}) + \iota\left(1 - \overline{b_{rj}}\right)\right)\right\}$ represent the complement of $\mathcal{A}_{rj}$.

Step 3: In this step, we aggregate the information obtained from step 2 by using the proposed notion of STCFRWA or STCFROWA or STCFRWG or SCFROWG operators.

Step 4: Find out the score values by using the formula given in definition 1.12.

Step 5: Rank the alternatives according to the result obtained through step 4 and obtain the best alternative according to ranking order.

To show the utilization of the developed approach, we have provided a case study of the developed approach in the following example.

4.4.2 Numerical example

Businesses are always looking for efficient financial solutions that promote growth and guarantee sustainability in the cutthroat economic environment of today. Rapid technology breakthroughs and dynamic changes in global marketplaces need creative ways to prioritize these instruments for the best outcomes. Financial tools, such as investment analysis, cash flow management, capital budgeting, and credit evaluation, are essential for helping companies weather changing market conditions and build long-term resilience. Adopting these technologies alone is no longer enough, though; businesses now need to prioritize and tailor them to their particular objectives, market needs, and risk tolerance.

Setting financial tool priorities entails striking a balance between short-term financial demands and long-term, strategic goals. To assess performance, forecast market trends, and pinpoint important growth areas, it is necessary to use cutting-edge approaches like data analytics, machine learning, and artificial intelligence. Furthermore, to satisfy the growing demand for environmental impact awareness and corporate responsibility, sustainable finance practices are crucial. Businesses can enhance their market positioning and foster stakeholder confidence by coordinating financial priorities with sustainability aims.

Developing an agile and adaptable culture within organizations is another aspect of innovative prioritization that helps them react quickly to new possibilities and challenges. To provide insights into how organizations might use financial tools to improve performance and generate long-term value in a constantly changing business environment, this chapter examines different strategies for prioritizing these tools for business growth and sustainability.

(1) *Cash flow management*

Managing cash flow is essential to preserving a company's financial stability. Businesses may make sure they have adequate cash on hand to handle both unforeseen costs and daily operations by monitoring their cash inflows and outflows. To maintain finances accessible for growth projects, this method uses forecasting, monitoring, and budgeting. Additionally, it aids in avoiding problems like excessive leverage and needless debt. A clear picture of financial stability may be obtained through effective cash flow management, which aids in decision-making for firms. In the end, it permits seamless operation free from monetary interruptions.

(2) *Financial forecasting*

A tool called financial forecasting uses past data and market patterns to project future revenues, costs, and capital requirements. Businesses may foresee changes in the market, prepare for expansion, and make proactive modifications thanks to this approach. By identifying possible cash shortages, forecasting enables organizations to make preparations before they become issues. Businesses can modify their plans and achieve their objectives more effectively by updating projections regularly. Because it gives a clear picture of financial expectations, financial forecasting also helps with risk management. Setting reasonable growth goals requires accurate forecasting.

(3) *Budgeting and variance analysis*

Setting financial objectives and constraints for different projects or departments as well as developing a plan for allocating resources are all part of budgeting. To find differences and potential areas for improvement, variance analysis then contrasts the actual performance with the allocated sums. This tool assists managers in adhering to budget plans and making necessary spending adjustments. Businesses can identify inefficiencies or unforeseen expenses that may affect profitability by examining deviations. By encouraging departmental accountability, this strategy makes sure every unit operates within its means. By maintaining financial alignment with strategic goals, regular budgeting and variance analysis promote sustainable growth.

(4) *Investment appraisal and risk assessment*

Investment appraisal examines the costs, anticipated returns, and related risks of certain projects or investments. This tool supports strategic growth decisions by assisting firms in identifying which investments are most likely to yield the highest returns. An essential component of investment appraisal, risk assessment takes into account variables like operational difficulties or market swings that may affect the project's performance. When taken as a whole, these evaluations offer a thorough understanding of an investment's feasibility and its effects. Businesses can minimize financial risk and prioritize sustainable growth by making data-driven investment decisions.

$\mathfrak{L}_1$ = *Cash flow management*

$\mathfrak{L}_2$ = *Financial forecasting*

$\mathfrak{L}_3$ = *Budgeting and variance analysis*

$\mathfrak{L}_4$ = *Investment appraisal and risk assessment*

Assume that these four financial tools for business growth and sustainability are assessed by the decision analyst based on the following attributes. Here are a few basic explanations of the four main characteristics of financial tools that are necessary for the expansion and sustainability of businesses.

* *Scalability*

Over time, financial tools ought to change to accommodate a company's expansion. They must be able to easily handle growing transaction volumes. Scalability allows for growth without requiring a complete overhaul of financial systems. It guarantees effective management as a company grows from small to huge. At every level of expansion, adaptable tools aid in preserving operational continuity.

* *Data accuracy and reliability*

Accurate data is necessary to make wise financial decisions. By using automated computations, financial instruments need to decrease errors. Accurate budgeting and forecasting are made possible by reliable data. Improved data integrity fosters stakeholder trust. It improves financial transparency and protects against compliance hazards.

* *Flexibility and customization*

Customizable technologies enable companies to adapt operations to particular requirements. Flexibility accommodates distinct workflows and a range of industrial requirements. For smooth operations, flexible tools can be integrated with other systems. They offer choices for adapting to shifting market conditions. Tailored financial instruments complement an organization's long-range objectives.

* *Cost efficiency*

Affordability and functionality should be balanced in effective financial tools. They optimize resource allocation and reduce wasteful spending. Sustainability and higher profit margins are two benefits of cost-effectiveness. Automation helps businesses by lowering operating costs. Cost-effective solutions free up funds for further investments in areas of expansion.

These attributes are denoted and given by

$\mathbb{T}_1$ = Scalability

$\mathbb{T}_2$ = Data accuracy and reliability

$\mathbb{T}_3$ = Flexibility and customization

$\mathbb{T}_4$ = Cost efficiency

Assume that the WVs of attributes are $\omega = (0.21, 0.18, 0.34, 0.27)$. Now based on this information, we have to utilize the proposed algorithm for the selection of the best alternative to show the applicability of the developed approach in decision making.

Step 1: The information provided by the decision analyst in the form of CFRNs is given in Table 4.1.

Table 4.1 CFR data.

	$\mathbb{T}_1$	$\mathbb{T}_2$	$\mathbb{T}_3$	$\mathbb{T}_4$
$\mathfrak{L}_1$	$\begin{pmatrix} 0.19+\iota 0.20, \\ 0.21+\iota\, 0.26 \end{pmatrix}$	$\begin{pmatrix} 0.18+\iota 0.19, \\ 0.11+\iota\, 0.16 \end{pmatrix}$	$\begin{pmatrix} 0.49+\iota 0.10, \\ 0.51+\iota\, 0.16 \end{pmatrix}$	$\begin{pmatrix} 0.24+\iota 0.19, \\ 0.34+\iota\, 0.26 \end{pmatrix}$
$\mathfrak{L}_2$	$\begin{pmatrix} 0.23+\iota 0.25, \\ 0.28+\iota\, 0.27 \end{pmatrix}$	$\begin{pmatrix} 0.15+\iota 0.30, \\ 0.11+\iota\, 0.21 \end{pmatrix}$	$\begin{pmatrix} 0.39+\iota 0.19, \\ 0.11+\iota\, 0.16 \end{pmatrix}$	$\begin{pmatrix} 0.19+\iota 0.30, \\ 0.29+\iota\, 0.36 \end{pmatrix}$
$\mathfrak{L}_3$	$\begin{pmatrix} 0.17+\iota 0.14, \\ 0.29+\iota\, 0.15 \end{pmatrix}$	$\begin{pmatrix} 0.39+\iota 0.24, \\ 0.41+\iota\, 0.23 \end{pmatrix}$	$\begin{pmatrix} 0.49+\iota 0.23, \\ 0.21+\iota\, 0.26 \end{pmatrix}$	$\begin{pmatrix} 0.39+\iota 0.30, \\ 0.41+\iota\, 0.36 \end{pmatrix}$
$\mathfrak{L}_4$	$\begin{pmatrix} 0.27+\iota 0.26, \\ 0.24+\iota\, 0.33 \end{pmatrix}$	$\begin{pmatrix} 0.59+\iota 0.27, \\ 0.18+\iota\, 0.28 \end{pmatrix}$	$\begin{pmatrix} 0.29+\iota 0.29, \\ 0.41+\iota\, 0.35 \end{pmatrix}$	$\begin{pmatrix} 0.59+\iota 0.10, \\ 0.17+\iota\, 0.16 \end{pmatrix}$

Step 2: No need to normalize the information given in Table 4.1 because all data is of benefit type.

Step 3: Utilize the notion of STCFRWA, STCFROWA, STCFRWG, and STCFROWG AOs to aggregate the information given in Table 4.1. The aggregated results are given in Table 4.2.

Table 4.2 Aggregated outcomes.

Methods	$\mathfrak{L}_1$	$\mathfrak{L}_2$	$\mathfrak{L}_3$	$\mathfrak{L}_4$
STCFRWA	$\begin{pmatrix} 0.468+\iota 0.253, \\ 0.4728+\iota\, 0.3239 \end{pmatrix}$	$\begin{pmatrix} 0.4080+\iota 0.3880, \\ 0.3146+\iota\, 0.3849 \end{pmatrix}$	$\begin{pmatrix} 0.5740+\iota 0.3600, \\ 0.4418+\iota\, 0.4015 \end{pmatrix}$	$\begin{pmatrix} 0.5630+\iota 0.3590, \\ 0.4012+\iota\, 0.4354 \end{pmatrix}$
STCFROWA	$\begin{pmatrix} 0.4170+\iota 0.2720, \\ 0.4388+\iota\, 0.3300 \end{pmatrix}$	$\begin{pmatrix} 0.4020+\iota 0.3910, \\ 0.2857+\iota\, 0.3680 \end{pmatrix}$	$\begin{pmatrix} 0.5600+\iota 0.3460, \\ 0.4764+\iota\, 0.3830 \end{pmatrix}$	$\begin{pmatrix} 0.5600+\iota 0.3530, \\ 0.3874+\iota\, 0.4310 \end{pmatrix}$
STCFRWG	$\begin{pmatrix} 0.4150+\iota 0.2400, \\ 0.4278+\iota\, 0.3110 \end{pmatrix}$	$\begin{pmatrix} 0.3680+\iota 0.3780, \\ 0.2679+\iota\, 0.3560 \end{pmatrix}$	$\begin{pmatrix} 0.5210+\iota 0.3440, \\ 0.4558+\iota\, 0.3770 \end{pmatrix}$	$\begin{pmatrix} 0.5190+\iota 0.3220, \\ 0.3778+\iota\, 0.4070 \end{pmatrix}$
STCFROWG	$\begin{pmatrix} 0.3620+\iota 0.2620, \\ 0.3500+\iota\, 0.3171 \end{pmatrix}$	$\begin{pmatrix} 0.3590+\iota 0.3800, \\ 0.2460+\iota\, 0.3434 \end{pmatrix}$	$\begin{pmatrix} 0.4970+\iota 0.3290, \\ 0.4470+\iota\, 0.3586 \end{pmatrix}$	$\begin{pmatrix} 0.5150+\iota 0.3170, \\ 0.3550+\iota\, 0.4046 \end{pmatrix}$

Step 4: The score values of the data given in Table 4.2 are calculated by the formula given in definition (1.12) and overall results are given in Table 4.3.

Table 4.3 Score values.

Methods	Scor. ($\mathfrak{L}_1$)	Scor. ($\mathfrak{L}_2$)	Scor. ($\mathfrak{L}_3$)	Scor. ($\mathfrak{L}_4$)	Ranking
STCFRW A	0.8790	0.8740	0.9440	0.9400	$\mathfrak{L}_3 > \mathfrak{L}_4 > \mathfrak{L}_1 > \mathfrak{L}_2$
STCFRO WA	0.8640	0.8620	0.9410	0.9330	$\mathfrak{L}_3 > \mathfrak{L}_4 > \mathfrak{L}_1 > \mathfrak{L}_2$
STCFRW G	0.8480	0.8430	0.9240	0.9060	$\mathfrak{L}_3 > \mathfrak{L}_4 > \mathfrak{L}_1 > \mathfrak{L}_2$
STCFRO WG	0.8230	0.8320	0.9080	0.8980	$\mathfrak{L}_3 > \mathfrak{L}_4 > \mathfrak{L}_2 > \mathfrak{L}_1$

Step 5: In the light of results given in Table 4.3 the ranking results are given in Table 4.4.

The graphical representation of the data given in Table 4.3 is represented in Figure 4.1.

Table 4.4 Ranking result.

Methods	Ranking
STCFRWA	$\mathfrak{L}_3 > \mathfrak{L}_4 > \mathfrak{L}_1 > \mathfrak{L}_2$
STCFROWA	$\mathfrak{L}_3 > \mathfrak{L}_4 > \mathfrak{L}_1 > \mathfrak{L}_2$
STCFRWG	$\mathfrak{L}_3 > \mathfrak{L}_4 > \mathfrak{L}_1 > \mathfrak{L}_2$
STCFROWG	$\mathfrak{L}_3 > \mathfrak{L}_4 > \mathfrak{L}_2 > \mathfrak{L}_1$

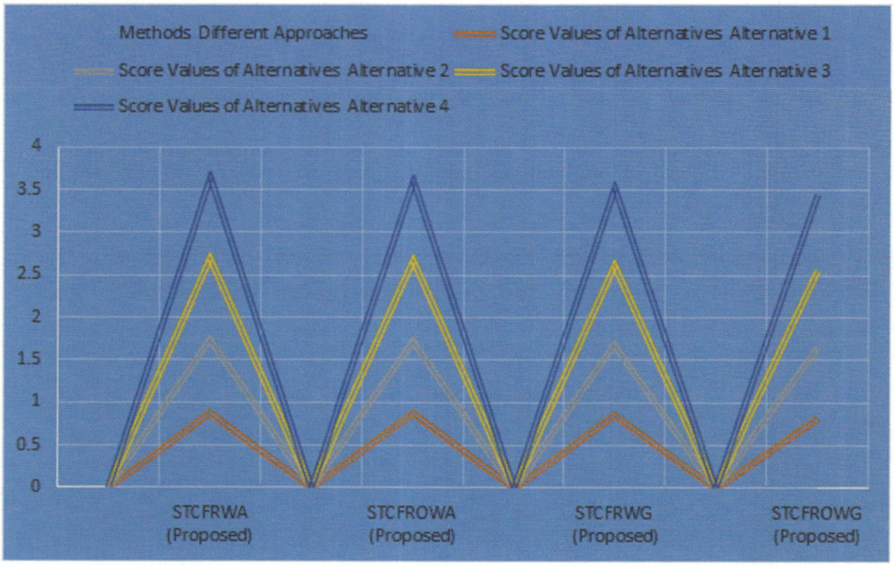

Figure 4.1 Graphical representation of data given in Table 4.3.

4.5 Comparative Analysis of the Proposed Study

In this section, we will discuss the comparative analysis of the proposed work with some existing notions that can help us to discuss the importance of the proposed work. We will compare our work with Khan et al. [14] approach, Bi et al. [17, 18] approach, Hussain et al. [19] approach, and Hu et al. [20] approach. Here in this section, we will discuss the results from Table 4.3.

1. Khan et al. [14] developed aggregation theory based on the polar form of CFRS which is limited because if the data is proposed in the form of the CFRN as produced in the developed approach then the necessary condition for a polar form of CFRS that is $r \in [0, 1]$ is violated and in this case, the defined theory becomes limited. For example, when data is given in the form of $(0.80 + \iota 0.98, 0.7 + \iota 0.76)$. Then observe

that $\sqrt{0.80^2+0.98^2}$ and $\sqrt{0.70^2+0.76^2} \notin [0,\ 1]$. Hence the defined theory is limited and established work is advanced.

2. Bi et al. [17, 18] diagnosed arithmetic AOs (AAOs) in the setting of CF sets. As we know the structure of CF sets is not rich enough to cope with upper and lower approximation of the data. The data given in Table 4.1 is based on CFRNs and in this case Bi et al. [17, 18] approach fails to handle such kind of information. While the developed approach can handle the information in Table 4.1 easily. Hence, in this case, we can say that the introduced approach is more advanced and it provides more space for decision-makers to take their information in the form of CFRNs in decision-making problems and utilize the proposed aggregation operators to solve theory problems.
3. The geometrical advantage of the CFRS is that it can cover more advanced information than that of the polar form of CFRS theory because we can observe that in the polar form of CFRS given in the form $\left\{\left(\underline{r}e^{2\pi\underline{\theta}}, \overline{r}e^{2\pi\overline{\theta}}\right)\right\}$ $\underline{r}$, $\overline{r}$, $\underline{\theta}$, and $\overline{\theta} \in [0,\ 1]$. But we can notice that if decision makers take the value $(0.98+\iota 0.81, 0.90+\iota 0.78)$, then we can see that $\underline{r} = \sqrt{0.98^2+0.81^2} = 1.6361 \notin [0,\ 1]$ and similarly $\overline{r} =$

Table 4.5 Comparative analysis results.

Methods	Score values				Ranking
	Scor. ($\mathfrak{L}_1$)	Scor. ($\mathfrak{L}_2$)	Scor. ($\mathfrak{L}_3$)	Scor. ($\mathfrak{L}_4$)	
Khan et al. [14] approach	No result	No result	No result	No result	No result
Bi et al. [17, 18] approach	No result	No result	No result	No result	No result
Hu et al. [19] approach	No result	No result	No result	No result	No result
Hussain et al. [20] approach	No result	No result	No result	No result	No result
STCFRWA AOs (proposed)	0.8790	0.8740	0.9440	0.9400	$\mathfrak{L}_3 > \mathfrak{L}_4 > \mathfrak{L}_1 > \mathfrak{L}_2$
STCFROWA AOs (proposed)	0.8640	0.8620	0.9410	0.9330	$\mathfrak{L}_3 > \mathfrak{L}_4 > \mathfrak{L}_1 > \mathfrak{L}_2$
STCFRWG AOs (proposed)	0.8480	0.8430	0.9240	0.9060	$\mathfrak{L}_3 > \mathfrak{L}_4 > \mathfrak{L}_1 > \mathfrak{L}_2$
STCFROWG AOs (proposed)	0.8230	0.8320	0.9080	0.8980	$\mathfrak{L}_3 > \mathfrak{L}_4 > \mathfrak{L}_2 > \mathfrak{L}_1$

$\sqrt{0.90^2 + 0.78^2} = 1.5084 \notin [0,\ 1]$. Hence, we can say that the data in Tamir's complex fuzzy form can never be handled by the idea proposed by Hussain et al. [19]. Hence Hussain et al. [19] approach is limited and it can never discuss the information $(0.98 + \iota 0.81, 0.90 + \iota 0.78)$. On the other hand, the proposed approach can discuss that kind of information. Hence we can say that the developed approach is very handy and attractive.

4. Hu et al. [20] approach is based on a fuzzy rough set and this approach cannot discuss the second dimension as well as upper and lower approximation in the data. So these weaknesses in this structure show the limitations of Hu et al. [20] approach.

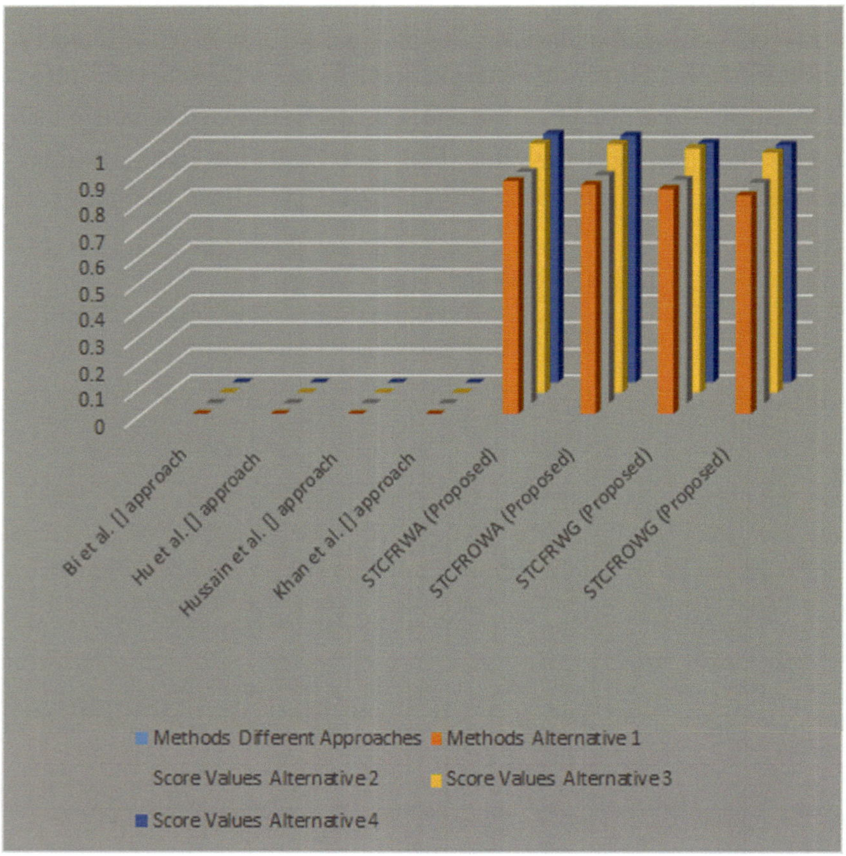

Figure 4.2 Graphical representation of results given in Table 4.5.

The overall results are given in Table 4.5.

The graphical representation of data given in Table 4.5 is represented in Figure 4.2.

4.6 Conclusion

The notion of the complex fuzzy rough set is a valuable and significant tool for discussing more advanced information. Aggregation theory plays a vital role in decision-making. In many decision-making situations, we have to deliver such kind of idea or structure that can handle more advanced data and in this case, the chance of data loss is reduced and more accurate results can be obtained. The fundamental laws for sine trigonometric aggregation operators based on CFRS have been delivered. Moreover based on these operational laws we have defined the notion of sine trigonometric complex fuzzy rough weighted averaging (STCFRWA), sine trigonometric complex fuzzy rough ordered weighted averaging (STCFROWA), sine trigonometric complex fuzzy rough hybrid averaging (STCFRHA), sine trigonometric complex fuzzy rough weighted geometric (STCFRWG), sine trigonometric complex fuzzy rough ordered weighted geometric (STCFROWG), and sine trigonometric complex fuzzy rough hybrid geometric (STCFRHG) operators. To discuss the application perspective of the developed theory, we have initiated an algorithm for the developed. Moreover, we have elaborated on the case study of prioritization of financial tools for business growth to strengthen the application of the developed theory. To discuss the results, we have established the comparative analysis section to deliver the validity and advancement of the initiated work.

5

A Framework for Prioritizing Tools and Techniques in Electrical Engineering Design and Analysis: An Application of Complex Fuzzy Rough Sets

Decision-making and system optimization are difficult in electrical engineering since the field frequently works with complicated systems that contain uncertainty, nonlinearity, and imprecise data. Unpredictable environmental circumstances and variable demand make it challenging to create precise models for problems like load forecasting, fault detection, and power system stability analysis. Conventional approaches frequently fail to capture the innate ambiguity of these systems. A workable answer is offered by fuzzy logic structures, which make it possible to describe complex relationships and uncertain variables. These issues can be resolved by using fuzzy sets and inference systems. For this purpose, we have delivered the basic operational laws for CFRNs based on Aczel-Alsina t-norm and t-conorm. Moreover, we have delivered the aggregation theory of the CFRNs consisting of complex fuzzy rough Aczel-Alsina weighted aggregation operator, complex fuzzy rough Aczel-Alsina ordered weighted aggregation operator, and complex fuzzy rough Aczel-Alsina hybrid aggregation operator. We have proposed the application of the delivered approaches by defining an algorithm. We provided an illustrative example through which we can classify the different technologies and tools in electrical engineering design and analysis. We have delivered a comparative analysis of the established work with existing theories to show the advantages of the devised theory.

5.1 Aczel-Alsina Operations of CFRNs

Based on the theory of Aczel-Alsina t-norm and t-conorm, in this section, we have delivered the theory of complex fuzzy rough Aczel-Alsina operational laws. Furthermore, based on these operations we have proved some fundamental properties. The overall discussion is given as

DOI: 10.1201/9788743807827-5

Definition 5.1: Let $\mathcal{A}_1 = \{(\overline{a_1} + \iota\overline{b_1},\ \underline{a_1} + \iota\underline{b_1})\}$ and $\mathcal{A}_2 = \{(\overline{a_2} + \iota\overline{b_2},\ \underline{a_2} + \iota\underline{b_2})\}$ be two CFRNs with $s > 0$ and $t \geq 1$, then the theory of Aczel-Alsina rules is defined by

1.

$$\mathcal{A}_1 \oplus \mathcal{A}_2 = \begin{pmatrix} 1 - e^{-((-\log(1-\overline{a_1}))^t + (-\log(1-\overline{a_2}))^t)^{\frac{1}{t}}} \\ +\iota\left(1 - e^{-((-\log(1-\overline{b_1}))^t + (-\log(1-\overline{b_2}))^t)^{\frac{1}{t}}}\right), \\ 1 - e^{-((-\log(1-\underline{a_1}))^t + (-\log(1-\underline{a_2}))^t)^{\frac{1}{t}}} \\ +\iota\left(1 - e^{-((-\log(1-\underline{b_1}))^t + (-\log(1-\underline{b_2}))^t)^{\frac{1}{t}}}\right) \end{pmatrix}.$$

2.

$$\mathcal{A}_1 \otimes \mathcal{A}_2 = \begin{pmatrix} e^{-((-\log(\overline{a_1}))^t + (-\log(\overline{a_2}))^t)^{\frac{1}{t}}} \\ +\iota\left(e^{-((-\log(\overline{b_1}))^t + (-\log(\overline{b_2}))^t)^{\frac{1}{t}}}\right), \\ e^{-((-\log(\underline{a_1}))^t + (-\log(\underline{a_2}))^t)^{\frac{1}{t}}} \\ +\iota\left(e^{-((-\log(\underline{b_1}))^t + (-\log(\underline{b_2}))^t)^{\frac{1}{t}}}\right) \end{pmatrix}.$$

3.

$$s\mathcal{A}_1 = \begin{pmatrix} 1 - e^{-(s(-\log(1-\overline{a_1}))^t)^{\frac{1}{t}}} + \iota\left(1 - e^{-(s(-\log(1-\overline{b_1}))^t)^{\frac{1}{t}}}\right), \\ 1 - e^{-(s(-\log(1-\underline{a_1}))^t)^{\frac{1}{t}}} + \iota\left(1 - e^{-(s(-\log(1-\underline{b_1}))^t)^{\frac{1}{t}}}\right) \end{pmatrix}.$$

4.

$$\mathcal{A}_1^s = \begin{pmatrix} e^{-(s(-\log|\overline{a_1}|)^t)^{\frac{1}{t}}} + \iota\left(e^{-(s(-\log|\overline{b_1}|)^t)^{\frac{1}{t}}}\right) \\ e^{-(s(-\log|\underline{a_1}|)^t)^{\frac{1}{t}}} + \iota\left(e^{-(s(-\log|\underline{b_1}|)^t)^{\frac{1}{t}}}\right) \end{pmatrix}.$$

Theorem 5.1: Let $\mathcal{A}_1 = \left\{\left(\overline{a_1} + \iota\overline{b_1}, \underline{a_1} + \iota\underline{b_1}\right)\right\}$ and $\mathcal{A}_2 = \left\{\left(\overline{a_2} + \iota\overline{b_2}, \underline{a_2} + \iota\underline{b_2}\right)\right\}$ be two CFRNs with $s, s_1, s_2 > 0$, we get:

(1) $\mathcal{A}_1 \oplus \mathcal{A}_2 = \mathcal{A}_2 \oplus \mathcal{A}_1$;
(2) $\mathcal{A}_1 \otimes \mathcal{A}_2 = \mathcal{A}_2 \otimes \mathcal{A}_1$;
(3) $s\left(\mathcal{A}_1 \oplus \mathcal{A}_2\right) = s\mathcal{A}_1 \oplus s\mathcal{A}_2$;
(4) $\left(s_1 + s_2\right)\mathcal{A}_1 = s_1\mathcal{A}_1 + s_2\mathcal{A}_1$;
(5) $\left(\mathcal{A}_1 \otimes \mathcal{A}_2\right)^{\varrho} = \mathcal{A}_1^{s} \otimes \mathcal{A}_2^{s}$;
(6) $\mathcal{A}_1^{s_1} \otimes \mathcal{A}_1^{s_2} = \mathcal{A}_1^{(s_1+s_2)}$.

Proof:

From the analysis of definition (5.1), we get:

(1)

$$\mathcal{A}_1 \oplus \mathcal{A}_2 = \begin{pmatrix} 1 - e^{-\left(\left(-\log\left(1-\overline{a_1}\right)\right)^t + \left(-\log\left(1-\overline{a_2}\right)\right)^t\right)^{\frac{1}{t}}} \\ +\iota\left(1 - e^{-\left(\left(-\log\left(1-\overline{b_1}\right)\right)^t + \left(-\log\left(1-\overline{b_2}\right)\right)^t\right)^{\frac{1}{t}}}\right) \\ 1 - e^{-\left(\left(-\log\left(1-\underline{a_1}\right)\right)^t + \left(-\log\left(1-\underline{a_2}\right)\right)^t\right)^{\frac{1}{t}}} \\ +\iota\left(1 - e^{-\left(\left(-\log\left(1-\underline{b_1}\right)\right)^t + \left(-\log\left(1-\underline{b_2}\right)\right)^t\right)^{\frac{1}{t}}}\right) \end{pmatrix}$$

$$= \begin{pmatrix} 1 - e^{-\left(\left(-\log\left(1-\overline{a_2}\right)\right)^t + \left(-\log\left(1-\overline{a_1}\right)\right)^t\right)^{\frac{1}{t}}} \\ +\iota\left(1 - e^{-\left(\left(-\log\left(1-\overline{b_2}\right)\right)^t + \left(-\log\left(1-\overline{b_1}\right)\right)^t\right)^{\frac{1}{t}}}\right) \\ 1 - e^{-\left(\left(-\log\left(1-\underline{a_2}\right)\right)^t + \left(-\log\left(1-\underline{a_1}\right)\right)^t\right)^{\frac{1}{t}}} \\ +\iota\left(1 - e^{-\left(\left(-\log\left(1-\underline{b_2}\right)\right)^t + \left(-\log\left(1-\underline{b_1}\right)\right)^t\right)^{\frac{1}{t}}}\right) \end{pmatrix}.$$

$$= \mathcal{A}_2 \oplus \mathcal{A}_1.$$

(2) Omitted.

(3) From the analysis of the definition (5.1), we get:

$$s\left(\mathcal{A}_1 \oplus \mathcal{A}_2\right) =$$

$$
s\left(\begin{array}{c} 1-e^{-\left(\left(-\log(1-\overline{a_1})\right)^t+\left(-\log(1-\overline{a_2})\right)^t\right)^{\frac{1}{t}}} \\ +\iota\left(1-e^{-\left(\left(-\log\left(1-\overline{b_1}\right)\right)^t+\left(-\log\left(1-\overline{b_2}\right)\right)^t\right)^{\frac{1}{t}}}\right) \\ 1-e^{-\left(\left(-\log\left(1-\underline{a_1}\right)\right)^t+\left(-\log\left(1-\underline{a_2}\right)\right)^t\right)^{\frac{1}{t}}} \\ +\iota\left(1-e^{-\left(\left(-\log\left(1-\underline{b_1}\right)\right)^t+\left(-\log\left(1-\underline{b_2}\right)\right)^t\right)^{\frac{1}{t}}}\right) \end{array}\right)
$$

$$
=\left(\begin{array}{c} 1-e^{-\left(s\left(-\log(1-\overline{a_1})\right)^t+\left(-\log(1-\overline{a_2})\right)^t\right)^{\frac{1}{t}}} \\ +\iota\left(1-e^{-\left(s\left(-\log\left(1-\overline{b_1}\right)\right)^t+\left(-\log\left(1-\overline{b_2}\right)\right)^t\right)^{\frac{1}{t}}}\right) \\ 1-e^{-\left(s\left(-\log\left(1-\underline{a_1}\right)\right)^t+\left(-\log\left(1-\underline{a_2}\right)\right)^t\right)^{\frac{1}{t}}} \\ +\iota\left(1-e^{-\left(s\left(-\log\left(1-\underline{b_1}\right)\right)^t+\left(-\log\left(1-\underline{b_2}\right)\right)^t\right)^{\frac{1}{t}}}\right) \end{array}\right)
$$

$$
=\left(\begin{array}{c} 1-e^{-\left(s\left(-\log(1-\overline{a_1})\right)^t\right)^{\frac{1}{t}}}+\iota\left(1-e^{-\left(s\left(-\log\left(1-\overline{b_1}\right)\right)^t\right)^{\frac{1}{t}}}\right), \\ 1-e^{-\left(s\left(-\log\left(1-\underline{a_1}\right)\right)^t\right)^{\frac{1}{t}}}+\iota\left(1-e^{-\left(s\left(-\log\left(1-\underline{b_1}\right)\right)^t\right)^{\frac{1}{t}}}\right) \end{array}\right)
$$

$$
\oplus\left(\begin{array}{c} 1-e^{-\left(s\left(-\log(1-\overline{a_2})\right)^t\right)^{\frac{1}{t}}}+\iota\left(1-e^{-\left(s\left(-\log\left(1-\overline{b_2}\right)\right)^t\right)^{\frac{1}{t}}}\right), \\ 1-e^{-\left(s\left(-\log\left(1-\underline{a_2}\right)\right)^t\right)^{\frac{1}{t}}}+\iota\left(1-e^{-\left(s\left(-\log\left(1-\underline{b_2}\right)\right)^t\right)^{\frac{1}{t}}}\right) \end{array}\right).
$$

$$
= s\mathcal{A}_1 \oplus s\mathcal{A}_2.
$$

(4) From the analysis of definition (5.1), we get:

$$
s_1\mathcal{A}_1 = \left(\begin{array}{c} 1-e^{-\left(s_1\left(-\log(1-\overline{a_1})\right)^t\right)^{\frac{1}{t}}}+\iota\left(1-e^{-\left(s_1\left(-\log\left(1-\overline{b_1}\right)\right)^t\right)^{\frac{1}{t}}}\right), \\ 1-e^{-\left(s_1\left(-\log\left(1-\underline{a_1}\right)\right)^t\right)^{\frac{1}{t}}}+\iota\left(1-e^{-\left(s_1\left(-\log\left(1-\underline{b_1}\right)\right)^t\right)^{\frac{1}{t}}}\right) \end{array}\right),
$$

$$s_2\mathcal{A}_1 = \begin{pmatrix} 1-e^{-\left(s_2\left(-\log(1-\overline{a_1})\right)^t\right)^{\frac{1}{t}}} + \iota\left(1-e^{-\left(s_2\left(-\log\left(1-\overline{b_1}\right)\right)^t\right)^{\frac{1}{t}}}\right), \\ 1-e^{-\left(s_2\left(-\log\left(1-\underline{a_1}\right)\right)^t\right)^{\frac{1}{t}}} + \iota\left(1-e^{-\left(s_2\left(-\log\left(1-\underline{b_1}\right)\right)^t\right)^{\frac{1}{t}}}\right) \end{pmatrix}.$$

Then,

$$s_1\mathcal{A}_1 \oplus s_2\mathcal{A}_1 =$$

$$\begin{pmatrix} 1-e^{-\left(s_1\left(-\log(1-\overline{a_1})\right)^t\right)^{\frac{1}{t}}} + \iota\left(1-e^{-\left(s_1\left(-\log\left(1-\overline{b_1}\right)\right)^t\right)^{\frac{1}{t}}}\right), \\ 1-e^{-\left(s_1\left(-\log\left(1-\underline{a_1}\right)\right)^t\right)^{\frac{1}{t}}} + \iota\left(1-e^{-\left(s_1\left(-\log\left(1-\underline{b_1}\right)\right)^t\right)^{\frac{1}{t}}}\right) \end{pmatrix}$$

$$\oplus \begin{pmatrix} 1-e^{-\left(s_2\left(-\log(1-\overline{a_1})\right)^t\right)^{\frac{1}{t}}} + \iota\left(1-e^{-\left(s_2\left(-\log\left(1-\overline{b_1}\right)\right)^t\right)^{\frac{1}{t}}}\right), \\ 1-e^{-\left(s_2\left(-\log\left(1-\underline{a_1}\right)\right)^t\right)^{\frac{1}{t}}} + \iota\left(1-e^{-\left(s_2\left(-\log\left(1-\underline{b_1}\right)\right)^t\right)^{\frac{1}{t}}}\right) \end{pmatrix}$$

$$= \begin{pmatrix} 1-e^{-\left((s_1+s_2)\left(-\log(1-\overline{a_1})\right)^t\right)^{\frac{1}{t}}} + \iota\left(1-e^{-\left((s_1+s_2)\left(-\log\left(1-\overline{b_1}\right)\right)^t\right)^{\frac{1}{t}}}\right), \\ 1-e^{-\left((s_1+s_2)\left(-\log\left(1-\underline{a_1}\right)\right)^t\right)^{\frac{1}{t}}} + \iota\left(1-e^{-\left((s_1+s_2)\left(-\log\left(1-\underline{b_1}\right)\right)^t\right)^{\frac{1}{t}}}\right) \end{pmatrix}.$$

$$= (s_1+s_2)\,\mathcal{A}_1.$$

(5) From the analysis of definition (5.1), we get:

$$\mathcal{A}_1 \otimes \mathcal{A}_2 =$$

$$\begin{pmatrix} e^{-\left(\left(-\log(\overline{a_1})\right)^t+\left(-\log(\overline{a_2})\right)^t\right)^{\frac{1}{t}}} + \iota\left(e^{-\left(\left(-\log\left(\overline{b_1}\right)\right)^t+\left(-\log\left(\overline{b_2}\right)\right)^t\right)^{\frac{1}{t}}}\right), \\ e^{-\left(\left(-\log\left(\underline{a_1}\right)\right)^t+\left(-\log\left(\underline{a_2}\right)\right)^t\right)^{\frac{1}{t}}} + \iota\left(e^{-\left(\left(-\log\left(\underline{b_1}\right)\right)^t+\left(-\log\left(\underline{b_2}\right)\right)^t\right)^{\frac{1}{t}}}\right) \end{pmatrix},$$

$$(\mathcal{A}_1 \otimes \mathcal{A}_2)^s$$

$$= \begin{pmatrix} e^{-\left(\left(-\log(\overline{a_1})\right)^t+\left(-\log(\overline{a_2})\right)^t\right)^{\frac{1}{t}}} + \iota\left(e^{-\left(\left(-\log\left(\overline{b_1}\right)\right)^t+\left(-\log\left(\overline{b_2}\right)\right)^t\right)^{\frac{1}{t}}}\right), \\ e^{-\left(\left(-\log\left(\underline{a_1}\right)\right)^t+\left(-\log\left(\underline{a_2}\right)\right)^t\right)^{\frac{1}{t}}} + \iota\left(e^{-\left(\left(-\log\left(\underline{b_1}\right)\right)^t+\left(-\log\left(\underline{b_2}\right)\right)^t\right)^{\frac{1}{t}}}\right) \end{pmatrix}^s$$

$$= \begin{pmatrix} e^{-\left(s(-\log(\overline{a_1}))^t + (-\log(\overline{a_2}))^t\right)^{1/t}} + \iota \left(e^{-\left(s(-\log(\overline{b_1}))^t + (-\log(\overline{b_2}))^t\right)^{\frac{1}{t}}} \right), \\ e^{-\left(s(-\log(\underline{a_1}))^t + (-\log(\underline{a_2}))^t\right)^{1/t}} + \iota \left(e^{-\left(s(-\log(\underline{b_1}))^t + (-\log(\underline{b_2}))^t\right)^{\frac{1}{t}}} \right) \end{pmatrix}$$

$$= \begin{pmatrix} e^{-\left(s(-\log|\overline{a_1}|)^t\right)^{\frac{1}{t}}} + \iota \left(e^{-\left(s(-\log|\overline{b_1}|)^t\right)^{\frac{1}{t}}} \right) \\ e^{-\left(s(-\log|\underline{a_1}|)^t\right)^{\frac{1}{t}}} + \iota \left(e^{-\left(s(-\log|\underline{b_1}|)^t\right)^{\frac{1}{t}}} \right) \end{pmatrix}$$

$$\otimes \begin{pmatrix} e^{-\left(s(-\log|\overline{a_2}|)^t\right)^{\frac{1}{t}}} + \iota \left(e^{-\left(s(-\log|\overline{b_2}|)^t\right)^{\frac{1}{t}}} \right) \\ e^{-\left(s(-\log|\underline{a_2}|)^t\right)^{\frac{1}{t}}} + \iota \left(e^{-\left(s(-\log|\underline{b_2}|)^t\right)^{\frac{1}{t}}} \right) \end{pmatrix}.$$

$$= \mathcal{A}_1^s \otimes \mathcal{A}_2^s.$$

(6) From the analysis of definition (5.1), we get:

$$\mathcal{A}_1^{s_1} = \begin{pmatrix} e^{-\left(s_1(-\log|\overline{a_1}|)^t\right)^{\frac{1}{t}}} + \iota \left(e^{-\left(s_1(-\log|\overline{b_1}|)^t\right)^{\frac{1}{t}}} \right) \\ e^{-\left(s_1(-\log|\underline{a_1}|)^t\right)^{\frac{1}{t}}} + \iota \left(e^{-\left(s_1(-\log|\underline{b_1}|)^t\right)^{\frac{1}{t}}} \right) \end{pmatrix},$$

$$\mathcal{A}_1^{s_2} = \begin{pmatrix} e^{-\left(s_2(-\log|\overline{a_1}|)^t\right)^{\frac{1}{t}}} + \iota \left(e^{-\left(s_2(-\log|\overline{b_1}|)^t\right)^{\frac{1}{t}}} \right) \\ e^{-\left(s_2(-\log|\underline{a_1}|)^t\right)^{\frac{1}{t}}} + \iota \left(e^{-\left(s_2(-\log|\underline{b_1}|)^t\right)^{\frac{1}{t}}} \right) \end{pmatrix},$$

then:

$$\mathcal{A}_1^{s_1} \otimes \mathcal{A}_1^{s_2} = \begin{pmatrix} e^{-\left(s_1(-\log|\overline{a_1}|)^t\right)^{\frac{1}{t}}} + \iota \left(e^{-\left(s_1(-\log|\overline{b_1}|)^t\right)^{\frac{1}{t}}} \right) \\ e^{-\left(s_1(-\log|\underline{a_1}|)^t\right)^{\frac{1}{t}}} + \iota \left(e^{-\left(s_1(-\log|\underline{b_1}|)^t\right)^{\frac{1}{t}}} \right) \end{pmatrix}$$

$$\otimes \begin{pmatrix} e^{-\left(s_2\left(-\log|\overline{a_1}|\right)^t\right)^{\frac{1}{t}}} + \iota\left(e^{-\left(s_2\left(-\log|\overline{b_1}|\right)^t\right)^{\frac{1}{t}}}\right) \\ e^{-\left(s_2\left(-\log|\underline{a_1}|\right)^t\right)^{\frac{1}{t}}} + \iota\left(e^{-\left(s_2\left(-\log|\underline{b_1}|\right)^t\right)^{\frac{1}{t}}}\right) \end{pmatrix}$$

$$= \left(\left(\begin{matrix} e^{-\left((s_1+s_2)\left(-\log|\overline{a_1}|\right)^t\right)^{\frac{1}{t}}} + \iota\left(e^{-\left((s_1+s_2)\left(-\log|\overline{b_1}|\right)^t\right)^{\frac{1}{t}}}\right) \\ e^{-\left((s_1+s_2)\left(-\log|\underline{a_1}|\right)^t\right)^{\frac{1}{t}}} + \iota\left(e^{-\left((s_1+s_2)\left(-\log|\underline{b_1}|\right)^t\right)^{\frac{1}{t}}}\right) \end{matrix}\right)\right).$$

$$= \mathcal{A}_1^{(s_1+s_2)}.$$

5.2 Aczel-Alsina Aggregation Operators using CFR Information

This section of the chapter is about the aggregation theory of CFRNs based on the developed operational laws for CFRNs. We have introduced the idea of CFRAAWA, CFRAAOWA, and CFRAAHA AOs. To Throughout in our next study, $\mathcal{A}_j = \left\{\left(\overline{a_j} + \iota\overline{b_j},\ \underline{a_j} + \iota\underline{b_j}\right)\right\}$ $(j = 1, 2, 3, \ldots, n)$ be a family of CFRNs and $\omega = (\omega_1, \omega_2, \ldots, \omega_n)$ be a weight vector of $\mathcal{A}_j$ $(j = 1, 2, .., n)$ with $\omega_j \in [0, 1]$ and $\sum_{j=1}^{n} \omega_j = 1$.

Definition 5.2: The notion of CFRAAWA AO is proposed as

$$\begin{aligned} \mathrm{CFRAAWA}_{\omega}(\mathcal{A}_1, \mathcal{A}_2, \ldots, \mathcal{A}_n) &= \bigoplus_{j=1}^{n} (\omega_j \mathcal{A}_j) \\ &= (\omega_1 \mathcal{A}_1) \oplus (\omega_2 \mathcal{A}_2) \oplus \ldots (\omega_n \mathcal{A}_n). \end{aligned} \quad (5.1)$$

Theorem 5.2: Let $\mathcal{A}_j$ be the family of CFRNs the aggregated results obtained by using the expression of eqn (5.1) is again CFRNs and it is given by

$$\mathrm{CFRAAWA}_{\omega}(\mathcal{A}_1, \mathcal{A}_2, \ldots, \mathcal{A}_n)$$

$$= \begin{pmatrix} 1 - e^{-\left(\sum_{j=1}^{n} \omega_j (-\log(1-\overline{a_j}))^t\right)^{\frac{1}{t}}} + \iota \left(1 - e^{-\left(\sum_{j=1}^{n} \omega_j (-\log(1-\overline{b_j}))^t\right)^{\frac{1}{t}}}\right) \\ 1 - e^{-\left(\sum_{j=1}^{n} \omega_j (-\log(1-\underline{a_j}))^t\right)^{\frac{1}{t}}} + \iota \left(1 - e^{-\left(\sum_{j=1}^{n} \omega_j (-\log(1-\underline{b_j}))^t\right)^{\frac{1}{t}}}\right) \end{pmatrix}. \tag{5.2}$$

Proof: We utilize the mathematical induction method for the analysis of the result in eqn (5.2)

Now $n = 2$, we get:

$$s_1\mathcal{A}_1 = \begin{pmatrix} 1 - e^{-\left(s_1(-\log(1-\overline{a_1}))^t\right)^{\frac{1}{t}}} + \iota \left(1 - e^{-\left(s_1(-\log(1-\overline{b_1}))^t\right)^{\frac{1}{t}}}\right), \\ 1 - e^{-\left(s_1(-\log(1-\underline{a_1}))^t\right)^{\frac{1}{t}}} + \iota \left(1 - e^{-\left(s_1(-\log(1-\underline{b_1}))^t\right)^{\frac{1}{t}}}\right) \end{pmatrix}.$$

$$s_2\mathcal{A}_2 = \begin{pmatrix} 1 - e^{-\left(s_2(-\log(1-\overline{a_2}))^t\right)^{\frac{1}{t}}} + \iota \left(1 - e^{-\left(s_2(-\log(1-\overline{b_2}))^t\right)^{\frac{1}{t}}}\right), \\ 1 - e^{-\left(s_2(-\log(1-\underline{a_2}))^t\right)^{\frac{1}{t}}} + \iota \left(1 - e^{-\left(s_2(-\log(1-\underline{b_2}))^t\right)^{\frac{1}{t}}}\right) \end{pmatrix},$$

then:

$$s_1\mathcal{A}_1 \oplus s_2\mathcal{A}_2 =$$

$$\begin{pmatrix} 1 - e^{-\left(s_1(-\log(1-\overline{a_1}))^t\right)^{\frac{1}{t}}} + \iota \left(1 - e^{-\left(s_1(-\log(1-\overline{b_1}))^t\right)^{\frac{1}{t}}}\right), \\ 1 - e^{-\left(s_1(-\log(1-\underline{a_1}))^t\right)^{\frac{1}{t}}} + \iota \left(1 - e^{-\left(s_1(-\log(1-\underline{b_1}))^t\right)^{\frac{1}{t}}}\right) \end{pmatrix}$$

$$\oplus \begin{pmatrix} 1 - e^{-\left(s_2(-\log(1-\overline{a_2}))^t\right)^{\frac{1}{t}}} + \iota \left(1 - e^{-\left(s_2(-\log(1-\overline{b_2}))^t\right)^{\frac{1}{t}}}\right), \\ 1 - e^{-\left(s_2(-\log(1-\underline{a_2}))^t\right)^{\frac{1}{t}}} + \iota \left(1 - e^{-\left(s_2(-\log(1-\underline{b_2}))^t\right)^{\frac{1}{t}}}\right) \end{pmatrix}$$

$$= \begin{pmatrix} 1 - e^{-\left(\sum_{j=1}^{2} \omega_j (-\log(1-\overline{a_j}))^t\right)^{\frac{1}{t}}} + \iota \left(1 - e^{-\left(\sum_{j=1}^{2} \omega_j (-\log(1-\overline{a_j}))^t\right)^{\frac{1}{t}}}\right) \\ 1 - e^{-\left(\sum_{j=1}^{2} \omega_j (-\log(1-\underline{a_j}))^t\right)^{\frac{1}{t}}} + \iota \left(1 - e^{-\left(\sum_{j=1}^{2} \omega_j (-\log(1-\underline{b_j}))^t\right)^{\frac{1}{t}}}\right) \end{pmatrix}.$$

Hence, for $n = 2$, eqn (5.2) is valid.
Now assume that for $n = r$, then eqn (5.2) is true, that is:

$$\mathrm{CFRAAWA}_{\omega}\left(\mathcal{A}_1,\, \mathcal{A}_2,\ldots,\, \mathcal{A}_r\right) = \bigoplus_{j=1}^{r}\left(\omega_j \mathcal{A}_j\right)$$

$$= \begin{pmatrix} 1-e^{-\left(\sum_{j=1}^{r}\omega_j\left(-\log\left(1-\overline{a_j}\right)\right)^t\right)^{\frac{1}{t}}} + \iota\left(1-e^{-\left(\sum_{j=1}^{r}\omega_j\left(-\log\left(1-\overline{b_j}\right)\right)^t\right)^{\frac{1}{t}}}\right) \\ 1-e^{-\left(\sum_{j=1}^{r}\omega_j\left(-\log\left(1-\underline{a_j}\right)\right)^t\right)^{\frac{1}{t}}} + \iota\left(1-e^{-\left(\sum_{j=1}^{r}\omega_j\left(-\log\left(1-\underline{b_j}\right)\right)^t\right)^{\frac{1}{t}}}\right) \end{pmatrix}.$$

Now we prove the result for $n = r + 1$, we get:

$$\mathrm{CFRAAWA}_{\omega}\left(\mathcal{A}_1,\, \mathcal{A}_2,\ldots,\, \mathcal{A}_{r+1}\right) = \bigoplus_{j=1}^{r+1}\left(\omega_j \mathcal{A}_j\right) \oplus \left(\omega_{r+1}\mathcal{A}_{r+1}\right)$$

$$= \begin{pmatrix} 1-e^{-\left(\sum_{j=1}^{r}\omega_j\left(-\log\left(1-\overline{a_j}\right)\right)^t\right)^{\frac{1}{t}}} + \iota\left(1-e^{-\left(\sum_{j=1}^{r}\omega_j\left(-\log\left(1-\overline{b_j}\right)\right)^t\right)^{\frac{1}{t}}}\right) \\ 1-e^{-\left(\sum_{j=1}^{r}\omega_j\left(-\log\left(1-\underline{a_j}\right)\right)^t\right)^{\frac{1}{t}}} + \iota\left(1-e^{-\left(\sum_{j=1}^{r}\omega_j\left(-\log\left(1-\underline{b_j}\right)\right)^t\right)^{\frac{1}{t}}}\right) \end{pmatrix}$$

$$\oplus \begin{pmatrix} 1-e^{-\left(s_{r+1}\left(-\log\left(1-\overline{a_{r+1}}\right)\right)^t\right)^{\frac{1}{t}}} + \iota\left(1-e^{-\left(s_{r+1}\left(-\log\left(1-\overline{b_{r+1}}\right)\right)^t\right)^{\frac{1}{t}}}\right), \\ 1-e^{-\left(s_{r+1}\left(-\log\left(1-\underline{a_{r+1}}\right)\right)^t\right)^{\frac{1}{t}}} + \iota\left(1-e^{-\left(s_{r+1}\left(-\log\left(1-\underline{b_{r+1}}\right)\right)^t\right)^{\frac{1}{t}}}\right) \end{pmatrix}$$

$$= \begin{pmatrix} 1-e^{-\left(\sum_{j=1}^{r+1}\omega_j\left(-\log\left(1-\overline{a_j}\right)\right)^t\right)^{\frac{1}{t}}} + \iota\left(1-e^{-\left(\sum_{j=1}^{r+1}\omega_j\left(-\log\left(1-\overline{b_j}\right)\right)^t\right)^{\frac{1}{t}}}\right) \\ 1-e^{-\left(\sum_{j=1}^{r+1}\omega_j\left(-\log\left(1-\underline{a_j}\right)\right)^t\right)^{\frac{1}{t}}} + \iota\left(1-e^{-\left(\sum_{j=1}^{r+1}\omega_j\left(-\log\left(1-\underline{b_j}\right)\right)^t\right)^{\frac{1}{t}}}\right) \end{pmatrix}.$$

Definition 5.3: The idea of CFRAAOWA AOs is delivered as

$$\mathrm{CFRAAOWA}_{\omega}\left(\mathcal{A}_1,\, \mathcal{A}_2,\ldots,\, \mathcal{A}_n\right) = \bigoplus_{j=1}^{n}\left(\omega_j \mathcal{A}_{\mathbb{O}(j)}\right) =$$

$$\left(\omega_1\mathcal{A}_{\mathbb{O}(1)}\right) \oplus \left(\omega_2\mathcal{A}_{\mathbb{O}(2)}\right) \oplus \ldots \left(\omega_n\mathcal{A}_{\mathbb{O}(n)}\right) =$$

$$\begin{pmatrix} 1-e^{-\left(\sum_{j=1}^{n}\omega_j\left(-\log\left(1-\overline{a_{\mathbb{O}(j)}}\right)\right)^t\right)^{\frac{1}{t}}} + \iota\left(1-e^{-\left(\sum_{j=1}^{n}\omega_j\left(-\log\left(1-\overline{a_{\mathbb{O}(j)}}\right)\right)^t\right)^{\frac{1}{t}}}\right) \\ 1-e^{-\left(\sum_{j=1}^{n}\omega_j\left(-\log\left(1-\underline{a_{\mathbb{O}(j)}}\right)\right)^t\right)^{\frac{1}{t}}} + \iota\left(1-e^{-\left(\sum_{j=1}^{n}\omega_j\left(-\log\left(1-\underline{b_{\mathbb{O}(j)}}\right)\right)^t\right)^{\frac{1}{t}}}\right) \end{pmatrix},$$

where, $(\mathbb{O}(1), \mathbb{O}(2), \mathbb{O}(3), \ldots, \mathbb{O}(n))$ are the permutation of $(j = 1, 2, .., n)$ for which $\mathcal{A}_{\mathbb{O}(j-1)} \geq \mathcal{A}_{\mathbb{O}(j)}\ \forall\, j$.

Definition 5.4: The idea of CFRAAHA AOs is given by

$$\text{CFRAAHA}_{\mathfrak{e},\omega}(\mathcal{A}_1, \mathcal{A}_2, \ldots, \mathcal{A}_n) = \bigoplus_{j=1}^{n}\left(\omega_j\mathcal{A}^*_{\mathbb{O}(j)}\right)$$

$$= \left(\omega_1\mathcal{A}^*_{\mathbb{O}(1)}\right) \oplus \left(\omega_2\mathcal{A}^*_{\mathbb{O}(2)}\right) \oplus \ldots \left(\omega_n\mathcal{A}^*_{\mathbb{O}(n)}\right)$$

$$= \begin{pmatrix} 1-e^{-\left(\sum_{j=1}^{n}\omega_j\left(-\log\left(1-\overline{a^*_{\mathbb{O}(j)}}\right)\right)^t\right)^{\frac{1}{t}}} + \iota\left(1-e^{-\left(\sum_{j=1}^{n}\omega_j\left(-\left(1-\overline{b^*_{\mathbb{O}(j)}}\right)\right)^t\right)^{\frac{1}{t}}}\right) \\ 1-e^{-\left(\sum_{j=1}^{n}\omega_j\left(-\log\left(1-\underline{a^*_{\mathbb{O}(j)}}\right)\right)^t\right)^{\frac{1}{t}}} + \iota\left(1-e^{-\left(\sum_{j=1}^{n}\omega_j\left(-\log\left(1-\underline{b^*_{\mathbb{O}(j)}}\right)\right)^t\right)^{\frac{1}{t}}}\right) \end{pmatrix},$$

where, $\mathcal{A}^*_{\mathbb{O}(j)} = n\mathfrak{e}_j\mathcal{A}_j$, $(j = 1, 2, 3, .., n)$, $\left(\mathcal{A}^*_{\mathbb{O}(1)}, \mathcal{A}^*_{\mathbb{O}(2)}, \ldots, \mathcal{A}^*_{\mathbb{O}(n)}\right)$ is any permutation of a collection of the weighted CFRNs $(\mathcal{A}^*_1, \mathcal{A}^*_2, \ldots, \mathcal{A}^*_n)$, such that $\mathcal{A}^*_{\mathbb{O}(j-1)} \geq \mathcal{A}^*_{\mathbb{O}(j)}\ \forall\, j$, $\mathfrak{e} = (\mathfrak{e}_1, \mathfrak{e}_2, \ldots, \mathfrak{e}_n)^T$ is the WV and n is the balancing coefficient.

5.3 Application of the Proposed Theory in Multiattribute Decision-making (MADM)

This section of the chapter is devoted to defining an algorithm that can help us to prose the utilization of introduced notions to solve decision-making problems. Here we have verified the utilization of established work by providing the application of initiated theory. The decision-making algorithm and its illustrative example are given by

5.3.1 Decision-making procedure

Assume that there are m alternatives and a set of alternatives is given by $\mathfrak{L} = \{\mathfrak{L}_1, \mathfrak{L}_2, \ldots, \mathfrak{L}_m\}$. The "$n$" attributes of these alternatives are denoted by $\mathbb{T} = \{\mathbb{T}_1, \mathbb{T}_2, \ldots, \mathbb{T}_n\}$. The weights of these attributes $\omega_j = (\omega_1, \omega_2, \ldots, \omega_n)^T$ such that $\sum_{j=1}^{n} \omega_j = 1$ and $\omega_j \in [0, 1]\ \forall\ j$. Assume that the decision analyst provides theory assessment in the form of CFRNs given by $\mathcal{A}_{ij} = \left\{\left(\overline{a_{ij}} + \iota\overline{b_{ij}},\ \underline{a_{ij}} + \iota\underline{b_{ij}}\right)\right\}$ for $i = 1, 2, 3, .., m$ and $j = 1, 2, 3, \ldots, n$. Now step-wise algorithm is given by

Step 1: Collect the information in the form of CFRNs proposed by decision makers and arrange it in the form of matric given by

$$\mathcal{M} = \begin{bmatrix} \mathcal{A}_{11} & \mathcal{A}_{12} & \ldots & \mathcal{A}_{1n} \\ \mathcal{A}_{21} & \mathcal{A}_{22} & \ldots & \mathcal{A}_{2n} \\ \vdots & \ddots & \ldots & \vdots \\ \mathcal{A}_{m1} & \mathcal{A}_{m2} & & \mathcal{A}_{mn} \end{bmatrix}.$$

Step 2: Utilize the following formula, if there is a need to normalize the information based on the information of cost type or benefit type attributes. The formulas are given by

$$\mathcal{N} = \begin{cases} \mathcal{A}_{ij} & \text{for benefit type attributes} \\ (\mathcal{A}_{ij})^c & \text{for cost type attributes} \end{cases},$$

where $(\mathcal{A}_{ij})^c = \left\{\left(\left(1 - \underline{a_{ij}}\right) + \iota\left(1 - \underline{b_{ij}}\right), (1 - \overline{a_{ij}}) + \iota\left(1 - \overline{b_{ij}}\right)\right)\right\}$ represent the complement of $\mathcal{A}_{ij}$.

Step 3: In this step, we aggregate the information obtained from step 2 by using the proposed notion of CFRAAWA or CFRAAOWA operators.

Step 4: Find out the score values by using the formula given in definition 1.12.

Step 5: Rank the alternatives according to the result obtained through step 4 and obtain the best alternative according to ranking order.

To show the utilization of the developed approach, we have provided a case study of the developed approach in the following example.

5.3.2 Illustrated example

Advanced technologies changed the design and analysis of electrical engineering. These technologies model and simulate systems with a high degree of accuracy and optimization analysis for complex systems. AI algorithms support predictive maintenance, fault detection, and energy management in smart grids and renewable energy systems. Internet of Things (IoT) devices and sensors facilitate real-time monitoring and control in industrial and household environments. Advancements in power electronics include high-efficiency inverters and wide-bandgap semiconductors, which result in energy-efficient systems. Additive manufacturing or 3D printing has made prototyping of customized electrical components cheaper in shorter times. Cloud computing allows design, storage, and scalability for computations which are often needed for big projects. The future generation of electronics and energy storage will be powered by advanced materials like graphene and superconductors. Next-generation electrical systems demand the inclusion of modern telecommunication networks into the electrical systems through the incorporation of high-speed communication protocols and fiber optics. The digital infrastructures are consequently being protected by cybersecurity frameworks through sensitive data. After all, these technologies are helping create sustainable, reliable, and intelligent electrical systems for today's demands.

Here we have discussed the four recent technologies used in electrical engineering and our basic motive is to choose the best alternative from these technologies. The description of each technology is given by

* *Artificial intelligence in power systems*

AI is revolutionizing power networks by predicting demand, optimizing energy use, and quickly identifying grid faults. Engineers employ AI to integrate renewable energy sources, enhance energy storage systems, and predict energy output based on weather data. AI-driven smart meters and fault detection systems contribute to the development of a more dependable and effective electrical infrastructure by reducing outages and improving reliability.

* *Smart grids*:

These state-of-the-art electrical networks use digital technologies to efficiently manage energy distribution and incorporate renewable energy sources like wind and solar. Smart grids enable real-time monitoring, load control, and demand response systems. They also incorporate energy storage technologies and boost system resilience to balance different renewable energy sources.

* *Internet of Things (IoT) in electrical engineering*:

Examples of networked devices that may exchange data and operate without interruption are smart appliances and industrial machinery, which are made possible by the Internet of Things. IoT-enabled smart grids and smart homes monitor energy use, boost productivity, and enable remote device control. By reducing energy use and providing information on usage patterns, these gadgets aid in the achievement of sustainability objectives.

* *Renewable energy technologies*:

Innovations in wind, solar, and hydroelectric power are increasing sustainability and efficiency. Engineers are also refining solar cells and creating other methods such as wave and tidal energy. These developments contribute to the global transition to renewable energy sources, reduce carbon emissions, and decrease reliance on fossil fuels.

The attributes of these technologies and their explanation are given in the following Table 5.1.

Assume that the WVs of attributes are $\omega = (0.29, 0.22, 0.21, 0.28)$. Now based on this information, we have to utilize the proposed algorithm for the selection of the best alternative to show the applicability of the developed approach in decision making.

Step 1: The information provided by the decision analyst in the form of CFRNs is given in Table 5.2.

Step 2: No need to normalize the information given in Table 5.2 because all data is of benefit type.

Step 3: Utilize the notion of CFRAAWA and CFRAAOWA to aggregate the information given in Table 5.2. The aggregated results are given in Table 5.3.

Step 4: The score values of the data given in Table 5.3 are calculated by the formula given in definition (1.12) and overall results are given in Table 5.4.

Step 5: In the light of results given in Table 5.4, the ranking results are given in Table 5.5.

From the analysis of Table 5.5, we can see that in the case of CFRAAWA AOs $\mathfrak{L}_4$ is the best alternative and in the case of CFRAAOWA AOs $\mathfrak{L}_1$ is the best alternative.

The graphical representation of the data given in Table 5.4 is depicted in Figure 5.1.

Table 5.1 Attributes and their explanations.

Attributes
(1) ***Energy efficiency*** Electrical engineering solutions seek to maximize energy efficiency by reducing energy loss during power generation, transmission, and consumption. For example, superconductors and other advanced materials lower resistive losses. Improvements in renewable energy sources, such as solar panels and wind turbines, highlight efficiency even more. Smart grids employ real-time data to enhance energy distribution and use. This emphasis reduces expenses while also minimizing the environmental impact.
(2) ***Automation and control*** Automation is incorporated into contemporary electrical systems to increase accuracy and decrease human involvement. Automated control in home and industrial applications is made possible by technologies such as microcontrollers and programmable logic controllers (PLCs). Automation in power systems guarantees quicker load balancing and fault detection. Predictive maintenance makes use of machine learning algorithms and sophisticated robotics. These developments improve the efficiency and dependability of the system.
(3) ***Miniaturization*** Electrical engineering technologies are always becoming smaller while retaining or improving functionality. Integrated circuits (ICs), a type of microelectronic innovation, have transformed everything from computers to medical implants. Wearable and portable electronics like smartwatches and smartphones are made possible via miniaturization. Additionally, it encourages the development of nanotechnology for uses such as high-performance sensors. Compact designs make systems more sustainable by using less energy and materials.
(4) ***Durability and reliability*** Technologies developed by electrical engineers are made to endure a variety of operating and environmental circumstances. Long-term use, stress absorption, and heat resistance are all prioritized in the materials and designs. Systems with high reliability are essential in fields like medical devices and aircraft. In critical situations, functionality is guaranteed via redundant systems and fail-safes. Increased durability boosts lifespan performance and lowers maintenance expenses.

Table 5.2 CFR data.

	$\mathbb{T}_1$	$\mathbb{T}_2$	$\mathbb{T}_3$	$\mathbb{T}_4$
$\mathfrak{L}_1$	$\begin{pmatrix} 0.23+\iota 0.10, \\ 0.24+\iota\, 0.16 \end{pmatrix}$	$\begin{pmatrix} 0.12+\iota 0.49, \\ 0.13+\iota\, 0.36 \end{pmatrix}$	$\begin{pmatrix} 0.59+\iota 0.20, \\ 0.41+\iota\, 0.66 \end{pmatrix}$	$\begin{pmatrix} 0.14+\iota 0.59, \\ 0.14+\iota\, 0.36 \end{pmatrix}$
$\mathfrak{L}_2$	$\begin{pmatrix} 0.25+\iota 0.15, \\ 0.27+\iota\, 0.17 \end{pmatrix}$	$\begin{pmatrix} 0.14+\iota 0.10, \\ 0.16+\iota\, 0.11 \end{pmatrix}$	$\begin{pmatrix} 0.69+\iota 0.59, \\ 0.71+\iota\, 0.56 \end{pmatrix}$	$\begin{pmatrix} 0.29+\iota 0.20, \\ 0.69+\iota\, 0.46 \end{pmatrix}$
$\mathfrak{L}_3$	$\begin{pmatrix} 0.37+\iota 0.24, \\ 0.49+\iota\, 0.19 \end{pmatrix}$	$\begin{pmatrix} 0.38+\iota 0.14, \\ 0.21+\iota\, 0.13 \end{pmatrix}$	$\begin{pmatrix} 0.39+\iota 0.33, \\ 0.21+\iota\, 0.36 \end{pmatrix}$	$\begin{pmatrix} 0.59+\iota 0.50, \\ 0.61+\iota\, 0.46 \end{pmatrix}$
$\mathfrak{L}_4$	$\begin{pmatrix} 0.57+\iota 0.16, \\ 0.64+\iota\, 0.13 \end{pmatrix}$	$\begin{pmatrix} 0.29+\iota 0.17, \\ 0.10+\iota\, 0.18 \end{pmatrix}$	$\begin{pmatrix} 0.19+\iota 0.19, \\ 0.21+\iota\, 0.15 \end{pmatrix}$	$\begin{pmatrix} 0.29+\iota 0.80, \\ 0.47+\iota\, 0.56 \end{pmatrix}$

Table 5.3 Aggregated results by using CFRAAWA or CFRAAOWA AOs.

Operators	$\mathfrak{L}_1$	$\mathfrak{L}_2$	$\mathfrak{L}_3$	$\mathfrak{L}_4$
CFRAAWA	$\begin{pmatrix} 0.1347 + \iota 0.1865, \\ 0.1080 + \iota 0.1952 \end{pmatrix}$	$\begin{pmatrix} 0.1805 + \iota 0.1298, \\ 0.2677 + \iota 0.1684 \end{pmatrix}$	$\begin{pmatrix} 0.2269 + \iota 0.1562, \\ 0.2159 + \iota 0.1439 \end{pmatrix}$	$\begin{pmatrix} 0.1811 + \iota 0.2248, \\ 0.2113 + \iota 01409 \end{pmatrix}$
CFRAAOWA	$\begin{pmatrix} 0.2838 + \iota 0.2227, \\ 0.3088 + \iota 0.1894 \end{pmatrix}$	$\begin{pmatrix} 0.2029 + \iota 0.2328, \\ 0.2075 + \iota 0.2118 \end{pmatrix}$	$\begin{pmatrix} 0.1442 + \iota 0.0969, \\ 0.1924 + \iota 0.1462 \end{pmatrix}$	$\begin{pmatrix} 0.0814 + \iota 0.1401, \\ 0.0870 + \iota 0.0971 \end{pmatrix}$

Table 5.4 Shown the SVs of the aggregated values.

Operators	$Scor.(\mathfrak{L}_1)$	$Scor.(\mathfrak{L}_2)$	$scor.(\mathfrak{L}_3)$	$scor.(\mathfrak{L}_4)$
CFRAAWA	0.1561	0.1866	0.1857	0.1894
CFRAAOWA	0.2512	0.2138	0.1449	0.1014

Table 5.5 Ranking results.

Operators	Ranking
CFRAAWA	$\mathfrak{L}_4 > \mathfrak{L}_2 > \mathfrak{L}_3 > \mathfrak{L}_1$
CFRAAOWA	$\mathfrak{L}_1 > \mathfrak{L}_2 > \mathfrak{L}_3 > \mathfrak{L}_4$

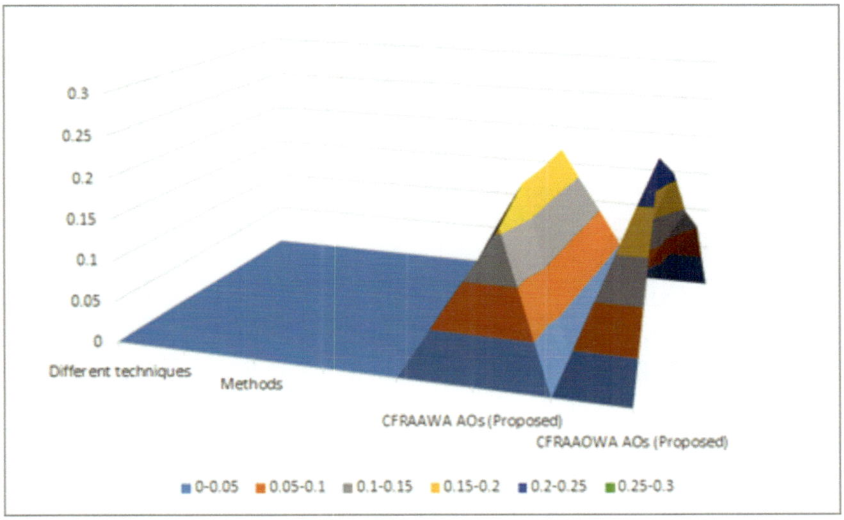

Figure 5.1 Graphical representation of data given in Table 5.4.

5.4 Comparative Analysis

We have compared our deliberated work with several existing studies, including Bi et al. [17], Bi et al. [18], Hu et al. [20], Khan et al. [14], Hussain et al. [19], and Mahmood et al. [21], to assess the influence and dominance of the diagnosed work. In this section, we have discussed the benefits of the established approach using the data from Table 5.3 and the results from Table 5.4.

Bi et al. [17] and Bi et al. [18] diagnosed arithmetic and geometric AOs for CF sets respectively which can deal with two-dimensional data but these notions are based on the polar form of CFS and this approach can never discuss the data of the $0.9+\iota 0.6$. We can notice that in the existing notion, the necessary condition is used that the amplitude term must belong to [0, 1] but in this case, we can observe that $\sqrt{0.9^2+0.6^2} \notin [0,\ 1]$. Hence in this case the limitation of the previous literature is obvious. We can say that the form of the CFR set can cover more advanced information and provide the opportunity for decision-makers to solve theory issues through the environment of the CFR structure.

Also, we can see that in the case of Bi et al. [17, 18] approaches, the chance of data loss increases because these approaches can never discuss the upper and lower approximation of information. The delivered approach can discover all these limitations in previous theories and provide a suitable way of finding the best alternative by using the advanced notion of CFRN. In this case, the chance of data loss decreases and decision-makers can rely more

Table 5.6 Mentioned the comparison between proposed and existing work.

Operators	Scor. $(\mathfrak{L}_1)$	Scor. $(\mathfrak{L}_2)$	Scor. $(\mathfrak{L}_3)$	Scor. $(\mathfrak{L}_4)$	**Ranking**
Bi et al. [17]	Failed	Failed	Failed	Failed	Failed
Bi et al. [18]	Failed	Failed	Failed	Failed	Failed
Hu et al. [20] approach	Failed	Failed	Failed	Failed	Failed
Khan et al. [14] approach	Failed	Failed	Failed	Failed	Failed
Hussain et al. [19] approach	Failed	Failed	Failed	Failed	Failed
Mahmood et al. [21]	Failed	Failed	Failed	Failed	Failed
CFRAAWA	0.1561	0.1866	0.1857	0.1894	$\mathfrak{L}_4 > \mathfrak{L}_2 > \mathfrak{L}_3 > \mathfrak{L}_1$
CFRAAOWA	0.2512	0.2138	0.1449	0.1014	$\mathfrak{L}_1 > \mathfrak{L}_2 > \mathfrak{L}_3 > \mathfrak{L}_4$

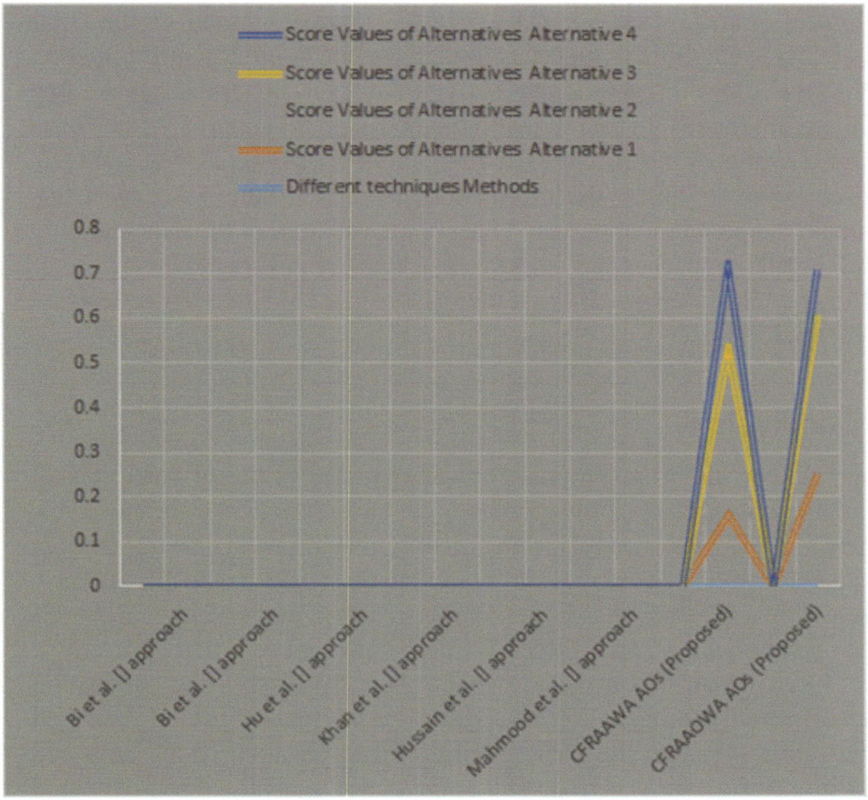

Figure 5.2 Graphical representation of data given in Table 5.6.

strongly on this structure. In the case of Hu et al. [20] we can see that this approach is based on a fuzzy rough set model and this approach can never discuss the two-dimensional information proposed in Table 5.2. The delivered approach can discuss this kind of information. So the devised approach is more suitable and reliable as compared to the Hu et al. [20] approach.

In the case of Khan et al. [14], we can observe that although this approach is more advanced than the approach of Hu et al. [20] because it can cover the upper and lower approximation, this approach can never discuss Tamir's complex fuzzy data and in this way, we can say that in fuzzy set theory the Tamir's complex fuzzy form can cover more advance information than the idea of polar form. Hence the established ideas are based on Tamir's complex fuzzy form so these theories are superior to existing notions developed by Khan et al. [14].

Hussain et al. [19] delivered the TOPSIS approach based on the polar form of CFRS and this approach has limitations due to its structure condition that the amplitude term belongs to [0, 1], while initiated approaches are free from these limitations. In the case of Mahmood et al. [21] approach, they have developed similarity measures based on a complex hesitant fuzzy set, and this approach can never discuss the information provided in Table 5.3 because this information is based on upper and lower approximation of the data and only the developed approaches can discuss these kinds of information.

The graphical representation of the results given in Table 5.6 is depicted in Figure 5.2.

5.5 Conclusion

In this chapter, we have proposed the importance of fuzzy structures in electrical engineering. For this purpose, we have determined the problems faced by technologies and tools in electrical engineering and discussed which tools and technology can play a role in solving these issues. For this purpose, we have delivered a novel aggregation theory based on fundamental Aczel-Alsina operational laws for CFRNs. We have delivered AOs like CFRAAWA AOs, CFRAAOWA AOs and CFRAAHA AOs. To discuss the application of the delivered approach, we have discussed an algorithm and delivered an illustrative example. We have proposed the application of the proposed theory in electrical engineering. The comparative analysis of the delivered approach with other existing theories shows the superiority and dominance of the initiated work.

6

Innovative AI Solutions through the Utilization of Complex Fuzzy Rough Set Theory

The introduction of innovative artificial intelligence (AI) solutions has changed different fields, including diagnostics, autonomous systems, and intelligent decision support systems. However, these advanced AI solutions that are used in real-world applications, have limitations in dealing with complex, uncertain, and rough information in MCDM problems. This chapter presents a new mathematical model that improves the ability of AI systems by incorporating the CFRS theory. We develop several sophisticated operators: There are complex fuzzy rough power averaging (CFRPA), complex fuzzy rough power weighted averaging (CFRPWA), complex fuzzy rough power geometric (CFRPG), and complex fuzzy rough power weighted geometric (CFRPWG). These operators are particularly developed to aggregate CFR in MCDM problems, which offers a stable framework to deal with uncertainty, roughness, and multidimensionality of data. In addition, we present a detailed MCDM approach that can efficiently handle problems with complex fuzzy rough data, especially concerning AI solution selection. The actual usefulness of the proposed theoretical framework is illustrated by a comprehensive case study devoted to the identification of the best AI solutions for enterprise deployment. A comparison of our approach with existing methodologies shows the effectiveness of the proposed approach in dealing with multiple decision parameters and uncertain information. This integrated framework not only improves the decision-making process for selecting AI solutions but also defines a new paradigm for AI solution evaluation and implementation in different domains.

DOI: 10.1201/9788743807827-6

6.1 Power AOs for CFRNs

Here, we interpret power AOs for aggregating CFR information, these operations are CFRPA, CFRPWA, CFRPG, and CFRPWG operators.

Definition 6.1: Let an assembly $\mathcal{A}_j = \left\{ \left(\overline{a_j} + \iota \overline{b_j},\ \underline{a_j} + \iota \underline{b_j} \right) \right\}, (j = 1,\ 2,\ 3,\ \ldots,\ n)$ of CFRNs. Then the CFRPA operator is scrutinized as

$$\text{CFRPA}\left(\mathcal{A}_1,\ \mathcal{A}_2,\ \mathcal{A}_3,\ \ldots,\ \mathcal{A}_n\right) = \bigoplus_{j=1}^{n} \frac{1 + T\left(\mathcal{A}_j\right)}{\sum_{j=1}^{n} \left(1 + T\left(\mathcal{A}_j\right)\right)} \mathcal{A}_j.$$

Observe that $\mathrm{T}\left(\mathcal{A}_j\right) = \sum_{\substack{j=1 \\ j \neq r}}^{n} \text{Sup}\left(\mathcal{A}_j,\ \mathcal{A}_r\right)$ and $\text{Sup}\left(\mathcal{A}_j,\ \mathcal{A}_r\right)$ infers the support for $\mathcal{A}_j$ from $\mathcal{A}_r$ with the axioms given below.

- $\text{Sup}\left(\mathcal{A}_j,\ \mathcal{A}_r\right) \in [0,\ 1]$;
- $\text{Sup}\left(\mathcal{A}_j,\ \mathcal{A}_r\right) = \text{Sup}\left(\mathcal{A}_r,\ \mathcal{A}_j\right)$;
- $\text{Sup}\left(\mathcal{A}_j,\ \mathcal{A}_r\right) \geq \text{Sup}\left(\mathcal{A}_{j'},\ \mathcal{A}_{r'}\right)$ if $đ\left(\mathcal{A}_j,\ \mathcal{A}_r\right) < đ\left(\mathcal{A}_{j'},\ \mathcal{A}_{r'}\right)$, đ can be a distance measure among CFRSs, that is:

$$đ\left(\mathcal{A}_1,\ \mathcal{A}_2\right) = \frac{1}{4}\left(\left|\overline{a_1} - \overline{a_2}\right| + \left|\overline{b_1} - \overline{b_2}\right| + \left|\underline{a_1} - \underline{a_2}\right| + \left|\underline{b_1} - \underline{b_2}\right| \right),$$

where $\mathcal{A}_j = \left\{ \left(\overline{a_j} + \iota \overline{b_j},\ \underline{a_j} + \iota \underline{b_j} \right) \right\},\ (j = 1,\ 2)$.

Theorem 6.1: Let an assembly $\mathcal{A}_j = \left\{ \left(\overline{a_j} + \iota \overline{b_j},\ \underline{a_j} + \iota \underline{b_j} \right) \right\}, (j = 1,\ 2,\ 3,\ \ldots,\ n)$ of CFRNs. Then the usage of the CFRPA operator over $\mathcal{A}_j$ will give a CFRN, that is:

$$\text{CFRPA}\left(\mathcal{A}_1,\ \mathcal{A}_2,\ \mathcal{A}_3,\ \ldots,\ \mathcal{A}_n\right) = \begin{pmatrix} 1 - \prod_{j=1}^{n} \left(1 - \overline{a_j}\right)^{\chi_j} + \iota \left(1 - \prod_{j=1}^{n} \left(1 - \overline{b_j}\right)^{\chi_j}\right), \\ 1 - \prod_{j=1}^{n} \left(1 - \underline{a_j}\right)^{\chi_j} + \iota \left(1 - \prod_{j=1}^{n} \left(1 - \underline{b_j}\right)^{\chi_j}\right) \end{pmatrix}. \quad (6.1)$$

Proof: Let $n = 2$. Then, we have:

$$\text{CFRPA}\left(\mathcal{A}_1,\ \mathcal{A}_2\right) = \chi_1 \mathcal{A}_1 \oplus \chi_2 \mathcal{A}_2,$$

and as

$$\chi_1\mathcal{A}_1 = \begin{pmatrix} \left(1-(1-\overline{a_1})^{\chi_1} + \iota\left(1-\ (1-\overline{b_1})^{\chi_1}\right)\right), \\ \left(1-(1-\underline{a_1})^{\chi_1} + \iota\ (1-\ (1-\underline{b_1})^{\chi_1})\right) \end{pmatrix},$$

$$\chi_2\mathcal{A}_2 = \begin{pmatrix} \left(1-(1-\overline{a_2})^{\chi_2} + \iota\left(1-\ (1-\overline{b_2})^{\chi_2}\right)\right), \\ \left(1-(1-\underline{a_2})^{\chi_2} + \iota\ (1-\ (1-\underline{b_2})^{\chi_2})\right) \end{pmatrix},$$

$$\chi_1\mathcal{A}_1 \oplus \chi_2\mathcal{A}_2 = \begin{pmatrix} \left(1-(1-\overline{a_1})^{\chi_1} + \iota\left(1-\ (1-\overline{b_1})^{\chi_1}\right)\right), \\ \left(1-(1-\underline{a_1})^{\chi_1} + \iota\ (1-\ (1-\underline{b_1})^{\chi_1})\right) \end{pmatrix}$$

$$\oplus \begin{pmatrix} \left(1-(1-\overline{a_2})^{\chi_2} + \iota\left(1-\ (1-\overline{b_2})^{\chi_2}\right)\right), \\ \left(1-(1-\underline{a_2})^{\chi_2} + \iota\ (1-\ (1-\underline{b_2})^{\chi_2})\right) \end{pmatrix}$$

$$= \begin{pmatrix} \left(1-(1-\overline{a_1})^{\chi_1}(1-\overline{a_2})^{\chi_2} + \iota\, 1-(1-\overline{b_1})^{\chi_1}(1-\overline{b_2})^{\chi_2}\right), \\ 1-(1-\underline{a_1})^{\chi_1}(1-\underline{a_2})^{\chi_2} + \iota\, 1-(1-\underline{b_1})^{\chi_1}(1-\underline{b_2})^{\chi_2} \end{pmatrix}$$

$$= \begin{pmatrix} 1-\prod_{j=1}^{2}(1-\overline{a_j})^{\chi_j} + \iota\left(1-\prod_{j=1}^{2}(1-\overline{b_j})^{\chi_j}\right), \\ 1-\prod_{j=1}^{2}\left(1-\underline{a_j}\right)^{\chi_j} + \iota\left(1-\prod_{j=1}^{2}\left(1-\underline{b_j}\right)^{\chi_j}\right) \end{pmatrix}.$$

Thus, eqn (6.1) holds for $n = 2$. Next let for $n = r$, eqn (6.1) holds. Then:

$$\text{CFRPA}\,(\mathcal{A}_1,\ \mathcal{A}_2,\ \mathcal{A}_3,\ \ldots,\ \mathcal{A}_r)$$
$$= \begin{pmatrix} 1-\prod_{j=1}^{r}(1-\overline{a_j})^{\chi_j} + \iota\left(1-\prod_{j=1}^{r}(1-\overline{b_j})^{\chi_j}\right), \\ 1-\prod_{j=1}^{r}\left(1-\underline{a_j}\right)^{\chi_j} + \iota\left(1-\prod_{j=1}^{r}\left(1-\underline{b_j}\right)^{\chi_j}\right) \end{pmatrix}.$$

Finally, let $n = r + 1$. Then:

$$\text{CFRPA}\,(\mathcal{A}_1,\ \mathcal{A}_2,\ \mathcal{A}_3,\ \ldots,\ \mathcal{A}_r,\ \mathcal{A}_{r+1})$$
$$= \begin{pmatrix} 1-\prod_{j=1}^{r}(1-\overline{a_j})^{\chi_j} + \iota\left(1-\prod_{j=1}^{r}(1-\overline{b_j})^{\chi_j}\right), \\ 1-\prod_{j=1}^{r}\left(1-\underline{a_j}\right)^{\chi_j} + \iota\left(1-\prod_{j=1}^{r}\left(1-\underline{b_j}\right)^{\chi_j}\right) \end{pmatrix}$$

$$\oplus\left(\begin{array}{c}\left(1-(1-\overline{a_{r+1}})^{\chi_{r+1}}+\iota\left(1-(1-\overline{b_{r+1}})^{\chi_{r+1}}\right)\right),\\ 1-\left(1-\underline{a_{r+1}}\right)^{\chi_{r+1}}+\iota\left(1-\left(1-\underline{b_{r+1}}\right)^{\chi_{r+1}}\right)\end{array}\right)$$

$$=\left(\begin{array}{c}1-\prod_{j=1}^{r+1}(1-\overline{a_j})^{\chi_j}+\iota\left(1-\prod_{j=1}^{r+1}(1-\overline{b_j})^{\chi_j}\right),\\ 1-\prod_{j=1}^{r+1}\left(1-\underline{a_j}\right)^{\chi_j}+\iota\left(1-\prod_{j=1}^{r+1}\left(1-\underline{b_j}\right)^{\chi_j}\right)\end{array}\right).$$

$\Longrightarrow$ Eqn (6.1) is true for n.

6.1.1 Properties of CFRPA operator

The notion of CFRPA satisfies the following properties.

Idempotency: Let an assembly $\mathcal{A}_j=\left\{\left(\overline{a_j}+\iota\overline{b_j},\ \underline{a_j}+\iota\underline{b_j}\right)\right\}, (j=1,\ 2,\ 3,\ \ldots,\ n)$ of CFRNs. If $\mathcal{A}_j=\mathcal{A}, \forall\ j$, then:

$$\text{CFRPA}\left(\mathcal{A}_1,\ \mathcal{A}_2,\ ..,\ \mathcal{A}_n\right)=\mathcal{A}.$$

Boundedness: Let an assembly $\mathcal{A}_j=\left(\overline{a_j}+\iota\,\overline{b_j},\underline{a_j}+\iota\underline{b_j}\right), (j=1,2,\ldots,n)$, of CFRNs and $\mathcal{A}^-=\left(\min_j\{\overline{a_j}\}+\iota\ \min_j\{\overline{b_j}\},\min_j\left\{\underline{a_j}\right\}+\iota\min_j\left\{\underline{b_j}\right\}\right)$, and $\mathcal{A}^+=\left(\max_j\{\overline{a_j}\}+\iota\ \max_j\{\overline{b_j}\},\max_j\left\{\underline{a_j}\right\}+\iota\ \max_j\left\{\underline{b_j}\right\}\right)$. Then:

$$\mathcal{A}^-\leq\text{CFRPA}\left(\mathcal{A}_1,\ \mathcal{A}_2,\ ..,\ \mathcal{A}_n\right)\leq\mathcal{A}^+.$$

Monotonicity: Let two assemblies $\mathcal{A}_j=\left(\overline{a_j}+\iota\,\overline{b_j},\underline{a_j}+\iota\underline{b_j}\right)$ and $\mathcal{A}'_j=\left(\overline{a'_j}+\iota\,\overline{b'_j},\underline{a'_j}+\iota\underline{b'_j}\right)$, $(j=1,\ 2,\ \ldots,\ n)$, of CFRNs. If $\underline{a_j}\leq\underline{a'_j}$, $\underline{b_j}\leq\underline{b'_j}$, $\overline{a_j}\leq\overline{a'_j}$, $\overline{b_j}\leq\overline{b'_j}\ \forall\ j$, then:

$$\text{CFRPA}\left(\mathcal{A}_1,\ \mathcal{A}_2,\ ..,\ \mathcal{A}_n\right)\leq\text{CFRPA}\left(\mathcal{A}'_1,\ \mathcal{A}'_2,\ ..,\ \mathcal{A}'_n\right).$$

Definition 6.2: Let an assembly $\mathcal{A}_j=\left\{\left(\overline{a_j}+\iota\overline{b_j},\ \underline{a_j}+\iota\underline{b_j}\right)\right\}, (j=1,\ 2,\ 3,\ \ldots,\ n)$ of CFRNs. Then the CFRPWA operator is scrutinized as

$$\text{CFRPWA}\left(\mathcal{A}_1,\ \mathcal{A}_2,\ \mathcal{A}_3,\ \ldots,\ \mathcal{A}_n\right)=\bigoplus_{j=1}^{n}\frac{\omega_j\left(1+T\left(\mathcal{A}_j\right)\right)}{\sum_{j=1}^{n}\omega_j\left(1+T\left(\mathcal{A}_j\right)\right)}\mathcal{A}_j.$$

Notice that $\omega = (\omega_1, \omega_2, \ldots, \omega_n)^T$ is a weight vector such that $\sum_{j=1}^{n} \omega_j = 1 \; \forall \, \omega_j$ and $0 \leq \omega_j \leq 1$.

Theorem 6.2: Let an assembly $\mathcal{A}_j = \left\{ \left(\overline{a_j} + \iota \overline{b_j}, \; \underline{a_j} + \iota \underline{b_j} \right) \right\}, (j = 1, 2, 3, \ldots, n)$ of CFRNs. Then the usage of CFRPWA operator over $\mathcal{A}_j$ will give a CFRN, that is:

$$\mathrm{CFRPWA}\left(\mathcal{A}_1, \mathcal{A}_2, \mathcal{A}_3, \ldots, \mathcal{A}_n\right) = \begin{pmatrix} 1 - \prod_{j=1}^{n} \left(1 - \overline{a_j}\right)^{\frac{\omega_j\left(1+T\left(\mathcal{A}_j\right)\right)}{\sum_{j=1}^{n} \omega_j\left(1+T\left(\mathcal{A}_j\right)\right)}} \\ +\iota \left(1 - \prod_{j=1}^{n} \left(1 - \overline{b_j}\right)^{\frac{\omega_j\left(1+T\left(\mathcal{A}_j\right)\right)}{\sum_{j=1}^{n} \omega_j\left(1+T\left(\mathcal{A}_j\right)\right)}}\right), \\ 1 - \prod_{j=1}^{n} \left(1 - \underline{a_j}\right)^{\frac{\omega_j\left(1+T\left(\mathcal{A}_j\right)\right)}{\sum_{j=1}^{n} \omega_j\left(1+T\left(\mathcal{A}_j\right)\right)}} \\ +\iota \left(1 - \prod_{j=1}^{n} \left(1 - \underline{b_j}\right)^{\frac{\omega_j\left(1+T\left(\mathcal{A}_j\right)\right)}{\sum_{j=1}^{n} \omega_j\left(1+T\left(\mathcal{A}_j\right)\right)}}\right) \end{pmatrix}.$$

6.1.2 Properties of CFRPWA operator

The notion of CFRPWA satisfies the following properties

Idempotency: Let an assembly $\mathcal{A}_j = \left\{ \left(\overline{a_j} + \iota \overline{b_j}, \; \underline{a_j} + \iota \underline{b_j} \right) \right\}, (j = 1, 2, 3, \ldots, n)$ of CFRNs. If $\mathcal{A}_j = \mathcal{A}, \forall \, j$, then:

$$\mathrm{CFRPWA}\left(\mathcal{A}_1, \mathcal{A}_2, .., \mathcal{A}_n\right) = \mathcal{A}.$$

Boundedness: Let an assembly $\mathcal{A}_j = \left(\overline{a_j} + \iota \overline{b_j}, \underline{a_j} + \iota \underline{b_j} \right), \; (j = 1, 2, \ldots, n)$, of CFRNs and $\mathcal{A}^- = \left(\min_j \left\{\overline{a_j}\right\} + \iota \min_j \left\{\overline{b_j}\right\}, \min_j \left\{\underline{a_j}\right\} + \iota \min_j \left\{\underline{b_j}\right\} \right)$, and $\mathcal{A}^+ = \left(\max_j \left\{\overline{a_j}\right\} + \iota \max_j \left\{\overline{b_j}\right\}, \max_j \left\{\underline{a_j}\right\} + \iota \max_j \left\{\underline{b_j}\right\} \right)$. Then:

$$\mathcal{A}^- \leq \mathrm{CFRPWA}\left(\mathcal{A}_1, \mathcal{A}_2, .., \mathcal{A}_n\right) \leq \mathcal{A}^+.$$

Monotonicity: Let two assemblies $\mathcal{A}_j = \left(\overline{a_j} + \iota\, \overline{b_j}, \underline{a_j} + \iota \underline{b_j}\right)$ and $\mathcal{A}'_j = \left(\overline{a'_j} + \iota\, \overline{b'_j}, \underline{a'_j} + \iota \underline{b'_j}\right),\ (j = 1,\ 2,\ \ldots,\ n)$, of CFRNs. If $\underline{a_j} \le \underline{a'_j}$, $\underline{b_j} \le \underline{b'_j}$, $\overline{a_j} \le \overline{a'_j}$, $\overline{b_j} \le \overline{b'_j}\ \forall\ j$, then:

$$\text{CFRPWA}\left(\mathcal{A}_1,\ \mathcal{A}_2,\ ..,\ \mathcal{A}_n\right) \le \text{CFRPWA}\left(\mathcal{A}'_1,\ \mathcal{A}'_2,\ ..,\ \mathcal{A}'_n\right).$$

Definition 6.3: Let an assembly $\mathcal{A}_j = \left\{\left(\overline{a_j} + \iota\overline{b_j},\ \underline{a_j} + \iota\underline{b_j}\right)\right\}, (j = 1,\ 2,\ 3,\ \ldots,\ n)$ of CFRNs. Then the CFRPG operator is scrutinized as

$$\text{CFRPG}\left(\mathcal{A}_1,\ \mathcal{A}_2,\ \mathcal{A}_3,\ \ldots,\ \mathcal{A}_n\right) = \bigotimes_{j=1}^{n} \left(\mathcal{A}_j\right)^{\frac{\left(1+T\left(\mathcal{A}_j\right)\right)}{\sum_{j=1}^{n}\left(1+T\left(\mathcal{A}_j\right)\right)}}.$$

Theorem 6.3: Let an assembly $\mathcal{A}_j = \left\{\left(\overline{a_j} + \iota\overline{b_j},\ \underline{a_j} + \iota\underline{b_j}\right)\right\}, (j = 1,\ 2,\ 3,\ \ldots,\ n)$ of CFRNs. Then the usage of the CFRPG operator over $\mathcal{A}_j$ will give a CFRN, that is:

$$\begin{aligned}
&\text{CFRPG}\left(\mathcal{A}_1,\ \mathcal{A}_2,\ \mathcal{A}_3,\ \ldots,\ \mathcal{A}_n\right)\\
&= \left(\prod_{j=1}^{n} \left(\overline{a_j}\right)^{\chi_j} + \iota\left(\prod_{j=1}^{n}\left(\overline{b_j}\right)^{\chi_j}\right), \prod_{j=1}^{n}\left(\underline{a_j}\right)^{\chi_j} + \iota\left(\prod_{j=1}^{n}\left(\underline{b_j}\right)^{\chi_j}\right)\right).
\end{aligned} \tag{6.2}$$

Proof: Let $n = 2$. Then we have:

$$\text{CFRPG}\left(\mathcal{A}_1,\ \mathcal{A}_2\right) = \left(\mathcal{A}_1\right)^{\chi_1} \otimes \left(\mathcal{A}_2\right)^{\chi_2},$$

and as

$$\begin{aligned}
\left(\mathcal{A}_1\right)^{\chi_1} &= \left(\left(\overline{a_1}\right)^{\chi_1} + \iota\left(\overline{b_1}\right)^{\chi_1},\ \left(\underline{a_1}\right)^{\chi_1} + \iota\left(\underline{b_1}\right)^{\chi_1}\right),\\
\left(\mathcal{A}_2\right)^{\chi_2} &= \left(\left(\overline{a_2}\right)^{\chi_2} + \iota\left(\overline{b_2}\right)^{\chi_2},\ \left(\underline{a_2}\right)^{\chi_2} + \iota\left(\underline{b_2}\right)^{\chi_2}\right),\\
\left(\mathcal{A}_1\right)^{\chi_1} \otimes \left(\mathcal{A}_2\right)^{\chi_2} &= \left(\left(\overline{a_1}\right)^{\chi_1} + \iota\left(\overline{b_1}\right)^{\chi_1},\ \left(\underline{a_1}\right)^{\chi_1} + \iota\left(\underline{b_1}\right)^{\chi_1}\right)\\
&\quad\otimes\left(\left(\overline{a_2}\right)^{\chi_2} + \iota\left(\overline{b_2}\right)^{\chi_2},\ \left(\underline{a_2}\right)^{\chi_2} + \iota\left(\underline{b_2}\right)^{\chi_2}\right)
\end{aligned}$$

$$= \begin{pmatrix} (\overline{a_1})^{\chi_1}(\overline{a_2})^{\chi_2} + \iota\,(\overline{b_1})^{\chi_1}(\overline{b_2})^{\chi_2}, \\ (\underline{a_1})^{\chi_1}(\underline{a_2})^{\chi_2} + \iota\,(\underline{b_1})^{\chi_1}(\underline{b_2})^{\chi_2} \end{pmatrix}$$

$$= \left(\prod_{j=1}^{2}(\overline{a_j})^{\chi_j} + \iota\left(\prod_{j=1}^{2}(\overline{b_j})^{\chi_j}\right),\right.$$

$$\left.\prod_{j=1}^{2}\left(\underline{a_j}\right)^{\chi_j} + \iota\left(\prod_{j=1}^{2}\left(\underline{b_j}\right)^{\chi_j}\right)\right).$$

Thus, eqn (6.2) holds for $n = 2$. Next let for $n = r$, eqn (6.2) holds.

$$\text{CFRPG}\,(\mathcal{A}_1,\ \mathcal{A}_2,\ \mathcal{A}_3,\ \ldots,\ \mathcal{A}_r)$$

$$= \left(\prod_{j=1}^{r}(\overline{a_j})^{\chi_j} + \iota\left(\prod_{j=1}^{r}(\overline{b_j})^{\chi_j}\right), \prod_{j=1}^{r}\left(\underline{a_j}\right)^{\chi_j} + \iota\left(\prod_{j=1}^{r}\left(\underline{b_j}\right)^{\chi_j}\right)\right).$$

Then finally, let $n = r + 1$. Then:

$$\text{CFRPG}\,(\mathcal{A}_1,\ \mathcal{A}_2,\ \mathcal{A}_3,\ \ldots,\ \mathcal{A}_r,\ \mathcal{A}_{r+1})$$

$$= \begin{pmatrix} \prod_{j=1}^{r}(\overline{a_j})^{\chi_j} + \iota\left(\prod_{j=1}^{r}(\overline{b_j})^{\chi_j}\right), \\ \prod_{j=1}^{r}\left(\underline{a_j}\right)^{\chi_j} + \iota\left(\prod_{j=1}^{r}\left(\underline{b_j}\right)^{\chi_j}\right) \end{pmatrix}$$

$$\otimes \begin{pmatrix} (\overline{a_{r+1}})^{\chi_{r+1}} + \iota\,(\overline{b_{r+1}})^{\chi_{r+1}} \\ \left(\underline{a_{r+1}}\right)^{\chi_{r+1}} + \iota\left(\underline{b_{r+1}}\right)^{\chi_{r+1}} \end{pmatrix}$$

$$= \left(\prod_{j=1}^{r+1}(\overline{a_j})^{\chi_j} + \iota\left(\prod_{j=1}^{r+1}(\overline{b_j})^{\chi_j}\right), \prod_{j=1}^{r+1}\left(\underline{a_j}\right)^{\chi_j} + \iota\left(\prod_{j=1}^{r+1}\left(\underline{b_j}\right)^{\chi_j}\right)\right).$$

$\Longrightarrow$ Eqn (6.2) is true for n.

6.1.3 Properties of CRFPG operator

The notion of CFRPG satisfies the following properties.

Idempotency: Let an assembly $\mathcal{A}_j = \left\{\left(\overline{a_j} + \iota\overline{b_j},\ \underline{a_j} + \iota\underline{b_j}\right)\right\}, (j = 1,\ 2,\ 3,\ \ldots,\ n)$ of CFRNs. If $\mathcal{A}_j = \mathcal{A}$, $\forall\ j$, then:

$$\text{CFRPG}\,(\mathcal{A}_1,\ \mathcal{A}_2,\ ..,\ \mathcal{A}_n) = \mathcal{A}.$$

Boundedness: Let an assembly $\mathcal{A}_j = \left(\overline{a_j} + \iota\, \overline{b_j}, \underline{a_j} + \iota \underline{b_j}\right)$, $(j = 1, 2, \ldots, n)$, of CFRNs and $\mathcal{A}^- = \left(\min_j \{\overline{a_j}\} + \iota \min_j \{\overline{b_j}\}, \min_j \{\underline{a_j}\} + \iota \min_j \{\underline{b_j}\}\right)$, and $\mathcal{A}^+ = \left(\max_j \{\overline{a_j}\} + \iota\, \max_j \{\overline{b_j}\}, \max_j \{\underline{a_j}\} + \iota\, \max_j \{\underline{b_j}\}\right)$. Then:

$$\mathcal{A}^- \leq \mathrm{CFRPG}\left(\mathcal{A}_1,\ \mathcal{A}_2,\ ..,\ \mathcal{A}_n\right) \leq \mathcal{A}^+.$$

Monotonicity: Let two assemblies $\mathcal{A}_j = \left(\overline{a_j} + \iota\, \overline{b_j}, \underline{a_j} + \iota \underline{b_j}\right)$ and $\mathcal{A}'_j = \left(\overline{a'_j} + \iota\, \overline{b'_j}, \underline{a'_j} + \iota \underline{b'_j}\right)$, $(j = 1,\ 2,\ \ldots,\ n)$, of CFRNs. If $\underline{a_j} \leq \underline{a'_j}$, $\underline{b_j} \leq \underline{b'_j}$, $\overline{a_j} \leq \overline{a'_j}$, $\overline{b_j} \leq \overline{b'_j}$ $\forall\, j$, then:

$$\mathrm{CFRPG}\left(\mathcal{A}_1,\ \mathcal{A}_2,\ ..,\ \mathcal{A}_n\right) \leq \mathrm{CFRPG}\left(\mathcal{A}'_1,\ \mathcal{A}'_2,\ ..,\ \mathcal{A}'_n\right).$$

Definition 6.4: Let an assembly $\mathcal{A}_j = \left\{\left(\overline{a_j} + \iota\overline{b_j},\ \underline{a_j} + \iota \underline{b_j}\right)\right\}$, $(j = 1,\ 2,\ 3,\ \ldots,\ n)$ of CFRNs. Then the CFRPWG operator is scrutinized as

$$\mathrm{CFRPWG}\left(\mathcal{A}_1,\ \mathcal{A}_2,\ \mathcal{A}_3,\ \ldots,\ \mathcal{A}_n\right) = \bigotimes_{j=1}^{n} \left(\mathcal{A}_j\right)^{\frac{\omega_j\left(1+T\left(\mathcal{A}_j\right)\right)}{\sum_{j=1}^{n}\omega_j\left(1+T\left(\mathcal{A}_j\right)\right)}}.$$

Theorem 6.4: Let an assembly $\mathcal{A}_j = \left\{\left(\overline{a_j}, + \iota\overline{b_j},\ \underline{a_j} + \iota \underline{b_j}\right)\right\}$, $(j = 1,\ 2,\ 3,\ \ldots,\ n)$ of CFRNs. Then the usage of the CFRPWG operator over $\mathcal{A}_j$ will give a CFRN, that is:

$$\mathrm{CFRPWG}\left(\mathcal{A}_1,\ \mathcal{A}_2,\ \mathcal{A}_3,\ \ldots,\ \mathcal{A}_n\right)$$

$$= \left(\begin{array}{c} \prod_{j=1}^{n} \left(\overline{a_j}\right)^{\frac{\omega_j\left(1+T\left(\mathcal{A}_j\right)\right)}{\sum_{j=1}^{n}\omega_j\left(1+T\left(\mathcal{A}_j\right)\right)}} + \iota \left(\prod_{j=1}^{n} \left(\overline{b_j}\right)^{\frac{\omega_j\left(1+T\left(\mathcal{A}_j\right)\right)}{\sum_{j=1}^{n}\omega_j\left(1+T\left(\mathcal{A}_j\right)\right)}}\right), \\ \prod_{j=1}^{n} \left(\underline{a_j}\right)^{\frac{\omega_j\left(1+T\left(\mathcal{A}_j\right)\right)}{\sum_{j=1}^{n}\omega_j\left(1+T\left(\mathcal{A}_j\right)\right)}} + \iota \left(\prod_{j=1}^{n} \left(\underline{b_j}\right)^{\frac{\omega_j\left(1+T\left(\mathcal{A}_j\right)\right)}{\sum_{j=1}^{n}\omega_j\left(1+T\left(\mathcal{A}_j\right)\right)}}\right) \end{array}\right).$$

6.1.4 Properties of CRFPWG operator

The notion of CFRPWG satisfies the following properties.

Idempotency: Let an assembly $\mathcal{A}_j = \left\{\left(\overline{a_j} + \iota\overline{b_j},\ \underline{a_j} + \iota\underline{b_j}\right)\right\}$, $(j = 1,\ 2,\ 3,\ \ldots,\ n)$ of CFRNs. If $\mathcal{A}_j = \mathcal{A}, \forall\, j$, then:

$$\mathrm{CFRPWG}\left(\mathcal{A}_1,\ \mathcal{A}_2,\ ..,\ \mathcal{A}_n\right) = \mathcal{A}.$$

Boundedness: Let an assembly $\mathcal{A}_j = \left(\overline{a_j} + \iota\,\overline{b_j}, \underline{a_j} + \iota\underline{b_j}\right)$, $(j = 1, 2, \ldots, n)$, of CFRNs and $\mathcal{A}^- = \left(\min_j\left\{\overline{a_j}\right\} + \iota\min_j\left\{\overline{b_j}\right\}, \min_j\left\{\underline{a_j}\right\} + \iota\min_j\left\{\underline{b_j}\right\}\right)$, and $\mathcal{A}^+ = \left(\max_j\left\{\overline{a_j}\right\} + \iota\ \max_j\left\{\overline{b_j}\right\}, \max_j\left\{\underline{a_j}\right\} + \iota\ \max_j\left\{\underline{b_j}\right\}\right)$. Then:

$$\mathcal{A}^- \leq \mathrm{CFRPWG}\left(\mathcal{A}_1,\ \mathcal{A}_2,\ ..,\ \mathcal{A}_n\right) \leq \mathcal{A}^+.$$

Monotonicity: Let two assemblies $\mathcal{A}_j = \left(\overline{a_j} + \iota\,\overline{b_j}, \underline{a_j} + \iota\underline{b_j}\right)$ and $\mathcal{A}'_j = \left(\overline{a'_j} + \iota\,\overline{b'_j}, \underline{a'_j} + \iota\underline{b'_j}\right)$, $(j = 1,\ 2,\ \ldots,\ n)$, of CFRNs. If $\underline{a_j} \leq \underline{a'_j}$, $\underline{b_j} \leq \underline{b'_j}$, $\overline{a_j} \leq \overline{a'_j}$, $\overline{b_j} \leq \overline{b'_j}\ \forall\, j$, then:

$$\mathrm{CFRPWG}\left(\mathcal{A}_1,\ \mathcal{A}_2,\ ..,\ \mathcal{A}_n\right) \leq \mathrm{CFRPWG}\left(\mathcal{A}'_1,\ \mathcal{A}'_2,\ ..,\ \mathcal{A}'_n\right).$$

6.2 MCDM Approach based on Power Operators within CFRS

Let $\mathfrak{L} = \{\mathfrak{L}_1,\ \mathfrak{L}_2, \ldots,\ \mathfrak{L}_m\}$ be an assembly of alternatives and for these alternatives, let $\mathbb{T} = \{\mathbb{T}_1,\ \mathbb{T}_2,\ \ldots,\ \mathbb{T}_n\}$ be an assembly of criteria that will be utilized for the assessment of the considered alternatives. In these alternatives, the decision analyst has to get the finest and best alternative. For that, the decision analyst will assess these alternatives based on their criteria and interpret their values in the framework of CFRNs that is $\mathcal{A} = \left(\overline{a} + \iota\overline{b}, \underline{a} + \iota\underline{b}\right)$, where $\underline{a}, \underline{b},\ \overline{a}, \overline{b} \in [0,\ 1]$. As each criterion has its weight the decision expert will provide the weight to each of the criteria which is $\omega_j = (\omega_1, \omega_2, \ldots, \omega_n)^T$ such that $\sum_{j=1}^{n} \omega_j = 1$ and $\omega_j \in [0,\ 1]\ \forall\, j$. Now to solve this, this MCDM approach has the underneath steps.

Step 1: As the assessment values are in the form of CFRNs, so develop a complex fuzzy rough decision matrix (CFRDM) $\mathfrak{D}$ by employing these assessment values. In this CFRDM, the first entry will represent the assessment value of the first alternative against the first criteria.

Step 2: Standardization of the CFRDM will be performed in this step by employing the given underneath formula. Standardization is needed because the data can be benefit and cost types.

$$D^{\mathcal{N}} = \begin{cases} \left(\overline{a} + \iota\overline{b}, \underline{a} + \iota\underline{b}\right) & \text{for benefit kind} \\ \left(\overline{a} + \iota\overline{b}, \underline{a} + \iota\underline{b}\right)^{c} & \text{for cost kind} \end{cases}.$$

Step 3: Here, the support of each $\mathcal{A}_j$ would be interpreted as

$$\text{Sup}\left(\mathcal{A}_{jr},\ \mathcal{A}_{jl}\right) = 1 - đ\left(\mathcal{A}_{jr},\ \mathcal{A}_{jl}\right),\ r,\ l = 1,\ 2,\ \ldots, n,\ r \neq l,$$

where $đ\left(\mathcal{A}_{jr},\ \mathcal{A}_{jl}\right) = \frac{1}{4}\left(\left|\overline{a_{jr}} - \overline{a_{jl}}\right| + \left|\overline{b_{jr}} - \overline{b_{jl}}\right| + \left|\underline{a_{jr}} - \underline{a_{jl}}\right| + \left|\underline{b_{jr}} - \underline{b_{jl}}\right|\right)$.

Step 4: Interpret

$$\text{T}\left(\mathcal{A}_{jr}\right) = \sum_{\substack{l=1 \\ l\neq r}}^{n} Sup\left(\mathcal{A}_{jr},\ \mathcal{A}_{jl}\right).$$

Noticed that $j = 1,\ 2,\ \ldots, m\ ; r,\ l = 1,\ 2,\ \ldots,\ n$ and $r \neq l$.

Step 5: Achieve the associated weight as follows

$$\chi_{jr} = \frac{\left(1 + T\left(\mathcal{A}_{jr}\right)\right)}{\sum_{l=1}^{n}\left(1 + T\left(\mathcal{A}_{jl}\right)\right)},$$

or

$$\chi'_{jr} = \frac{\hat{\text{W}}_{\omega-jr}\left(1 + T\left(\mathcal{A}_{jr}\right)\right)}{\sum_{l=1}^{n}\hat{\text{W}}_{\omega-jl}\left(1 + T\left(\mathcal{A}_{jl}\right)\right)}.$$

Step 6: Aggregate the CFRDM with the assistance of any of the devised operators that is CFRPA, CFRPWA, CFRPG, and CFRPWG operators.

Step 7: Employing score function to achieve the score values of aggregated outcomes of each alternative. In case of the same score values, achieve the accuracy values by employing the accuracy function.

Step 8: Rank all alternatives by considering their score or accuracy values and select the finest and best alternative.

6.2.1 Case study (selection of AI solution)

Global Tech Services (GTS) is a multinational technology company that is looking forward to enhancing the customer service department by introducing an intelligent customer service solution. The company deals with more than 1000 customers' contacts per day through email, chat, and voice communication. The management has to identify the right AI solution that will improve customer experience, cut response time, and minimize costs.

Decision context: The company is to choose from four different AI solutions and to do that, it has to take into account several factors that would reflect its strategic goals. This decision will affect their customer relations service delivery, cost of operations, and customer satisfaction over the next 5 years. The company shortlisted four AI solutions which are devised in Table 6.1.

Table 6.1 The AI solutions along with an explanation.

Notations	AI solutions	Explanation
$\mathbb{A}_1$	SmartServe AI	An AI solution that incorporates a complete package from a company with 10 years of experience in the industry. Enables natural language processing, supports multiple languages, and has sentiment analysis, voice recognition, and auto responder for sending responses.
$\mathbb{A}_2$	ResponsePro AI	An innovative product from a relatively young company with state-of-the-art machine learning algorithms for pattern matching, predictive analytics for customer behavior, and real-time customer feedback processing.
$\mathbb{A}_3$	OmniAI Assistant	An omnichannel support integration solution for enterprises, which offers advanced customer journey mapping, and analytics for ticket prioritization and routing, and has been successfully deployed in large enterprises.
$\mathbb{A}_4$	CustoCare AI	Flexible and modular, customizable for your business needs, based on visual tools for designing the chatbot experience, includes robust workflow automation and seamless integration with your CRM, famous for its scalability and high achievements in performance.

To assess these AI solutions, the decision analyst considered 4 criteria, which are displayed in Table 6.2.

The decision analyst will assess these AI solutions and provide their values in the form of CFRNs. Also, the expert provides the weight to the criteria based on their preference that weight is $(0.23,\ 0.16,\ 0.34,\ 0.27)$. To solve this, we have the underneath steps.

Table 6.2 The criteria of the AI solutions.

Notations	Criteria	Explanation
$\mathbb{C}_1$	Response accuracy	Calculates the frequency and quality of errors in AI's given answers to customers' questions in terms of error rate and response quality. Critically important for sustaining high levels of service quality.
$\mathbb{C}_2$	Implementation cost	The largest consideration of an ERP involves acquiring software and license fees, hardware, training of employees, and maintenance and updates in the future.
$\mathbb{C}_3$	Scalability	Assesses the system's capacity to improve upon the throughput, managing the system at the peak and the performance stability under different circumstances.
$\mathbb{C}_4$	Integration capability	Evaluate how it will fit into the current system environment, how well it interfaces with existing technologies, and flexibility toward new technologies in the future.

Step 1: The decision analyst assessed the AI solutions and provided their values in the structure of CFRNs which form CFRDM as shown in Table 6.3.

Table 6.3 The assessment values of AI solutions are interpreted by experts.

	$\mathbb{C}_1$	$\mathbb{C}_2$	$\mathbb{C}_3$	$\mathbb{C}_4$
$\mathbb{A}_1$	$\begin{pmatrix} 0.83+\iota\,0.35, \\ 0.26+\iota\,0.62 \end{pmatrix}$	$\begin{pmatrix} 0.73+\iota\,0.64, \\ 0.13+\iota\,0.32 \end{pmatrix}$	$\begin{pmatrix} 0.52+\iota\,0.64, \\ 0.84+\iota\,0.24 \end{pmatrix}$	$\begin{pmatrix} 0.26+\iota\,0.69, \\ 0.73+\iota\,0.52 \end{pmatrix}$
$\mathbb{A}_2$	$\begin{pmatrix} 0.53+\iota\,0.63, \\ 0.25+\iota\,0.75 \end{pmatrix}$	$\begin{pmatrix} 0.72+\iota\,0.45, \\ 0.21+\iota\,0.15 \end{pmatrix}$	$\begin{pmatrix} 0.73+\iota\,0.17, \\ 0.82+\iota\,0.67 \end{pmatrix}$	$\begin{pmatrix} 0.85+\iota\,0.72, \\ 0.22+\iota\,0.14 \end{pmatrix}$
$\mathbb{A}_3$	$\begin{pmatrix} 0.34+\iota\,0.37, \\ 0.62+\iota\,0.72 \end{pmatrix}$	$\begin{pmatrix} 0.63+\iota\,0.63, \\ 0.74+\iota\,0.25 \end{pmatrix}$	$\begin{pmatrix} 0.63+\iota\,0.39, \\ 0.63+\iota\,0.53 \end{pmatrix}$	$\begin{pmatrix} 0.27+\iota\,0.63, \\ 0.71+\iota\,0.26 \end{pmatrix}$
$\mathbb{A}_4$	$\begin{pmatrix} 0.66+\iota\,0.37, \\ 0.52+\iota\,0.27 \end{pmatrix}$	$\begin{pmatrix} 0.45+\iota\,0.73, \\ 0.52+\iota\,0.63 \end{pmatrix}$	$\begin{pmatrix} 0.25+\iota\,0.83, \\ 0.63+\iota\,0.36 \end{pmatrix}$	$\begin{pmatrix} 0.88+\iota\,0.37, \\ 0.28+\iota\,0.83 \end{pmatrix}$

Step 2: As the data is benefit-kind, so after the standardization, the CFRDM will remain the same.

Step 3: The support of each $\mathbb{A}_j$ for $j = 1$

$$\mathrm{Sup}\left(\mathbb{A}_{11},\ \mathbb{A}_{12}\right) = 0.833, \mathrm{Sup}\left(\mathbb{A}_{11},\ \mathbb{A}_{13}\right) = 0.61, \mathrm{Sup}\left(\mathbb{A}_{11},\ \mathbb{A}_{14}\right) = 0.63,$$

$$\mathrm{Sup}\left(\mathbb{A}_{12},\ \mathbb{A}_{11}\right) = 0.833, \mathrm{Sup}\left(\mathbb{A}_{12},\ \mathbb{A}_{13}\right) = 0.768, \mathrm{Sup}\left(\mathbb{A}_{12},\ \mathbb{A}_{14}\right) = 0.788,$$

$$\mathrm{Sup}\left(\mathbb{A}_{13},\ \mathbb{A}_{11}\right) = 0.61, \mathrm{Sup}\left(\mathbb{A}_{13},\ \mathbb{A}_{12}\right) = 0.768, \mathrm{Sup}\left(\mathbb{A}_{13},\ \mathbb{A}_{14}\right) = 0.825,$$

$$\mathrm{Sup}\left(\mathbb{A}_{14},\ \mathbb{A}_{11}\right) = 0.63, \mathrm{Sup}\left(\mathbb{A}_{14},\ \mathbb{A}_{12}\right) = 0.788, \mathrm{Sup}\left(\mathbb{A}_{14},\ \mathbb{A}_{13}\right) = 0.825,$$

for $j = 2$

$$\mathrm{Sup}(\mathbb{A}_{21}, \mathbb{A}_{22}) = 0.748, \mathrm{Sup}(\mathbb{A}_{21}, \mathbb{A}_{23}) = 0.673, \mathrm{Sup}(\mathbb{A}_{21}, \mathbb{A}_{24}) = 0.738,$$

$$\mathrm{Sup}(\mathbb{A}_{22}, \mathbb{A}_{21}) = 0.748, \mathrm{Sup}(\mathbb{A}_{22}, \mathbb{A}_{23}) = 0.645, \mathrm{Sup}(\mathbb{A}_{22}, \mathbb{A}_{24}) = 0.895,$$

$$\mathrm{Sup}(\mathbb{A}_{23}, \mathbb{A}_{21}) = 0.673, \mathrm{Sup}(\mathbb{A}_{23}, \mathbb{A}_{22}) = 0.645, \mathrm{Sup}(\mathbb{A}_{23}, \mathbb{A}_{24}) = 0.55,$$

$$\mathrm{Sup}(\mathbb{A}_{24}, \mathbb{A}_{21}) = 0.595, \mathrm{Sup}(\mathbb{A}_{24}, \mathbb{A}_{22}) = 0.895, \mathrm{Sup}(\mathbb{A}_{24}, \mathbb{A}_{23}) = 0.55,$$

for $j = 3$

$$\mathrm{Sup}(\mathbb{A}_{31}, \mathbb{A}_{32}) = 0.715, \mathrm{Sup}(\mathbb{A}_{31}, \mathbb{A}_{33}) = 0.873, \mathrm{Sup}(\mathbb{A}_{31}, \mathbb{A}_{34}) = 0.78,$$

$$\mathrm{Sup}(\mathbb{A}_{32}, \mathbb{A}_{31}) = 0.873, \mathrm{Sup}(\mathbb{A}_{32}, \mathbb{A}_{33}) = 0.843, \mathrm{Sup}(\mathbb{A}_{32}, \mathbb{A}_{34}) = 0.9,$$

$$\mathrm{Sup}(\mathbb{A}_{33}, \mathbb{A}_{31}) = 0.873, \mathrm{Sup}(\mathbb{A}_{33}, \mathbb{A}_{32}) = 0.843, \mathrm{Sup}(\mathbb{A}_{33}, \mathbb{A}_{34}) = 0.763,$$

$$\mathrm{Sup}(\mathbb{A}_{34}, \mathbb{A}_{31}) = 0.708, \mathrm{Sup}(\mathbb{A}_{34}, \mathbb{A}_{32}) = 0.9, \mathrm{Sup}(\mathbb{A}_{34}, \mathbb{A}_{33}) = 0.763,$$

for $j = 4$

$$\mathrm{Sup}(\mathbb{A}_{41}, \mathbb{A}_{42}) = 0.768, \mathrm{Sup}(\mathbb{A}_{41}, \mathbb{A}_{43}) = 0.733, \mathrm{Sup}(\mathbb{A}_{41}, \mathbb{A}_{44}) = 0.745,$$

$$\mathrm{Sup}(\mathbb{A}_{42}, \mathbb{A}_{41}) = 0.768, \mathrm{Sup}(\mathbb{A}_{42}, \mathbb{A}_{43}) = 0.83, \mathrm{Sup}(\mathbb{A}_{42}, \mathbb{A}_{44}) = 0.693,$$

$$\mathrm{Sup}(\mathbb{A}_{43}, \mathbb{A}_{41}) = 0.733, \mathrm{Sup}(\mathbb{A}_{43}, \mathbb{A}_{42}) = 0.83, \mathrm{Sup}(\mathbb{A}_{43}, \mathbb{A}_{44}) = 0.523,$$

$$\mathrm{Sup}(\mathbb{A}_{44}, \mathbb{A}_{41}) = 0.673, \mathrm{Sup}(\mathbb{A}_{44}, \mathbb{A}_{42}) = 0.693, \mathrm{Sup}(\mathbb{A}_{44}, \mathbb{A}_{43}) = 0.523.$$

Step 4: Interpreted $T(\mathbb{A}_{jr})$

$$T(\mathbb{A}_{11}) = 2.073, \mathrm{T}(\mathbb{A}_{12}) = 2.388, \mathrm{T}(\mathbb{A}_{13}) = 2.203, \mathrm{T}(\mathbb{A}_{14}) = 2.243,$$

$$\mathrm{T}(\mathbb{A}_{21}) = 2.158, \mathrm{T}(\mathbb{A}_{22}) = 2.288, \mathrm{T}(\mathbb{A}_{23}) = 1.868, \mathrm{T}(\mathbb{A}_{24}) = 2.04,$$

$$\mathrm{T}(\mathbb{A}_{31}) = 2.368, \mathrm{T}(\mathbb{A}_{32}) = 2.458, \mathrm{T}(\mathbb{A}_{33}) = 2.478, \mathrm{T}(\mathbb{A}_{34}) = 2.37,$$

$$\mathrm{T}(\mathbb{A}_{41}) = 2.245, \mathrm{T}(\mathbb{A}_{42}) = 2.29, \mathrm{T}(\mathbb{A}_{43}) = 2.085, \mathrm{T}(\mathbb{A}_{44}) = 1.888.$$

Step 5: The associated weights are:

$$\chi_{11} = 0.238, \chi_{12} = 0.262, \chi_{13} = 0.249, \chi_{14} = 0.251,$$

$$\chi_{21} = 0.256, \chi_{22} = 0.266, \chi_{23} = 0.232, \chi_{24} = 0.246,$$

$$\chi_{31} = 0.247, \chi_{32} = 0.253, \chi_{33} = 0.254, \chi_{34} = 0.246,$$

$$\chi_{41} = 0.259, \chi_{42} = 0.263, \chi_{43} = 0.247, \chi_{44} = 0.231.$$

After that analyst weight of each criterion is $(0.23,\ 0.16,\ 0.34,\ 0.27)$, the associated weights are:

$$\chi'_{11} = 0.22, \chi'_{12} = 0.169, \chi'_{13} = 0.339, \chi'_{14} = 0.272,$$
$$\chi'_{21} = 0.238, \chi'_{22} = 0.173, \chi'_{23} = 0.32, \chi'_{24} = 0.269,$$
$$\chi'_{31} = 0.226, \chi'_{32} = 0.162, \chi'_{33} = 0.345, \chi'_{34} = 0.267,$$
$$\chi'_{41} = 0.241, \chi'_{42} = 0.17, \chi'_{43} = 0.338, \chi'_{44} = 0.251,$$

Step 6: The aggregated outcome of each AI solution after employing CFRPA, CFRPWA, CFRPG, and CFRPWG operators is displayed in Table 6.4.

Table 6.4 The aggregated outcomes of AI solutions.

Operators	$\mathbb{A}_1$	$\mathbb{A}_2$	$\mathbb{A}_3$	$\mathbb{A}_4$
CFRYPA	$\begin{pmatrix}0.641 + \iota\, 0.601,\\ 0.65 + \iota\, 0.528\end{pmatrix}$	$\begin{pmatrix}0.728 + \iota\, 0.537,\\ 0.449 + \iota\, 0.5\end{pmatrix}$	$\begin{pmatrix}0.495 + \iota\, 0.521,\\ 0.679 + \iota\, 0.48\end{pmatrix}$	$\begin{pmatrix}0.631 + \iota\, 0.635,\\ 0.506 + \iota\, 0.578\end{pmatrix}$
CFRYPWA	$\begin{pmatrix}0.61 + \iota\, 0.606,\\ 0.689 + \iota\, 0.492\end{pmatrix}$	$\begin{pmatrix}0.735 + \iota\, 0.524,\\ 0.516 + \iota\, 0.529\end{pmatrix}$	$\begin{pmatrix}0.442 + \iota\, 0.479,\\ 0.636 + \iota\, 0.451\end{pmatrix}$	$\begin{pmatrix}0.629 + \iota\, 0.65,\\ 0.513 + \iota\, 0.568\end{pmatrix}$
CFRYWG	$\begin{pmatrix}0.534 + \iota\, 0.565,\\ 0.541 + \iota\, 0.472\end{pmatrix}$	$\begin{pmatrix}0.696 + \iota\, 0.489,\\ 0.305 + \iota\, 0.315\end{pmatrix}$	$\begin{pmatrix}0.439 + \iota\, 0.489,\\ 0.637 + \iota\, 0.397\end{pmatrix}$	$\begin{pmatrix}0.502 + \iota\, 0.54,\\ 0.473 + \iota\, 0.47\end{pmatrix}$
CFRYPWG	$\begin{pmatrix}0.505 + \iota\, 0.572,\\ 0.576 + \iota\, 0.431\end{pmatrix}$	$\begin{pmatrix}0.703 + \iota\, 0.405,\\ 0.343 + \iota\, 0.349\end{pmatrix}$	$\begin{pmatrix}0.458 + \iota\, 0.52,\\ 0.697 + \iota\, 0.443\end{pmatrix}$	$\begin{pmatrix}0.479 + \iota\, 0.546,\\ 0.475 + \iota\, 0.456\end{pmatrix}$

Step 7: The score values of AI solutions are interpreted in Table 6.5.

Table 6.5 The score values of AI solutions.

Operators	$\text{Scor}.(\mathbb{A}_1)$	$\text{Scor}.(\mathbb{A}_2)$	$\text{Scor}.(\mathbb{A}_3)$	$\text{Scor}.(\mathbb{A}_4)$
CFRPA	0.605	0.553	0.544	0.588
CFRPWA	0.599	0.576	0.502	0.590
CFRPG	0.528	0.439	0.500	0.496
CFRPWG	0.521	0.450	0.529	0.489

Step 8: The ranking of AI solutions is devised in Table 6.6.

Table 6.6 The ranking of AI solutions.

Operators	Ranking
CFRYPA	$\mathbb{A}_1 > \mathbb{A}_4 > \mathbb{A}_2 > \mathbb{A}_1$
CFRYPWA	$\mathbb{A}_1 > \mathbb{A}_4 > \mathbb{A}_2 > \mathbb{A}_1$
CFRYPG	$\mathbb{A}_1 > \mathbb{A}_4 > \mathbb{A}_2 > \mathbb{A}_1$
CFRYPWG	$\mathbb{A}_1 > \mathbb{A}_4 > \mathbb{A}_2 > \mathbb{A}_1$

From the ranking of AI solutions, the analyst decided that $\mathbb{A}_1$ is the finest and best framework. The graphical interpretation of AI solutions can be seen in Figure 6.1.

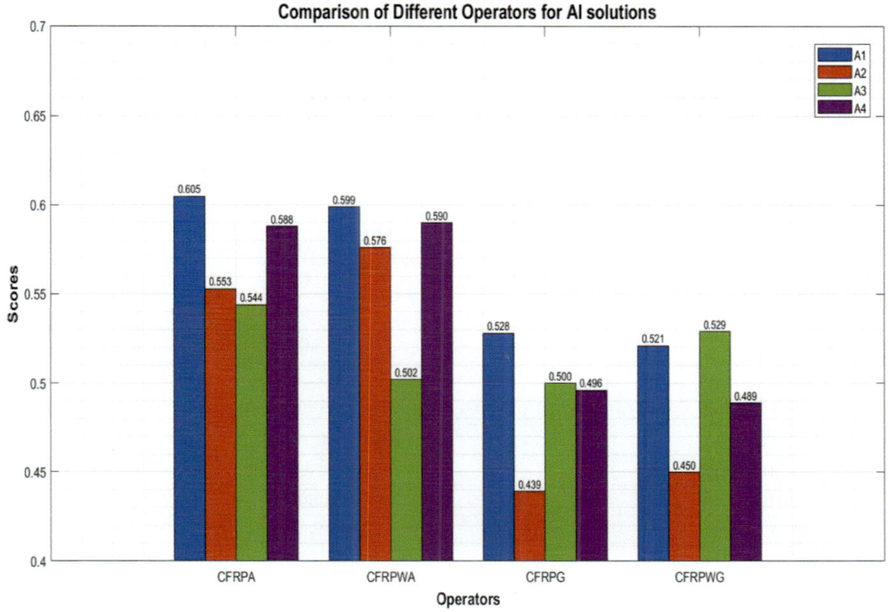

Figure 6.1 The graphical interpretation of the score values and ranking of the AI solutions through different proposed operators.

6.3 Comparative Analysis

To prove the effectiveness of the suggested operators and methods, we compare them with several theoretical frameworks of the field. These include power geometric operators by Xu and Yager [22], probability complex fuzzy AOs and MCDM methods by Rehman [23] for complex and two-dimensional information aggregation, power AOs by Hu et al. [24] for complex information aggregation in polar form, AOs and MCDM problems by Khan et al. [25] for complex fuzzy rough information in polar form, and the TOPSIS approach within complex fuzzy rough information developed by Hussain et al. [26]. The comparison is based on the complex fuzzy rough information shown in Table 6.3, using different operators for aggregation and methods for the last ranking. The comparative results are summarized in Tables 6.7 and 6.8 and Figure 6.2

The comparative analysis of the results obtained and presented in Tables 6.7 and 6.8 and Figure 6.2 shows that existing methods have significant limitations. The power geometric operators are shown to have limited use in practice and are only suitable for crisp information handling, but not

Table 6.7 The score values of existing and proposed theory.

Operators	$\mathbf{Scor}.(\mathbb{A}_1)$	$\mathbf{Scor}.(\mathbb{A}_2)$	$\mathbf{Scor}.(\mathbb{A}_3)$	$\mathbf{Scor}.(\mathbb{A}_4)$
Xu and Yager [22]	No result	No result	No result	No result
Rehman [23]	No result	No result	No result	No result
Hu et al. [24]	No result	No result	No result	No result
Khan et al. [25]	No result	No result	No result	No result
Hussain et al. [26]	No result	No result	No result	No result
CFRPA	0.605	0.553	0.544	0.588
CFRPWA	0.599	0.576	0.502	0.59
CFRPG	0.528	0.439	0.5	0.496
CFRPWG	0.521	0.45	0.529	0.489

Table 6.8 The ranking of proposed theories and existing ones.

Operators	**Ranking result**
Xu and Yager [22]	No result
Rehman [23]	No result
Hu et al. [24]	No result
Khan et al. [25]	No result
Hussain et al. [26]	No result
CFRPA	$\mathbb{A}_1 > \mathbb{A}_4 > \mathbb{A}_2 > \mathbb{A}_1$
CFRPWA	$\mathbb{A}_1 > \mathbb{A}_4 > \mathbb{A}_2 > \mathbb{A}_1$
CFRPG	$\mathbb{A}_1 > \mathbb{A}_4 > \mathbb{A}_2 > \mathbb{A}_1$
CFRPWG	$\mathbb{A}_1 > \mathbb{A}_4 > \mathbb{A}_2 > \mathbb{A}_1$

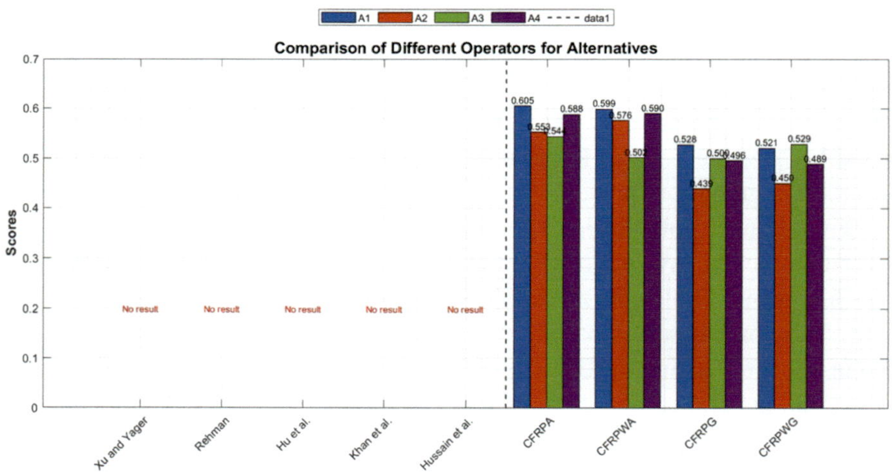

Figure 6.2 The comparison of the score values of AI solutions obtained by existing and proposed work.

uncertainty, roughness, or two-dimensional aspects. Our proposed approach, however, goes beyond these limitations, and it is capable of processing both crisp information and other types of data. Likewise, probability complex fuzzy operators can deal with two-dimensional and uncertain information but they fail to deal with roughness, which our proposed work does by handling two-dimensional and uncertain information with and without considering the roughness. The complex fuzzy rough operators are characterized by a significant limitation of their capacity to aggregate only the polar form of the complex information while being incapable of handling the Tamir's complex fuzzy information.

One of the most important findings of the critical observation of current AI solution selection processes is the lack of consideration of roughness and uncertainties, which undermines the quality of final decisions to a great extent. Our approach fills this gap through a proposed framework that can tackle roughness, 2D information, and uncertainty at the same time. This integrated approach makes decision-making in AI solution selection sounder and more reliable as compared to existing methods and thus represents a major improvement. This enhanced version offers a superior and comprehensive framework to address the complexities of decision-making in selecting AI solutions for applications and overcome the shortcomings of the previous methods in addressing the issues encountered in this field.

6.4 Conclusion

This chapter is a major contribution to the theory of MCDM by proposing new operators and approaches for managing FRI in AI solutions selection. The development of CFRPA, CFRPWA, CFRPG, and CFRPWG operators is a significant contribution to the literature on decision-making models. The findings of our study show that these operators can overcome the problems of traditional methods in dealing with uncertainty, roughness, and two-dimensional data in Cartesian. The operators used in the development of the proposed MCDM technique offer decision-makers a reliable method of assessing and selecting the most suitable AI solutions based on multiple criteria. The practicality of our proposed framework is demonstrated through an extensive case study of AI solution selection where the methodology was able to successfully traverse the decision parameters to make informed decisions. The comparative analysis with existing methods reveals the superior capabilities of our approach in several key aspects: First of all, unlike most conventional approaches that can address only certain kinds of information, our framework shows great versatility in terms of the kind of intricate data it can process at once. Second, the incorporation of roughness and uncertainty aspects into the decision-making process improves the reliability and efficiency of the decision-making process in arriving at the final choices. Third, the proposed operators have better aggregation performance compared to the existing methods, especially in cases with multidimensional and uncertain information.

7

Advanced Data Science Techniques with Complex Fuzzy Rough Sets: Applications and Insights

Data science advancements have changed aerospace engineering. It now helps in accurate decision-making and optimization of complex systems. This chapter introduces advanced data science techniques integrated with the Complex Fuzzy Rough WASPAS (weighted aggregated sum product assessment) approach for solving multicriteria decision-making problems in aerospace applications. We developed the Einstein aggregation theory based on CFRNs and then used these aggregation operators to develop the WASPAS approach. The proposed approach utilizes complex fuzzy rough sets to provide a means of dealing with data uncertainties and imprecise natures, combined with the computational effectiveness of the WASPAS method for robust evaluation and ranking of alternatives. These outcomes show that this hybrid method provides more accuracy along with adaptability, giving opportunities for intelligent and resilient solutions in aerospace.

7.1 Einstein Operators for CFRS

In this section, we are going to diagnose Einstein's operations in the setting of CFRS and study their significant outcomes.

Definition 7.1: Let $\mathcal{A}_1 = \left\{\left(\overline{a_1} + \iota\overline{b_1}, \underline{a_1} + \iota\underline{b_1}\right)\right\}$ and $\mathcal{A}_2 = \left\{\left(\overline{a_2} + \iota\overline{b_2}, \underline{a_2} + \iota\underline{b_2}\right)\right\}$ be two CFRNs and $s \geq 0$, the Einstein operational laws for CFRNs are given by

1. $$\mathcal{A}_1 \oplus \mathcal{A}_2 = \begin{pmatrix} \frac{\overline{a_1}+\overline{a_2}}{1+\overline{a_1}\,\overline{a_2}} + \iota\,\frac{\overline{b_1}+\overline{b_2}}{1+\overline{b_1}\,\overline{b_2}}, \\ \frac{\underline{a_1}+\underline{a_2}}{1+\underline{a_1}\,\underline{a_2}} + \iota\,\frac{\underline{b_1}+\underline{b_2}}{1+\underline{b_1}\,\underline{b_2}} \end{pmatrix}.$$

$$2.\ \mathcal{A}_1 \otimes \mathcal{A}_2 = \left(\begin{array}{c} \frac{\overline{a_1}\ \overline{a_2}}{1+(1-\overline{a_1})(1-\overline{a_2})} + \iota \frac{\overline{b_1}\ \overline{b_2}}{1+\left(1-\overline{b_1}\right)\left(1-\overline{b_2}\right)}, \\ \frac{\underline{a_1}\ \underline{a_2}}{1+\left(1-\underline{a_1}\right)\left(1-\underline{a_2}\right)} + \iota \frac{\underline{b_1}\ \underline{b_2}}{1+\left(1-\underline{b_1}\right)\left(1-\underline{b_2}\right)} \end{array} \right).$$

$$3.\ (\mathcal{A}_1)^s = \left(\begin{array}{c} \frac{2(\overline{a_1})^s}{(2-\overline{a_1})^s+(\overline{a_1})^s} + \iota \frac{2\left(\overline{b_1}\right)^s}{\left(2-\overline{b_1}\right)^s+\left(\overline{b_1}\right)^s}, \\ \frac{2\left(\underline{a_1}\right)^s}{\left(2-\underline{a_1}\right)^s+\left(\underline{a_1}\right)^s} + \iota \frac{2\left(\underline{b_1}\right)^s}{\left(2-\underline{b_1}\right)^s+\left(\underline{b_1}\right)^s} \end{array} \right).$$

$$4.\ s\mathcal{A}_1 = \left(\begin{array}{c} \frac{(1+\overline{a_1})^s-(1-\overline{a_1})^s}{(1+\overline{a_1})^s+(1-\overline{a_1})^s} + \iota \frac{\left(1+\overline{b_1}\right)^s-\left(1-\overline{b_1}\right)^s}{\left(1+\overline{b_1}\right)^s+\left(1-\overline{b_1}\right)^s}, \\ \frac{\left(1+\underline{a_1}\right)^s-\left(1-\underline{a_1}\right)^s}{\left(1+\underline{a_1}\right)^s+\left(1-\underline{a_1}\right)^s} + \iota \frac{\left(1+\underline{b_1}\right)^s-\left(1-\underline{b_1}\right)^s}{\left(1+\underline{b_1}\right)^s+\left(1-\underline{b_1}\right)^s} \end{array} \right).$$

Theorem 7.1: Let $\mathcal{A}_1 = \left\{\left(\overline{a_1} + \iota\overline{b_1},\ \underline{a_1} + \iota\underline{b_1}\right)\right\}$ and $\left\{\left(\overline{a_2} + \iota\overline{b_2}\ ,\ \underline{a_2} + \iota\underline{b_2}\right)\right\}$ be two CFRNs and $s,\ s_1, s_2\ \geq 0$, then:

1. $\mathcal{A}_1 \oplus \mathcal{A}_2 = \mathcal{A}_2 \oplus \mathcal{A}_1$
2. $\mathcal{A}_1 \otimes \mathcal{A}_2 = \mathcal{A}_2 \otimes \mathcal{A}_1$
3. $(\mathcal{A}_1 \otimes \mathcal{A}_2)^s = (\mathcal{A}_1)^s \otimes (\mathcal{A}_1)^s$
4. $s\,(\mathcal{A}_1 \oplus \mathcal{A}_2) =\ s\mathcal{A}_1 \oplus s\mathcal{A}_2$
5. $(\mathcal{A}_1)^{s_1} \oplus (\mathcal{A}_1)^{s_1}\ = (\mathcal{A}_1)^{s_1+s_2}$
6. $s_1\mathcal{A}_1 \otimes s_2\mathcal{A}_1 = (s_1 + s_2)\,\mathcal{A}_1$
7. $((\mathcal{A}_1)^{s_1})^{s_2} = (\mathcal{A}_1)^{s_1 s_2}$
8. $s_1\,(s_2\mathcal{A}_1) = (s_1 s_2)\,\mathcal{A}_1$

Proof: Omitted.

7.2 CFR Einstein Weighted Average and Geometric Aggregation Operators

Aggregation operators are the fundamental tool that can convert the overall information into a single value that can further help to discuss the decision-making problems. Here in this section, we have delivered the notion of complex fuzzy rough Einstein weighted average (CFREWA) and complex fuzzy rough weighted geometric (CFRWG) aggregation operators.

Definition 7.2: Let $\mathcal{A}_j\ =\ \left\{\left(\overline{a_j} + \iota\overline{b_j},\ \underline{a_j} + \iota\underline{b_j}\right)\right\}\ j\ =\ 1,\ 2,\ldots,\ n$ be the collection of CFRNs and $\omega\ =\ (\omega_1,\ \omega_2,\ldots,\ \omega_n)$ be a weight vector of $\mathcal{A}_j\ (j = 1,\ 2,..,\ n)$ with $\omega_j\ \in\ [0,\ 1]$ and $\sum_{j=1}^{n} \omega_j\ =\ 1$, then the notion CFREWA operator is introduced by

$$\text{CFREWA}\,(\mathcal{A}_1,\ \mathcal{A}_2,\ \ldots,\ \mathcal{A}_n) = \omega_1\mathcal{A}_1 \oplus \omega_2\mathcal{A}_2 \oplus \ldots \oplus \omega_n\mathcal{A}_n. \quad (7.1)$$

Theorem 7.2: The results after applying the notion of eqn (7.1) are again CFRNs:

$$\mathrm{CFREWA}\,(\mathcal{A}_1,\ \mathcal{A}_2,\ \ldots,\ \mathcal{A}_n)$$

$$= \begin{pmatrix} \dfrac{\prod_{j=1}^{n}(1+\overline{a_j})^{\omega_j}-\prod_{j=1}^{n}(1-\overline{a_j})^{\omega_j}}{\prod_{j=1}^{n}(1+\overline{a_j})^{\omega_j}+\prod_{j=1}^{n}(1-\overline{a_j})^{\omega_j}} + \iota\dfrac{\prod_{j=1}^{n}\left(1+\overline{b_j}\right)^{\omega_j}-\prod_{j=1}^{n}\left(1-\overline{b_j}\right)^{\omega_j}}{\prod_{j=1}^{n}\left(1+\overline{b_j}\right)^{\omega_j}+\prod_{j=1}^{n}\left(1-\overline{b_j}\right)^{\omega_j}}, \\ \dfrac{\prod_{j=1}^{n}\left(1+\underline{a_j}\right)^{\omega_j}-\prod_{j=1}^{n}\left(1-\underline{a_j}\right)^{\omega_j}}{\prod_{j=1}^{n}\left(1+\underline{a_j}\right)^{\omega_j}+\prod_{j=1}^{n}\left(1-\underline{a_j}\right)^{\omega_j}} + \iota\dfrac{\prod_{j=1}^{n}\left(1+\underline{b_j}\right)^{\omega_j}-\prod_{j=1}^{n}\left(1-\underline{b_j}\right)^{\omega_j}}{\prod_{j=1}^{n}\left(1+\underline{b_j}\right)^{\omega_j}+\prod_{j=1}^{n}\left(1-\underline{b_j}\right)^{\omega_j}} \end{pmatrix}. \quad (7.2)$$

Proof: This result is proved with the help of the mathematical induction method.

For $n = 2$, then we find:

$$\mathrm{CFREWA}\,(\mathcal{A}_1,\ \mathcal{A}_2) = \omega_1\mathcal{A}_1 \oplus \omega_2\mathcal{A}_2.$$

We have:

$$\omega_1\mathcal{A}_1 = \begin{pmatrix} \dfrac{(1+\overline{a_1})^{\omega_1}-(1-\overline{a_1})^{\omega_1}}{(1+\overline{a_1})^{\omega_1}+(1-\overline{a_1})^{\omega_1}} + \iota\,\dfrac{\left(1+\overline{b_1}\right)^{\omega_1}-\left(1-\overline{b_1}\right)^{\omega_1}}{\left(1+\overline{b_1}\right)^{\omega_1}+\left(1-\overline{b_1}\right)^{\omega_1}}, \\ \dfrac{\left(1+\underline{a_1}\right)^{\omega_{w1}}-\left(1-\underline{a_1}\right)^{\omega_1}}{\left(1+\underline{a_1}\right)^{\omega_1}+\left(1-\underline{a_1}\right)^{\omega_1}} + \iota\,\dfrac{\left(1+\underline{b_1}\right)^{\omega_1}-\left(1-\underline{b_1}\right)^{\omega_1}}{\left(1+\underline{b_1}\right)^{\omega_1}+\left(1-\underline{b_1}\right)^{\omega_1}} \end{pmatrix},$$

and

$$\omega_2\mathcal{A}_2 = \begin{pmatrix} \dfrac{(1+\overline{a_2})^{\omega_2}-(1-\overline{a_2})^{\omega_2}}{(1+\overline{a_2})^{\omega_2}+(1-\overline{a_2})^{\omega_2}} + \iota\,\dfrac{\left(1+\overline{b_2}\right)^{\omega_2}-\left(1-\overline{b_2}\right)^{\omega_2}}{\left(1+\overline{b_2}\right)^{\omega_2}+\left(1-\overline{b_2}\right)^{\omega_2}}, \\ \dfrac{\left(1+\underline{a_2}\right)^{\omega_2}-\left(1-\underline{a_2}\right)^{\omega_2}}{\left(1+\underline{a_2}\right)^{\omega_2}+\left(1-\underline{a_2}\right)^{\omega_2}} + \iota\,\dfrac{\left(1+\underline{b_2}\right)^{\omega_2}-\left(1-\underline{b_2}\right)^{\omega_2}}{\left(1+\underline{b_2}\right)^{\omega_2}+\left(1-\underline{b_2}\right)^{\omega_2}} \end{pmatrix},$$

then,

$$\omega_1\mathcal{A}_1 \oplus \omega_2\mathcal{A}_2 = \begin{pmatrix} \dfrac{(1+\overline{a_1})^{\omega_1}-(1-\overline{a_1})^{\omega_1}}{(1+\overline{a_1})^{\omega_1}+(1-\overline{a_1})^{\omega_1}} + \iota\,\dfrac{\left(1+\overline{b_1}\right)^{\omega_1}-\left(1-\overline{b_1}\right)^{\omega_1}}{\left(1+\overline{b_1}\right)^{\omega_1}+\left(1-\overline{b_1}\right)^{\omega_1}}, \\ \dfrac{\left(1+\underline{a_1}\right)^{\omega_{w1}}-\left(1-\underline{a_1}\right)^{\omega_1}}{\left(1+\underline{a_1}\right)^{\omega_1}+\left(1-\underline{a_1}\right)^{\omega_1}} + \iota\,\dfrac{\left(1+\underline{b_1}\right)^{\omega_1}-\left(1-\underline{b_1}\right)^{\omega_1}}{\left(1+\underline{b_1}\right)^{\omega_1}+\left(1-\underline{b_1}\right)^{\omega_1}} \end{pmatrix}$$

$$\oplus \begin{pmatrix} \dfrac{(1+\overline{a_2})^{\omega_2}-(1-\overline{a_2})^{\omega_2}}{(1+\overline{a_2})^{\omega_2}+(1-\overline{a_2})^{\omega_2}} + \iota\,\dfrac{\left(1+\overline{b_2}\right)^{\omega_2}-\left(1-\overline{b_2}\right)^{\omega_2}}{\left(1+\overline{b_2}\right)^{\omega_2}+\left(1-\overline{b_2}\right)^{\omega_2}}, \\ \dfrac{\left(1+\underline{a_2}\right)^{\omega_2}-\left(1-\underline{a_2}\right)^{\omega_2}}{\left(1+\underline{a_2}\right)^{\omega_2}+\left(1-\underline{a_2}\right)^{\omega_2}} + \iota\,\dfrac{\left(1+\underline{b_2}\right)^{\omega_2}-\left(1-\underline{b_2}\right)^{\omega_2}}{\left(1+\underline{b_2}\right)^{\omega_2}+\left(1-\underline{b_2}\right)^{\omega_2}} \end{pmatrix}$$

$$= \left(\begin{array}{c} \frac{\prod_{j=1}^{2} (1+\overline{a_j})^{\omega_j} - \prod_{j=1}^{2} (1-\overline{a_j})^{\omega_j}}{\prod_{j=1}^{2} (1+\overline{a_j})^{\omega_j} + \prod_{j=1}^{2} (1-\overline{a_j})^{\omega_j}} + + \iota \frac{\prod_{j=1}^{2} \left(1+\overline{b_j}\right)^{\omega_j} - \prod_{j=1}^{2} \left(1-\overline{b_j}\right)^{\omega_j}}{\prod_{j=1}^{2} \left(1+\overline{b_j}\right)^{\omega_j} + \prod_{j=1}^{2} \left(1-\overline{b_j}\right)^{\omega_j}}, \\ \frac{\prod_{j=1}^{2} \left(1+\underline{a_j}\right)^{\omega_j} - \prod_{j=1}^{2} \left(1-\underline{a_j}\right)^{\omega_j}}{\prod_{j=1}^{2} \left(1+\underline{a_j}\right)^{\omega_j} + \prod_{j=1}^{2} \left(1-\underline{a_j}\right)^{\omega_j}} + + \iota \frac{\prod_{j=1}^{2} \left(1+\underline{b_j}\right)^{\omega_j} - \prod_{j=1}^{2} \left(1-\underline{b_j}\right)^{\omega_j}}{\prod_{j=1}^{2} \left(1+\underline{b_j}\right)^{\omega_j} + \prod_{j=1}^{2} \left(1-\underline{b_j}\right)^{\omega_j}} \end{array} \right).$$

$\Rightarrow$ Eqn (7.2) is valid for $n = 2$.

Assume that eqn (7.2) is valid for $n =$ r, then we have:

$$\text{CFREWA}\left(\mathcal{A}_1,\ \mathcal{A}_2,\ \ldots,\ \mathcal{A}_r\right)$$

$$= \left(\begin{array}{c} \frac{\prod_{j=1}^{r} (1+\overline{a_j})^{\omega_j} - \prod_{j=1}^{r} (1-\overline{a_j})^{\omega_j}}{\prod_{j=1}^{r} (1+\overline{a_j})^{\omega_j} + \prod_{j=1}^{r} (1-\overline{a_j})^{\omega_j}} + \iota \frac{\prod_{j=1}^{r} \left(1+\overline{b_j}\right)^{\omega_j} - \prod_{j=1}^{r} \left(1-\overline{b_j}\right)^{\omega_j}}{\prod_{j=1}^{r} \left(1+\overline{b_j}\right)^{\omega_j} + \prod_{j=1}^{r} \left(1-\overline{b_j}\right)^{\omega_j}} \\ \frac{\prod_{j=1}^{r} \left(1+\underline{a_j}\right)^{\omega_j} - \prod_{j=1}^{r} \left(1-\underline{a_j}\right)^{\omega_j}}{\prod_{j=1}^{r} \left(1+\underline{a_j}\right)^{\omega_j} + \prod_{j=1}^{r} \left(1-\underline{a_j}\right)^{\omega_j}} + \iota \frac{\prod_{j=1}^{r} \left(1+\underline{b_j}\right)^{\omega_j} - \prod_{j=1}^{r} \left(1-\underline{b_j}\right)^{\omega_j}}{\prod_{j=1}^{r} \left(1+\underline{b_j}\right)^{\omega_j} + \prod_{j=1}^{r} (1-\underline{b})^{\omega_j}} \end{array} \right).$$

Now we prove that eqn (7.2) is valid for $n =$ r + 1. Then,

$$\text{CFREWA}\left(\mathcal{A}_1,\ \mathcal{A}_2,\ \ldots,\ \mathcal{A}_r,\ \mathcal{A}_{r+1}\right) = \text{CFREWA}\left(\mathcal{A}_1,\ \mathcal{A}_2,\ \ldots,\ \mathcal{A}_r\right) \oplus \mathcal{A}_{r+1}$$

$$= \left(\begin{array}{c} \frac{\prod_{j=1}^{r} (1+\overline{a_j})^{\omega_j} - \prod_{j=1}^{r} (1-\overline{a_j})^{\omega_j}}{\prod_{j=1}^{r} (1+\overline{a_j})^{\omega_j} + \prod_{j=1}^{r} (1-\overline{a_j})^{\omega_j}} + \iota \frac{\prod_{j=1}^{r} (1+\overline{b_j})^{\omega_j} - \prod_{j=1}^{r} (1-\overline{b_j})^{\omega_j}}{\prod_{j=1}^{r} (1+\overline{b_j})^{\omega_j} + \prod_{j=1}^{r} (1-\overline{b_j})^{\omega_j}}, \\ \frac{\prod_{j=1}^{r} \left(1+\underline{a_j}\right)^{\omega_j} - \prod_{j=1}^{r} \left(1-\underline{a_j}\right)^{\omega_j}}{\prod_{j=1}^{r} \left(1+\underline{a_j}\right)^{\omega_j} + \prod_{j=1}^{r} \left(1-\underline{a_j}\right)^{\omega_j}} + \iota \frac{\prod_{j=1}^{r} \left(1+\underline{b_j}\right)^{\omega_j} - \prod_{j=1}^{r} \left(1-\underline{b_j}\right)^{\omega_j}}{\prod_{j=1}^{r} \left(1+\underline{b_j}\right)^{\omega_j} + \prod_{j=1}^{r} \left(1-\underline{b_j}\right)^{\omega_j}} \end{array} \right)$$

$$\oplus \left(\begin{array}{c} \frac{\left(1+\overline{a_{r+1}}\right)^{\omega_{r+1}} - \left(1-\overline{a_{r+1}}\right)^{\omega_{r+1}}}{\left(1+\overline{a_{r+1}}\right)^{\omega_{r+1}} + \left(1-\overline{a_{r+1}}\right)^{\omega_{r+1}}} + \iota \frac{\left(1+\overline{b_{r+1}}\right)^{\omega_{r+1}} - \left(1-\overline{b_{r+1}}\right)^{\omega_{r+1}}}{\left(1+\overline{b_{r+1}}\right)^{\omega_{r+1}} + \left(1-\overline{b_{r+1}}\right)^{\omega_{r+1}}}, \\ \frac{\left(1+\underline{a_{r+1}}\right)^{\omega_{r+1}} - \left(1-\underline{a_{r+1}}\right)^{\omega_{r+1}}}{\left(1+\underline{a_{r+1}}\right)^{\omega_{r+1}} + \left(1-\underline{a_{r+1}}\right)^{\omega_{r+1}}} + \iota \frac{\left(1+\underline{b_{r+1}}\right)^{\omega_{r+1}} - \left(1-\underline{b_{r+1}}\right)^{\omega_{r+1}}}{\left(1+\underline{b_{r+1}}\right)^{\omega_{r+1}} + \left(1-\underline{b_{r+1}}\right)^{\omega_{r+1}}} \end{array} \right)$$

$$= \left(\begin{array}{c} \frac{\prod_{j=1}^{r+1} (1+\overline{a_j})^{\omega_j} - \prod_{j=1}^{r+1} (1-\overline{a_j})^{\omega_j}}{\prod_{j=1}^{r+1} (1+\overline{a_j})^{\omega_j} + \prod_{j=1}^{r+1} (1-\overline{a_j})^{\omega_j}} + \iota \frac{\prod_{j=1}^{r+1} (1+\overline{b_j})^{\omega_j} - \prod_{j=1}^{r+1} (1-\overline{b_j})^{\omega_j}}{\prod_{j=1}^{r+1} (1+\overline{b_j})^{\omega_j} + \prod_{j=1}^{r+1} (1-\overline{b_j})^{\omega_j}} \\ \frac{\prod_{j=1}^{r+1} \left(1+\underline{a_j}\right)^{\omega_j} - \prod_{j=1}^{r+1} \left(1-\underline{a_j}\right)^{\omega_j}}{\prod_{j=1}^{r+1} \left(1+\underline{a_j}\right)^{\omega_j} + \prod_{j=1}^{r+1} \left(1-\underline{a_j}\right)^{\omega_j}} + \iota \frac{\prod_{j=1}^{r+1} \left(1+\underline{b_j}\right)^{\omega_j} - \prod_{j=1}^{r+1} \left(1-\underline{b_j}\right)^{\omega_j}}{\prod_{j=1}^{r+1} \left(1+\underline{b_j}\right)^{\omega_j} + \prod_{j=1}^{r+1} \left(1-\underline{b_j}\right)^{\omega_j}} \end{array} \right).$$

Hence, eqn (7.2) is valid $\forall\ j$.

7.2.1 Properties of CFREWA AOs

Now we explore the properties of the CFREWA operator. These properties are idempotency, boundedness, and monotonicity, respectively.

- Let $\mathcal{A}_j = \left\{\left(\overline{a_j} + \iota\overline{b_j},\ \underline{a_j} + \iota\underline{b_j}\right)\right\}$ $j = 1,\ 2, \ldots,\ n$ be the collection of CFRNs, and if $\mathcal{A}_j = \mathcal{A}$ for all j then:

$$\text{CFREWA}\left(\mathcal{A}_1,\ \mathcal{A}_2,\ \ldots,\ \mathcal{A}_n\right) = \mathcal{A}.$$

Proof: Since all $\mathcal{A}_j = \mathcal{A}$ that is $\overline{a_j} = \overline{a},\ \overline{b_j} = \overline{b},\ \underline{a_j} = \underline{a}$ and $\underline{b_j} = \underline{b}$, then, we get:

$$\begin{aligned}
&\text{CFREWA}\left(\mathcal{A}_1,\ \mathcal{A}_2,\ \ldots,\ \mathcal{A}_n\right)\\
&= \left(\begin{array}{c}
\dfrac{\prod_{j=1}^{r+1}(1+\overline{a_j})^{\omega_j} - \prod_{j=1}^{r+1}(1-\overline{a_j})^{\omega_j}}{\prod_{j=1}^{r+1}(1+\overline{a_j})^{\omega_j} + \prod_{j=1}^{r+1}(1-\overline{a_j})^{\omega_j}} + \iota\dfrac{\prod_{j=1}^{r+1}(1+\overline{b_j})^{\omega_j} - \prod_{j=1}^{r+1}(1-\overline{b_j})^{\omega_j}}{\prod_{j=1}^{r+1}(1+\overline{b_j})^{\omega_j} + \prod_{j=1}^{r+1}(1-\overline{b_j})^{\omega_j}} \\
\dfrac{\prod_{j=1}^{r+1}\left(1+\underline{a_j}\right)^{\omega_j} - \prod_{j=1}^{r+1}\left(1-\underline{a_j}\right)^{\omega_j}}{\prod_{j=1}^{r+1}\left(1+\underline{a_j}\right)^{\omega_j} + \prod_{j=1}^{r+1}\left(1-\underline{a_j}\right)^{\omega_j}} + \iota\dfrac{\prod_{j=1}^{r+1}\left(1+\underline{b_j}\right)^{\omega_j} - \prod_{j=1}^{r+1}\left(1-\underline{b_j}\right)^{\omega_j}}{\prod_{j=1}^{r+1}\left(1+\underline{b_j}\right)^{\omega_j} + \prod_{j=1}^{r+1}(1-\underline{b})^{\omega_j}}
\end{array}\right)\\
&= \left(\begin{array}{c}
\dfrac{(1+\overline{a})-(1-\overline{a})}{(1+\overline{a})+(1-\overline{a})} + \iota\dfrac{(1+\overline{b})-(1-\overline{b})}{(1+\overline{b})+(1-\overline{b})} \\
\dfrac{(1+\underline{a})-(1-\underline{a})}{(1+\underline{a})+(1-\underline{a})} + \iota\dfrac{(1+\underline{b})-(1-\underline{b})}{(1+\underline{b})+(1-\underline{b})}
\end{array}\right)\\
&= \left(\overline{a} + \iota\overline{b}, \underline{a} + \iota\underline{b}\right) = \mathcal{A}.
\end{aligned}$$

- Let $\mathcal{A}_j = \left\{\left(\overline{a_j} + \iota\overline{b_j},\ \underline{a_j} + \iota\underline{b_j}\right)\right\}$ $j = 1,\ 2, \ldots,\ n$ be the collection of CFRNs, and $\mathcal{A}^- = \left(\min_j\left\{\overline{a_j}\right\} + \iota\ \min_j\left\{\overline{b_j}\right\},\ \min_j\left\{\underline{a_j}\right\} + \iota\ \min_j\left\{\underline{b_j}\right\}\right)$, and $\mathcal{A}^+ = \left(\max_j\left\{\overline{a_j}\right\} + \iota\max_j\left\{\overline{b_j}\right\},\ \max_j\left\{\underline{a_j}\right\} + \iota\ \max_j\left\{\underline{b_j}\right\}\right)$, then:

$$\mathcal{A}^- \leq \text{CFREWA}\left(\mathcal{A}_1,\ \mathcal{A}_2,\ \ldots,\ \mathcal{A}_n\right) \leq \mathcal{A}^+.$$

Proof: Assume that $\boldsymbol{f}(\mathfrak{e}) = \frac{1-\mathfrak{e}}{1+\mathfrak{e}}$ for $\mathfrak{e} \in [0,\ 1]$ then $\boldsymbol{f}'(\mathfrak{e}) = \frac{-2}{1+\mathfrak{e}^2} < 0$. Hence $f(x)$ is a decreasing function. As

$\overline{a_{\min}} \leq \overline{a_j} \leq \overline{a_{\max}}$ for all j, then $f\left(\overline{a_{\max}}\right) \leq f\left(\overline{a_j}\right) \leq f\left(\overline{a_{\min}}\right)$ for $j = 1, 2, \ldots, n$ that is $\frac{1-\overline{a_{\max}}}{1+\overline{a_{\max}}} \leq \frac{1-\overline{a_j}}{1+\overline{a_j}} \leq \frac{1-\overline{a_{\min}}}{1+\overline{a_{\min}}}$.

Now if ω_j be the weight vector for $\mathcal{A}_j$, then:

$$\left(\frac{1-\overline{a_{\max}}}{1+\overline{a_{\max}}}\right)^{\omega_j} \leq \left(\frac{1-\overline{a_j}}{1+\overline{a_j}}\right)^{\omega_j} \leq \left(\frac{1-\overline{a_{\min}}}{1+\overline{a_{\min}}}\right)^{\omega_j}$$

$$\prod_{j=1}^{n}\left(\frac{1-\overline{a_{\max}}}{1+\overline{a_{\max}}}\right)^{\omega_j} \leq \prod_{j=1}^{n}\left(\frac{1-\overline{a_j}}{1+\overline{a_j}}\right)^{\omega_j} \leq \prod_{j=1}^{n}\left(\frac{1-\overline{a_{\min}}}{1+\overline{a_{\min}}}\right)^{\omega_j}$$

$$\Leftrightarrow \sum_{j=1}^{n}\left(\frac{1-\overline{a_{\max}}}{1+\overline{a_{\max}}}\right)^{\omega_j} \leq \prod_{j=1}^{n}\left(\frac{1-\overline{a_j}}{1+\overline{a_j}}\right)^{\omega_j} \leq \sum_{j=1}^{n}\left(\frac{1-\overline{a_{\min}}}{1+\overline{a_{\min}}}\right)^{\omega_j}$$

$$\Leftrightarrow \left(\frac{1-\overline{a_{\max}}}{1+\overline{a_{\max}}}\right) \leq \prod_{j=1}^{n}\left(\frac{1-\overline{a_j}}{1+\overline{a_j}}\right)^{\omega_j} \leq \left(\frac{1-\overline{a_{\min}}}{1+\overline{a_{\min}}}\right)$$

$$\Leftrightarrow \left(\frac{2}{1+\overline{a_{\max}}}\right) \leq 1+\prod_{j=1}^{n}\left(\frac{1-\overline{a_j}}{1+\overline{a_j}}\right)^{\omega_j} \leq \left(\frac{2}{1+\overline{a_{\min}}}\right)$$

$$\Leftrightarrow \left(\frac{1+\overline{a_{\min}}}{2}\right) \leq \frac{1}{1+\prod\limits_{j=1}^{n}\left(\frac{1-\overline{a_j}}{1+\overline{a_j}}\right)^{\omega_j}} \leq \frac{1+\overline{a_{\max}}}{2}$$

$$\Leftrightarrow 1+\overline{a_{\min}} \leq \frac{2}{1+\prod\limits_{j=1}^{n}\left(\frac{1-\overline{a_j}}{1+\overline{a_j}}\right)^{\omega_j}} \leq 1+\overline{a_{\max}}$$

$$\Leftrightarrow \overline{a_{\min}} \leq \frac{2}{1+\prod\limits_{j=1}^{n}\left(\frac{1-\overline{a_j}}{1+\overline{a_j}}\right)^{\omega_j}} - 1 \leq \overline{a_{\max}}.$$

That is:

$$\Leftrightarrow \overline{a_{\min}} \leq \frac{\prod\limits_{j=1}^{n}\left(1+\overline{a_j}\right)^{\omega_j} - \prod\limits_{j=1}^{n}\left(1-\overline{a_j}\right)^{\omega_j}}{\prod\limits_{j=1}^{n}\left(1+\overline{a_j}\right)^{\omega_j} + \prod\limits_{j=1}^{n}\left(1-\overline{a_j}\right)^{\omega_j}} \leq \overline{a_{\max}}.$$

Similarly, we can get:

$$\overline{b_{\min}} \leq \frac{\prod\limits_{j=1}^{n}\left(1+\overline{b_j}\right)^{\omega_j} - \prod\limits_{j=1}^{n}\left(1-\overline{b_j}\right)^{\omega_j}}{\prod\limits_{j=1}^{n}\left(1+\overline{b_j}\right)^{\omega_j} + \prod\limits_{j=1}^{n}\left(1-\overline{b_j}\right)^{\omega_j}} \leq \overline{b_{\max}}.$$

Similar is the case for lower parts $\underline{a_j}$ and $\underline{b_j}$. Hence, we can conclude that:

$$\mathcal{A}^- \leq \text{CFREWA}\left(\mathcal{A}_1,\ \mathcal{A}_2,\ \ldots,\ \mathcal{A}_n\right) \leq \mathcal{A}^+.$$

- Let $\mathcal{A}_j = \left\{\left(\overline{a_j} + \iota\overline{b_j},\ \underline{a_j} + \iota\underline{b_j}\right)\right\}$ and $\mathcal{A}_j^* = \left\{\left(\overline{a_j^*} + \iota\overline{b_j^*},\ \underline{a_j^*} + \iota\underline{b_j^*}\right)\right\}$ $j = 1,\ 2, \ldots,\ n$ be the two families CFRNs, and $\overline{a_j} \leq \overline{a_j^*}, \overline{b_j} \leq \overline{b_j^*}$, $\underline{a_j} \leq \underline{a_j^*}$ and $\underline{b_j} \leq \underline{b_j^*}$, then:

$$\text{CFREWA}\left(\mathcal{A}_1,\ \mathcal{A}_2,\ \ldots,\ \mathcal{A}_n\right) \leq \text{CFREWA}\left(\mathcal{A}_1^*,\ \mathcal{A}_2^*,\ \ldots,\ \mathcal{A}_n^*\right).$$

Proof: Assume that $\boldsymbol{f}\left(\mathfrak{e}\right) = \frac{1-\mathfrak{e}}{1+\mathfrak{e}}$ for $\mathfrak{e} \in [0,\ 1]$. Hence $f\left(x\right)$ is a decreasing function. Now for $\overline{a_j} \leq \overline{a_j^*}$, we get $f\left(\overline{a_j^*}\right) \leq f\left(\overline{a_j}\right)$ for $j = 1,\ 2, \ldots,\ n$ that is $\frac{1-\overline{a_j^*}}{1+\overline{a_j^*}} \leq \frac{1-\overline{a_j}}{1+\overline{a_j}}$. Now if ω_j be the WVs for $\mathcal{A}_j$, then:

$$\left(\frac{1-\overline{a_j^*}}{1+\overline{a_j^*}}\right)^{\omega_j} \leq \left(\frac{1-\overline{a_j}}{1+\overline{a_j}}\right)^{\omega_j}$$

$$\prod_{j=1}^{n}\left(\frac{1-\overline{a_j^*}}{1+\overline{a_j^*}}\right)^{\omega_j} \leq \prod_{j=1}^{n}\left(\frac{1-\overline{a_j}}{1+\overline{a_j}}\right)^{\omega_j}$$

$$\Leftrightarrow 1+\prod_{j=1}^{n}\left(\frac{1-\overline{a_j^*}}{1+\overline{a_j^*}}\right)^{\omega_j} \leq 1+\prod_{j=1}^{n}\left(\frac{1-\overline{a_j}}{1+\overline{a_j}}\right)^{\omega_j}$$

$$\Leftrightarrow \frac{1}{1+\prod\limits_{j=1}^{n}\left(\frac{1-\overline{a_j}}{1+\overline{a_j}}\right)^{\omega_j}} \leq \frac{1}{1+\prod\limits_{j=1}^{n}\left(\frac{1-\overline{a_j^*}}{1+\overline{a_j^*}}\right)^{\omega_j}}$$

$$\Leftrightarrow \frac{2}{1+\prod\limits_{j=1}^{n}\left(\frac{1-\overline{a_j}}{1+\overline{a_j}}\right)^{\omega_j}} \leq \frac{2}{1+\prod\limits_{j=1}^{n}\left(\frac{1-\overline{a_j^*}}{1+\overline{a_j^*}}\right)^{\omega_j}}$$

$$\Leftrightarrow \frac{2}{1+\prod\limits_{j=1}^{n}\left(\frac{1-\overline{a_j}}{1+\overline{a_j}}\right)^{\omega_j}} - 1 \leq \frac{2}{1+\prod\limits_{j=1}^{n}\left(\frac{1-\overline{a_j^*}}{1+\overline{a_j^*}}\right)^{\omega_j}} - 1.$$

That is:

$$\frac{\prod_{j=1}^{n}(1+\overline{a_j})^{\omega_j}-\prod_{j=1}^{n}(1-\overline{a_j})^{\omega_j}}{\prod_{j=1}^{n}(1+\overline{a_j})^{\omega_j}+\prod_{j=1}^{n}(1-\overline{a_j})^{\omega_j}}\leq\frac{\prod_{j=1}^{n}\left(1+\overline{a_j^*}\right)^{\omega_j}-\prod_{j=1}^{n}\left(1-\overline{a_j^*}\right)^{\omega_j}}{\prod_{j=1}^{n}\left(1+\overline{a_j^*}\right)^{\omega_j}+\prod_{j=1}^{n}\left(1-\overline{a_j^*}\right)^{\omega_j}}.$$

Similarly:

$$\frac{\prod_{j=1}^{n}\left(1+\overline{b_j}\right)^{\omega_j}-\prod_{j=1}^{n}\left(1-\overline{b_j}\right)^{\omega_j}}{\prod_{j=1}^{n}\left(1+\overline{b_j}\right)^{\omega_j}+\prod_{j=1}^{n}\left(1-\overline{b_j}\right)^{\omega_j}}\leq\frac{\prod_{j=1}^{n}\left(1+\overline{b_j^*}\right)^{\omega_j}-\prod_{j=1}^{n}\left(1-\overline{b_j^*}\right)^{\omega_j}}{\prod_{j=1}^{n}\left(1+\overline{b_j^*}\right)^{\omega_j}+\prod_{j=1}^{n}\left(1-\overline{b_j^*}\right)^{\omega_j}}.$$

Similar is the case for lower values $\underline{a_j}$ and $\underline{b_j}$.
Hence, we conclude that:

$$\text{CFREWA}\left(\mathcal{A}_1,\ \mathcal{A}_2,\ \ldots,\ \mathcal{A}_n\right)\leq\text{CFREWA}\left(\mathcal{A}_1^*,\ \mathcal{A}_2^*,\ \ldots,\ \mathcal{A}_n^*\right).$$

7.2.2 CFREWG AOs

In this section, we have explored the idea of CFREWG AOs.

Definition 7.3: Let $\mathcal{A}_j = \left\{\left(\overline{a_j}+\iota\overline{b_j},\ \underline{a_j}+\iota\underline{b_j}\right)\right\}\ j = 1,\ 2,\ldots,\ n$ be the collection of CFRNs and $\omega = (\omega_1,\ \omega_2,\ldots,\ \omega_n)$ be a WV of $\mathcal{A}_j\ (j = 1,\ 2,..,\ n)$ with $\omega_j \in [0,\ 1]$ and $\sum_{j=1}^{n}\omega_j = 1$, then the notion CFREWG AOs is introduced by

$$\text{CFREWG}\left(\mathcal{A}_1,\ \mathcal{A}_2,\ \ldots,\ \mathcal{A}_n\right) = (\mathcal{A}_1)^{\omega_1}\otimes(\mathcal{A}_2)^{\omega_2}\otimes\cdots\otimes(\mathcal{A}_n)^{\omega_n}. \quad (7.3)$$

Theorem 7.3: The results after applying the notion of eqn (7.3) are again CFRNs:

$$\text{CFREWG}\left(\mathcal{A}_1,\ \mathcal{A}_2,\ \ldots,\ \mathcal{A}_n\right) = \left(\begin{array}{c}\frac{2\prod_{j=1}^{n}(\overline{a_j})^{\omega_j}}{\prod_{j=1}^{n}(2-\overline{a_j})^{\omega_j}+\prod_{j=1}^{n}(\overline{a_j})^{\omega_j}}+\iota\frac{2\prod_{j=1}^{n}\left(\overline{b_j}\right)^{\omega_j}}{\prod_{j=1}^{n}\left(2-\overline{b_j}\right)^{\omega_j}+\prod_{j=1}^{n}\left(\overline{b_j}\right)^{\omega_j}},\\ \frac{2\prod_{j=1}^{n}\left(\underline{a_j}\right)^{\omega_j}}{\prod_{j=1}^{n}\left(2-\underline{a_j}\right)^{\omega_j}+\prod_{j=1}^{n}\left(\underline{a_j}\right)^{\omega_j}}+\iota\frac{2\prod_{j=1}^{n}\left(\overline{b_j}\right)^{\omega_j}}{\prod_{j=1}^{n}\left(2-\underline{b_j}\right)^{\omega_j}+\prod_{j=1}^{n}\left(\underline{b_j}\right)^{\omega_j}},\end{array}\right). \quad (7.4)$$

Proof: It would be proved with the assistance of mathematical induction.

Assume $n = 2$, then we find:

$$\text{CFREWG}\left(\mathcal{A}_1,\ \mathcal{A}_2\right) = \left(\mathcal{A}_1\right)^{\omega_1} \otimes \left(\mathcal{A}_2\right)^{\omega_2}.$$

We have:

$$\left(\mathcal{A}_1\right)^{\omega_1} = \left(\begin{array}{c} \frac{2(\overline{a_1})^{\omega_1}}{(2-\overline{a_1})^{\omega_1}+(\overline{a_1})^{\omega_1}} + \iota\,\frac{2\left(\overline{b_1}\right)^{\omega_1}}{\left(2-\overline{b_1}\right)^{\omega_1}+\left(\overline{b_1}\right)^{\omega_1}}, \\ \frac{2\left(\underline{a_1}\right)^{\omega_1}}{\left(2-\underline{a_1}\right)^{\omega_1}+\left(\underline{a_1}\right)^{\omega_1}} + \iota\,\frac{2\left(\underline{b_1}\right)^{\omega_1}}{\left(2-\underline{b_1}\right)^{\omega_1}+\left(\underline{b_1}\right)^{\omega_1}} \end{array}\right),$$

and

$$\left(\mathcal{A}_2\right)^{\omega_2} = \left(\begin{array}{c} \frac{2(\overline{a_2})^{\omega_1}}{(2-\overline{a_2})^{\omega_1}+(\overline{a_2})^{\omega_1}} + \iota\,\frac{2\left(\overline{b_2}\right)^{\omega_1}}{\left(2-\overline{b_2}\right)^{\omega_1}+\left(\overline{b_2}\right)^{\omega_1}}, \\ \frac{2\left(\underline{a_2}\right)^{\omega_1}}{\left(2-\underline{a_2}\right)^{\omega_1}+\left(\underline{a_2}\right)^{\omega_1}} + \iota\,\frac{2\left(\underline{b_2}\right)^{\omega_1}}{\left(2-\underline{b_2}\right)^{\omega_1}+\left(\underline{b_2}\right)^{\omega_1}} \end{array}\right).$$

Then,

$$\begin{aligned} &\left(\mathcal{A}_1\right)^{\omega_1} \otimes \left(\mathcal{A}_2\right)^{\omega_2} \\ &= \left(\begin{array}{c} \frac{2(\overline{a_1})^{\omega_1}}{(2-\overline{a_1})^{\omega_1}+(\overline{a_1})^{\omega_1}} + \iota\,\frac{2\left(\overline{b_1}\right)^{\omega_1}}{\left(2-\overline{b_1}\right)^{\omega_1}+\left(\overline{b_1}\right)^{\omega_1}}, \\ \frac{2\left(\underline{a_1}\right)^{\omega_1}}{\left(2-\underline{a_1}\right)^{\omega_1}+\left(\underline{a_1}\right)^{\omega_1}} + \iota\,\frac{2\left(\underline{b_1}\right)^{\omega_1}}{\left(2-\underline{b_1}\right)^{\omega_1}+\left(\underline{b_1}\right)^{\omega_1}} \end{array}\right) \\ &\otimes \left(\begin{array}{c} \frac{2(\overline{a_2})^{\omega_1}}{(2-\overline{a_2})^{\omega_1}+(\overline{a_2})^{\omega_1}} + \iota\,\frac{2\left(\overline{b_2}\right)^{\omega_1}}{\left(2-\overline{b_2}\right)^{\omega_1}+\left(\overline{b_2}\right)^{\omega_1}}, \\ \frac{2\left(\underline{a_2}\right)^{\omega_1}}{\left(2-\underline{a_2}\right)^{\omega_1}+\left(\underline{a_2}\right)^{\omega_1}} + \iota\,\frac{2\left(\underline{b_2}\right)^{\omega_1}}{\left(2-\underline{b_2}\right)^{\omega_1}+\left(\underline{b_2}\right)^{\omega_1}} \end{array}\right) \\ &= \left(\begin{array}{c} \frac{2\prod_{j=1}^{2}(\overline{a_j})^{\omega_j}}{\prod_{j=1}^{2}(2-\overline{a_j})^{\omega_j}+\prod_{j=1}^{2}(\overline{a_j})^{\omega_j}} + \iota\,\frac{2\prod_{j=1}^{2}\left(\overline{b_j}\right)^{\omega_j}}{\prod_{j=1}^{2}\left(2-\overline{b_j}\right)^{\omega_j}+\prod_{j=1}^{2}\left(\overline{b_j}\right)^{\omega_j}}, \\ \frac{2\prod_{j=1}^{2}\left(\underline{a_j}\right)^{\omega_j}}{\prod_{j=1}^{2}\left(2-\underline{a_j}\right)^{\omega_j}+\prod_{j=1}^{2}\left(\underline{a_j}\right)^{\omega_j}} + \iota\,\frac{2\prod_{j=1}^{2}\left(\underline{b_j}\right)^{\omega_j}}{\prod_{j=1}^{2}\left(2-\underline{b_j}\right)^{\omega_j}+\prod_{j=1}^{2}\left(\underline{b_j}\right)^{\omega_j}} \end{array}\right). \\ &= CFREWG\left(\mathcal{A}_1,\ \mathcal{A}_2\right) \end{aligned}$$

Hence, eqn (7.4) is true for $n = 2$.

Now assume that eqn (7.4) is true for $n = k$, then we have:

$$\text{CFREWG}\left(\mathcal{A}_1,\ \mathcal{A}_2,\ \ldots,\ \mathcal{A}_k\right)$$

$$
= \begin{pmatrix}
\dfrac{2\prod_{j=1}^{k}(\overline{a_j})^{\omega_j}}{\prod_{j=1}^{k}(2-\overline{a_j})^{\omega_j}+\prod_{j=1}^{k}(\overline{a_j})^{\omega_j}} + \iota\,\dfrac{2\prod_{j=1}^{k}(\overline{b_j})^{\omega_j}}{\prod_{j=1}^{k}(2-\overline{b_j})^{\omega_j}+\prod_{j=1}^{k}(\overline{b_j})^{\omega_j}}, \\
\dfrac{2\prod_{j=1}^{k}(\underline{a_j})^{\omega_j}}{\prod_{j=1}^{k}(2-\underline{a_j})^{\omega_j}+\prod_{j=1}^{k}(\underline{a_j})^{\omega_j}} + \iota\,\dfrac{2\prod_{j=1}^{k}(\underline{b_j})^{\omega_j}}{\prod_{j=1}^{k}(2-\underline{b_j})^{\omega_j}+\prod_{j=1}^{k}(\underline{b_j})^{\omega_j}}
\end{pmatrix}
$$

Now we prove that eqn (7.4) is valid for $n = k + 1$. Then:

$$
\begin{aligned}
&\mathrm{CFEWG}(\mathcal{A}_1, \mathcal{A}_2, \ldots, \mathcal{A}_k, \mathcal{A}_{k+1}) \\
&= \mathrm{CFREWG}(\mathcal{A}_1, \mathcal{A}_2, \ldots, \mathcal{A}_k) \otimes \mathcal{A}_{k+1}
\end{aligned}
$$

$$
= \begin{pmatrix}
\dfrac{2\prod_{j=1}^{k}(\overline{a_j})^{\omega_j}}{\prod_{j=1}^{k}(2-\overline{a_j})^{\omega_j}+\prod_{j=1}^{k}(\overline{a_j})^{\omega_j}} + \iota\,\dfrac{2\prod_{j=1}^{k}(\overline{b_j})^{\omega_j}}{\prod_{j=1}^{k}(2-\overline{b_j})^{\omega_j}+\prod_{j=1}^{k}(\overline{b_j})^{\omega_j}}, \\
\dfrac{2\prod_{j=1}^{k}(\underline{a_j})^{\omega_j}}{\prod_{j=1}^{k}(2-\underline{a_j})^{\omega_j}+\prod_{j=1}^{k}(\underline{a_j})^{\omega_j}} + \iota\,\dfrac{2\prod_{j=1}^{2}(\underline{b_j})^{\omega_j}}{\prod_{j=1}^{k}(2-\underline{b_j})^{\omega_j}+\prod_{j=1}^{k}(\underline{b_j})^{\omega_j}}
\end{pmatrix}
$$

$$
\otimes \begin{pmatrix}
\dfrac{2(\overline{a_{k+1}})^{\omega_{k+1}}}{(2-\overline{a_{k+1}})^{\omega_1}+(\overline{a_{k+1}})^{\omega_{k+1}}} + \iota\,\dfrac{2(\overline{b_{k+1}})^{\omega_{k+1}}}{(2-\overline{b_{k+1}})^{\omega_{k+1}}+(\overline{b_{k+1}})^{\omega_{k+1}}}, \\
\dfrac{2(\underline{a_{k+1}})^{\omega_{k+1}}}{(2-\underline{a_{k+1}})^{\omega_1}+(\underline{a_{k+1}})^{\omega_{k+1}}} + \iota\,\dfrac{2(\underline{b_{k+1}})^{\omega_{k+1}}}{(2-\underline{b_{k+1}})^{\omega_{k+1}}+(\underline{b_{k+1}})^{\omega_{k+1}}}
\end{pmatrix}
$$

$$
= \begin{pmatrix}
\dfrac{2\prod_{j=1}^{k+1}(\overline{a_j})^{\omega_j}}{\prod_{j=1}^{k+1}(2-\overline{a_j})^{\omega_j}+\prod_{j=1}^{k+1}(\overline{a_j})^{\omega_j}} + \iota\,\dfrac{2\prod_{j=1}^{k+1}(\overline{b_j})^{\omega_j}}{\prod_{j=1}^{k}(2-\overline{b_j})^{\omega_j}+\prod_{j=1}^{k}(\overline{b_j})^{\omega_j}}, \\
\dfrac{2\prod_{j=1}^{k+1}(\underline{a_j})^{\omega_j}}{\prod_{j=1}^{k+1}(2-\underline{a_j})^{\omega_j}+\prod_{j=1}^{k+1}(\underline{a_j})^{\omega_j}} + \iota\,\dfrac{2\prod_{j=1}^{k+1}(\underline{b_j})^{\omega_j}}{\prod_{j=1}^{k+1}(2-\underline{b_j})^{\omega_j}+\prod_{j=1}^{k+1}(\underline{b_j})^{\omega_j}}
\end{pmatrix}.
$$

Hence, eqn (7.4) is valid $\forall\, j$.

Remark 7.1. The notion of CFREWG AOs satisfies the properties of idempotency, monotonicity, and boundedness.

7.3 The WASPAS Technique based on CFRE AOs

This section of the chapter is devoted to defining the idea of the WASPAS approach for CFRNs. Here, we have used the notion of CFREWA and CFREWG AOs.

7.3.1 Algorithm of the proposed study

Assume that there are m alternatives and a set of alternatives is given by $\mathfrak{L} = \{\mathfrak{L}_1, \mathfrak{L}_2, \ldots, \mathfrak{L}_m\}$. The n attributes of these alternatives are denoted by $\mathbb{T} = \{\mathbb{T}_1, \mathbb{T}_2, \ldots, \mathbb{T}_n\}$. The weights of these attributes $\omega_j = (\omega_1, \omega_2, \ldots, \omega_n)^T$ such that $\sum_{j=1}^{n} \omega_j = 1$ and $\omega_j \in [0, 1]\ \forall\, j$. Assume that the decision analyst provides theory assessment in the form of CFRNs given by $\mathcal{A}_{ij} = \left\{\left(\overline{a_{ij}} + \iota\overline{b_{ij}},\ \underline{a_{ij}} + \iota\underline{b_{ij}}\right)\right\}$ for $i = 1, 2, .., m$ and $j = 1, 2, \ldots, n$. Now, the step-wise algorithm is given by

Step 1: Collect the information in the form of CFRNs proposed by decision makers and arrange it in the form of matric given by

$$\mathcal{M} = \begin{bmatrix} \mathcal{A}_{11} & \mathcal{A}_{12} & \cdots & \mathcal{A}_{1n} \\ \mathcal{A}_{21} & \mathcal{A}_{22} & \cdots & \mathcal{A}_{2n} \\ \vdots & \ddots & \cdots & \vdots \\ \mathcal{A}_{m1} & \mathcal{A}_{m2} & & \mathcal{A}_{mn} \end{bmatrix}.$$

Step 2: Utilize the following formula, if there is a need to normalize the information based on the information of cost type or benefit type attributes. The formulas are given by

$$\mathcal{N} = \begin{cases} \mathcal{A}_{ij} & \text{for benefit type attributes} \\ (\mathcal{A}_{ij})^c & \text{for cost type attributes} \end{cases},$$

where $(\mathcal{A}_{ij})^c = \left\{\left(\left(1 - \underline{a_{ij}}\right) + \iota\left(1 - \underline{b_{ij}}\right), (1 - \overline{a_{ij}}) + \iota\left(1 - \overline{b_{ij}}\right)\right)\right\}$ represent the complement of $\mathcal{A}_{ij}$.

Step 3: Find out the relative importance of the alternatives relying on the WSM by the formula given by

$$(\mathcal{A}_j)^{WS} = \text{CFREWA}\left(\mathcal{A}_1, \mathcal{A}_2, \ldots, \mathcal{A}_n\right)$$
$$= \begin{pmatrix} \dfrac{\prod_{j=1}^{n}(1+\overline{a_j})^{\omega_j} - \prod_{j=1}^{n}(1-\overline{a_j})^{\omega_j}}{\prod_{j=1}^{n}(1+\overline{a_j})^{\omega_j} + \prod_{j=1}^{n}(1-\overline{a_j})^{\omega_j}} + \iota\dfrac{\prod_{j=1}^{n}(1+\overline{b_j})^{\omega_j} - \prod_{j=1}^{n}(1-\overline{b_j})^{\omega_j}}{\prod_{j=1}^{n}(1+\overline{b_j})^{\omega_j} + \prod_{j=1}^{n}(1-\overline{b_j})^{\omega_j}}, \\ \dfrac{\prod_{j=1}^{n}\left(1+\underline{a_j}\right)^{\omega_j} - \prod_{j=1}^{n}\left(1-\underline{a_j}\right)^{\omega_j}}{\prod_{j=1}^{n}\left(1+\underline{a_j}\right)^{\omega_j} + \prod_{j=1}^{n}\left(1-\underline{a_j}\right)^{\omega_j}} + \iota\dfrac{\prod_{j=1}^{n}\left(1+\underline{b_j}\right)^{\omega_j} - \prod_{j=1}^{n}\left(1-\underline{b_j}\right)^{\omega_j}}{\prod_{j=1}^{n}\left(1+\underline{b_j}\right)^{\omega_j} + \prod_{j=1}^{n}\left(1-\underline{b_j}\right)^{\omega_j}} \end{pmatrix}.$$

Step 4: Find out the relative importance of the alternatives relying on the WSP by the formula given by

$$(\mathcal{A}_j)^{WP} = \text{CFREWG}\,(\mathcal{A}_1,\, \mathcal{A}_2,\, \ldots,\, \mathcal{A}_n)$$

$$= \begin{pmatrix} \dfrac{2\prod\limits_{j=1}^{n} (\overline{a_j})^{\omega_j}}{\prod\limits_{j=1}^{n} (2-\overline{a_j})^{\omega_j} + \prod\limits_{j=1}^{n} (\overline{a_j})^{\omega_j}} + \iota\, \dfrac{2\prod\limits_{j=1}^{n} \left(\overline{b_j}\right)^{\omega_j}}{\prod\limits_{j=1}^{n} \left(2-\overline{b_j}\right)^{\omega_j} + \prod\limits_{j=1}^{n} \left(\overline{b_j}\right)^{\omega_j}}, \\ \dfrac{2\prod\limits_{j=1}^{n} \left(\underline{a_j}\right)^{\omega_j}}{\prod\limits_{j=1}^{n} \left(2-\underline{a_j}\right)^{\omega_j} + \prod\limits_{j=1}^{n} \left(\underline{a_j}\right)^{\omega_j}} + \iota\, \dfrac{2\prod\limits_{j=1}^{n} \left(\overline{b_j}\right)^{\omega_j}}{\prod\limits_{j=1}^{n} \left(2-\underline{b_j}\right)^{\omega_j} + \prod\limits_{j=1}^{n} \left(\underline{b_j}\right)^{\omega_j}}, \end{pmatrix}.$$

Step 5: The importance of each alternative is evaluated by using the WASPAS technique using the following formula

$$\mathcal{A}_j = \frac{(\mathcal{A}_j)^{WS} + (\mathcal{A}_j)^{WP}}{2}.$$

Step 6: Find out the score values by using the formula given in definition (1.12).

Step 7: Rank the alternatives according to the result obtained through step 6 and obtain the best alternative according to ranking order.

7.3.2 Numerical example

Modern aviation systems are highly complex, and therefore, data science techniques need to be integrated into aerospace. The data the aerospace industry generates is enormous and, thus, it would be of great value in making decisions and achieving efficiency in the use of aircraft technology, such as satellite systems, as well as space exploration. In the field of aerospace, data-driven approaches can predict aircraft maintenance time. This can reduce downtime and operational costs while increasing safety. Data science also assists in optimizing flight paths for fuel consumption and minimization of environmental impact. Space exploration utilizes machine learning and statistical models to analyze astronomical data, simulate missions, and develop autonomous navigation systems for spacecraft. This will enhance the capability of designing and testing newer materials and structures, making them stronger and more resourceful. Techniques in artificial intelligence, neural networks, and big data analytics increase the capacity of the aerospace industry for innovation concerning solving complex issues at affordable costs. In the age of technology, it is the face of data science that gives the competitive edge to meet the demands that aerospace engineering and exploration require.

Four different data science techniques are given, and we want to classify these techniques based on the proposed algorithms.

(1) *Predictive maintenance with machine learning*

With machine learning methods, the sensor data from airplanes is used by a decision tree and neural networks to predict equipment breakdown. Pattern recognition and anomaly leads to proactive maintenance, thus diminishing downtime and safety. Some methods for monitoring wear and tear across time include anomaly detection, as well as time-series analysis. Predictive maintenance prolongs the life of aerospace equipment and reduces operating expenses. Even replacement part schedules can be optimized using algorithms to optimize the process to its maximum level. For instance, in engines, IoT sensors can send real-time data for training predictive models. Maintenance for commercial and military aerospace industries has been changed as a result.

(2) *Analysis of finite elements for structural integrity*

Finite element analysis is a computer-based prediction about stress behavior in structures under physical forces such as vibration. It also reduces difficult aerospace parts into smaller pieces for detailed analysis. Data science enhances FEA through the automation of simulation processes to improve accuracy using AI-driven optimization. Engineers can try materials and designs virtually with no need for expensive prototype models. FEA ensures that the safety of critical parts such as wings and sections of fuselage is met. The results can be interpreted by advanced data visualization tools, and weak points are determined. This method assists in developing lightweight materials for aerospace designs that can last.

(3) *An optimization algorithm for designing flight paths*

Data science uses the optimization techniques of genetic algorithms and linear programming to provide efficient flight paths. Optimization parameters include fuel consumption, patterns in weather, air traffic, and aircraft performance. Such algorithms will always find optimal solutions, such as taking less time to travel with fewer costs, while not compromising on safety. Optimization is done in real time to change the flight path. For example, satellite information helps in the accuracy of routes. Airlines benefit from saving fuel and reducing emissions, contributing to sustainability goals.

Such techniques are also important for unmanned aerial vehicles (UAVs) in autonomous navigation.

(4) *A neural language process for communicating in air traffic*

These NLP techniques process and analyze unstructured textual data coming from air traffic control communications, maintenance logs, and safety reports. Transcribing in real-time conversations between pilots and controllers with speech-to-text models is one technique for processing such data to find improvements in safety due to the detection of stress or miscommunication patterns. NLP tools such as sentiment analysis and topic modeling shed light on recurring issues with flight operations. Advanced transformer-based NLP models summarize long reports and flag significant concerns. In aerospace manufacturing, NLP helps in parsing technical documents to facilitate streamlined design and testing. The technique guarantees smooth communication in pressure situations, which contributes to better efficiency.

Based on these alternatives the attributes of these techniques and their explanation are given in the following Table 7.1.

Assume that the WVs for these attributes are $(0.23,\ 0.29,\ 0.28,\ 0.20)$. Now we utilize the step-wise algorithm and find out the best alternative based on this information.

Step 1: Collect the information in the form of CFRNs proposed by decision makers and arrange it in the form of a matrix given in Table 7.2.

Step 2: No need to normalize the information, all the attributes are benefit type.

Step 3: Find out the relative importance of the alternatives by using the formula given in eqn (7.3):

$$(\mathcal{A}_1)^{WS} = \begin{pmatrix} 0.\ 336 + \iota\, 0.3400\ , \\ 0.2767 + \iota\, 0.6518 \end{pmatrix}, (\mathcal{A}_2)^{WS} = \begin{pmatrix} 0.\ 2610 + \iota\, 0.\ 2570, \\ 0.2781 + \iota\, 0.4444 \end{pmatrix},$$

$$(\mathcal{A}_3)^{WS} = \begin{pmatrix} 0.2340\ + \iota\, 0.3160, \\ 0.3057 + \iota\, 0.3304 \end{pmatrix}, (\mathcal{A}_4)^{WS} = \begin{pmatrix} 0.\ 3730 + \iota\, 0.\ 3150, \\ 0.2290 + \iota\, 0.3511 \end{pmatrix}.$$

Step 4: Find out the relative importance of the alternatives by using the formula given in eqn (7.4):

$$(\mathcal{A}_1)^{WP} = \begin{pmatrix} 0.\ 298 + \iota\, 0.\ 315, \\ 0.\ 2403 + \iota\, 0.3981 \end{pmatrix}, (\mathcal{A}_2)^{WP} = \begin{pmatrix} 0.\ 2580 + \iota\, 0.\ 2310, \\ 0.\ 2703 + \iota\, 0.3365 \end{pmatrix},$$

Table 7.1 Description of attributes.

Attributes	Description	Examples in aerospace	Impact
Predictive accuracy	Data science techniques leverage machine learning algorithms and statistical models to make highly accurate predictions.	Predicting component failure, optimizing flight paths, and forecasting weather patterns.	Enhances safety, reduces costs, and improves operational efficiency.
Real-time Processing	Ability to analyze and process data in real-time or near real-time for quick decision-making.	Real-time flight monitoring, air traffic control analytics, fault detection systems	Enables immediate response to critical situations and improves safety and reliability.
Scalability	Techniques are capable of handling massive datasets generated by modern aerospace systems like satellites and sensors.	Analyzing satellite imagery, processing terabytes of flight sensor data.	Facilitates insights from large-scale operations and supports mission-critical decisions.
Integration with models	Seamlessly integrates with physics-based models and domain knowledge for more accurate and explainable results.	Hybrid modeling for aerodynamics, flight dynamics simulations.	Combines computational accuracy with expert knowledge,

Table 7.2 Data proposed by experts in the form of CFRNs.

	$\mathbb{T}_1$	$\mathbb{T}_2$	$\mathbb{T}_3$	$\mathbb{T}_4$
$\mathfrak{L}_1$	$\begin{pmatrix} 0.123+\iota\,0.241, \\ 0.516+\iota\,0.261 \end{pmatrix}$	$\begin{pmatrix} 0.387+\iota\,0.234, \\ 0.219+\iota\,0.962 \end{pmatrix}$	$\begin{pmatrix} 0.283+\iota\,0.334, \\ 0.218+\iota\,0.362 \end{pmatrix}$	$\begin{pmatrix} 0.543+\iota\,0.574, \\ 0.119+\iota\,0.192 \end{pmatrix}$
$\mathfrak{L}_2$	$\begin{pmatrix} 0.287+\iota\,0.134, \\ 0.219+\iota\,0.162 \end{pmatrix}$	$\begin{pmatrix} 0.289+\iota\,0.234, \\ 0.269+\iota\,0.662 \end{pmatrix}$	$\begin{pmatrix} 0.261+\iota\,0.434, \\ 0.232+\iota\,0.562 \end{pmatrix}$	$\begin{pmatrix} 0.187+\iota\,0.164, \\ 0.419+\iota\,0.152 \end{pmatrix}$
$\mathfrak{L}_3$	$\begin{pmatrix} 0.126+\iota\,0.140, \\ 0.219+\iota\,0.120 \end{pmatrix}$	$\begin{pmatrix} 0.207+\iota\,0.534, \\ 0.299+\iota\,0.462 \end{pmatrix}$	$\begin{pmatrix} 0.233+\iota\,0.334, \\ 0.215+\iota\,0.462 \end{pmatrix}$	$\begin{pmatrix} 0.387+\iota\,0.124, \\ 0.519+\iota\,0.152 \end{pmatrix}$
$\mathfrak{L}_4$	$\begin{pmatrix} 0.297+\iota\,0.144, \\ 0.269+\iota\,0.152 \end{pmatrix}$	$\begin{pmatrix} 0.227+\iota\,0.334, \\ 0.239+\iota\,0.262 \end{pmatrix}$	$\begin{pmatrix} 0.298+\iota\,0.534, \\ 0.271+\iota\,0.662 \end{pmatrix}$	$\begin{pmatrix} 0.687+\iota\,0.124, \\ 0.110+\iota\,0.152 \end{pmatrix}$

$$(\mathcal{A}_3)^{WP} = \begin{pmatrix} 0.2180+\iota\,0.2650\,, \\ 0.2865+\iota\,0.2641 \end{pmatrix}, (\mathcal{A}_4)^{WP} = \begin{pmatrix} 0.3320+\iota\,0.2650, \\ 0.2192+\iota\,0.2656 \end{pmatrix}.$$

Step 5: The evaluated overall significance of every alternative is:

$$\mathcal{A}_1 = \begin{pmatrix} 0.3170+\iota\,0.3280\,, \\ 0.2586+\iota\,0.5737 \end{pmatrix}, \mathcal{A}_2 = \begin{pmatrix} 0.2600+\iota\,0.2440, \\ 0.2742+\iota\,0.3918 \end{pmatrix}$$

$$\mathcal{A}_{A3} = \begin{pmatrix} 0.\ 2260 + \iota\ 0.\ 2910, \\ 0.2961 + \iota\ 0.2976 \end{pmatrix}, \mathcal{A}_4 = \begin{pmatrix} 0.\ 3530 + \iota\ 0.\ 2900, \\ 0.2241 + \iota\ 0.3090 \end{pmatrix}.$$

Step 6: Find out the score values by using the formula given in definition (1.12). Hence score value for each alternative. $\mathcal{A}_j,\ j = 1,\ 2,\ 3,\ 4$ are given by

$$\text{Scor.}\,(\mathcal{A}_1) = 0.8600,\ \text{Scor.}\,(\mathcal{A}_2) = 0.7920,$$
$$\text{Scor.}\,(\mathcal{A}_3) = 0.7780,\ \text{Scor.}\,(\mathcal{A}_4) = 0.7940.$$

Step 7: Rank the alternatives according to the result obtained through step 6 and obtain the best alternative according to ranking order. Based on the results we can conclude that the ranking results are $\mathcal{A}_1 > \mathcal{A}_4 > \mathcal{A}_2 > \mathcal{A}_3$. Thus, $\mathcal{A}_1$ is the best alternative.

Furthermore, the graphical analysis of the results is given in Figure 7.1.

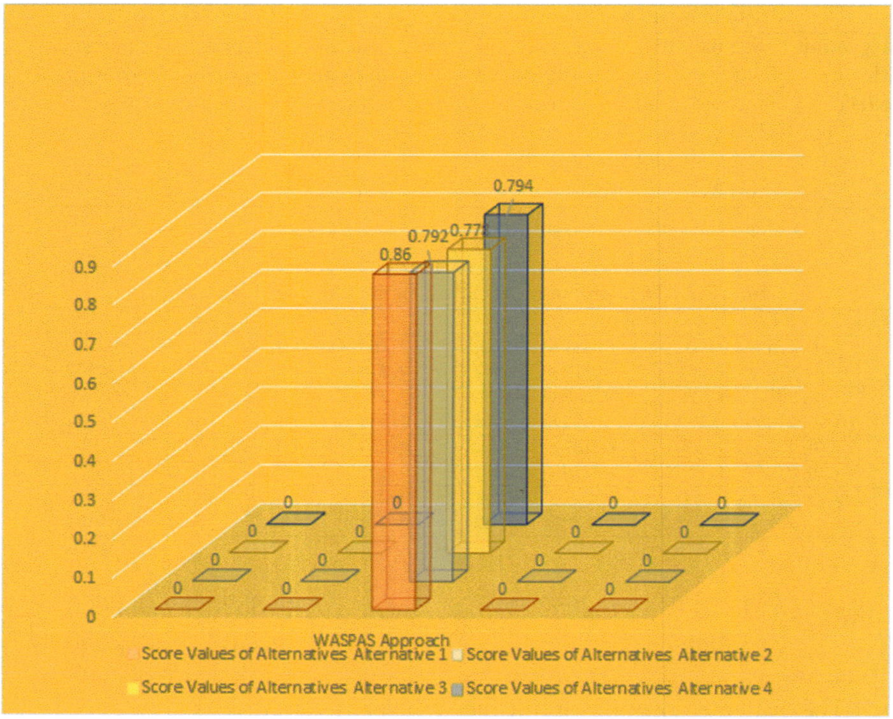

Figure 7.1 Graphical representation of results.

Table 7.3 Overall results.

Methods	**Score values**	**Ranking results**
Bi et al. [17] approach	No result	No result
Bi et al. [18] approach	No result	No result
Hu et al. [20] approach	No result	No result
CFREWA AOs (proposed)	$\text{Scor.}(\mathcal{A}_1) = 0.4013$ $\text{Scor.}(\mathcal{A}_2) = 0.3101$ $\text{Scor.}(\mathcal{A}_3) = 0.2965$ $\text{Scor.}(\mathcal{A}_4) = 0.3170$	$\mathcal{A}_1 > \mathcal{A}_4 > \mathcal{A}_2 > \mathcal{A}_3$
CFREWG AOs (proposed)	$\text{Scor.}(\mathcal{A}_1) = 0.3128$ $\text{Scor.}(\mathcal{A}_2) = 0.2739$ $\text{Scor.}(\mathcal{A}_3) = 0.2584$ $\text{Scor.}(\mathcal{A}_4) = 0.2704$	$\mathcal{A}_1 > \mathcal{A}_2 > \mathcal{A}_4 > \mathcal{A}_3$
The WASPAS approach (proposed)	$\text{Scor.}(\mathcal{A}_1) = 0.8600$ $\text{Scor.}(\mathcal{A}_2) = 0.7920$ $\text{Scor.}(\mathcal{A}_3) = 0.7780$ $\text{Scor.}(\mathcal{A}_4) = 0.7940$	$\mathcal{A}_1 > \mathcal{A}_4 > \mathcal{A}_2 > \mathcal{A}_3$

7.4 Comparative Analysis

In this section, we will discuss the comparative analysis of the proposed study by exploring the advantages of the delivered approaches. We have discussed the superiority of the initiated work to discuss the efficiency of the proposed theory.

1. If we consider the fuzzy Einstein weighted average (FEWA) AOs and fuzzy Einstein weighted geometric (FEWG) AOs, then we can see that these AOs are less applicable than proposed AOs because FEWA and FEWG AOs can only discuss the membership grade while the delivered approaches consist of two-dimensional information and this information provide more space to decision makers. Also, all the other aggregation operators that are based on fuzzy structure can never discuss the complex fuzzy rough data showing the weakness of these existing notions. While in comparison to these existing notions, the delivered AOs are more suitable to handle the two-dimensional information and rough data easily.
2. When we consider the fuzzy rough Einstein weighted average (FREWA) AOs and fuzzy rough Einstein weighted geometric (FREWG) AOs, we can see that although these AOs can handle the rough information these operators are free to handle the two-dimensional information in the form of CFRNs. So all those aggregation operators that are based on FR structure can never discuss the CFR data. Hence in these types of

existing notions, the chance of data loss increases and one can never rely on these weak structures. Hu et al. [20] approach is based on FR structure and hence it cannot discuss the CFR data given in Table 7.2.

3. If we compare our work with complex fuzzy aggregation theory, then we can see that these aggregation operators are based on the Polar form of the complex fuzzy idea, and in the case of the Polar form of CFS, the range of membership grade is unit circle. The delivered approaches are based on Tamir's et al. [5] idea in which the range of membership grade is unit square and these approaches can handle more advanced information. Be et al. [17, 18] approaches are based on CF information. These approaches are less applicable due to restrictions in their structure.
4. Hence in all these cases, the delivered approach is a more suitable and advance structure to handle the MCDM problems.

The overall results of the comparative study are given in Table 7.3.

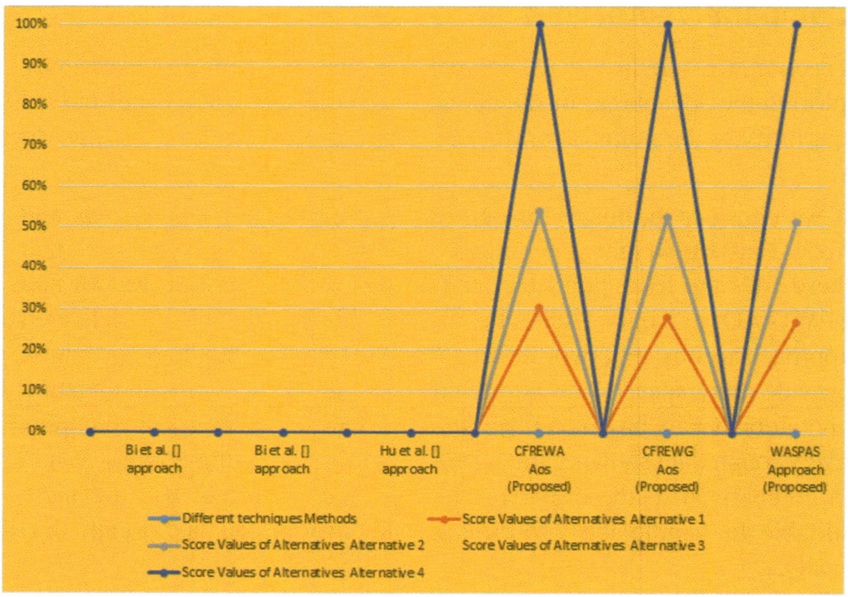

Figure 7.2 Graphical representation of results given in Table 7.3.

Moreover, the graphical analysis of the results of Table 7.3 is given in Figure 7.2.

7.5 Conclusion

The research focuses on sophisticated methods in complex fuzzy rough Einstein aggregation and WASPAS, which aim at enhancing decision-making techniques within the aerospace domain. Make the best use of these methods to classify data science methodologies appropriate for this field effectively. Fuzzy logic and aggregation operators are strong tools with the ability to manage uncertainty and imprecision present in aerospace data. The complex fuzzy rough Einstein aggregation captures the multicriteria information and the WASPAS approach optimizes conflicting criteria. These contributions give a novel perspective in aerospace research, particularly in systems optimization and predictive modeling. Significant improvements are in the classification accuracy and also in decision-making efficiency. This proposed framework also finds scalability in various aerospace applications. This work establishes the foundation for further advancement in the application of fuzzy logic to challenging, real-world problems.

8

Tackling the Challenges of Environmental Complexity: A Complex Fuzzy Rough Set Approach to Ecosystem Management

Management of ecosystems is currently one of the most difficult areas in decision-making concerning the environment since it involves biological systems, human activities, and other environmental factors. The nature of ecosystem data is complex and uncertain, and since environmental systems are constantly evolving, robust mathematical models are required for efficient decision-making support. This chapter presents a new strategy to address these environmental challenges by proposing the complex fuzzy rough set theory to design new sophisticated aggregation operators. We propose four innovative operators: The novel operators include complex fuzzy rough Dombi power averaging (CFRDPA), complex fuzzy rough Dombi power weighted averaging (CFRDPWA), complex fuzzy rough Dombi power geometric (CFRDPG), and complex fuzzy rough Dombi power weighted geometric (CFRDPWG). These operators are particularly tailored to address the specific requirements of ecosystem data by efficiently managing fuzzy rough information in MCDM issues. The integration of Dombi operations with complex fuzzy rough sets improves the operators' ability to identify uncertainty and complicated dependencies inherent in ecological systems. Based on these operators, we construct an integrated MCDM method for environmental decision-making situations involving fuzzy rough data. The applicability of our approach is illustrated through an extended case study that deals with the choice of the best forest management policies. This chapter demonstrates that the proposed framework handles the complexity of the ecosystem management decisions, the uncertainty of data, and the existence of multiple stakeholders and interdependencies. Moreover, we perform a detailed comparison of our proposed approach with other existing methods in environmental decision-making. The results show that our

DOI: 10.1201/9788743807827-8

framework outperforms the other approaches in addressing the issues of complexity and uncertainty in ecosystem management problems. This comparative study confirms the theoretical benefits of the proposed approach and demonstrates its practical relevance to enhancing the quality of environmental decision-making.

8.1 Dombi AOs within the Framework of CFRS

In this section of this chapter, we first discuss Dombi t-norm and t-conorm, and algebraic operations based on these t-norm and t-conorm in the structure of CFRSs. After that, we interpret Dombi power AOs in the setting of CFRS which are CFRDPA, CFRDPWA, CFRDPG, and CFRDPWG operators.

Definition 8.1 [28]: Let real numbers $\phi_1,\ \phi_2$. Then the Dombi t-norms and t-conorm are interpreted as

$$T_N\left(\phi_1,\ \phi_2\right)=\frac{1}{1+\left\{\left(\frac{1-\phi_1}{\phi_1}\right)^{\varsigma}+\left(\frac{1-\phi_2}{\phi_2}\right)^{\varsigma}\right\}^{\frac{1}{\varsigma}}},$$

$$T_{CN}\left(\phi_1,\ \phi_2\right)=1-\frac{1}{1+\left\{\left(\frac{\phi_1}{1-\phi_1}\right)^{\varsigma}+\left(\frac{\phi_2}{1-\phi_2}\right)^{\varsigma}\right\}^{\frac{1}{\varsigma}}}.$$

Definition 8.2: For two CFRNs $\mathcal{A}_1=\left\{\left(\overline{a_1}+\iota\overline{b_1},\ \underline{a_1}+\iota\underline{b_1}\right)\right\}$ and $\mathcal{A}_2=\left\{\left(\overline{a_2}+\iota\overline{b_2},\ \underline{a_2}+\iota\underline{b_2}\right)\right\}$,$\varsigma\geq 1$ and $s>0$, the algebraic operations by employing Dombi t-norm and co-norm are inferred as

(1)

$$\mathcal{A}_1\oplus\mathcal{A}_2=$$

$$\left(\begin{array}{c}1-\frac{1}{1+\left\{\left(\frac{\overline{a_1}}{1-\overline{a_1}}\right)^{\varsigma}+\left(\frac{\overline{a_2}}{1-\overline{a_2}}\right)^{\varsigma}\right\}^{\frac{1}{\varsigma}}}+\iota\left(1-\frac{1}{1+\left\{\left(\frac{\overline{b_1}}{1-\overline{b_1}}\right)^{\varsigma}+\left(\frac{\overline{b_2}}{1-\overline{b_2}}\right)^{\varsigma}\right\}^{\frac{1}{\varsigma}}}\right),\\ 1-\frac{1}{1+\left\{\left(\frac{\underline{a_1}}{1-\underline{a_1}}\right)^{\varsigma}+\left(\frac{\underline{a_2}}{1-\underline{a_2}}\right)^{\varsigma}\right\}^{\frac{1}{\varsigma}}}+\iota\left(1-\frac{1}{1+\left\{\left(\frac{\underline{b_1}}{1-\underline{b_1}}\right)^{\varsigma}+\left(\frac{\underline{b_2}}{1-\underline{b_2}}\right)^{\varsigma}\right\}^{\frac{1}{\varsigma}}}\right)\end{array}\right).$$

(2)

$$\mathcal{A}_1 \otimes \mathcal{A}_2 = \begin{pmatrix} \frac{1}{1+\left\{\left(\frac{1-\overline{a_1}}{\overline{a_1}}\right)^{\zeta}+\left(\frac{1-\overline{a_2}}{\overline{a_2}}\right)^{\zeta}\right\}^{\frac{1}{\zeta}}} + \iota \frac{1}{1+\left\{\left(\frac{1-\overline{b_1}}{\overline{b_1}}\right)^{\zeta}+\left(\frac{1-\overline{b_2}}{\overline{b_2}}\right)^{\zeta}\right\}^{\frac{1}{\zeta}}}, \\ \frac{1}{1+\left\{\left(\frac{1-\underline{a_1}}{\underline{a_1}}\right)^{\zeta}+\left(\frac{1-\underline{a_2}}{\underline{a_2}}\right)^{\zeta}\right\}^{\frac{1}{\zeta}}} + \iota \frac{1}{1+\left\{\left(\frac{1-\underline{b_1}}{\underline{b_1}}\right)^{\zeta}+\left(\frac{1-\underline{b_2}}{\underline{b_2}}\right)^{\zeta}\right\}^{\frac{1}{\zeta}}} \end{pmatrix}.$$

(3)

$$s\mathcal{A}_1 = \begin{pmatrix} 1 - \frac{1}{1+\left\{s\left(\frac{\overline{a_1}}{1-\overline{a_1}}\right)^{\zeta}\right\}^{\frac{1}{\zeta}}} + \iota \left(1 - \frac{1}{1+\left\{s\left(\frac{\overline{b_1}}{1-\overline{b_1}}\right)^{\zeta}\right\}^{\frac{1}{\zeta}}}\right), \\ 1 - \frac{1}{1+\left\{s\left(\frac{\underline{a_1}}{1-\underline{a_1}}\right)^{\zeta}\right\}^{\frac{1}{\zeta}}} + \iota \left(1 - \frac{1}{1+\left\{s\left(\frac{\underline{b_1}}{1-\underline{b_1}}\right)^{\zeta}\right\}^{\frac{1}{\zeta}}}\right) \end{pmatrix}.$$

(4)

$$\mathcal{A}_1{}^{s} = \begin{pmatrix} \frac{1}{1+\left\{s\left(\frac{1-\overline{a_1}}{\overline{a_1}}\right)^{\zeta}\right\}^{\frac{1}{\zeta}}} + \iota \frac{1}{1+\left\{s\left(\frac{1-\overline{b_1}}{\overline{b_1}}\right)^{\zeta}\right\}^{\frac{1}{\zeta}}}, \\ \frac{1}{1+\left\{s\left(\frac{1-\underline{a_1}}{\underline{a_1}}\right)^{\zeta}\right\}^{\frac{1}{\zeta}}} + \iota \frac{1}{1+\left\{s\left(\frac{1-\underline{b_1}}{\underline{b_1}}\right)^{\zeta}\right\}^{\frac{1}{\zeta}}} \end{pmatrix}.$$

Definition 8.3: Let an assembly $\mathcal{A}_j = \left\{\left(\overline{a_j} + \iota\overline{b_j},\ \underline{a_j} + \iota\underline{b_j}\right)\right\}$, $(j = 1, 2, 3, \ldots, n)$ of CFRNs. Then the CFRDPA operator is scrutinized as

$$\mathrm{CFRDPA}\left(\mathcal{A}_1,\ \mathcal{A}_2,\ \ldots,\ \mathcal{A}_n\right) = \bigoplus_{j=1}^{n} \frac{1 + T\left(\mathcal{A}_j\right)}{\sum_{j=1}^{n}\left(1 + T\left(\mathcal{A}_j\right)\right)\mathcal{A}_j}.$$

Observe that $\mathrm{T}\left(\varkappa_j\right) = \sum_{\substack{j=1 \\ j\neq r}}^{n} \mathrm{Sup}\left(\mathcal{A}_j,\ \mathcal{A}_r\right)$ and $\mathrm{Sup}\left(\mathcal{A}_j, \mathcal{A}_r\right)$ infers the support for $\mathcal{A}_j$ from $\mathcal{A}_r$ with the axioms given below.

- $\mathrm{Sup}\left(\mathcal{A}_j, \mathcal{A}_r\right) \in [0, 1]$;

- $\text{Sup}(\mathcal{A}_j, \mathcal{A}_r) = \text{Sup}(\mathcal{A}_r, \mathcal{A}_j)$;
- $\text{Sup}(\mathcal{A}_j, \mathcal{A}_r) \geq \text{Sup}\left(\mathcal{A}_{j'}, \mathcal{A}_{r'}\right)$ if $\text{đ}(\mathcal{A}_j, \mathcal{A}_r) < \text{đ}\left(\mathcal{A}_{j'}, \mathcal{A}_{r'}\right)$, đ can be a distance measure among CFRSs.

Theorem 8.1: Let an assembly $\mathcal{A}_j = \left\{\left(\overline{a_j} + \iota\overline{b_j}, \underline{a_j} + \iota\underline{b_j}\right)\right\}$, $(j = 1, 2, 3, \ldots, n)$ of CFRNs. Then the usage of the CFRDPA operator over $\mathcal{A}_j$ will give a CFRN, that is:

$$\text{CFRDPA}(\mathcal{A}_1, \mathcal{A}_2, \mathcal{A}_3, \ldots, \mathcal{A}_n) = \begin{pmatrix} 1 - \frac{1}{1+\left\{\sum_{j=1}^{n} \chi_j\left(\frac{\overline{a_j}}{1-\overline{a_j}}\right)^{\varsigma}\right\}^{\frac{1}{\varsigma}}} + \iota\left(1 - \frac{1}{1+\left\{\sum_{j=1}^{n} \chi_j\left(\frac{\overline{b_j}}{1-\overline{b_j}}\right)^{\varsigma}\right\}^{\frac{1}{\varsigma}}}\right), \\ 1 - \frac{1}{1+\left\{\sum_{j=1}^{n} \chi_j\left(\frac{\underline{a_j}}{1-\underline{a_j}}\right)^{\varsigma}\right\}^{\frac{1}{\varsigma}}} + \iota\left(1 - \frac{1}{1+\left\{\sum_{j=1}^{n} \chi_j\left(\frac{\underline{b_j}}{1-\underline{b_j}}\right)^{\varsigma}\right\}^{\frac{1}{\varsigma}}}\right) \end{pmatrix}. \tag{8.1}$$

Proof: Let $n = 2$. Then, we have:

$$\text{CFRDPA}(\mathcal{A}_1, \mathcal{A}_2) = \chi_1\mathcal{A}_1 \oplus \chi_1\mathcal{A}_2$$

$$= \begin{pmatrix} 1 - \frac{1}{1+\left\{\chi_1\left(\frac{\overline{a_1}}{1-\overline{a_1}}\right)^{\varsigma}+\chi_2\left(\frac{\overline{a_2}}{1-\overline{a_2}}\right)^{\varsigma}\right\}^{\frac{1}{\varsigma}}} + \iota\left(1 - \frac{1}{1+\left\{\chi_1\left(\frac{\overline{b_1}}{1-\overline{b_1}}\right)^{\varsigma}+\chi_2\left(\frac{\overline{b_2}}{1-\overline{b_2}}\right)^{\varsigma}\right\}^{\frac{1}{\varsigma}}}\right), \\ 1 - \frac{1}{1+\left\{\chi_1\left(\frac{\underline{a_1}}{1-\underline{a_1}}\right)^{\varsigma}+\chi_2\left(\frac{\underline{a_2}}{1-\underline{a_2}}\right)^{\varsigma}\right\}^{\frac{1}{\varsigma}}} + \iota\left(1 - \frac{1}{1+\left\{\chi_1\left(\frac{\underline{b_1}}{1-\underline{b_1}}\right)^{\varsigma}+\chi_2\left(\frac{\underline{b_2}}{1-\underline{b_2}}\right)^{\varsigma}\right\}^{\frac{1}{\varsigma}}}\right) \end{pmatrix}$$

$$= \begin{pmatrix} 1 - \frac{1}{1+\left\{\sum_{j=1}^{2} \chi_j\left(\frac{\overline{a_j}}{1-\overline{a_j}}\right)^{\varsigma}\right\}^{\frac{1}{\varsigma}}} + \iota\left(1 - \frac{1}{1+\left\{\sum_{j=1}^{2} \chi_j\left(\frac{\overline{b_j}}{1-\overline{b_j}}\right)^{\varsigma}\right\}^{\frac{1}{\varsigma}}}\right), \\ 1 - \frac{1}{1+\left\{\sum_{j=1}^{2} \chi_j\left(\frac{\underline{a_j}}{1-\underline{a_j}}\right)^{\varsigma}\right\}^{\frac{1}{\varsigma}}} + \iota\left(1 - \frac{1}{1+\left\{\sum_{j=1}^{2} \chi_j\left(\frac{\underline{b_j}}{1-\underline{b_j}}\right)^{\varsigma}\right\}^{\frac{1}{\varsigma}}}\right) \end{pmatrix}.$$

Thus, eqn (8.1) holds for $n = 2$. Next let for $n = r$, eqn (8.1) holds. Then:

$$\text{CFRDPA}\left(\mathcal{A}_1,\, \mathcal{A}_2,\, \mathcal{A}_3,\, \ldots,\, \mathcal{A}_r\right) = \bigoplus_{j=1}^{r}\left(\chi_j \mathcal{A}_j\right)$$

$$= \begin{pmatrix} 1 - \dfrac{1}{1+\left\{\sum\limits_{j=1}^{r}\chi_j\left(\frac{\overline{a_j}}{1-\overline{a_j}}\right)^{\zeta}\right\}^{\frac{1}{\zeta}}} + \left(1 - \dfrac{1}{1+\left\{\sum\limits_{j=1}^{r}\chi_j\left(\frac{\overline{b_j}}{1-\overline{b_j}}\right)^{\zeta}\right\}^{\frac{1}{\zeta}}}\right), \\ 1 - \dfrac{1}{1+\left\{\sum\limits_{j=1}^{r}\chi_j\left(\frac{\underline{a_j}}{1-\underline{a_j}}\right)^{\zeta}\right\}^{\frac{1}{\zeta}}} + \iota\left(1 - \dfrac{1}{1+\left\{\sum\limits_{j=1}^{r}\chi_j\left(\frac{\underline{b_j}}{1-\underline{b_j}}\right)^{\zeta}\right\}^{\frac{1}{\zeta}}}\right) \end{pmatrix}.$$

Finally, let $n = r + 1$. Then:

$$\text{CFRDPA}\left(\mathcal{A}_1,\, \mathcal{A}_2,\, \mathcal{A}_3,\, \ldots,\, \mathcal{A}_{r+1}\right) = \bigoplus_{j=1}^{r}\left(\chi_j \mathcal{A}_j\right) \oplus \left(\chi_{r+1}\mathcal{A}_{r+1}\right)$$

$$= \begin{pmatrix} 1 - \dfrac{1}{1+\left\{\sum\limits_{j=1}^{r}\chi_j\left(\frac{\overline{a_j}}{1-\overline{a_j}}\right)^{\zeta}\right\}^{\frac{1}{\zeta}}} + \iota\left(1 - \dfrac{1}{1+\left\{\sum\limits_{j=1}^{r}\chi_j\left(\frac{\overline{b_j}}{1-\overline{b_j}}\right)^{\zeta}\right\}^{\frac{1}{\zeta}}}\right), \\ 1 - \dfrac{1}{1+\left\{\sum\limits_{j=1}^{r}\chi_j\left(\frac{\underline{a_j}}{1-\underline{a_j}}\right)^{\zeta}\right\}^{\frac{1}{\zeta}}} + \iota\left(1 - \dfrac{1}{1+\left\{\sum\limits_{j=1}^{r}\chi_j\left(\frac{\underline{b_j}}{1-\underline{b_j}}\right)^{\zeta}\right\}^{\frac{1}{\zeta}}}\right) \end{pmatrix}$$

$$\oplus$$

$$\begin{pmatrix} 1 - \dfrac{1}{1+\left\{\chi_{r+1}\left(\frac{\overline{a_{r+1}}}{1-\overline{a_{r+1}}}\right)^{\zeta}\right\}^{\frac{1}{\zeta}}} + \iota\left(1 - \dfrac{1}{1+\left\{\chi_{r+1}\left(\frac{\overline{b_{r+1}}}{1-\overline{b_{r+1}}}\right)^{\zeta}\right\}^{\frac{1}{\zeta}}}\right), \\ 1 - \dfrac{1}{1+\left\{\chi_{r+1}\left(\frac{\underline{a_{r+1}}}{1-\underline{a_{r+1}}}\right)^{\zeta}\right\}^{\frac{1}{\zeta}}} + \iota\left(1 - \dfrac{1}{1+\left\{\chi_{r+1}\left(\frac{\underline{b_{r+1}}}{1-\underline{b_{r+1}}}\right)^{\zeta}\right\}^{\frac{1}{\zeta}}}\right) \end{pmatrix}$$

$$
= \left(\begin{array}{c} 1 - \dfrac{1}{1+\left\{ \sum\limits_{j=1}^{r+1} \chi_j \left(\frac{\overline{a_j}}{1-\overline{a_j}} \right)^{\zeta} \right\}^{\frac{1}{\zeta}}} + \iota \left(1 - \dfrac{1}{1+\left\{ \sum\limits_{j=1}^{r+1} \chi_j \left(\frac{\overline{b_j}}{1-\overline{b_j}} \right)^{\zeta} \right\}^{\frac{1}{\zeta}}} \right), \\ 1 - \dfrac{1}{1+\left\{ \sum\limits_{j=1}^{r+1} \chi_j \left(\frac{\underline{a_j}}{1-\underline{a_j}} \right)^{\zeta\zeta} \right\}^{\frac{1}{\zeta}}} + \iota \left(1 - \dfrac{1}{1+\left\{ \sum\limits_{j=1}^{r+1} \chi_j \left(\frac{\underline{b_j}}{1-\underline{b_j}} \right)^{\zeta} \right\}^{\frac{1}{\zeta}}} \right) \end{array} \right).
$$

$\Longrightarrow$ Eqn (8.1) is true for n.

8.1.1 Properties of CFRDPA operator

The notion of CFRDPA satisfies the following properties.

Idempotency: Let an assembly $\mathcal{A}_j = \left\{ \left(\overline{a_j} + \iota\overline{b_j},\ \underline{a_j} + \iota\underline{b_j} \right) \right\}, (j = 1, 2, 3, \ldots, n)$ of CFRNs. If $\mathcal{A}_j = \mathcal{A}, \forall\ j$, then:

$$\text{CFRDPA}\left(\mathcal{A}_1,\ \mathcal{A}_2,\ ..,\ \mathcal{A}_n\right) = \mathcal{A}.$$

Boundedness: Let an assembly $\mathcal{A}_j = \left(\overline{a_j} + \iota\overline{b_j}, \underline{a_j} + \iota\underline{b_j} \right), (j = 1, 2, \ldots, n)$, of CFRNs and $\mathcal{A}^- = \left(\min_j \left\{\overline{a_j}\right\} + \iota \min_j \left\{\overline{b_j}\right\}, \min_j \left\{\underline{a_j}\right\} + \iota \min_j \left\{\underline{b_j}\right\} \right)$, and $\mathcal{A}^+ = \left(\max_j \left\{\overline{a_j}\right\} + \iota\ \max_j \left\{\overline{b_j}\right\}, \max_j \left\{\underline{a_j}\right\} + \iota\ \max_j \left\{\underline{b_j}\right\} \right)$. Then:

$$\mathcal{A}^- \leq \text{CFRDPA}\left(\mathcal{A}_1,\ \mathcal{A}_2,\ ..,\ \mathcal{A}_n\right) \leq \mathcal{A}^+.$$

Monotonicity: Let two assemblies $\mathcal{A}_j = \left(\overline{a_j} + \iota\,\overline{b_j}, \underline{a_j} + \iota\underline{b_j} \right)$ and $\mathcal{A}_j^{'} = \left(\overline{a_j^{'}} + \iota\,\overline{b_j^{'}}, \underline{a_j^{'}} + \iota\underline{b_j^{'}} \right)$, $(j = 1,\ 2,\ \ldots,\ n)$, of CFRNs. If $\underline{a_j} \leq \underline{a_j^{'}}$, $\underline{b_j} \leq \underline{b_j^{'}}$, $\overline{a_j} \leq \overline{a_j^{'}}$, $\overline{b_j} \leq \overline{b_j^{'}}\ \forall\ j$, then:

$$\text{CFRDPA}\left(\mathcal{A}_1,\ \mathcal{A}_2,\ ..,\ \mathcal{A}_n\right) \leq CFRDPA\left(\mathcal{A}_1^{'},\ \mathcal{A}_2^{'},\ ..,\ \mathcal{A}_n^{'}\right).$$

Definition 8.4: Let an assembly $\mathcal{A}_j = \left\{ \left(\overline{a_j} + \iota\overline{b_j},\ \underline{a_j} + \iota\underline{b_j} \right) \right\}, (j = 1, 2, 3, \ldots, n)$ of CFRNs. Then the CFRDPWA operator is scrutinized as

$$\text{CFRDPWA}\left(\mathcal{A}_1,\ \mathcal{A}_2,\ \mathcal{A}_3,\ \ldots,\ \mathcal{A}_n\right) = \bigoplus_{j=1}^{n} \frac{\omega_j\left(1 + T\left(\mathcal{A}_j\right)\right)}{\sum\limits_{j=1}^{n} \omega_j\left(1 + T\left(\mathcal{A}_j\right)\right)} \mathcal{A}_j.$$

Theorem 8.2: Let an assembly $\mathcal{A}_j = \left\{\left(\overline{a_j} + \iota\overline{b_j},\ \underline{a_j} + \iota\underline{b_j}\right)\right\}, (j = 1, 2, 3, \ldots, n)$ of CFRNs. Then the usage of the CFRDPWA operator over $\mathcal{A}_j$ will give a CFRN, that is:

$$
\begin{aligned}
&\text{CFRDPWA}\left(\mathcal{A}_1,\ \mathcal{A}_2,\ \mathcal{A}_3,\ \ldots,\ \mathcal{A}_n\right) \\
&= \begin{pmatrix}
\left(1 - \dfrac{1}{1+\left\{\sum_{j=1}^{n} \frac{\omega_j(1+T(\mathcal{A}_j))}{\sum_{j=1}^{n}\omega_j(1+T(\mathcal{A}_j))}\left(\frac{\overline{a_j}}{1-\overline{a_j}}\right)^{\varsigma}\right\}^{\frac{1}{\varsigma}}} + \iota\left(1 - \dfrac{1}{1+\left\{\sum_{j=1}^{n} \frac{\omega_j(1+T(\mathcal{A}_j))}{\sum_{j=1}^{n}\omega_j(1+T(\mathcal{A}_j))}\left(\frac{\overline{b_j}}{1-\overline{b_j}}\right)^{\varsigma}\right\}^{\frac{1}{\varsigma}}}\right)\right), \\
1 - \dfrac{1}{1+\left\{\sum_{j=1}^{n} \frac{\omega_j(1+T(\mathcal{A}_j))}{\sum_{j=1}^{n}\omega_j(1+T(\mathcal{A}_j))}\left(\frac{\underline{a_j}}{1-\underline{a_j}}\right)^{\varsigma}\right\}^{\frac{1}{\varsigma}}} + \iota\left(1 - \dfrac{1}{1+\left\{\sum_{j=1}^{n} \frac{\omega_j(1+T(\mathcal{A}_j))}{\sum_{j=1}^{n}\omega_j(1+T(\mathcal{A}_j))}\left(\frac{\underline{b_j}}{1-\underline{b_j}}\right)^{\varsigma}\right\}^{\frac{1}{\varsigma}}}\right)
\end{pmatrix}.
\end{aligned}
$$

The notion of CFRDPWA satisfies idempotency, boundedness, and monotonicity properties.

Definition 8.5: Let an assembly$\mathcal{A}_j = \left\{\left(\overline{a_j} + \iota\overline{b_j},\ \underline{a_j} + \iota\underline{b_j}\right)\right\}, (j = 1, 2, 3, \ldots, n)$ of CFRNs. Then the CFRDPG operator is scrutinized as

$$
\text{CFRDPG}\left(\mathcal{A}_1,\ \mathcal{A}_2,\ \mathcal{A}_3,\ \ldots,\ \mathcal{A}_n\right) = \bigotimes_{j=1}^{n} \left(\mathcal{A}_j\right)^{\frac{(1+T(\mathcal{A}_j))}{\sum_{j=1}^{n}(1+T(\mathcal{A}_j))}}.
$$

Theorem 8.3: Let an assembly $\mathcal{A}_j = \left\{\left(\overline{a_j} + \iota\overline{b_j},\ \underline{a_j} + \iota\underline{b_j}\right)\right\}, (j = 1, 2, 3, \ldots, n)$ of CFRNs. Then the usage of the CFRDPG operator over $\mathcal{A}_j$ will give a CFRN, that is:

$$
\text{CFRDPG}\left(\mathcal{A}_1,\ \mathcal{A}_2,\ \mathcal{A}_3,\ \ldots,\ \mathcal{A}_n\right)
$$

$$= \begin{pmatrix} \frac{1}{1+\left\{\sum_{j=1}^{n} \chi_j \left(\frac{1-\overline{a_j}}{\overline{a_j}}\right)^{\zeta}\right\}^{\frac{1}{\zeta}}} + \iota \frac{1}{1+\left\{\sum_{j=1}^{n} \chi_j \left(\frac{1-\overline{b_j}}{\overline{b_j}}\right)^{\zeta}\right\}^{\frac{1}{\zeta}}}, \\ \frac{1}{1+\left\{\sum_{j=1}^{n} \chi_j \left(\frac{1-\underline{a_j}}{\underline{a_j}}\right)^{\zeta}\right\}^{\frac{1}{\zeta}}} + \iota \frac{1}{1+\left\{\sum_{j=1}^{n} \chi_j \left(\frac{1-\underline{b_j}}{\underline{b_j}}\right)^{\zeta}\right\}^{\frac{1}{\zeta}}} \end{pmatrix}. \tag{8.2}$$

Proof: Let $n = 2$. Then we have:

$$\text{CFRDPG}\,(\mathcal{A}_1,\, \mathcal{A}_2) = (\mathcal{A}_1)^{\chi_1} \otimes (\mathcal{A}_2)^{\chi_2}$$

$$= \begin{pmatrix} \frac{1}{1+\left\{\chi_1\left(\frac{1-\overline{a_1}}{\overline{a_1}}\right)^{\zeta}+\chi_2\left(\frac{1-\overline{a_2}}{\overline{a_2}}\right)^{\zeta}\right\}^{\frac{1}{\zeta}}} + \iota \frac{1}{1+\left\{\chi_1\left(\frac{1-\overline{b_1}}{\overline{b_1}}\right)^{\zeta}+\chi_2\left(\frac{1-\overline{b_2}}{\overline{b_2}}\right)^{\zeta}\right\}^{\frac{1}{\zeta}}}, \\ \frac{1}{1+\left\{\chi_1\left(\frac{1-\underline{a_1}}{\underline{a_1}}\right)^{\zeta}+\chi_2\left(\frac{1-\underline{a_2}}{\underline{a_2}}\right)^{\zeta}\right\}^{\frac{1}{\zeta}}} + \iota \frac{1}{1+\left\{\chi_1\left(\frac{1-\underline{b_1}}{\underline{b_1}}\right)^{\zeta}+\chi_2\left(\frac{1-\underline{b_2}}{\underline{b_2}}\right)^{\zeta}\right\}^{\frac{1}{\zeta}}} \end{pmatrix}$$

$$= \begin{pmatrix} \frac{1}{1+\left\{\sum_{j=1}^{2} \chi_j \left(\frac{1-\overline{a_j}}{\overline{a_j}}\right)^{\zeta}\right\}^{\frac{1}{\zeta}}} + \iota \frac{1}{1+\left\{\sum_{j=1}^{2} \chi_j \left(\frac{1-\overline{b_j}}{\overline{b_j}}\right)^{\zeta}\right\}^{\frac{1}{\zeta}}}, \\ \frac{1}{1+\left\{\sum_{j=1}^{2} \chi_j \left(\frac{1-\underline{a_j}}{\underline{a_j}}\right)^{\zeta}\right\}^{\frac{1}{\zeta}}} + \iota \frac{1}{1+\left\{\sum_{j=1}^{2} \chi_j \left(\frac{1-\underline{b_j}}{\underline{b_j}}\right)^{\zeta}\right\}^{\frac{1}{\zeta}}} \end{pmatrix}.$$

Thus, eqn (8.2) holds for $n = 2$. Next let for $n = r$, eqn (8.2) holds.

$$\text{CFRDPG}\,(\mathcal{A}_1,\, \mathcal{A}_2,\, \mathcal{A}_3,\, \ldots,\, \mathcal{A}_r) = \bigotimes_{j=1}^{r} (\mathcal{A}_j)^{\chi_j}$$

$$= \begin{pmatrix} \frac{1}{1+\left\{\sum_{j=1}^{r} \chi_j \left(\frac{1-\overline{a_j}}{\overline{a_j}}\right)^{\zeta}\right\}^{\frac{1}{\zeta}}} + \iota \frac{1}{1+\left\{\sum_{j=1}^{r} \chi_j \left(\frac{1-\overline{b_j}}{\overline{b_j}}\right)^{\zeta}\right\}^{\frac{1}{\zeta}}}, \\ \frac{1}{1+\left\{\sum_{j=1}^{r} \chi_j \left(\frac{1-\underline{a_j}}{\underline{a_j}}\right)^{\zeta}\right\}^{\frac{1}{\zeta}}} + \iota \frac{1}{1+\left\{\sum_{j=1}^{r} \chi_j \left(\frac{1-\underline{b_j}}{\underline{b_j}}\right)^{\zeta}\right\}^{\frac{1}{\zeta}}} \end{pmatrix}.$$

Then, finally, let $n = r + 1$. Then:

$$\text{CFRDPG}\,(\mathcal{A}_1,\, \mathcal{A}_2,\, \mathcal{A}_3,\, \ldots,\, \mathcal{A}_{r+1}) = \bigotimes_{j=1}^{r} (\mathcal{A}_j)^{\chi_j} \otimes (\mathcal{A}_{r+1})^{\chi_{r+1}}$$

$$= \left(\begin{array}{c} \frac{1}{1+\left\{ \sum_{j=1}^{r} \chi_j \left(\frac{1-\overline{a_j}}{\overline{a_j}} \right)^{\zeta} \right\}^{\frac{1}{\zeta}}} + \iota \frac{1}{1+\left\{ \sum_{j=1}^{r} \chi_j \left(\frac{1-\overline{b_j}}{\overline{b_j}} \right)^{\zeta} \right\}^{\frac{1}{\zeta}}}, \\ \frac{1}{1+\left\{ \sum_{j=1}^{r} \chi_j \left(\frac{1-\underline{a_j}}{\underline{a_j}} \right)^{\zeta} \right\}^{\frac{1}{\zeta}}} + \iota \frac{1}{1+\left\{ \sum_{j=1}^{r} \chi_j \left(\frac{1-\underline{b_j}}{\underline{b_j}} \right)^{\zeta} \right\}^{\frac{1}{\zeta}}} \end{array} \right)$$

$$\otimes \left(\begin{array}{c} \frac{1}{1+\left\{ \chi_{r+1} \left(\frac{1-\overline{a_{r+1}}}{\overline{a_{r+1}}} \right)^{\zeta} \right\}^{\frac{1}{\zeta}}} + \iota \frac{1}{1+\left\{ \chi_{r+1} \left(\frac{1-\overline{b_{r+1}}}{\overline{b_{r+1}}} \right)^{\zeta} \right\}^{\frac{1}{\zeta}}}, \\ \frac{1}{1+\left\{ \chi_{r+1} \left(\frac{1-\underline{a_{r+1}}}{\underline{a_{r+1}}} \right)^{\zeta} \right\}^{\frac{1}{\zeta}}} + \iota \frac{1}{1+\left\{ \chi_{r+1} \left(\frac{1-\underline{b_{r+1}}}{\underline{b_{r+1}}} \right)^{\zeta} \right\}^{\frac{1}{\zeta}}} \end{array} \right)$$

$$= \left(\begin{array}{c} \frac{1}{1+\left\{ \sum_{j=1}^{r+1} \chi_j \left(\frac{1-\overline{a_j}}{\overline{a_j}} \right)^{\zeta} \right\}^{\frac{1}{\zeta}}} + \iota \frac{1}{1+\left\{ \sum_{j=1}^{r+1} \chi_j \left(\frac{1-\overline{b_j}}{\overline{b_j}} \right)^{\zeta} \right\}^{\frac{1}{\zeta}}}, \\ \frac{1}{1+\left\{ \sum_{j=1}^{r+1} \chi_j \left(\frac{1-\underline{a_j}}{\underline{a_j}} \right)^{\zeta} \right\}^{\frac{1}{\zeta}}} + \iota \frac{1}{1+\left\{ \sum_{j=1}^{r+1} \chi_j \left(\frac{1-\underline{b_j}}{\underline{b_j}} \right)^{\zeta} \right\}^{\frac{1}{\zeta}}} \end{array} \right).$$

$\Longrightarrow$ Eqn (8.2) is true for n.

8.1.2 Properties of CRFDPG operator

The notion of CFRDPG satisfies the following properties.

Idempotency: Let an assembly $\mathcal{A}_j = \left\{ \left(\overline{a_j} + \iota \overline{b_j},\ \underline{a_j} + \iota \underline{b_j} \right) \right\}$, $(j = 1,\ 2,\ 3,\ \ldots,\ n)$ of CFRNs. If $\mathcal{A}_j = \mathcal{A}, \forall\ j$, then:

$$\text{CFRDPG}\left(\mathcal{A}_1,\ \mathcal{A}_2,\ ..,\ \mathcal{A}_n\right) = \mathcal{A}.$$

Boundedness: Let an assembly $\mathcal{A}_j = \left(\overline{a_j} + \iota \overline{b_j}, \underline{a_j} + \iota \underline{b_j} \right), (j = 1, 2, \ldots, n)$. of CFRNs and $\mathcal{A}^- = \left(\min_j \left\{ \overline{a_j} \right\} + \iota \min_j \left\{ \overline{b_j} \right\}, \min_j \left\{ \underline{a_j} \right\} + \iota \min_j \left\{ \underline{b_j} \right\} \right)$, and $\mathcal{A}^+ = \left(\max_j \left\{ \overline{a_j} \right\} + \iota \max_j \left\{ \overline{b_j} \right\}, \max_j \left\{ \underline{a_j} \right\} + \iota \max_j \left\{ \underline{b_j} \right\} \right)$. Then:

$$\mathcal{A}^- \le \text{CFRDPG}\left(\mathcal{A}_1,\ \mathcal{A}_2,\ ..,\ \mathcal{A}_n\right) \le \mathcal{A}^+.$$

Monotonicity: Let two assemblies $\mathcal{A}_j = \left(\overline{a_j} + \iota \overline{b_j}, \underline{a_j} + \iota \underline{b_j} \right)$ and $\mathcal{A}_j' = \left(\overline{a_j'} + \iota \overline{b_j'}, \underline{a_j'} + \iota \underline{b_j'} \right)$, $(j = 1,\ 2,\ \ldots,\ n)$, of CFRNs. If $\underline{a_j} \le \underline{a_j'}$, $\underline{b_j} \le \underline{b_j'}$,

$\overline{a_j} \leq \overline{a_j^{'}}, \overline{b_j} \leq \overline{b_j^{'}}\ \forall\ j$, then:

$$\text{CFRDPG}\left(\mathcal{A}_1,\ \mathcal{A}_2,\ ..,\ \mathcal{A}_n\right) \leq \text{CFRDPG}\left(\mathcal{A}_1^{'},\ \mathcal{A}_2^{'},\ ..,\ \mathcal{A}_n^{'}\right).$$

Definition 8.6: Let an assembly $\mathcal{A}_j = \left\{\left(\overline{a_j} + \iota\overline{b_j},\ \underline{a_j} + \iota\underline{b_j}\right)\right\}$, $(j = 1,\ 2,\ 3,\ \ldots,\ n)$ of CFRNs. Then the CFRDPWG operator is scrutinized as

$$\text{CFRDPWG}\left(\mathcal{A}_1,\ \mathcal{A}_2,\ \mathcal{A}_3,\ \ldots,\ \mathcal{A}_n\right) = \bigotimes_{j=1}^{n} \left(\mathcal{A}_j\right)^{\frac{\omega_j\left(1+T\left(\mathcal{A}_j\right)\right)}{\sum_{j=1}^{n}\omega_j\left(1+T\left(\mathcal{A}_j\right)\right)}}.$$

Theorem 8.4: Let an assembly $\mathcal{A}_j = \left\{\left(\overline{a_j} + \iota\overline{b_j},\ \underline{a_j} + \iota\underline{b_j}\right)\right\}$, $(j = 1,\ 2,\ 3,\ \ldots,\ n)$ of CFRNs. Then the usage of the CFRDPWG operator over $\mathcal{A}_j$ will give a CFRN, that is:

$$\text{CFRDPWG}\left(\mathcal{A}_1,\ \mathcal{A}_2,\ \mathcal{A}_3,\ \ldots,\ \mathcal{A}_n\right) = \bigotimes_{j=1}^{n} \left(\mathcal{A}_\text{j}\right)^{\frac{\omega_j\left(1+T\left(\mathcal{A}_j\right)\right)}{\sum_{j=1}^{n}\omega_j\left(1+T\left(\mathcal{A}_j\right)\right)}}$$

$$= \left(\begin{array}{c} \frac{1}{1+\left\{\sum_{j=1}^{n}\frac{\omega_j\left(1+T\left(\mathcal{A}_j\right)\right)}{\sum_{j=1}^{n}\omega_j\left(1+T\left(\mathcal{A}_j\right)\right)}\left(\frac{1-\overline{a_j}}{\overline{a_j}}\right)^{\zeta}\right\}^{\frac{1}{\zeta}}} \\ +\iota\frac{1}{1+\left\{\sum_{j=1}^{n}\frac{\omega_j\left(1+T\left(\mathcal{A}_j\right)\right)}{\sum_{j=1}^{n}\omega_j\left(1+T\left(\mathcal{A}_j\right)\right)}\left(\frac{1-\overline{b_j}}{\overline{b_j}}\right)^{\zeta}\right\}^{\frac{1}{\zeta}}}, \\ \frac{1}{1+\left\{\sum_{j=1}^{n}\frac{\omega_j\left(1+T\left(\mathcal{A}_j\right)\right)}{\sum_{j=1}^{n}\omega_j\left(1+T\left(\mathcal{A}_j\right)\right)}\left(\frac{1-\underline{a_j}}{\underline{a_j}}\right)^{\zeta}\right\}^{\frac{1}{\zeta}}} \\ +\iota\frac{1}{1+\left\{\sum_{j=1}^{n}\frac{\omega_j\left(1+T\left(\mathcal{A}_j\right)\right)}{\sum_{j=1}^{n}\omega_j\left(1+T\left(\mathcal{A}_j\right)\right)}\left(\frac{1-\underline{b_j}}{\underline{b_j}}\right)^{\zeta}\right\}^{\frac{1}{\zeta}}} \end{array}\right).$$

8.2 MCDM Approach based on Dombi Power Operators within CFRS

Let $\mathfrak{L} = \{\mathfrak{L}_1, \mathfrak{L}_2, \ldots, \mathfrak{L}_m\}$ be an assembly of alternatives and for these alternatives, let $\mathbb{T} = \{\mathbb{T}_1, \mathbb{T}_2, \ldots, \mathbb{T}_n\}$ be an assembly of criteria that will be utilized for the assessment of the considered alternatives. In these alternatives, the decision analyst has to get the finest and best alternative. For that, the decision analyst will assess these alternatives based on their criteria and interpret their values in the framework of CFRNs, that is, $\mathcal{A} = \left(\overline{a} + \iota\overline{b}, \underline{a} + \iota\underline{b}\right)$, where $\underline{a}, \underline{b}, \ \overline{a}, \overline{b} \in [0,\ 1]$. As each criterion has its weight the decision expert will provide the weight to each of the criteria which is $\omega_j = (\omega_1, \omega_2, \ldots, \omega_n)^T$ such that $\sum\limits_{j=1}^{n} \omega_j$ and $\omega_j \in [0,\ 1]\ \forall\ j$. Now to solve this, this MCDM approach has the underneath steps.

Step 1: As the assessment values are in the form of CFRNs, so develop a complex fuzzy rough decision matrix (CFRDM) $\mathfrak{D}$ by employing these assessment values. In this CFRDM, the first entry will represent the assessment value of the first alternative against the first criteria.

Step 2: Standardization of the CFRDM will be performed in this step by employing the given underneath formula. Standardization is needed because the data can be benefit and cost types:

$$D^{\mathcal{N}} = \begin{cases} \left(\overline{a} + \iota\overline{b}, \underline{a} + \iota\underline{b}\right) & \text{for benefit kind} \\ \left(\overline{a} + \iota\overline{b}, \underline{a} + \iota\underline{b}\right)^c & \text{for cost kind} \end{cases}.$$

Step 3: Here, the support of each $\mathcal{A}_j$would be interpreted as

$$\operatorname{Sup}\left(\mathcal{A}_{jr},\ \mathcal{A}_j l\right) = 1 - đ\left(\mathcal{A}_{jr},\ \mathcal{A}_j l\right),\ r,\ l = 1,\ 2,\ \ldots, n,\ r \neq l,$$

where $đ\left(\mathcal{A}_{jr},\ \mathcal{A}_{jl}\right) = \frac{1}{4}\left(\left|\overline{a_{jr}} - \overline{a_{jl}}\right| + \left|\overline{b_{jr}} - \overline{b_{jl}}\right| + \left|\underline{a_{jr}} - \underline{a_{jl}}\right| + \left|\underline{b_{jr}} - \underline{b_{jl}}\right|\right)$.

Step 4: Interpret

$$\mathrm{T}\left(\mathcal{A}_{jr}\right) = \sum_{\substack{l=1 \\ l \neq r}}^{n} Sup\left(\mathcal{A}_{jr},\ \mathcal{A}_{jl}\right).$$

Noticed that $j = 1,\ 2,\ \ldots, m$; $r,\ l = 1,\ 2,\ \ldots,\ n$ and $r \neq l$.

Step 5: Achieve the associated weight as follows:

$$\chi_{jr} = \frac{\left(1 + T\left(\mathcal{A}_{jr}\right)\right)}{\sum\limits_{l=1}^{n} \left(1 + T\left(\mathcal{A}_{jl}\right)\right)},$$

or

$$\chi_{jr}^{'} = \frac{\hat{W}_{\omega-jr}\left(1+T\left(\mathcal{A}_{jr}\right)\right)}{\sum_{l=1}^{n}\hat{W}_{\omega-jl}\left(1+T\left(\mathcal{A}_{jl}\right)\right)}.$$

Step 6: Aggregate the CFRDM with the assistance of any of the devised operators that is CFRDPA, CFRYPDA, CFRDPG, and CFRDPWG operators.

Step 7: Employing score function to achieve the score values of aggregated outcomes of each alternative. In case of the same score values, achieve the accuracy values by employing the accuracy function.

Step 8: Rank all alternatives by considering their score or accuracy values and select the finest and best alternative.

8.2.1 Case study (selection of protected forest management strategy in national reserve)

ABC Republic's Department of Forest Management and Conservation (DFMC) together with the National Environmental Protection Agency (NEPA) is responsible for choosing the best management strategy for the XYZ National Reserve covering an area of 8500 hectares. This protected area, in the Eastern Province, has experienced escalating threats in the last decade: logging, human-wildlife conflict, and habitat degradation. It has several endemic species and has water catchment importance to neighboring communities. A specialized decision-making committee has been established, consisting of:

- Director General of DFMC
- Senior scientists from the National Institute of Environmental Studies (NIES)
- Representatives from NEPA
- Conservationists from different countries
- Members of the regional community council
- Economists from the Ministry of Planning for Economic Development.

This committee provided four management strategies which are displayed in Table 8.1.

To assess these strategies, the committee considered four criteria, which are displayed in Table 8.2.

The committee will assess these management strategies and provide their values in the form of CFRNs. Also, the expert of the committee

Table 8.1 The forest management strategies with explanation.

Notations	Management strategies	Explanation
$\mathbb{L}_1$	Zoned management system	This strategy categorizes the reserve into different management units of different levels of protection and utilization. It sets up strict protection core areas, regulated-use buffer zones, and community-use zones. The approach comprises monitoring procedures, community forest guard, and sustainable resource utilization strategies. It is implemented in a phased manner with a year's time frame and annual review.
$\mathbb{L}_2$	Smart forest management framework	This approach uses advanced technology in the protection and monitoring of the forests. It includes satellite monitoring systems, artificial intelligence tracking of wildlife, digital patrol management, and early warning systems for illegality. It involves staff development programs and needs cooperation with the National Technology Institute.
$\mathbb{L}_3$	Participatory forest management model	This strategy is focused on the community-based management of the resources. They are; the formation of village forest committees, the use of indigenous knowledge and information, and the development of community-based enterprises. It is based on the capacity development, documentation of traditional practices, and collaborative forest protection activities facilitated by the community engagement unit of the DFMC.
$\mathbb{L}_4$	Multistakeholder partnership approach	This strategy develops a system of cooperation between the government other stakeholders and the local population. They are conservation agreements, eco-tourism development, and market-based conservation incentives. The approach defines the governance structures, benefits distribution, and performance evaluation frameworks.

provides weight to the criteria based on their preference that weight is $(0.31,\ 0.22,\ 0.18,\ 0.29)$. To solve this, we have the underneath steps.

Step 1: The committee assessed the strategies and provided their values in the structure of CFRNs which form CFRDM as shown in Table 8.3.

Step 2: As the data is benefit-kind, so after the standardization, the CFRDM will remain the same.

Step 3: The support of each $\mathcal{A}_j$
for $j = 1$

$$\mathrm{Sup}\left(\mathbb{L}_{11},\ \mathbb{L}_{12}\right) = 0.863, \mathrm{Sup}\left(\mathbb{L}_{11},\ \mathbb{L}_{13}\right) = 0.788, \mathrm{Sup}\left(\mathbb{L}_{11},\ \mathbb{L}_{14}\right) = 0.633,$$

Table 8.2 The criteria of forest management strategies.

Notations	Criteria	Explanation
C_1	Ecological integrity index	This criterion measures how well each strategy will address the conservation, as well as improvement of the forests' ecosystem. It includes the density of forest cover, wildlife population, fragmentation, and ecosystem service assessment. These parameters are monitored by the research division of DFMC through the ecological surveys conducted every 6 months and habitat surveys conducted every month. The measurements are consistent with ABC Republic's National Biodiversity Strategy and other global conservation obligations.
C_2	Community development impact	This criterion established the extent to which each strategy fosters the development of locals while preserving tradition. It includes an assessment of livelihood prospects, forest resource availability to the community, and cultural and economic returns. The Regional Development Authority has to perform detailed social impact studies and economic cost-benefit analyses on these aspects.
C_3	Operational viability	This criterion evaluates the actual realization potential within current governmental structures. It assesses the adequacy of skilled manpower, needed facilities, compliance with present environmental legislation, and compatibility with existing management systems. The assessment also involves capability evaluation of the staff of DFMC and resource requirement analysis by NEPA's planning division.
C_4	Resource sustainability	This criterion looks at the sustainable financial and resource needs in the next fifteen years. It refers to the cost, degree of complexity, ability to begin to generate revenue, and continued fiscal capability. The National Planning Commission regression analyzes and assesses several funding sources and methods inclusive of government and conservation international grants.

$$\mathrm{Sup}\left(\mathbb{L}_{12},\ \mathbb{L}_{11}\right) = 0.863, \mathrm{Sup}\left(\mathbb{L}_{12},\ \mathbb{L}_{13}\right) = 0.72, \mathrm{Sup}\left(\mathbb{L}_{12},\ \mathbb{L}_{14}\right) = 0.59,$$

$$\mathrm{Sup}\left(\mathbb{L}_{13},\ \mathbb{L}_{11}\right) = 0.788, \mathrm{Sup}\left(\mathbb{L}_{13},\ \mathbb{L}_{12}\right) = 0.72, \mathrm{Sup}\left(\mathbb{L}_{13},\ \mathbb{L}_{14}\right) = 0.77,$$

$$\mathrm{Sup}\left(\mathbb{L}_{14},\ \mathbb{L}_{11}\right) = 0.633, \mathrm{Sup}\left(\mathbb{L}_{14},\ \mathbb{L}_{12}\right) = 0.59,\ \mathrm{Sup}\left(\mathbb{L}_{14},\ \mathbb{L}_{13}\right) = 0.77,$$

for $j = 2$

$$\mathrm{Sup}\left(\mathbb{L}_{21},\ \mathbb{L}_{22}\right) = 0.605, \mathrm{Sup}\left(\mathbb{L}_{21},\ \mathbb{L}_{23}\right) = 0.788, \mathrm{Sup}\left(\mathbb{L}_{21},\ \mathbb{L}_{24}\right) = 0.68,$$

Table 8.3 The assessment values of forest management strategies are interpreted by the experts of the committee.

	C_1	C_2	C_3	C_4
$\mathbb{L}_1$	$\begin{pmatrix} 0.23+\iota 0.35, \\ 0.53+\iota 0.83 \end{pmatrix}$	$\begin{pmatrix} 0.29+\iota 0.45, \\ 0.84+\iota 0.75 \end{pmatrix}$	$\begin{pmatrix} 0.71+\iota 0.21, \\ 0.52+\iota 0.61 \end{pmatrix}$	$\begin{pmatrix} 0.98+\iota 0.39, \\ 0.54+\iota 0.16 \end{pmatrix}$
$\mathbb{L}_2$	$\begin{pmatrix} 0.57+\iota 0.48, \\ 0.38+\iota 0.82 \end{pmatrix}$	$\begin{pmatrix} 0.23+\iota 0.32, \\ 0.89+\iota 0.25 \end{pmatrix}$	$\begin{pmatrix} 0.45+\iota 0.78, \\ 0.45+\iota 0.46 \end{pmatrix}$	$\begin{pmatrix} 0.23+\iota 0.14, \\ 0.29+\iota 0.31 \end{pmatrix}$
$\mathbb{L}_3$	$\begin{pmatrix} 0.24+\iota 0.45, \\ 0.21+\iota 0.78 \end{pmatrix}$	$\begin{pmatrix} 0.45+\iota 0.56, \\ 0.14+\iota 0.12 \end{pmatrix}$	$\begin{pmatrix} 0.18+\iota 0.19, \\ 0.84+\iota 0.45 \end{pmatrix}$	$\begin{pmatrix} 0.46+\iota 0.51, \\ 0.73+\iota 0.21 \end{pmatrix}$
$\mathbb{L}_4$	$\begin{pmatrix} 0.62+\iota 0.12, \\ 0.87+\iota 0.25 \end{pmatrix}$	$\begin{pmatrix} 0.41+\iota 0.22, \\ 0.21+\iota 0.32 \end{pmatrix}$	$\begin{pmatrix} 0.41+\iota 0.52, \\ 0.21+\iota 0.74 \end{pmatrix}$	$\begin{pmatrix} 0.12+\iota 0.32, \\ 0.29+\iota 0.85 \end{pmatrix}$

$$\mathrm{Sup}\,(\mathbb{L}_{22},\ \mathbb{L}_{21}) = 0.605, \mathrm{Sup}\,(\mathbb{L}_{22},\ \mathbb{L}_{23}) = 0.668, \mathrm{Sup}\,(\mathbb{L}_{22},\ \mathbb{L}_{24}) = 0.79,$$

$$\mathrm{Sup}\,(\mathbb{L}_{23},\ \mathbb{L}_{21}) = 0.788, \mathrm{Sup}\,(\mathbb{L}_{23},\ \mathbb{L}_{22}) = 0.668, \mathrm{Sup}\,(\mathbb{L}_{23},\ \mathbb{L}_{24}) = 0.708,$$

$$\mathrm{Sup}\,(\mathbb{L}_{24},\ \mathbb{L}_{21}) = 0.743,\ \mathrm{Sup}\,(\mathbb{L}_{24},\ \mathbb{L}_{22}) = 0.79, \mathrm{Sup}\,(\mathbb{L}_{24},\ \mathbb{L}_{23}) = 0.708,$$

for $j = 3$

$$\mathrm{Sup}\,(\mathbb{L}_{31},\ \mathbb{L}_{32}) = 0.738, \mathrm{Sup}\,(\mathbb{L}_{31},\ \mathbb{L}_{33}) = 0.68, \mathrm{Sup}\,(\mathbb{L}_{31},\ \mathbb{L}_{34}) = 0.658,$$

$$\mathrm{Sup}\,(\mathbb{L}_{32},\ \mathbb{L}_{31}) = 0.738, \mathrm{Sup}\,(\mathbb{L}_{32},\ \mathbb{L}_{33}) = 0.583, \mathrm{Sup}\,(\mathbb{L}_{32},\ \mathbb{L}_{34}) = 0.815,$$

$$\mathrm{Sup}\,(\mathbb{L}_{33},\ \mathbb{L}_{31}) = 0.68, \mathrm{Sup}\,(\mathbb{L}_{33},\ \mathbb{L}_{32}) = 0.583, \mathrm{Sup}\,(\mathbb{L}_{33},\ \mathbb{L}_{34}) = 0.763,$$

$$\mathrm{Sup}\,(\mathbb{L}_{34},\ \mathbb{L}_{31}) = 0.7, \mathrm{Sup}\,(\mathbb{L}_{34},\ \mathbb{L}_{32}) = 0.815, \mathrm{Sup}\,(\mathbb{L}_{34},\ \mathbb{L}_{33}) = 0.763,$$

for $j = 4$

$$\mathrm{Sup}\,(\mathbb{L}_{41},\ \mathbb{L}_{42}) = 0.74, \mathrm{Sup}\,(\mathbb{L}_{41},\ \mathbb{L}_{43}) = 0.56, \mathrm{Sup}\,(\mathbb{L}_{41},\ \mathbb{L}_{44}) = 0.53,$$

$$\mathrm{Sup}\,(\mathbb{L}_{42},\ \mathbb{L}_{41}) = 0.74, \mathrm{Sup}\,(\mathbb{L}_{42},\ \mathbb{L}_{43}) = 0.82, \mathrm{Sup}\,(\mathbb{L}_{42},\ \mathbb{L}_{44}) = 0.75,$$

$$\mathrm{Sup}\,(\mathbb{L}_{43},\ \mathbb{L}_{41}) = 0.56, \mathrm{Sup}\,(\mathbb{L}_{43},\ \mathbb{L}_{42}) = 0.82, \mathrm{Sup}\,(\mathbb{L}_{43},\ \mathbb{L}_{44}) = 0.83,$$

$$\mathrm{Sup}\,(\mathbb{L}_{44},\ \mathbb{L}_{41}) = 0.62, \mathrm{Sup}\,(\mathbb{L}_{44},\ \mathbb{L}_{42}) = 0.75, \mathrm{Sup}\,(\mathbb{L}_{44},\ \mathbb{L}_{43}) = 0.83,$$

Step 4: Interpreted $T\,(\mathbb{L}_{jr})$

$$T\,(\mathbb{L}_{11}) = 2.283\mathrm{T}\,(\mathbb{L}_{12}) = 2.173,\ \mathrm{T}\,(\mathbb{L}_{13}) = 2.278,\ \mathrm{T}\,(\mathbb{L}_{14}) = 1.993,$$

$$\mathrm{T}\,(\mathbb{L}_{21}) = 2.073,\ \mathrm{T}\,(\mathbb{L}_{22}) = 2.063,\ \mathrm{T}\,(\mathbb{L}_{23}) = 2.163,\ \mathrm{T}\,(\mathbb{L}_{24}) = 2.24,$$

$$\mathrm{T}\,(\mathbb{L}_{31}) = 2.075,\ \mathrm{T}\,(\mathbb{L}_{32}) = 2.135,\ \mathrm{T}\,(\mathbb{L}_{33}) = 2.025,\ \mathrm{T}\,(\mathbb{L}_{34}) = 2.278,$$

$$\mathrm{T}\,(\mathbb{L}_{41}) = 1.83,\ \mathrm{T}\,(\mathbb{L}_{42}) = 2.31,\ \mathrm{T}\,(\mathbb{L}_{43}) = 2.21,\ \mathrm{T}\,(\mathbb{L}_{44}) = 2.2,$$

Step 5: The associated weights are:

$$\chi_{11} = 0.238, \chi_{12} = 0.262, \chi_{13} = 0.249, \chi_{14} = 0.251,$$

$$\chi_{21} = 0.256, \chi_{22} = 0.266, \chi_{23} = 0.232, \chi_{24} = 0.246,$$

$$\chi_{31} = 0.247, \chi_{32} = 0.253, \chi_{33} = 0.253, \chi_{34} = 0.246,$$

$$\chi_{41} = 0.259, \chi_{42} = 0.263, \chi_{43} = 0.247, \chi_{44} = 0.231,$$

After that analyst weight of each criterion is $(0.31,\ 0.22,\ 0.18,\ 0.29)$, the associated weights are:

$$\chi'_{11} = 0.22, \chi'_{12} = 0.169, \chi'_{13} = 0.339, \chi'_{14} = 0.272,$$

$$\chi'_{21} = 0.238, \chi'_{22} = 0.173, \chi'_{23} = 0.32, \chi'_{24} = 0.269,$$

$$\chi'_{31} = 0.226, \chi'_{32} = 0.162, \chi'_{33} = 0.345, \chi'_{34} = 0.267,$$

$$\chi'_{41} = 0.241, \chi'_{42} = 0.17, \chi'_{43} = 0.338, \chi'_{44} = 0.251.$$

Step 6: The aggregated outcome of each management strategy after employing CFRDPA, CFRDPWA, CFRDPG, and CFRDPWG operators are displayed in Table 8.4.

Table 8.4 The aggregated outcomes of management strategy.

Operators	$\mathbb{L}_1$	$\mathbb{L}_2$	$\mathbb{L}_3$	$\mathbb{L}_4$
CFRDPA	$\begin{pmatrix} 0.997 + \iota\, 0.154, \\ 0.803 + \iota\, 0.812 \end{pmatrix}$	$\begin{pmatrix} 0.246 + \iota\, 0.615, \\ 0.899 + \iota\, 0.735 \end{pmatrix}$	$\begin{pmatrix} 0.161 + \iota\, 0.3, \\ 0.815 + \iota\, 0.622 \end{pmatrix}$	$\begin{pmatrix} 0.32 + \iota\, 0.155, \\ 0.864 + \iota\, 0.826 \end{pmatrix}$
CFRDPWA	$\begin{pmatrix} 0.997 + \iota\, 0.135, \\ 0.741 + \iota\, 0.792 \end{pmatrix}$	$\begin{pmatrix} 0.251 + \iota\, 0.681, \\ 0.854 + \iota\, 0.724 \end{pmatrix}$	$\begin{pmatrix} 0.146 + \iota\, 0.265, \\ 0.852 + \iota\, 0.607 \end{pmatrix}$	$\begin{pmatrix} 0.308 + \iota\, 0.19, \\ 0.845 + \iota\, 0.845 \end{pmatrix}$
CFRDWG	$\begin{pmatrix} 0.629 + \iota\, 0.124, \\ 0.189 + \iota\, 0.157 \end{pmatrix}$	$\begin{pmatrix} 0.285 + \iota\, 0.202, \\ 0.138 + \iota\, 0.085 \end{pmatrix}$	$\begin{pmatrix} 0.071 + \iota\, 0.054, \\ 0.106 + \iota\, 0.157 \end{pmatrix}$	$\begin{pmatrix} 0.104 + \iota\, 0.054, \\ 0.069 + \iota\, 0.051 \end{pmatrix}$
CFRDPWG	$\begin{pmatrix} 0.6 + \iota\, 0.116, \\ 0.22 + \iota\, 0.134 \end{pmatrix}$	$\begin{pmatrix} 0.268 + \iota\, 0.23, \\ 0.152 + \iota\, 0.082 \end{pmatrix}$	$\begin{pmatrix} 0.097 + \iota\, 0.071, \\ 0.091 + \iota\, 0.126 \end{pmatrix}$	$\begin{pmatrix} 0.103 + \iota\, 0.251, \\ 0.064 + \iota\, 0.057 \end{pmatrix}$

Step 7: The score values of management strategies are interpreted in Table 8.5.

Table 8.5 The score values of forest management strategies.

Operators	Scor. $(\mathbb{L}_1)$	Scor. $(\mathbb{L}_2)$	Scor. $(\mathbb{L}_3)$	Scor. $(\mathbb{L}_4)$
CFRDPA	0.692	0.624	0.475	0.539
CFRDPWA	0.666	0.628	0.468	0.547
CFRDPG	0.775	0.678	0.597	0.611
CFRDPWG	0.768	0.683	0.569	0.619

Table 8.6 The ranking of management strategies.

Operators	Ranking
CFRDPA	$\mathbb{L}_1 > \mathbb{L}_2 > \mathbb{L}_4 > \mathbb{L}_3$
CFRDPWA	$\mathbb{L}_1 > \mathbb{L}_2 > \mathbb{L}_4 > \mathbb{L}_3$
CFRDPG	$\mathbb{L}_1 > \mathbb{L}_2 > \mathbb{L}_4 > \mathbb{L}_3$
CFRDPWG	$\mathbb{L}_1 > \mathbb{L}_2 > \mathbb{L}_4 > \mathbb{L}_3$

Step 8: The ranking of management strategies is devised in Table 8.6.

From the ranking of management strategies, the committee decided that $\mathbb{L}_1$ is the finest and best strategy. The graphical interpretation of score values of forest management strategies is given in Figure 8.1.

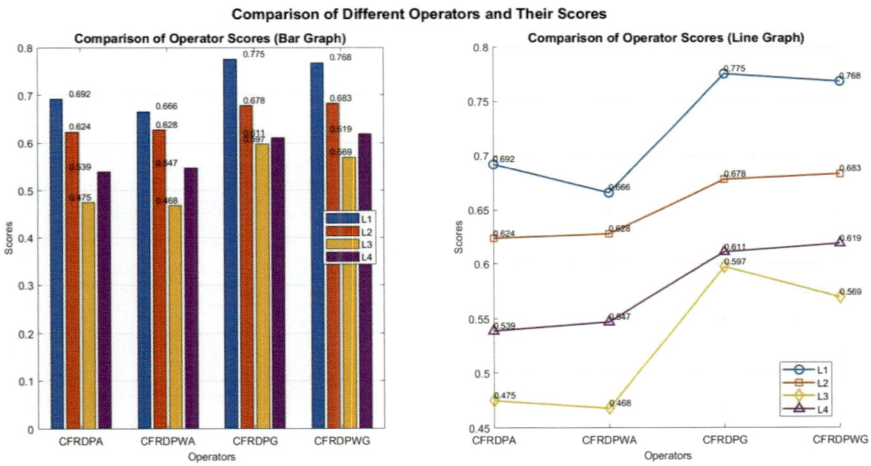

Figure 8.1 The graphical interpretation of score values of forest management strategies.

8.3 Comparative Study

To show the applicability of the proposed operators and methods, a comparison with several other theories in the field is performed. These include Xu and Yager's power geometric operators [22], Rehman's probability complex fuzzy aggregation operators (AOs) and MCDM methods [23] for two-dimensional and complex information aggregation, Hu et al.'s power AOs [24] designed for complex information in polar form, Khan et al.'s AOs and MCDM techniques [25] addressing complex fuzzy rough information in polar form, and Hussain et al. [26] approach for CFR information in polar form. The comparison is done using the complex fuzzy rough information highlighted in Table 8.3 with the help of different AOs and ranking techniques. The findings of the comparative analysis are presented in Tables 8.7, 8.8, and Figure 8.2.

Table 8.7 The score values of existing and proposed theory.

Operators	**Scor.** $(\mathbb{L}_1)$	**Scor.** $(\mathbb{L}_2)$	**Scor.** $(\mathbb{L}_3)$	**Scor.** $(\mathbb{L}_4)$
Xu and Yager [22]	No result	No result	No result	No result
Rehman [23]	No result	No result	No result	No result
Hu et al. [24]	No result	No result	No result	No result
Khan et al. [25]	No result	No result	No result	No result
Hussain et al. [25]	No result	No result	No result	No result
CFRDPA	0.692	0.624	0.475	0.539
CFRDPWA	0.666	0.628	0.468	0.547
CFRDPG	0.775	0.678	0.597	0.611
CFRDPWG	0.768	0.683	0.569	0.619

Table 8.8 The ranking of proposed theories and existing ones.

Operators	**Ranking result**
Xu and Yager [22]	No result
Rehman [23]	No result
Hu et al. [24]	No result
Khan et al. [25]	No result
Hussain et al. [25]	No result
CFRDPA	$\mathbb{L}_1 > \mathbb{L}_2 > \mathbb{L}_4 > \mathbb{L}_3$
CFRDPWA	$\mathbb{L}_1 > \mathbb{L}_2 > \mathbb{L}_4 > \mathbb{L}_3$
CFRDPG	$\mathbb{L}_1 > \mathbb{L}_2 > \mathbb{L}_4 > \mathbb{L}_3$
CFRDPWG	$\mathbb{L}_1 > \mathbb{L}_2 > \mathbb{L}_4 > \mathbb{L}_3$

The findings shown in Tables 8.7, 8.8, and Figure 8.2 indicate several major shortcomings of the current approaches. Power geometric operators, which are efficient for dealing with crisp information, cannot be applied to uncertainty, roughness, or two-dimensional cases. However, the proposed approach goes beyond these limitations and can handle both crisp information and other data types. Likewise, probability complex fuzzy operators are good at handling two-dimensional and uncertain data while having low performance in dealing with roughness. The proposed framework can also manage two-dimensional and uncertain information and it also considers the roughness and is therefore more robust than the previous solution. One more limitation is seen in more complex fuzzy rough operators: these are capable of handling only polar forms of complex information and are useless in Tamir's complex fuzzy form. This restricts their applicability to a great extent in dealing with various formats in which data may be available. One of the key lessons from this comparative study is that the existing approaches to forest management are insufficient in terms of roughness and uncertainty. This oversight undermines the quality of decisions, particularly in complex environmental conditions. The following framework fills this gap by incorporating roughness, 2D information, and uncertainty into the decision-making procedure. This enhances the reliability and soundness of strategies for forest management by a large measure, thus overcoming the limitations of current approaches. Therefore, it provides an enhanced and comprehensive system for decision-making in the management of forests as compared to previous models.

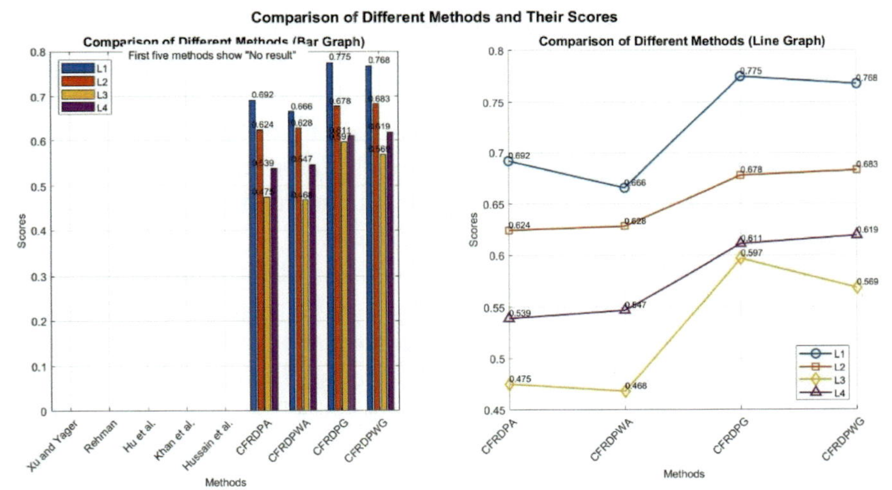

Figure 8.2 The graphical interpretation of score values obtained by proposed and existing methods.

8.4 Conclusion

This chapter has introduced a brand new mathematical approach for dealing with the challenges associated with ecosystem management using complex fuzzy rough Dombi power aggregation operators. The research has several important implications for both theory and application in environmental decision-making. First, the introduction of the CFRDPA, CFRDPWA,

CFRDPG, and CFRDPWG operators is a theoretical innovation in dealing with complicated fuzzy rough information. These operators are well suited to model the uncertainty, imprecision, and interconnectivity inherent in ecosystem data and environmental systems in general. The combination of Dombi operations with CFRSs has been found to be especially useful in the modeling of the complex interdependencies that are often found in ecological data. The analysis of the forest management strategy case proves the effectiveness of our framework in actual environmental decision-making. The results indicate that our approach effectively solves some of the most important problems of ecosystem management, such as the consideration of multiple perspectives, the processing of uncertain ecological data, and the analysis of the interactions between the components of the environment. The fact that the methodology can handle fuzzy rough information and is computationally efficient makes it ideal for large-scale environmental decision support systems. The analysis of our approach in comparison with the existing methodologies shows several significant benefits of the proposed approach. The proposed operators show higher performance in dealing with uncertainty and complexity as compared to the traditional approaches as they offer more accurate and detailed results. This superiority is especially noticeable in situations where there is a lot of data uncertainty and intricate interdependence between species, which is typical for ecosystem management.

In addition, the study provides a strong background for future advancements in environmental decision support systems. The proposed framework is therefore flexible and can be extended to incorporate other factors that may arise in ecosystem management for example effects of climate change and other dynamic processes. The strength of the approach is that it is highly mathematical and yet can be applied in the real world by environmental managers and decision-makers. The findings also support the use of higher mathematical methods in decision-making on environmental issues. Since the complex fuzzy rough set approach was useful in addressing the issues of ecosystem management, likely, other areas of environmental science and management may also benefit from the use of similar mathematical models.

9

Empowering Robotic Decision-making with Complex Fuzzy Rough Sets: Toward Autonomous Industrial Applications

The ever-growing pace of developing industrial automation technologies and the growing complexity of robotic autonomous systems have raised the demand for complex decision-making models that can address complex information environments. This chapter aims to overcome this challenge by proposing a novel theoretical framework for enhancing robotic decision-making using CFRS, especially in the context of autonomous industrial environments where uncertainty, roughness, and complexity of information are inevitable. We introduce a novel suite of aggregation operators: complex fuzzy rough Frank power averaging (CFRFPA), complex fuzzy rough Frank power weighted averaging (CFRFPWA), complex fuzzy rough Frank power geometric (CFRFPG), and complex fuzzy rough Frank power weighted geometric (CFRFPWG) operators. These operators are intended for the management and summarization of CFR information in MCDM conditions. The theoretical background of these operators is well grounded, their basic characteristics and peculiarities of functioning are described. Based on these operators, we propose a complex MCDM methodology for the cases with the use of CFR information. As a proof of concept for our framework, we provide an extensive real-world example that is centered on the identification of robotic autonomous solutions for industrial uses. This chapter demonstrates how the proposed approach can be applied to solve practical problems in industrial automation decision-making where uncertainty and imprecision are inevitable. The usefulness of the proposed framework is also demonstrated by comparing it to the existing approaches in the area. The results clearly show that our approach outperforms the benchmark in terms of its ability to capture

DOI: 10.1201/9788743807827-9

the interactions between uncertainty, roughness, and the underlying information complexity of the robotic autonomous system selection problem. This comparative analysis also shows that the proposed framework offers more comprehensive and accurate decision support for applications of industrial automation.

9.1 Frank AOs within the Framework of CFRSs

Here, we first revise the Frank t-norm and t-conorm and then discuss the algebraic operations based on these in the framework of CFRSs. After that, we devise Frank AOs in the setting of CFRSs that are CFRFPA, CFRFPWA, CFRFPG, and CFRFPWG operators.

Definition 9.1 [29]: The Frank t-norm and t-conorm is diagnosed as

$$\phi_1 \oplus \phi_2 = 1 - \log_\theta \left(1 + \frac{\left(\theta^{1-\phi_1} - 1\right)\left(\theta^{1-\phi_2} - 1\right)}{\theta - 1}\right),$$

$$\phi_1 \bigotimes \phi_2 = \log_\theta \left(1 + \frac{\left(\theta^{1-\phi_1} - 1\right)\left(\theta^{1-\phi_2} - 1\right)}{\theta - 1}\right)$$

for all $(\phi_1, \phi_2) \in [0, 1] \times [0, 1]$ and $\theta > 1$.

Note: Here, we take $\log_\theta 0 = 1, \theta > 1$.

The algebraic operations based on Frank t-norm and co-norm are interpreted as

Definition 9.2: For two CFRNs $\mathcal{A}_1 = \left\{\left(\overline{a_1} + \iota\overline{b_1},\ \underline{a_1} + \iota\underline{b_1}\right)\right\}$ and $\mathcal{A}_2 = \left\{\left(\overline{a_2} + \iota\overline{b_2},\ \underline{a_2} + \iota\underline{b_2}\right)\right\}$, the algebraic operations by employing Frank t-norm and co-norm are inferred as, where $s > 0$ and $\theta > 0$,

1. $\mathcal{A}_1 \oplus \mathcal{A}_2 =$

$$\begin{pmatrix} 1 - \log_\theta\left(1 + \frac{\left(\theta^{1-\overline{a_1}}-1\right)\left(\theta^{1-\overline{a_2}}-1\right)}{\theta-1}\right) \\ +\iota 1 - \log_\theta\left(1 + \frac{\left(\theta^{1-\overline{b_1}}-1\right)\left(\theta^{1-\overline{b_2}}-1\right)}{\theta-1}\right), \\ 1 - \log_\theta\left(1 + \frac{\left(\theta^{1-\underline{a_1}}-1\right)\left(\theta^{1-\underline{a_2}}-1\right)}{\theta-1}\right) \\ +\iota 1 - \log_\theta\left(1 + \frac{\left(\theta^{1-\underline{b_1}}-1\right)\left(\theta^{1-\underline{b_2}}-1\right)}{\theta-1}\right) \end{pmatrix}.$$

2. $\mathcal{A}_1 \otimes \mathcal{A}_2 =$

$$\left(\begin{array}{c} \log_\theta\left(1+\frac{\left(\theta^{\overline{a_1}}-1\right)\left(\theta^{\overline{a_2}}-1\right)}{\theta-1}\right) \\ +\iota\log_\theta\left(1+\frac{\left(\theta^{\overline{b_1}}-1\right)\left(\theta^{\overline{b_2}}-1\right)}{\theta-1}\right), \\ \log_\theta\left(1+\frac{\left(\theta^{\underline{a_1}}-1\right)\left(\theta^{\underline{a_2}}-1\right)}{\theta-1}\right) \\ +\iota\log_\theta\left(1+\frac{\left(\theta^{\underline{b_1}}-1\right)\left(\theta^{\underline{b_2}}-1\right)}{\theta-1}\right) \end{array}\right).$$

3. $s\mathcal{A}_1 =$

$$\left(\begin{array}{c} 1-\log_\theta\left(1+\frac{\left(\theta^{1-\overline{a_1}}-1\right)^s}{(\theta-1)^{s-1}}\right)+\iota 1-\log_\theta\left(1+\frac{\left(\theta^{1-\overline{b_1}}-1\right)^s}{(\theta-1)^{s-1}}\right), \\ 1-\log_\theta\left(1+\frac{\left(\theta^{1-\underline{a_1}}-1\right)^s}{(\theta-1)^{s-1}}\right)+\iota 1-\log_\theta\left(1+\frac{\left(\theta^{1-\underline{b_1}}-1\right)^s}{(\theta-1)^{s-1}}\right) \end{array}\right).$$

4. $$(\mathcal{A}_1)^s = \left(\begin{array}{c} \log_\theta\left(1+\frac{\left(\theta^{\overline{a_1}}-1\right)^s}{(\theta-1)^{s-1}}\right)+\iota\log_\theta\left(1+\frac{\left(\theta^{\overline{b_1}}-1\right)^{\iota\ddagger}}{(\theta-1)^{s-1}}\right), \\ \log_\theta\left(1+\frac{\left(\theta^{\underline{a_1}}-1\right)^s}{(\theta-1)^{s-1}}\right)+\iota\log_\theta\left(1+\frac{\left(\theta^{\underline{b_1}}-1\right)^s}{(\theta-1)^{s-1}}\right) \end{array}\right).$$

Definition 9.3: Let an assembly $\mathcal{A}_j = \left\{\left(\overline{a_j}+\iota\overline{b_j},\ \underline{a_j}+\iota\underline{b_j}\right)\right\}, (j = 1,\ 2,\ 3,\ \ldots,\ n)$ of CFRNs. Then the CFRFPA operator is scrutinized as

$$\mathrm{CFRFPA}(\mathcal{A}_1,\ \mathcal{A}_2,\ \mathcal{A}_3,\ \ldots,\ \mathcal{A}_n) = \bigoplus_{j=1}^{n} \frac{1+T(\mathcal{A}_j)}{\sum_{j=1}^{n}(1+T(\mathcal{A}_j))}\mathcal{A}_j.$$

Observe that $\mathrm{T}(\mathcal{A}_j) = \sum_{\substack{j=1 \\ j\neq r}}^{n} \mathrm{Sup}(\mathcal{A}_j,\ \mathcal{A}_r)$ and $\mathrm{Sup}(\mathcal{A}_j,\ \mathcal{A}_r)$ infers the support for $\mathcal{A}_j$ from $\mathcal{A}_r$ with the axioms given below:

- $\mathrm{Sup}(\mathcal{A}_j,\ \mathcal{A}_r) \in [0,\ 1]$;
- $\mathrm{Sup}(\mathcal{A}_j,\ \mathcal{A}_r) = \mathrm{Sup}(\mathcal{A}_r,\ \mathcal{A}_j)$;
- $\mathrm{Sup}(\mathcal{A}_j,\ \mathcal{A}_r) \geq \mathrm{Sup}\left(\mathcal{A}_{j'},\ \mathcal{A}_{r'}\right)$ if $đ(\mathcal{A}_j,\ \mathcal{A}_r) < đ\left(\mathcal{A}_{j'},\ \mathcal{A}_{r'}\right)$, $đ$ can be a distance measure among CFRSs, that is:

$$đ(\mathcal{A}_1,\ \mathcal{A}_2) = \frac{1}{4}\left(\left|\overline{a_1}-\overline{a_2}\right|+\left|\overline{b_1}-\overline{b_2}\right|+\left|\underline{a_1}-\underline{a_2}\right|+\left|\underline{b_1}-\underline{b_2}\right|\right),$$

where $\mathcal{A}_j = \left\{\left(\overline{a_j} + \iota\overline{b_j},\ \underline{a_j} + \iota\underline{b_j}\right)\right\}$, $(j = 1,\ 2)$.

Theorem 9.1: Let an assembly $\mathcal{A}_j = \left\{\left(\overline{a_j} + \iota\overline{b_j}, \underline{a_j} + \iota\underline{b_j}\right)\right\}, (j = 1,\ 2,\ 3,\ \ldots,\ n)$ of CFRNs.

Then the usage of the CFRFPA operator over $\mathcal{A}_j$ will give a CFRN, that is:

$$\mathrm{CFRFPA}\left(\mathcal{A}_1,\ \mathcal{A}_2,\ \mathcal{A}_3,\ \ldots,\ \mathcal{A}_n\right) = \left(\begin{array}{l} 1 - \left(\log_\theta\left(1 + \prod_{j=1}^{n}\left(\theta^{1-\overline{a_j}} - 1\right)^{\chi_j}\right)\right) \\ \qquad +\iota\left(1 - \left(\log_\theta\left(1 + \prod_{j=1}^{n}\left(\theta^{1-\overline{b_j}} - 1\right)^{\chi_j}\right)\right),\right) \\ 1 - \left(\log_\theta\left(1 + \prod_{j=1}^{n}\left(\theta^{1-\underline{a_j}} - 1\right)^{\chi_j}\right)\right) \\ \qquad +\iota\left(1 - \left(\log_\theta\left(1 + \prod_{j=1}^{n}\left(\theta^{1-\underline{b_j}} - 1\right)^{\chi_j}\right)\right)\right), \end{array}\right). \tag{9.1}$$

Proof: Let $n = 2$. Then, we have:

$$\mathrm{CFRFPA}\left(\mathcal{A}_1,\ \mathcal{A}_2\right) = \chi_1\mathcal{A}_1 \oplus \chi_2\mathcal{A}_2 =$$

$$\left(\begin{array}{l} 1 - \log_\theta\left(1 + \frac{\left(\theta^{1-\overline{a_j}}-1\right)^{\chi_1}}{(\theta-1)^{\chi_1-1}}\right)\iota\left(1 - \log_\theta\left(1 + \frac{\left(\theta^{1-\overline{b_j}}-1\right)^{\chi_1}}{(\theta-1)^{\chi_1-1}}\right)\right), \\ 1 - \log_\theta\left(1 + \frac{\left(\theta^{1-\underline{a_j}}-1\right)^{\chi_1}}{(\theta-1)^{\chi_1-1}}\right)\iota\left(1 - \log_\theta\left(1 + \frac{\left(\theta^{1-\underline{b_j}}-1\right)^{\chi_1}}{(\theta-1)^{\chi-1^{1}}}\right)\right) \end{array}\right)$$

$$\oplus\left(\begin{array}{l} 1 - \log_\theta\left(1 + \frac{\left(\theta^{1-\overline{a_j}}-1\right)^{\chi_2}}{(\theta-1)^{\chi_2-1}}\right)\iota\left(1 - \log_\theta\left(1 + \frac{\left(\theta^{1-\overline{b_j}}-1\right)^{\chi_2}}{(\theta-1)^{\chi-2^{1}}}\right)\right), \\ 1 - \log_\theta\left(1 + \frac{\left(\theta^{1-\underline{a_j}}-1\right)^{\chi_2}}{(\theta-1)^{\chi_2-1}}\right)\iota\left(1 - \log_\theta\left(1 + \frac{\left(\theta^{1-\underline{b_j}}-1\right)^{\chi_2}}{(\theta-1)^{\chi_2-1}}\right)\right) \end{array}\right)$$

$$= \left(\begin{array}{l} \left(\begin{array}{l} 1 - \log_\theta \left(1 + \frac{\prod_{j=1}^{2} \left(\theta^{1-\overline{a_j}} - 1 \right)^{\chi_j}}{(\theta - 1)^{\sum_{j=1}^{2} \chi_j - 1}} \right) \\ \quad + \iota \left(1 - \log_\theta \left(1 + \frac{\prod_{j=1}^{2} \left(\theta^{1-\overline{b_j}} - 1 \right)^{\chi_j}}{(\theta - 1)^{\sum_{j=1}^{2} \chi - j - 1}} \right) \right) \end{array} \right), \\ \left(\begin{array}{l} 1 - \log_\theta \left(1 + \frac{\prod_{j=1}^{2} \left(\theta^{1-\underline{a_j}} - 1 \right)^{\chi_j}}{(\theta - 1)^{\sum_{j=1}^{2} \chi_j 1}} \right) \\ \quad + \iota \left(1 - \log_\theta \left(1 + \frac{\prod_{j=1}^{2} \left(\theta^{1-\underline{b_j}} - 1 \right)^{\chi_j}}{(\theta - 1)^{\sum_{j=1}^{2} \chi_j - 1}} \right) \right) \end{array} \right) \end{array} \right).$$

Thus, eqn (9.1) holds for $n = 2$. Next let for $n = r$, eqn (9.1) holds. Then:

$$\text{CFRFPA}(\mathcal{A}_1, \mathcal{A}_2, \ldots, \mathcal{A}_r)$$

$$= \left(\begin{array}{l} \left(\begin{array}{l} 1 - \log_\theta \left(1 + \frac{\prod_{j=1}^{r} \left(\theta^{1-\overline{a_j}} - 1 \right)^{\chi_j}}{(\theta - 1)^{\sum_{j=1}^{r} \chi_j - 1}} \right) \\ \quad + \iota \left(1 - \log_\theta \left(1 + \frac{\prod_{j=1}^{r} \left(\theta^{1-\overline{b_j}} - 1 \right)^{\chi_j}}{(\theta - 1)^{\sum_{j=1}^{r} \chi_j - 1}} \right) \right) \end{array} \right), \\ \left(\begin{array}{l} 1 - \log_\theta \left(1 + \frac{\prod_{j=1}^{r} \left(\theta^{1-\underline{a_j}} - 1 \right)^{\chi_j}}{(\theta - 1)^{\sum_{j=1}^{r} \chi_j - 1}} \right) \\ \quad + \iota \left(1 - \log_\theta \left(1 + \frac{\prod_{j=1}^{r} \left(\theta^{1-\underline{b_j}} - 1 \right)^{\chi_j}}{(\theta - 1)^{\sum_{j=1}^{r} \chi_j - 1}} \right) \right) \end{array} \right) \end{array} \right).$$

Finally, let $n = r + 1$. Then:

$$\text{CFRFPA}(\mathcal{A}_1, \mathcal{A}_2, \ldots, \mathcal{A}_r, \mathcal{A}_{r+1}) = \text{CFRFPA}(\mathcal{A}_1, \mathcal{A}_2, \ldots, \mathcal{A}_r) \oplus \chi_{r+1} \mathcal{A}_{r+1}$$

$$= \begin{pmatrix} 1-\log_\theta\left(1+\dfrac{\prod_{j=1}^{r}\left(\theta^{1-\overline{a_j}}-1\right)^{\chi_j}}{(\theta-1)^{\sum_{j=1}^{r}\chi_j-1}}\right)+\iota\left(1-\log_\theta\left(1+\dfrac{\prod_{j=1}^{r}\left(\theta^{1-\overline{b_j}}-1\right)^{\chi_j}}{(\theta-1)^{\sum_{j=1}^{r}\chi_j-1}}\right)\right), \\ 1-\log_\theta\left(1+\dfrac{\prod_{j=1}^{r}\left(\theta^{1-\underline{a_j}}-1\right)^{\chi_j}}{(\theta-1)^{\sum_{j=1}^{r}\chi_j-1}}\right)+\iota\left(1-\log_\theta\left(1+\dfrac{\prod_{j=1}^{r}\left(\theta^{1-\underline{b_j}}-1\right)^{\chi_j}}{(\theta-1)^{\sum_{j=1}^{r}\chi_j-1}}\right)\right) \end{pmatrix}$$

$$\bigoplus \begin{pmatrix} 1-\log_\theta\left(1+\dfrac{\left(\theta^{1-\overline{a_{r+1}}}-1\right)^{\chi_{r+1}}}{(\theta-1)^{\chi_1-r+1}}\right) \\ +\iota\left(1-\log_\theta\left(1+\dfrac{\left(\theta^{1-\overline{b_{r+1}}}-1\right)^{\chi_{r+1}}}{(\theta-1)^{\chi-1-r+1}}\right)\right), \\ 1-\log_\theta\left(1+\dfrac{\left(\theta^{1-\underline{a_{r+1}}}-1\right)^{\chi_{r+1}}}{(\theta-1)^{\chi_1-r+1}}\right) \\ +\iota\left(1-\log_\theta\left(1+\dfrac{\left(\theta^{1-\underline{b_{r+1}}}-1\right)^{\chi_{r+1}}}{(\theta-1)^{\chi_1-r+1}}\right)\right) \end{pmatrix}$$

$$= (A,\ B),$$

where

$$A = \begin{pmatrix} 1-\log_\theta\left(1+\dfrac{\left(\theta^{\log_\theta\left(1+\frac{\prod_{j=1}^{r}\left(\theta^{1-\overline{a_j}}-1\right)^{\chi_j}}{(\theta-1)^{\sum_{j=1}^{r}\chi_j-1}}\right)}-1\right)\left(\theta^{\log_\theta\left(1+\frac{\left(\theta^{1-\overline{a_j}}-1\right)^{\chi_{r+1}}}{(\theta-1)^{\chi_{r+1}-1}}\right)}-1\right)}{\theta-1}\right) \\ +\iota\, 1-\log_\theta\left(1+\dfrac{\left(\theta^{\log_\theta\left(1+\frac{\prod_{j=1}^{r}\left(\theta^{1-\overline{b_j}}-1\right)^{\chi_j}}{(\theta-1)^{\sum_{j=1}^{r}\chi_j-1}}\right)}-1\right)\left(\theta^{\log_\theta\left(1+\frac{\left(\theta^{1-\overline{b_j}}-1\right)^{\chi_{r+1}}}{(\theta-1)^{\chi_{r+1}-1}}\right)}-1\right)}{\theta-1}\right) \end{pmatrix},$$

and

$$B = \begin{pmatrix} 1 - \log_\theta \left(1 + \dfrac{\left(\theta^{\log_\theta \left(1 + \frac{\prod_{j=1}^{r} \left(\theta^{1-\underline{a}_j} 1 \right)^{\chi_j}}{(\theta-1)^{\sum_{j=1}^{r} \chi_j - 1}} \right)} - 1 \right) \left(\theta^{\log_\theta \left(1 + \frac{\left(\theta^{1-\underline{a}_j} - 1 \right)^{\chi_{r+1}}}{(\theta-1)^{\chi_{r+1} - 1}} \right)} - 1 \right)}{\theta - 1} \right) \\ + \iota\, 1 - \log_\theta \left(1 + \dfrac{\left(\theta^{\log_\theta \left(1 + \frac{\prod_{j=1}^{r} \left(\theta^{1-\underline{b}_j} - 1 \right)^{\chi_{-j}}}{(\theta-1)^{\sum_{j=1}^{r} \chi_j - 1}} \right)} - 1 \right) \left(\theta^{\log_\theta \left(1 + \frac{\left(\theta^{1-\underline{b}_j} - 1 \right)^{\chi_{r+1}}}{(\theta-1)^{\chi_{r+1} - 1}} \right)} - 1 \right)}{\theta - 1} \right) \end{pmatrix}$$

$$= \begin{pmatrix} 1 - \log_\theta \left(1 + \dfrac{\prod_{j=1}^{r+1} \left(\theta^{1-\overline{a_j}} - 1 \right)^{\chi_j}}{(\theta-1)^{\sum_{j=1}^{r+1} \chi_j - 1}} \right) \\ + \iota \left(1 - \log_\theta \left(1 + \dfrac{\prod_{j=1}^{r+1} \left(\theta^{1-\overline{b_j}} - 1 \right)^{\chi_j}}{(\theta-1)^{\sum_{j=1}^{r+1} \chi_j - 1}} \right) \right), \\ 1 - \log_\theta \left(1 + \dfrac{\prod_{j=1}^{r+1} \left(\theta^{1-\underline{a}_j} - 1 \right)^{\chi_j}}{(\theta-1)^{\sum_{j=1}^{r+1} \chi_j - 1}} \right) \\ + \iota \left(1 - \log_\theta \left(1 + \dfrac{\prod_{j=1}^{r+1} \left(\theta^{1-\underline{b}_j} - 1 \right)^{\chi_j}}{(\theta-1)^{\sum_{j=1}^{r+1} \chi_j - 1}} \right) \right) \end{pmatrix}.$$

$\Longrightarrow$ Eqn (9.1) is true for n.

9.1.1 Properties of CFRFPA operator

The notion of CFRFPA satisfies the following properties.

Idempotency:Let an assembly$\mathcal{A}_j = \left\{\left(\overline{a_j} + \iota\overline{b_j},\ \underline{a_j} + \iota\underline{b_j}\right)\right\}, (j = 1,\ 2,\ 3,\ \ldots,\ n)$ of CFRNs. If $\mathcal{A}_j = \mathcal{A}$, $\forall\ j$, then:

$$\mathrm{CFRFPA}\left(\mathcal{A}_1,\ \mathcal{A}_2,\ ..,\ \mathcal{A}_n\right) = \mathcal{A}.$$

Boundedness: Let an assembly $\mathcal{A}_j = \left(\overline{a_j} + \iota\,\overline{b_j}, \underline{a_j} + \iota\underline{b_j}\right), (j = 1, 2, \ldots, n)$, of CFRNs and $\mathcal{A}^- = \left(\min_j\left\{\overline{a_j}\right\} + \iota\min_j\left\{\overline{b_j}\right\},\ \min_j\left\{\underline{a_j}\right\} + \iota\min_j\left\{\underline{b_j}\right\}\right)$ and $\mathcal{A}^+ = \left(\max_j\left\{\overline{a_j}\right\} + \iota\max_j\left\{\overline{b_j},\quad \max_j\left\{\underline{a_j}\right\} + \iota\max_j\left\{\underline{b_j}\right\}\right\}\right)$. Then:

$$\mathcal{A}^- \leq \mathrm{CFRFPA}\left(\mathcal{A}_1,\ \mathcal{A}_2,\ ..,\ \mathcal{A}_n\right) \leq \mathcal{A}^+.$$

Monotonicity: Let two assemblies $\mathcal{A}_j = \left(\overline{a_j} + \iota\,\overline{b_j}, \underline{a_j} + \iota\underline{b_j}\right)$ and $\mathcal{A}_j^{'} = \left(\overline{a_j^{'}} + \iota\,\overline{b_j^{'}}, \underline{a_j^{'}} + \iota\underline{b_j^{'}}\right),\ (j = 1,\ 2,\ \ldots,\ n)$, of CFRNs. If $\underline{a_j} \leq \underline{a_j^{'}}$, $\underline{b_j} \leq \underline{b_j^{'}}$, $\overline{a_j} \leq \overline{a_j^{'}}$, $\overline{b_j} \leq \overline{b_j^{'}}\forall\ j$, then:

$$\mathrm{CFRFPA}\left(\mathcal{A}_1,\ \mathcal{A}_2,\ ..,\ \mathcal{A}_n\right) \leq \mathrm{CFRFPA}\left(\mathcal{A}_1^{'},\ \mathcal{A}_2^{'},\ ..,\ \mathcal{A}_n^{'}\right).$$

Definition 9.4: Let an assembly $\mathcal{A}_j = \left\{\left(\overline{a_j} + \iota\overline{b_j},\ \underline{a_j} + \iota\underline{b_j}\right)\right\},\ (j = 1,\ 2,\ 3,\ \ldots,\ n)$ of CFRNs.

Then the CFRFPWA operator is scrutinized as

$$\mathrm{CFRFPWA}\left(\mathcal{A}_1,\ \mathcal{A}_2,\ \mathcal{A}_3,\ \ldots,\ \mathcal{A}_n\right) = \underset{j=1}{\overset{n}{\oplus}} \frac{\omega_j\left(1 + T\left(\mathcal{A}_j\right)\right)}{\sum\limits_{j=1}^{n}\omega_j\left(1 + T\left(\mathcal{A}_j\right)\right)}\mathcal{A}_j.$$

Theorem 9.2: Let an assembly $\mathcal{A}_j = \left\{\left(\overline{a_j} + \iota\overline{b_j},\ \underline{a_j} + \iota\underline{b_j}\right)\right\},\ (j = 1,\ 2,\ 3,\ \ldots,\ n)$ of CFRNs. Then the usage of the CFRFPWA operator over $\mathcal{A}_j$ will give a CFRN, that is:

$$\mathrm{CFRFPWA}\left(\mathcal{A}_1,\ \mathcal{A}_2,\ \ldots,\ \mathcal{A}_n\right) =$$

$$\left(\begin{array}{c} 1-\left(\log_\theta\left(1+\prod_{j=1}^{n}\left(\theta^{1-\overline{a_j}}-1\right)^{\frac{\omega_j\left(1+T\left(\mathcal{A}_j\right)\right)}{\sum_{j=1}^{n}\omega_j\left(1+T\left(\mathcal{A}_j\right)\right)}}\right)\right) \\ +\iota\left(1-\left(\log_\theta\left(1+\prod_{j=1}^{n}\left(\theta^{1-\overline{b_j}}-1\right)^{\frac{\omega_j\left(1+T\left(\mathcal{A}_j\right)\right)}{\sum_{j=1}^{n}\omega_j\left(1+T\left(\mathcal{A}_j\right)\right)}}\right)\right)\right), \\ 1-\left(\log_\theta\left(1+\prod_{j=1}^{n}\left(\theta^{1-\underline{a_j}}-1\right)^{\frac{\omega_j\left(1+T\left(\mathcal{A}_j\right)\right)}{\sum_{j=1}^{n}\omega_j\left(1+T\left(\mathcal{A}_j\right)\right)}}\right)\right) \\ +\iota\left(1-\left(\log_\theta\left(1+\prod_{j=1}^{n}\left(\theta^{1-\underline{b_j}}-1\right)^{\frac{\omega_j\left(1+T\left(\mathcal{A}_j\right)\right)}{\sum_{j=1}^{n}\omega_j\left(1+T\left(\mathcal{A}_j\right)\right)}}\right)\right)\right), \end{array}\right).$$

9.1.2 Properties of CFRFPWA operator

The notion of CFRFPWA satisfies the following properties.

Idempotency:Let an assembly $\mathcal{A}_j = \left\{\left(\overline{a_j} + \iota\overline{b_j},\ \underline{a_j} + \iota\underline{b_j}\right)\right\}$, $(j = 1,\ 2,\ 3,\ \ldots,\ n)$ of CFRNs. If $\mathcal{A}_j = \mathcal{A}$, $\forall\ j$, then:

$$\text{CFRFPWA}\left(\mathcal{A}_1,\ \mathcal{A}_2,\ ..,\ \mathcal{A}_n\right) = \mathcal{A}.$$

Boundedness: Let an assembly $\mathcal{A}_j = \left(\overline{a_j} + \iota\overline{b_j}, \underline{a_j} + \iota\underline{b_j}\right)$, $(j = 1, 2, \ldots, n)$, of CFRNs and $\mathcal{A}^- = \left(\min_j\left\{\overline{a_j}\right\} + \iota\min_j\left\{\overline{b_j}\right\}, \min_j\left\{\underline{a_j}\right\} + \iota\min_j\left\{\underline{b_j}\right\}\right)$, and $\mathcal{A}^+ = \left(\max_j\left\{\overline{a_j}\right\} + \iota\max_j\left\{\overline{b_j}\right\}, \max_j\left\{\underline{a_j}\right\} + \iota\max_j\left\{\underline{b_j}\right\}\right)$. Then:

$$\mathcal{A}^- \leq \text{CFRFPWA}\left(\mathcal{A}_1,\ \mathcal{A}_2,\ ..,\ \mathcal{A}_n\right) \leq \mathcal{A}^+.$$

Monotonicity: Let two assemblies $\mathcal{A}_j = \left(\overline{a_j} + \iota\,\overline{b_j}, \underline{a_j} + \iota\underline{b_j}\right)$ and $\mathcal{A}_j' = \left(\overline{a_j'} + \iota\,\overline{b_j'}, \underline{a_j'} + \iota\underline{b_j'}\right)$, $(j = 1,\ 2,\ \ldots,\ n)$, of CFRNs. If $\underline{a_j} \leq \underline{a_j'}$, $\underline{b_j} \leq \underline{b_j'}$, $\overline{a_j} \leq \overline{a_j'}$, $\overline{b_j} \leq \overline{b_j'} \forall\ j$, then:

$$\text{CFRFPWA}\left(\mathcal{A}_1,\ \mathcal{A}_2,\ ..,\ \mathcal{A}_n\right) \leq \text{CFRFPWA}\left(\mathcal{A}_1^{'},\ \mathcal{A}_2^{'},\ ..,\ \mathcal{A}_n^{'}\right).$$

Definition 9.5: Let an assembly $\mathcal{A}_j = \left\{\left(\overline{a_j} + \iota\overline{b_j},\ \underline{a_j} + \iota\underline{b_j}\right)\right\}, (j = 1,\ 2,\ 3,\ \ldots,\ n)$ of CFRNs. Then, the CFRFPG operator is scrutinized as

$$\text{CFRFPG}\left(\mathcal{A}_1,\ \mathcal{A}_2,\ \mathcal{A}_3,\ \ldots,\ \mathcal{A}_n\right) = \bigotimes_{j=1}^{n}\left(\mathcal{A}_j\right)^{\frac{\left(1+T\left(\mathcal{A}_j\right)\right)}{\sum_{j=1}^{n}\left(1+T\left(\mathcal{A}_j\right)\right).}}$$

Theorem 9.3: Let an assembly $\mathcal{A}_j = \left\{\left(\overline{a_j} + \iota\overline{b_j},\ \underline{a_j} + \iota\underline{b_j}\right)\right\},\ (j = 1,\ 2,\ 3,\ \ldots,\ n)$ of CFRNs. Then the usage of the CFRFPG operator over $\mathcal{A}_j$ will give a CFRN, that is:

$$\text{CFRFPG}\left(\mathcal{A}_1,\ \mathcal{A}_2,\ \ldots,\ \mathcal{A}_n\right) =$$
$$\left(\begin{array}{c}\left(\log_\theta\left(1+\prod_{j=1}^{n}\left(\theta^{1-\overline{a_j}}-1\right)^{\chi_j}\right)\right)+\iota\left(\log_\theta\left(1+\prod_{j=1}^{n}\left(\theta^{1-\overline{b_j}}-1\right)^{\chi_j}\right)\right),\\ \left(\log_\theta\left(1+\prod_{j=1}^{n}\left(\theta^{1-\underline{a_j}}-1\right)^{\chi_j}\right)\right)+\iota\left(\log_\theta\left(1+\prod_{j=1}^{n}\left(\theta^{1-\underline{b_j}}-1\right)^{\chi_j}\right)\right),\end{array}\right).$$

Definition 9.6: Let an assembly $\mathcal{A}_j = \left\{\left(\overline{a_j} + \iota\overline{b_j},\ \underline{a_j} + \iota\underline{b_j}\right)\right\},\ (j = 1,\ 2,\ 3,\ \ldots,\ n)$ of CFRNs. Then the CFRFPWG operator is scrutinized as

$$\text{CFRFPWG}\left(\mathcal{A}_1,\ \mathcal{A}_2,\ \mathcal{A}_3,\ \ldots,\ \mathcal{A}_n\right) = \bigotimes_{j=1}^{n}\left(\mathcal{A}_j\right)^{\frac{\omega_j\left(1+T\left(\mathcal{A}_j\right)\right)}{\sum_{j=1}^{n}\omega_j\left(1+T\left(\mathcal{A}_j\right)\right)}}.$$

Theorem 9.4: Let an assembly $\mathcal{A}_j = \left\{\left(\overline{a_j}, +\iota\overline{b_j},\ \underline{a_j} + \iota\underline{b_j}\right)\right\},\ (j = 1,\ 2,\ 3,\ \ldots,\ n)$ of CFRNs. Then the usage of the CFRFPWG operator over $\mathcal{A}_j$ will give a CFRN, that is:

$$\text{CFRFPWG}\left(\mathcal{A}_1,\ \mathcal{A}_2,\ \ldots,\ \mathcal{A}_n\right) =$$

$$
\left(\begin{array}{c}
\left(\log_{\theta}\left(1+\prod_{j=1}^{n}\left(\theta^{1-\overline{a_j}}-1\right)^{\frac{\omega_j\left(1+T\left(\mathcal{A}_j\right)\right)}{\sum_{j=1}^{n}\omega_j\left(1+T\left(\mathcal{A}_j\right)\right)}}\right)\right)\\
+\iota\left(\log_{\theta}\left(1+\prod_{j=1}^{n}\left(\theta^{1-\overline{b_j}}-1\right)^{\frac{\omega_j\left(1+T\left(\mathcal{A}_j\right)\right)}{\sum_{j=1}^{n}\mathcal{A}_j\left(1+T\left(\mathcal{A}_j\right)\right)}}\right)\right),\\
\left(\log_{\theta}\left(1+\prod_{j=1}^{n}\left(\theta^{1-\underline{a_j}}-1\right)^{\frac{\omega_j\left(1+T\left(\mathcal{A}_j\right)\right)}{\sum_{j=1}^{n}\omega_j\left(1+T\left(\mathcal{A}_j\right)\right)}}\right)\right)\\
+\iota\left(\log_{\theta}\left(1+\prod_{j=1}^{n}\left(\theta^{1-\underline{b_j}}-1\right)^{\frac{\omega_j\left(1+T\left(\mathcal{A}_j\right)\right)}{\sum_{j=1}^{n}\omega_j\left(1+T\left(\mathcal{A}_j\right)\right)}}\right)\right),
\end{array}\right).
$$

9.1.3 MADM Approach for the Developed Notions

Let $\mathfrak{L} = \{\mathfrak{L}_1, \mathfrak{L}_2, \ldots, \mathfrak{L}\}$ be an assembly of alternatives and for these alternatives, let $\mathfrak{C} = \{\mathfrak{C}_1, \mathfrak{C}_2, \ldots, \mathfrak{C}_n\}$ be an assembly of criteria that will be utilized for the assessment of the considered alternatives. In these alternatives, the decision analyst has to get the finest and best alternative. For that, the decision analyst will assess these alternatives based on their criteria and interpret their values in the framework of CFRNs, that is $\mathcal{A} = \left(\overline{a} + \iota\overline{b}, \underline{a} + \iota\underline{b}\right)$, where $\underline{a}, \underline{b}, \overline{a}, \overline{b} \in [0, 1]$. As each criterion has its weight the decision expert will provide the weight to each of the criteria, which is $\omega_j = (\omega_1, \omega_2, \ldots, \omega_n)^T$ such that $\sum_{j=1}^{n} \omega_j = 1$ and $\omega_j \in [0, 1]\ \forall\ j$. Now to solve this, this MCDM approach has the underneath steps.

Step 1: As the assessment values are in the form of CFRNs, so develop a complex fuzzy rough decision matrix (CFRDM) $\mathfrak{D}$ by employing these assessment values. In this CFRDM, the first entry will represent the assessment value of the first alternative against the first criteria.

Step 2: Standardization of the CFRDM will be performed in this step by employing the given underneath formula. Standardization is needed because the data can be benefit and cost types.

$$D^{\mathcal{N}} = \begin{cases} \left(\overline{a} + \iota\overline{b}, \underline{a} + \iota\underline{b}\right) & \text{for benefit kind} \\ \left(\overline{a} + \iota\overline{b}, \underline{a} + \iota\underline{b}\right)^{c} & \text{for cost kind} \end{cases}.$$

Step 3: Here the support of each $\mathcal{A}_j$ would be interpreted as

$$\text{Sup}\left(\mathcal{A}_{jr},\ \mathcal{A}_{jl}\right) = 1 - \text{đ}\left(\mathcal{A}_{jr},\ \mathcal{A}_{jl}\right),\ r,\ l = 1,\ 2,\ \ldots, n,\ r \neq l,$$

where $\text{đ}\left(\mathcal{A}_{jr},\ \mathcal{A}_{jl}\right) = \frac{1}{4}\left(\left|\overline{a_{jr}} - \overline{a_{jl}}\right| + \left|\overline{b_{jr}} - \overline{b_{jl}}\right| + \left|\underline{a_{jr}} - \underline{a_{jl}}\right| + \left|\underline{b_{jr}} - \underline{b_{jl}}\right|\right).$

Step 4: Interpret

$$\text{T}\left(\mathcal{A}_{jr}\right) = \sum_{\substack{l=1 \\ l \neq r}}^{n} Sup\left(\mathcal{A}_{jr},\ \mathcal{A}_{jl}\right).$$

Noticed that $j = 1,\ 2,\ \ldots, m\ ;\ r,\ l = 1,\ 2,\ \ldots,\ n$ and $r \neq l$.

Step 5: Achieve the associated weight as follows

$$\chi_{jr} = \frac{\left(1 + T\left(\mathcal{A}_{jr}\right)\right)}{\sum_{l=1}^{n}\left(1 + T\left(\mathcal{A}_{jl}\right)\right)},$$

Or

$$\chi'_{jr} = \frac{\hat{\text{W}}_{\omega - jr}\left(1 + T\left(\mathcal{A}_{jr}\right)\right)}{\sum_{l=1}^{n}\hat{\text{W}}_{\omega - jl}\left(1 + T\left(\mathcal{A}_{jl}\right)\right)}.$$

Step 6: Aggregate the CFRDM with the assistance of any of the devised operators that is CFRPA, CFRYPA, CFRPG, and CFRPWG operators.

Step 7: Employing score function to achieve the score values of aggregated outcomes of each alternative. In case of the same score values, achieve the accuracy values by employing the accuracy function.

Step 8: Rank all alternatives by considering their score or accuracy values and select the finest and best alternative.

9.1.4 Case study (selection of robotic automation solution)

Techno-Robotics Solutions (TRS) is a medium B2B manufacturing firm founded in 2010 that focuses on manufacturing precision electronic parts for automobiles and aerospace applications. TRS is based in Stuttgart, Germany, and has developed a solid customer base that includes many of the continent's largest manufacturers. TRS has been experiencing stable growth in the past ten years; the company's annual revenue is €50 million, and the number of employees is 200 people.

Recently, TRS has been under pressure from global counterparts in the areas of production costs and productivity. The current semiautomated production line was established in 2015, and it has become inefficient and cannot satisfy the increased demand for higher accuracy and shorter cycle times. In the same way, the COVID-19 outbreak also exposed the necessity of improving the degree of automation in manufacturing operations.

Problem statement: Due to the current increase in customer demand, TRS has to update its main production line by installing an advanced robotic system to remain competitive in the market. The company must choose the best robotic automation solution that can achieve several goals at once, such as accuracy in manufacturing, cost, and expandability. The decision is strategic because it involves a large amount of money (€2-3 million) and will affect the company's activities in the next 7-10 years. For this, the decision analyst of the company shortlisted 4 robotic solutions which are devised in Table 9.1.

Table 9.1 The robotic solutions along with an explanation.

Notations	Robotic solutions	Explanation
$\mathbb{R}_1$	KUKA iSeries Pro	A modern robotic system with artificial intelligence, the ability to monitor the quality of products in real-time, and predict the need for maintenance. This system provides full data analysis and cloud integration for monitoring and managing the system from a distance.
$\mathbb{R}_2$	ABB Flex Assembly	Flexible assembly system, which can be easily adapted to different product types and easily changed to meet the requirements of new product types. It incorporates smart vision systems and exclusive software for interfacing with the manufacturing execution systems in place.
$\mathbb{R}_3$	Fanuc Smart-factory	An automation solution from part picking to testing with machine learning integrated into the system that focuses on high-precision assembly. Some of these are self-organizing error control and self-tuning control systems.
$\mathbb{R}_4$	Yaskawa Nexus	A low-cost approach that is designed to be dependable and easy to manage. It has minimum artificial intelligence features with possibilities of future enhancements and is compatible with other parts.

To assess these solutions the decision analyst considered four criteria, which are displayed in Table 9.2

Table 9.2 The criteria of robotic solutions.

Notations	Criteria	Explanation	Important context
$\mathfrak{C}_1$	Technical capability	Initial cost, costs of installation, cost of maintenance, energy used, and expected costs of upgrade within 7 years. This is arrived at as a net present value (NPV) of all the financial impacts.	Critically important for financial management to guarantee that the ROI is within the goals set by the company.
$\mathfrak{C}_2$	Total cost of ownership	Determines the flexibility of the system toward new products, compatibility with the new technologies, and capacity for growth with the business. Such as flexibility of programming and modularity of the hardware.	Able to be used for long-term planning and sustaining a competitive edge in the market.
$\mathfrak{C}_3$	Future adaptability	Analyzes possible hazards in implementation, training of personnel, loss of output during the change-over, and compatibility issues with other systems. Consists of vendor credibility and support service quality.	Vital for continuity and continuity management with little interference to the normal running of the business.
$\mathfrak{C}_4$	Implementation risk	Initial cost, costs of installation, cost of maintenance, energy used, and expected costs of upgrade within 7 years. This is arrived at as a net present value (NPV) of all the financial impacts.	Critically important for financial management to guarantee that the ROI is within the goals set by the company.

The decision expert will assess these robotic solutions and provide their values in the form of CFRNs. Also, the expert provides the weight to the criteria based on their preference that weight is $(0.2, 0.15, 0.3, 0.35)$. To solve this, we have the underneath steps.

Step 1:The decision analyst assessed the robotic solutions and provided their values in the structure of CFRNs which form CFRDM as shown in Table 9.3.

Step 2: As the data is benefit-kind, so after the standardization, the CFRDM will remain the same.

Table 9.3 The assessment values of robotic solutions are interpreted by experts.

	$\mathfrak{C}_1$	$\mathfrak{C}_2$	$\mathfrak{C}_3$	$\mathfrak{C}_4$
$\mathbb{R}_1$	$\begin{pmatrix} 0.11+\iota 0.33, \\ 0.62+\iota 0.36 \end{pmatrix}$	$\begin{pmatrix} 0.35+\iota 0.31, \\ 0.21+\iota 0.51 \end{pmatrix}$	$\begin{pmatrix} 0.84+\iota 0.74, \\ 0.62+\iota 0.52 \end{pmatrix}$	$\begin{pmatrix} 0.31+\iota 0.02, \\ 0.71+\iota 0.13 \end{pmatrix}$
$\mathbb{R}_2$	$\begin{pmatrix} 0.41+\iota 0.43, \\ 0.45+\iota 0.48 \end{pmatrix}$	$\begin{pmatrix} 0.79+\iota 0.41, \\ 0.48+\iota 0.55 \end{pmatrix}$	$\begin{pmatrix} 0.11+\iota 0.22, \\ 0.88+\iota 0.21 \end{pmatrix}$	$\begin{pmatrix} 0.32+\iota 0.23, \\ 0.52+\iota 0.41 \end{pmatrix}$
$\mathbb{R}_3$	$\begin{pmatrix} 0.74+\iota 0.20, \\ 0.45+\iota 0.19 \end{pmatrix}$	$\begin{pmatrix} 0.63+\iota 0.67, \\ 0.76+\iota 0.45 \end{pmatrix}$	$\begin{pmatrix} 0.84+\iota 0.12, \\ 0.45+\iota 0.27 \end{pmatrix}$	$\begin{pmatrix} 0.16+\iota 0.42, \\ 0.96+\iota 0.40 \end{pmatrix}$
$\mathbb{R}_4$	$\begin{pmatrix} 0.41+\iota 0.27, \\ 0.59+\iota 0.61 \end{pmatrix}$	$\begin{pmatrix} 0.87+\iota 0.51, \\ 0.22+\iota 0.41 \end{pmatrix}$	$\begin{pmatrix} 0.44+\iota 0.61, \\ 0.52+\iota 0.18 \end{pmatrix}$	$\begin{pmatrix} 0.87+\iota 0.64, \\ 0.54+\iota 0.23 \end{pmatrix}$

Step 3: The support of each $\mathbb{R}_j$
for $j = 1$

$$\text{Sup}\,(\mathbb{R}_{11}, \mathbb{R}_{12}) = 0.795, \text{Sup}\,(\mathbb{R}_{11}, \mathbb{R}_{13}) = 0.675, \text{Sup}\,(\mathbb{R}_{11}, \mathbb{R}_{14}) = 0.84,$$

$$\text{Sup}\,(\mathbb{R}_{12}, \mathbb{R}_{11}) = 0.795, \text{Sup}\,(\mathbb{R}_{12}, \mathbb{R}_{13}) = 0.665, \text{Sup}\,(\mathbb{R}_{12}, \mathbb{R}_{14}) = 0.645,$$
$$\text{Sup}\,(\mathbb{R}_{13}, \mathbb{R}_{11}) = 0.675, \text{Sup}\,(\mathbb{R}_{13}, \mathbb{R}_{12}) = 0.665, \text{Sup}\,(\mathbb{R}_{13}, \mathbb{R}_{14}) = 0.515,$$
$$\text{Sup}\,(\mathbb{R}_{14}, \mathbb{R}_{11}) = 0.84, \text{Sup}\,(\mathbb{R}_{14}, \mathbb{R}_{12}) = 0.645, \text{Sup}\,(\mathbb{R}_{14}, \ \mathbb{R}_{13}) = 0.515,$$

for $j = 2$

$$\text{Sup}\,(\mathbb{R}_{21}, \mathbb{R}_{22}) = 0.85, \text{Sup}\,(\mathbb{R}_{21}, \mathbb{R}_{23}) = 0.698, \text{Sup}\,(\mathbb{R}_{21}, \mathbb{R}_{24}) = 0.675,$$

$$\text{Sup}\,(\mathbb{R}_{22}, \mathbb{R}_{21}) = 0.85, \text{Sup}\,(\mathbb{R}_{22}, \mathbb{R}_{23}) = 0.573, \text{Sup}\,(\mathbb{R}_{22}, \mathbb{R}_{24}) = 0.745,$$
$$\text{Sup}\,(\mathbb{R}_{23}, \ \mathbb{R}_{21}) = 0.698, \text{Sup}\,(\mathbb{R}_{23}, \mathbb{R}_{22}) = 0.573, \text{Sup}\,(\mathbb{R}_{23}, \mathbb{R}_{24}) = 0.508,$$
$$\text{Sup}\,(\mathbb{R}_{24}, \mathbb{R}_{21}) = 0.763, \ \text{Sup}\,(\mathbb{R}_{24}, \mathbb{R}_{22}) = 0.745, \text{Sup}\,(\mathbb{R}_{24}, \ \mathbb{R}_{23}) = 0.508,$$

for $j = 3$

$$\text{Sup}\,(\mathbb{R}_{31}, \mathbb{R}_{32}) = 0.713, \text{Sup}\,(\mathbb{R}_{31}, \mathbb{R}_{33}) = 0.935, \text{Sup}\,(\mathbb{R}_{31}, \mathbb{R}_{34}) = 0.62,$$

$$\text{Sup}\,(\mathbb{R}_{32}, \mathbb{R}_{31}) = 0.713, \text{Sup}\,(\mathbb{R}_{32}, \mathbb{R}_{33}) = 0.688, \text{Sup}\,(\mathbb{R}_{32}, \mathbb{R}_{34}) = 0.758,$$
$$\text{Sup}\,(\mathbb{R}_{33}, \mathbb{R}_{31}) = 0.935, \text{Sup}\,(\mathbb{R}_{33}, \mathbb{R}_{32}) = 0.688, \text{Sup}\,(\mathbb{R}_{33}, \mathbb{R}_{34}) = 0.595,$$
$$\text{Sup}\,(\mathbb{R}_{34}, \mathbb{R}_{31}) = 0.685, \text{Sup}\,(\mathbb{R}_{34}, \ \mathbb{R}_{32}) = 0.758, \text{Sup}\,(\mathbb{R}_{34}, \ \mathbb{R}_{33}) = 0.595,$$

for $j = 4$

$$\text{Sup}\,(\mathbb{R}_{41}, \mathbb{R}_{42}) = 0.683, \text{Sup}\,(\mathbb{R}_{41}, \mathbb{R}_{43}) = 0.783, \text{Sup}\,(\mathbb{R}_{41}, \mathbb{R}_{44}) = 0.685,$$

$$\text{Sup}\,(\mathbb{R}_{42}, \mathbb{R}_{41}) = 0.683, \text{Sup}\,(\mathbb{R}_{42}, \mathbb{R}_{43}) = 0.735, \text{Sup}\,(\mathbb{R}_{42}, \mathbb{R}_{44}) = 0.843,$$
$$\text{Sup}\,(\mathbb{R}_{43}, \mathbb{R}_{41}) = 0.783, \text{Sup}\,(\mathbb{R}_{43}, \mathbb{R}_{42}) = 0.735, \text{Sup}\,(\mathbb{R}_{43}, \mathbb{R}_{44}) = 0.868,$$

$\mathrm{Sup}\left(\mathbb{R}_{44},\ \mathbb{R}_{41}\right) = 0.768, \mathrm{Sup}\left(\mathbb{R}_{44},\ \mathbb{R}_{42}\right) = 0.843, \mathrm{Sup}\left(\mathbb{R}_{44},\ \mathbb{R}_{43}\right) = 0.868,$

Step 4: Interpreted $T\left(\mathbb{R}_{jr}\right)$

$$T\left(\mathbb{R}_{11}\right) = 2.31, \mathrm{T}\left(\mathbb{R}_{12}\right) = 2.105,\ \mathrm{T}\left(\mathbb{R}_{13}\right) = 1.855, \mathrm{T}\left(\mathbb{R}_{14}\right) = 2.0,$$

$$\mathrm{T}\left(\mathbb{R}_{21}\right) = 2.223, \mathrm{T}\left(\mathbb{R}_{22}\right) = 2.168,\ \mathrm{T}\left(\mathbb{R}_{23}\right) = 1.778, \mathrm{T}\left(\mathbb{R}_{24}\right) = 2.015,$$

$$\mathrm{T}\left(\mathbb{R}_{31}\right) = 2.268, \mathrm{T}\left(\mathbb{R}_{32}\right) = 2.158,\ \mathrm{T}\left(\mathbb{R}_{33}\right) = 2.218, \mathrm{T}\left(\mathbb{R}_{34}\right) = 2.038,$$

$$\mathrm{T}\left(\mathbb{R}_{41}\right) = 2.15, \mathrm{T}\left(\mathbb{R}_{42}\right) = 2.26,\ \mathrm{T}\left(\mathbb{R}_{43}\right) = 2.385, \mathrm{T}\left(\mathbb{R}_{44}\right) = 2.478,$$

Step 5: The associated weights are:

$$\chi_{11} = 0.27, \chi_{12} = 0.253, \chi_{13} = 0.233, \chi_{14} = 0.244,$$

$$\chi_{21} = 0.265, \chi_{22} = 0.26, \chi_{23} = 0.228, \chi_{24} = 0.247,$$

$$\chi_{31} = 0.258, \chi_{32} = 0.249, \chi_{33} = 0.253, \chi_{34} = 0.24,$$

$$\chi_{41} = 0.237, \chi_{42} = 0.246, \chi_{43} = 0.255, \chi_{44} = 0.262.$$

After that analyst weight of each criterion is $(0.2,\ 0.15,\ 0.3,\ 0.35)$, the associated weights are:

$$\chi_{11}^{'} = 0.218, \chi_{12}^{'} = 0.154, \chi_{13}^{'} = 0.282, \chi_{14}^{'} = 0.346,$$

$$\chi_{21}^{'} = 0.214, \chi_{22}^{'} = 0.158, \chi_{23}^{'} = 0.277, \chi_{24}^{'} = 0.351,$$

$$\chi_{31}^{'} = 0.207, \chi_{32}^{'} = 0.15, \chi_{33}^{'} = 0.306, \chi_{34}^{'} = 0.337,$$

$$\chi_{41}^{'} = 0.188, \chi_{42}^{'} = 0.146, \chi_{43}^{'} = 0.303, \chi_{44}^{'} = 0.363.$$

Step 6: The aggregated outcome of each robotic solution after employing CFRFPA, CFRFPWA, CFRFPG, and CFRFPWG operators is displayed in Table 9.4.

Table 9.4 The aggregated outcomes of robotic solutions.

Operators	$\mathbb{R}_1$	$\mathbb{R}_2$	$\mathbb{R}_3$	$\mathbb{R}_4$
CFRFPA	$\begin{pmatrix} 0.428 + \iota\, 0.394, \\ 0.567 + \iota\, 0.394 \end{pmatrix}$	$\begin{pmatrix} 0.688 + \iota\, 0.476, \\ 0.571 + \iota\, 0.371 \end{pmatrix}$	$\begin{pmatrix} 0.659 + \iota\, 0.383, \\ 0.752 + \iota\, 0.332 \end{pmatrix}$	$\begin{pmatrix} 0.723 + \iota\, 0.528, \\ 0.428 + \iota\, 0.371 \end{pmatrix}$
CFRFPWA	$\begin{pmatrix} 0.454 + \iota\, 0.397, \\ 0.609 + \iota\, 0.366 \end{pmatrix}$	$\begin{pmatrix} 0.672 + \iota\, 0.506, \\ 0.528 + \iota\, 0.314 \end{pmatrix}$	$\begin{pmatrix} 0.638 + \iota\, 0.346, \\ 0.79 + \iota\, 0.329 \end{pmatrix}$	$\begin{pmatrix} 0.724 + \iota\, 0.557, \\ 0.506 + \iota\, 0.331 \end{pmatrix}$
CFRFPG	$\begin{pmatrix} 0.24 + \iota\, 0.208, \\ 0.495 + \iota\, 0.339 \end{pmatrix}$	$\begin{pmatrix} 0.464 + \iota\, 0.419, \\ 0.455 + \iota\, 0.309 \end{pmatrix}$	$\begin{pmatrix} 0.523 + \iota\, 0.29, \\ 0.622 + \iota\, 0.31 \end{pmatrix}$	$\begin{pmatrix} 0.62 + \iota\, 0.491, \\ 0.442 + \iota\, 0.318 \end{pmatrix}$
CFRFPWG	$\begin{pmatrix} 0.236 + \iota\, 0.166, \\ 0.557 + \iota\, 0.301 \end{pmatrix}$	$\begin{pmatrix} 0.436 + \iota\, 0.431, \\ 0.435 + \iota\, 0.257 \end{pmatrix}$	$\begin{pmatrix} 0.465 + \iota\, 0.268, \\ 0.637 + \iota\, 0.311 \end{pmatrix}$	$\begin{pmatrix} 0.622 + \iota\, 0.523, \\ 0.479 + \iota\, 0.282 \end{pmatrix}$

Step 7: The score values of robotic solutions are interpreted in Table 9.5.

Table 9.5 The score values of neural network frameworks.

Operators	**Scor.** $(\mathbb{R}_1)$	**Scor.** $(\mathbb{R}_2)$	**Scor.** $(\mathbb{R}_3)$	**Scor.** $(\mathbb{R}_4)$
CFRFPA	0.446	0.527	0.532	0.526
CFRFPWA	0.457	0.519	0.526	0.529
CFRFPG	0.321	0.412	0.436	0.468
CFRFPWG	0.315	0.39	0.42	0.477

Step 8: The ranking of robotic solutions is devised in Table 9.6.

Table 9.6 The ranking of robotic solutions.

Operators	**Ranking**
CFRFPA	$\mathbb{R}_3 > \mathbb{R}_2 > \mathbb{R}_4 > \mathbb{R}_1$
CFRFPWA	$\mathbb{R}_4 > \mathbb{R}_3 > \mathbb{R}_2 > \mathbb{R}_1$
CFRFPG	$\mathbb{R}_4 > \mathbb{R}_3 > \mathbb{R}_2 > \mathbb{R}_1$
CFRFPWG	$\mathbb{R}_4 > \mathbb{R}_3 > \mathbb{R}_2 > \mathbb{R}_1$

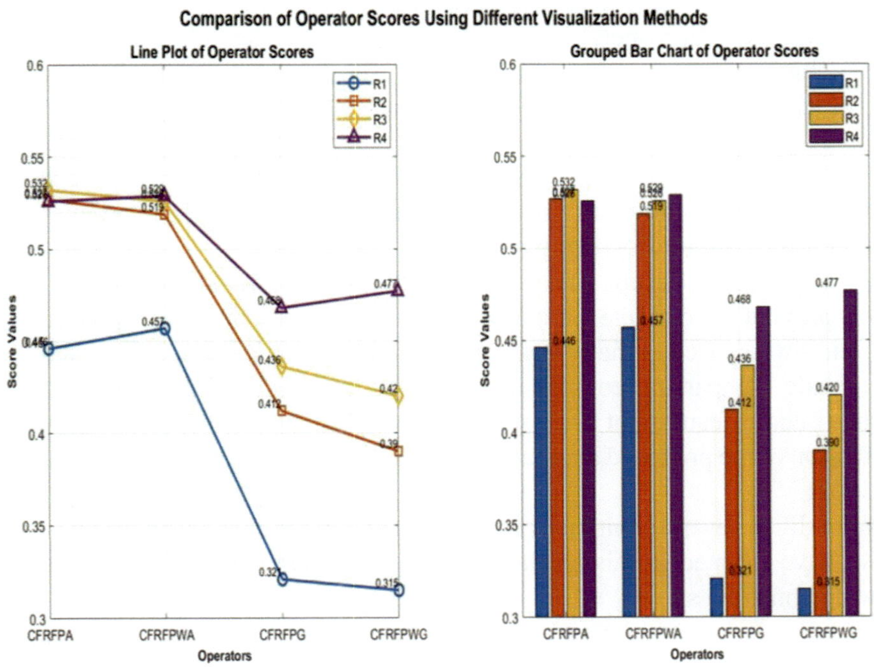

Figure 9.1 The graphical representation of score values of robotic systems.

From the ranking of robotic solutions, when the analyst used CFRFPA operator for aggregating the value, they found that that $\mathbb{R}_3$ is the finest and best solution, while using other operators, $\mathbb{R}_4$ is the finest and best solution. For graphical interpretation, see Figure 9.1.

9.2 Comparative Study

To check the efficiency and applicability of the proposed methodological framework, we performed a detailed comparison of our work with several well-known theoretical approaches. The analysis uses the CFR information given in Table 9.3 and compares the performance of various AOs and ranking methods in these frameworks. This chapter presents a comparative analysis of various theories that are used in the context of the given problem and which offer different approaches to the analysis of complex information. We considered Xu and Yager's power geometric operators [22] which gave preliminary work for power-based aggregation. This was further supported by Rehman's work [23] on probability complex fuzzy aggregation operators which added probability aspects into complex and two-dimensional information processing. The analysis also included the integration of Hu et al.'s [24] new power aggregation operators for polar forms of complex information. To further enhance the comparative analysis, we also incorporated the following works of Khan et al. [25]: AOs for CFR information in polar form and MCDM methodologies for CFR information. The analytical spectrum was enriched by integrating Hussain et al.'s [26] modification of the TOPSIS approach within the framework of CFR framework and Yahya et al.'s [27] creation of Frank AOs for intuitionistic fuzzy rough sets (IFRSs).

The comparative results presented in Table 9.7 and Table 9.8 and Figure 9.2 provide a complete picture of the effectiveness of these different approaches when used in the analysis of the same CFR information set. Such a systematic comparison enables us to assess the comparative advantages and the specific features of each method, as well as to define the specific contribution of the proposed approach within the framework of the theoretical framework.

We outlined several limitations in the current methodological approaches that we have adopted in this chapter. The critical examination revealed the following constraints:

- Power geometric operators have limited practical relevance as they work well only when the information is clear and precise, and do not account for uncertainty, roughness, or the two-dimensional nature of many decision problems.

Table 9.7 The score values of existing and proposed theories.

Operators	$\mathbf{Scor}.(\mathbb{A}_1)$	$\mathbf{Scor}.(\mathbb{A}_2)$	$\mathbf{Scor}.(\mathbb{A}_3)$	$\mathbf{Scor}.(\mathbb{A}_4)$
Xu and Yager [22]	No result	No result	No result	No result
Rehman [23]	No result	No result	No result	No result
Hu et al. [24]	No result	No result	No result	No result
Khan et al. [25]	No result	No result	No result	No result
Hussain et al. [26]	No result	No result	No result	No result
Yahya et al. [27]	No result	No result	No result	No result
CFRFPA	0.446	0.527	0.532	0.526
CFRFPWA	0.457	0.519	0.526	0.529
CFRFPG	0.321	0.412	0.436	0.468
CFRFPWG	0.315	0.39	0.42	0.477

Table 9.8 The ranking of proposed theories and existing ones.

Operators	**Ranking result**
Xu and Yager [22]	No result
Rehman [23]	No result
Hu et al. [24]	No result
Khan et al. [25]	No result
Hussain et al. [26]	No result
Yahya et al. [3]	No result
CFRFPA	$\mathbb{R}_3 > \mathbb{R}_2 > \mathbb{R}_4 > \mathbb{R}_1$
CFRFPWA	$\mathbb{R}_4 > \mathbb{R}_3 > \mathbb{R}_2 > \mathbb{R}_1$
CFRFPG	$\mathbb{R}_4 > \mathbb{R}_3 > \mathbb{R}_2 > \mathbb{R}_1$
CFRFPWG	$\mathbb{R}_4 > \mathbb{R}_3 > \mathbb{R}_2 > \mathbb{R}_1$

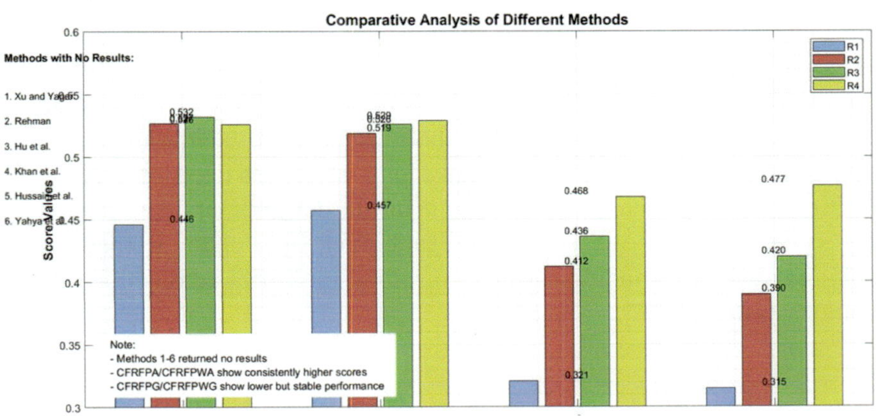

Figure 9.2 The graphical interpretation of comparison.

- Probability complex fuzzy operators are capable of handling two-dimensional and uncertain information but they are inadequate in handling roughness components, which leads to a major gap in holistic decision-making.
- Complex fuzzy rough operators are quite powerful, they have a major weakness in that they are only able to work on polar form complex information and not Tamir's complex information.
- While the Frank aggregation operators are efficient in dealing with information roughness within intuitionistic fuzzy rough sets, they fail to handle other fuzzy information components.

A critical evaluation of modern robotic autonomous solution selection methods shows that roughness and uncertainties are completely ignored in the selection process, which greatly reduces the overall quality of the decisions made. To overcome these drawbacks, the proposed framework uses an integrated approach that handles roughness, two-dimensional information (extra fuzzy information), and uncertainty at the same time. This broad approach improves the decision-making process of choosing robotic autonomous solutions, especially in industries that require high levels of accuracy and dependability. This advanced methodological framework provides a more complex and comprehensive approach to the strategies required to select robotic autonomous solutions. It offers decision-makers a better way to assess and choose autonomous robotic systems, especially in situations where other approaches are not feasible due to their inability to address multiple layers of decision-making at once. The ability of the framework to deal with different kinds of information – clear data, fuzzy rough sets, etc., is especially beneficial in the contemporary industrial environment where robotic self-sufficient solutions have to work in various and often adverse conditions. The advantage of this approach is that it provides more accurate and detailed outcomes in the choice of robotic autonomous solutions, which directly eliminates the weaknesses that have long influenced decision-making in this area. This is a major advancement in the development of decision support systems for robotic automation and offers a sounder framework for making strategic technological investments in industrial automation and autonomous systems.

9.3 Conclusion

This chapter provides a detailed theoretical model that enhances the field of robotic decision-making by combining CFRSs with Frank operators. The research presented in this chapter provides several significant advancements to theoretical frameworks and real-world decision-making in industrial automation. First, we have successfully developed and mathematically validated a new family of AOs: the CFRFPA, CFRFPWA, CFRFPG, and CFRFPWG operators. These operators show high ability in dealing with the complexity of CFR information, which offers strong theoretical support for the processing of multidimensional uncertainty in decision-making. The algebraic characteristics of these operators have been analyzed and their validity has been demonstrated, both in terms of theory and real-life application. The MCDM methodology presented in this research work is a major contribution to decision support systems for robotic autonomous solutions. Thus, by applying CFRSs with Frank operators, the proposed approach eliminates the shortcomings of the existing frameworks in the simultaneous consideration of uncertainty, roughness, and complex information organization. This integration makes decision-making more accurate and precise, which is very important in the area of industrial automation. The framework is best illustrated by our case study on the selection of robotic autonomous solutions. The results show how our approach can systematically assess and rank options and take into account multiple objectives in conditions of vagueness and fuzziness. This more practical form of validation supports the framework and shows that it can be applied in industrial environments. A comparison with other existing approaches demonstrates the effectiveness of the proposed framework. In contrast to previous approaches that can address only certain aspects of uncertainty or complexity, our methodology offers an integrated approach that can be used to address multiple aspects of information complexity at once. This leads to the development of more accurate and sound decision-making procedures which is very important in the case of industrial automation decisions.

References

[1] Zadeh, L. A. (1965). Fuzzy sets. Information and control, 8(3), 338-353.

[2] Pawlak, Z. (1995). Vagueness and uncertainty: a rough set perspective. Computational intelligence, 11(2), 227-232.

[3] Dubois, D., & Prade, H. (1990). Rough fuzzy sets and fuzzy rough sets. International Journal of General System, 17(2-3), 191-209.

[4] Ramot, D., Milo, R., Friedman, M., & Kandel, A. (2002). Complex fuzzy sets. IEEE transactions on fuzzy systems, 10(2), 171-186.

[5] Tamir, D. E., Rishe, N. D., & Kandel, A. (2015). Complex fuzzy sets and complex fuzzy logic an overview of theory and applications. Fifty years of fuzzy logic and its applications, 661-681.

[6] Yi, J., Ahmmad, J., Mahmood, T., Ur Rehman, U., & Zeng, S. (2024). Complex Fuzzy Rough Set: An Application in Digital Marketing for Business Growth. IEEE Access, 12, 66453-66465, DOI:10.1109/ACCESS.2024.3397699.

[7] Butnariu, D., & Klement, E. P. (1993). Triangular norm-based measures and games with fuzzy coalitions (Vol. 10). Springer Science & Business Media.

[8] Klement, E.P., Mesiar, R. and Pap, E. (2000) Triangular Norms. Trends in Logic-Studia Logica Library. Vol. 8, Kluwer Academic Publishers, Dordrecht.

[9] Hamacher H., Uber logische Verknupfungen unscharfer Aussagen und deren Zugehotige Bewertungs-funktionen, in Progress in Cybernetics and Systems Research, Vol. 3 (R. Trappl, G. J. Klir, and L. Ricciardi, Eds.), Hemisphere, New York, 1978, pp. 276-287.

[10] Klement, E. P., & Mesiar, R. (Eds.). (2005). Logical, algebraic, analytic and probabilistic aspects of triangular norms. Elsevier, https://doi.org/10.1016/B978-0-444-51814-9.X5000-9.

[11] Aczel, J., & Alsina, C. (1982). Characterizations of some classes of quasilinear functions with applications to triangular norms and to synthesizing judgments. Aequationes mathematicae, 25(1), 313-315.

[12] Menger, K. (1942). Statistical metrics. Proceedings of the National Academy of Sciences of the United States of America 28(12), 535.
[13] Mardani, A., Nilashi, M., Zavadskas, E. K., Awang, S. R., Zare, H., & Jamal, N. M. (2018). Decision-making methods based on fuzzy aggregation operators: Three decades review from 1986 to 2017. International Journal of Information Technology & Decision Making, 17(02), 391-466.
[14] Khan, F. M., Bibi, N., Abdullah, S., & Ullah, A. (2023). Complex Fuzzy Rough Aggregation Operators and their Applications in Multi-Criteria Group Decision-Making. International Journal of Fuzzy Logic and Intelligent Systems, 23(3), 270-293.
[15] Hadi, A., Khan, W., & Khan, A. (2021). A novel approach to MADM problems using Fermatean fuzzy Hamacher aggregation operators. International Journal of Intelligent Systems, 36(7), 3464-3499.
[16] Zhou, L., Zhao, X., & Wei, G. (2014). Hesitant fuzzy Hamacher aggregation operators and their application to multiple attribute decision making. Journal of Intelligent & Fuzzy Systems, 26(6), 2689-2699.
[17] Bi, L., Dai, S., Hu, B., & Li, S. (2019). Complex fuzzy arithmetic aggregation operators. Journal of Intelligent & Fuzzy Systems, 36(3), 2765-2771.
[18] Bi, L., Dai, S., & Hu, B. (2018). Complex fuzzy geometric aggregation operators. Symmetry, 10(7), 251.
[19] Hussain, A., Ullah, K., Senapati, T., & Moslem, S. (2024). Energy supplier selection by TOPSIS method based on multi-attribute decision-making by using novel ideas of complex fuzzy rough information. Energy Strategy Reviews, 54, 101442.
[20] Hu, Q., Zhang, L., An, S., Zhang, D., & Yu, D. (2011). On robust fuzzy rough set models. IEEE Transactions on Fuzzy Systems, 20(4), 636-651.
[21] Mahmood, T., Ur Rehman, U., Ali, Z., & Mahmood, T. (2021). Hybrid vector similarity measures based on complex hesitant fuzzy sets and their applications to pattern recognition and medical diagnosis. Journal of Intelligent & Fuzzy Systems, 40(1) , 625-646.
[22] Xu, Z., & Yager, R. R. (2009). Power-geometric operators and their use in group decision-making. IEEE Transactions on Fuzzy Systems, 18(1), 94-105.
[23] ur Rehman, U. (2023). Selection of database management system by using multi-attribute decision-making approach based on probability complex fuzzy aggregation operators. Journal of Innovative Research in Mathematical and Computational Sciences, 2(1), 1-16.

[24] Hu, B., Bi, L., & Dai, S. (2019). Complex fuzzy power aggregation operators. Mathematical problems in Engineering, 2019, 1-7.
[25] Khan, F. M., Bibi, N., Abdullah, S., & Ullah, A. (2023). Complex Fuzzy Rough Aggregation Operators and their Applications in Multi-Criteria Group Decision-Making. International Journal of Fuzzy Logic and Intelligent Systems, 23(3), 270-293.
[26] Hussain, A., Ullah, K., Senapati, T., & Moslem, S. (2024). Energy supplier selection by TOPSIS method based on multi-attribute decision-making by using novel ideas of complex fuzzy rough information. Energy Strategy Reviews, 54, 1001442.
[27] Yahya, M., Naeem, M., Abdullah, S., Qiyas, M., & Aamir, M. (2021). A Novel Approach on the Intuitionistic Fuzzy Rough Frank Aggregation Operator-Based EDAS Method for Multicriteria Group Decision-Making. Complexity, 2021(1), 5534381.
[28] Dombi, J. (1982). A general class of fuzzy operators, the DeMorgan class of fuzzy operators, and fuzziness measures induced by fuzzy operators. Fuzzy sets and systems, 8(2), 149-163.
[29] Beliakov, G., Pradera, A., & Calvo, T. (2007). Aggregation functions: A guide for practitioners (Vol. 221). Heidelberg, Berlin, New York: Springer.

Index

A

Aczel-Alsina, 7, 9, 73, 79, 90
aggregation operator, xxi, 8, 11, 20, 30, 33, 55, 57, 60, 72, 79, 109, 125, 129, 148, 151, 167
alternatives, 23, 25, 27, 44, 63, 67, 83, 84, 99, 100, 118, 122, 139
artificial Intelligence, xi, 3, 25, 33, 54, 64, 84, 91, 141, 161, 177

C

computational intelligence, 8, 171, 178
complex fuzzy rough set, xiii, xxi, 5, 11, 33, 55, 71, 109, 129, 149
cybersecurity, xii, 8, 11, 27, 32, 84

D

data science, 9, 109, 120, 121, 127
decision-making, 2, 8, 10, 11, 54, 63, 83, 107, 127, 148, 149

F

forest management, 129, 140, 142, 143, 147
fuzzy rough set, 4, 32, 70, 109, 149, 168
fuzzy set, xi, 1, 2, 5, 8, 73, 89, 90, 173
fuzzy sets and systems, 173

M

membership grade, xiii, 2, 4, 125, 126
machine learning, 3, 47, 54, 64, 86, 101, 120, 121

R

rough set, xi, xxi, 2, 33, 89, 91, 129, 149, 171

S

score values, 25, 29, 30, 46, 52, 67, 85, 100, 104, 120, 140, 147, 165, 167

T

t-norm, xiv, 6, 7, 11, 73, 130, 150

W

WASPAS, xxiii, 8, 10, 11, 23, 25, 30, 109, 118, 125, 127

About the Authors

Tahir Mahmood is an associate professor of Mathematics at the Department of Mathematics and Statistics, International Islamic University Islamabad, Pakistan. He received his Ph.D. degree in Mathematics from Quaid-i-Azam University Islamabad, Pakistan in 2012 in the field of Fuzzy Algebra. His areas of interest are algebraic structures, fuzzy algebraic structures, decision-making, and generalizations of fuzzy sets. Around 360 research publications are on his credit with more than 10,500 citations, 850 impact factor, 50 h-index, and around 200 i10-index. He has produced 63 M.S. students and 9 Ph.D. students. Currently, he is working as an editorial board member of 3 impact factor journals and as editor-in-chief of the journal "Journal of Innovative Research in Mathematical and Computational Sciences."

Jabbar Ahmmad received his M.Sc., M.S., and Ph.D. degrees in Mathematics from International Islamic University Islamabad, Pakistan, in 2018, 2020, and 2024, respectively. His research interests include fuzzy sets and their generalizations, fuzzy algebraic structures, aggregation operators, similarity measures, fuzzy decision-making, rough sets, soft sets, decision-making theory, and machine learning. He has published more than 35 articles in well-reputed peer-reviewed journals.

Ubaid ur Rehman working as an assistant professor at the Department of Mathematics, University of Management and Technology, Lahore, Pakistan. He received his Ph.D. degree in Mathematics from the International Islamic University Islamabad, Pakistan in 2023. His research interests include fuzzy sets and their generalizations, aggregation operators, similarity measures, fuzzy decision-making, rough sets, soft sets, decision-making theory, and artificial intelligence. He has published more than 80 articles in well-reputed peer-reviewed journals with 250+ impact factor. He has been a member of the academic board of Global Open Share Publishing since 2024.

Harish Garg working as an associate professor at Thapar Institute of Engineering & Technology, Patiala, Punjab, India. He is ranked in the World's Top 2% Scientist List and India Rank #1 & World Rank #163 published by Stanford University in the consecutive six years 2020-2025. He received the Most Outstanding Researcher award in the field of Mathematics from Carrer 360 Academy. He is also the recipient of the International Obada-Prize 2022 – Young Distinguished Researchers. He is also the recipient of the Top-Cited paper by an India-based author (2015–2019) from Elsevier Publisher. He also serves as an advisory board member of the Universal Scientific Education and Research Network (USERN). He is a Research Fellow at INTI International University, Malaysia; Adjunct Professor at the School of Mathematical Sciences, Sunway University, Malaysia; Adjunct Researcher at International Center for AI and Cyber Security Research and Innovations at Asia University, Taiwan.

Dr. Garg's research interests include computational intelligence, multi-criteria decision-making, evolutionary algorithms, reliability analysis, expert systems and decision support systems, computing with words, and soft computing. He has authored more than 540 papers (over 520 are SCI) published in refereed International Journals including IEEE Transactions, Elsevier, and Springer. His Google citations are over 31,100 with H-index- 95. He is one of the leading researchers in the world related to reliability, MCDM, and soft computing approaches.

Dr. Garg also serves on editorial boards of several leading international journals, this includes the founding editor-in-chief of the Journal of Computational and Cognitive Engineering. He is also the associate editor of Alexandria Engineering Journal, Journal of Industrial & Management Optimization, CAAI Transactions on Intelligence Technology, etc. For more details about him, kindly follow his webpage https://sites.google.com/site/harishg58iitr/home

For Product Safety Concerns and Information please contact our EU representative GPSR@taylorandfrancis.com Taylor & Francis Verlag GmbH, Kaufingerstraße 24, 80331 München, Germany